D0620903

Fuzzy,
Holographic, and
Parallel Intelligence

Sixth-Generation Computer Technology Series

Branko Souček, Editor
University of Zagreb

Fuzzy, Holographic, and Parallel Intelligence

The Sixth-Generation Breakthrough

BRANKO SOUČEK
and
The IRIS GROUP

A Wiley-Interscience Publication

JOHN WILEY & SONS, INC.

New York-Chichester-Brisbane-Toronto-Singapore

In recognition of the importance of preserving what has been
written, it is a policy of John Wiley & Sons, Inc., to have books
of enduring value published in the United States printed on
acid-free paper, and we exert our best efforts to that end.

Copyright © 1992 by John Wiley & Sons, Inc.

All rights reserved. Published simultaneously in Canada.

Reproduction or translation of any part of this work
beyond that permitted by Section 107 or 108 of the
1976 United States Copyright Act without the permission
of the copyright owner is unlawful. Requests for
permission or further information should be addressed to
the Permissions Department, John Wiley & Sons, Inc.

Library of Congress Cataloging in Publication Data:

Fuzzy, holographic, and parallel intelligence: the sixth-
   generation breakthrough / by Branko Souček and IRIS Group.
      p.   cm.—(Sixth-generation computer technology series)
   Includes bibliographical references and index.
    1. Electronic digital computers. 2. Artificial intelligence.
  I. Souček, Branko. II. IRIS Group. III. Series.
  QA76.5.F89 1992
  006.3—dc20   91-28310
  ISBN 0-471-54772-7   CIP

Printed in the United States of America

10 9 8 7 6 5 4 3 2 1

Printed and bound by Courier Companies, Inc.

CONTRIBUTORS

The IRIS Group presents a forum for international cooperation in research development and applications of intelligent systems. The IRIS International Center is involved in projects, design, measurements, and experiments, as well as in teaching courses and workshops, and consulting. The IRIS invites inquiries and operates under the auspices of the Star Service S.p.A., director V. L. Plantamura. The IRIS research coordinator is Professor B. Souček, IRIS, Star Service—Via Amendola 162/1, 70126—Bari, Italy.

J. DIAMOND
INTEL Corporation
Santa Clara
California

JANET EFSTATHIOU
Department of Engineering
University of Oxford
United Kingdom

D. J. EVANS
Department of Computer Studies
Loughborough University of
* Technology*
Loughborough, Licestershire
United Kingdom

K. E. GROSSPIETSCH
Gesellschaft für Mathematik
und Datenverarbeitung mbH
Sankt Augustin, Germany

E. KATONA
Cellware, Ltd.
Budapest, Hungary

R. D. MCLEOD
Department of Electrical and
* Computer Engineering*
University of Manitoba
Canada

W. PEDRYCZ
Department of Electrical and
  Computer Engineering
University of Manitoba
Canada

BRANKO SOUCEK
IRIS International Center
Bari, Italy

DARKO STIPANICEV
Department of Electrical
  Engineering
University of Split
Split, Croatia

JOHN G. SUTHERLAND
AND Corporation
Ontario, Canada

KARL-HEINZ ZIMMERMAN
Mathematical Institute
University of Bayereuth
Bayereuth, Germany

CONTENTS

PREFACE

This book describes the *New Wave* of applied intelligent systems. The New Wave offers the features that are well beyond the capability of earlier intelligent, neural, and vision techniques. The New Wave represents the melding of two groups of advanced computer technologies, one in hardware, the other in software. Together, these two technologies improve the intelligent systems' performances and result in near-human judgements, in quality of performance, and in robustness in perception, at super-human speeds and tolerances.

New hardware technologies include massively parallel processors; special high speed implementation of fuzzy cognitive systems; innovative concept of associative processors and content addressable memory that directly access the data without searching; and cellular accelerators for personal computers with up to 2000 MOPS.

New software technologies include advanced, invariant, higher-order, temporal, holographic neural networks; fuzzy expert systems; fuzzy content addressable holographic memory; packages for fuzzy reasoning, decision making, and control; programming methods for vision associative and cellular processors; and object-oriented software environment and user-oriented adaptive application tools.

New Wave of intelligent systems can deal with the *complex, noisy, confusing, and highly varying problems* in management, financing, manufacturing, shape recognition, adaptive instrumentation, process control and robotics, diagnostics, intelligent data bases, data delivery, and dictionary machines. The market and application area for practical and versatile intelligent systems are rapidly growing.

In addition to New Wave, another described technique and method which opens up a new paradigm in computing is *Processing and Reasoning by Association and by Analogy.*

This new paradigm is a strong competitor to connectionist neural networks, to rule-based reasoning and to current parallel processing. Its main features include:

- It does not require a detailed mathematical model of the process to formulate the algorithm.
- It has more robust and adaptive capability.
- It is capable to operate for a large range of inputs.
- It is cheaper.
- It is fast and stable and therefore results in reliable learning, which is superior to standard neural networks.
- It accepts and handles incomplete and/or imprecise input information (not realizable in standard architectures of neural networks).
- It is focussed and a flexible form of information processing (such as the specification of user defined prototypes).
- It has a self-flagging character of results obtained in the structure (explicit articulation of generalization capabilities).
- It has parallelism in information processing.
- It uses VLSI implementation and fault tolerance of digital implementation.

This book is divided into two parts.

PART I *HOLOGRAPHIC, FUZZY, AND PARALLEL SYSTEMS* introduces major breakthroughs in machine cognition. The new holographic neural method is described. Experiments reveal speed up factors of 10 to 100 times compared to other learning paradigms. Holographic neural technology employs a novel concept in which information is represented by vector orientation on a Riemann plane where very large sets of fuzzy associations may be enfolded within the same set of cells. Stimulus-response associations are both learned and expressed in one noniterative transformation. The holographic neural process ideally embodies the concept of content addressable memory. Multiple pattern associations, at nearly arbitrary levels of complexity, may be enfolded onto a neural cell. Encoded responses or "outputs" may subsequently be generated or accessed from the cell via content of input. Input fields may be representative of addressing schemes or "syntax," and are transformed in an inherently parallel manner through all of the content "addresses" enfolded within the cell. In response to an address or stimulus signal, the cell regenerates the associated output data field, indicating also the degree of confidence in that output association. The holographic process can be structured to operate directly within the context of content addressable memory, whereby input-output associations enfolded within a given memory "cell" are expressed directly through content of input.

The holographic network is capable of enfolding associations in the sense that input of one pattern prototype will induce the issuance of the second, thus subsequently inducing the issuance of a third, and so on. Patterns generated within a recurrent data flow may express a linear sequence of associations, each pattern association connected through its encoding within one temporal frame (i.e., associations are linked by their proximity in time). This process of linear association may be considered to be somewhat analogous to the associative reasoning processes in animal cognition, where a thought train may be expressed through a sequence of associations initially learned over time. For example, the image of a fork may invoke the impression of plate, subsequently invoking an impression response in association to a kitchen table or food, for instance. In this manner, the holographic system courses through a sequence of sensory impressions, each of which has been formed by associations temporally connected.

Realizing this capability, one may construct expert or automated reasoning systems along an associative network, in which each neuron cell functions, in an analog sense, as one unit of content addressable memory. Expressed associations may propagate along several neural pathways either within feedforward configuration or within a recurrent structure. Such neural based systems may be configured to form, for instance, the operational kernel of an inference engine for applications within expert or diagnostic systems. For instance, an input field consisting of, say, 1000 values, may store the state conditions for a particular diagnostic system. The holographic system may enfold a vast number of scenarios for those state conditions and associated diagnostic responses onto the neural system. In this manner, the expert system need not parse through a logical or heuristic tree structure. The holographic process permits all input/output scenarios to be enfolded onto the same correlation elements, and one stimulus pass through the neural system will generate the closest associated response.

Fuzzy reasoning in planning, decision making, and control is presented. Neural–fuzzy cognitive hybrids are described. A three layer structure consisting of a matching layer, a neural network, and an inverse matching layer is explored. A VLSI implementation and resulting chip-set is presented. Described applications include: interpretation of sensory information; and process/robot dynamics and man/machine communication using natural language.

An innovative concept for associative (content–addressable access) using functional blocks for the execution of 1-bit operations is presented. Its main idea is the extension of a content–addressable memory by architectural features, such as, combining RAM and CAM; introducing 1-bit operations; extension of the memory structure by adder elements.

Cellular algorithms and their implementation on very high speed processors are described. Hardware implementation techniques of cellular arrays, pipeline processing, modeling, partitioning, and I/O management are presented.

PART II *PARALLEL ALGORITHMS* deals with matrix and vector operations that could further enhance the previously described holographic, fuzzy, and parallel processing.

An optimal partitioning method for parallel algorithms is introduced. An algorithm is decomposed into subalgorithms, which efficiently use multiprocessor systems. It is shown that linear schedules can be used to schedule the operations of every subalgorithm.

The new parallel matrix strategies, known as quadrant interlocking and quadrant iterative interlocking are introduced and applications are presented. The triangular decomposition and the quadrant interlocking matrix methods are compared. Practical implementations of new parallel algorithms are described. Described algorithms open new possibilities in multiprocessor-based learning and in intelligent, real-time, signal and image processing, fuzzy associators, robotics and control.

This book presents unified treatment of material that is otherwise scattered over many publications and research reports. Previously unpublished methods and results based on research of Integrated Reasoning Information Systems, IRIS Group, are presented. IRIS Group brings together the results from leading American, European, and Japanese laboratories and projects. Each chapter focuses on two items:

- Detailed explanation of underlying principles in processes and in systems.
- Presentation of concrete results, applications and speed-up factors.

This book has been written as a textbook for students as well as a reference for practicing engineers and scientists. A minimal undergraduate-level background is assumed, although many fundamentals are reviewed. The treatment is kept as straightforward as possible emphasizing functions, systems, and applications. The treatment is rounded out with a large number of examples, experimental results, details of working systems, illustrations, flowcharts, program listings and a bibliography of over 200 items. The examples are designed as practical exercises for students and for intelligent system designers and users. Readers interested in complementary solutions, in other related topics, and in background on neural, concurrent, and intelligent systems, should combine this book with the other Sixth-Generation Computer Technology Series books listed on the page opposite the title page. These books are independent mutually supporting volumes.

BRANKO SOUČEK

Bari, Italy
February 1992

ACKNOWLEDGMENTS

We acknowledge the encouragement, discussions, and support received from our teachers, collaborators, friends, and colleagues. We are grateful for the grants supporting our research. We thank the institutions where we performed the experiments and research with intelligent systems. The institutions are listed next to the contributors' names. Special thanks to Mrs. Vladimira Zlatić, Mrs. Lisa Van Horn, and John Wiley's editors and reviewers, for an outstanding job in preparation, supervising, and copyediting the manuscript.

PART I ————————————————

Holographic, Fuzzy, and Parallel Systems

Processing and Reasoning by Association

Holographic Neural Method

Fuzzy Reasoning in Planning, Decision Making, and Control: Intelligent Robots, Vision, Natural Language

Fuzzy Cognitive Structure: Foundation, Application, and VLSI Implementations

Intelligent Systems by Means of Associative Processing

Cellular Processing

CHAPTER 1 ———————————————

Processing and Reasoning by Association

BRANKO SOUČEK

1.1 INTRODUCTION

In the past decades, man-made intelligence has been channeled into two tracks, symbolic artificial intelligence (knowledge, expert systems) and neural networks (adaptive, learning systems). These two tracks, together with fuzzy reasoning, are now melding into one track. Important breakthroughs have been recently achieved in the following crucial areas:

- Soft information processing: fast learning, fuzzy associations, fuzzy reasoning and control, generalization
- Massively parallel information processing: concurrent, parallel, associative, cellular hardware and related software and algorithms

This book presents the latest advances in the above areas. The new wave of applied intelligent systems is described, that is well beyond the capability of earlier intelligent, neural, vision, and reasoning techniques. Speedup factors of 10 to 100 times have been achieved.

The described techniques lead in the direction of reasoning systems whose behavior resembles that of a human mind. The systems should be able to describe, evaluate, and approximate information with some degree of fuzziness, uncertainty, or incompleteness. The ultimate goal is intuitive information processing that humans display: unconscious, integrated, analog, parallel, and distributed reasoning; pattern recognition; probabilistic reasoning; inductive reasoning in situations of incomplete or fuzzy information.

Fuzzy, Holographic, and Parallel Intelligence, By Branko Souček and the IRIS Group.
ISBN 0-471-54772-7 © 1992 John Wiley & Sons, Inc.

The future reasoning systems envision billions of processors having autonomous computation and information-processing/memory functions. Communication and reliability become crucial issue. Fuzzy, invariant, neural, holographic, parallel, associative, cellular techniques offer new approaches toward complex intelligent hardware and software systems based on an entirely different set of paradigms from those used in classical computing.

Major breakthroughs in intelligent systems design and applications have occurred recently in the following five areas, described in references [1–5]:

1. Biological models; neural and massively parallel computers
2. Concurrent computing; intelligent real-time systems
3. Integration of reasoning, informing, and serving
4. Fast learning and invariant object recognition
5. Dynamic, genetic, and chaotic programming

Building on the above, this book presents the latest breakthroughs in these two areas:

1. Fuzzy and holographic learning and associations
2. Parallel reasoning

This chapter introduces processing and reasoning by association. Chapters 2 to 9 give a detailed description of new paradigms, systems, and applications.

1.2   FUZZY ASSOCIATIONS

Associations present the basic for intelligent behavior of living organisms. Received sound invokes the shape of an animal in the night; smell invokes the kind of food; a broken branch signifies that a dangerous predator may have passed through.

Both, symbolic and neural, computing have difficulty in expressing associations. It seems that holographic neural technology, described by Sutherland in Chapter 2 presents the major breakthrough in fuzzy associations. A holographic network superimposes a very large set of analog stimulus–response associations within the individual neuron cell. The holographic process involves representation of information within the stimulus and response field by vector orientations in a generalized complex domain. The holographic process utilizes the inherent properties of vector transforms to enfold very large numbers of stimulus–response associations onto an identical set of complex vectors. Digitization of the information enfolding process facilitates a neural system whereby easily thousands of analog stimulus–response associations may be enfolded onto a single neuron of relatively small size. Simulation results for holographic systems indicate data storage capacities and effective rates of processing at a level that is orders of magnitude beyond current existing neural network theory and practice. Holographic neural technology is based on matrix operations. For the latest advances in parallel matrix algorithms, see Chapter 8 and 9.

It is interesting to compare a fuzzy associative system, such as described in

Chapter 2, with the newly developed "crisp" associative system described in Chapter 5.

1.3 FUZZY REASONING AND CONTROL

Fuzzy or soft reasoning and processing refers to the machine's ability to describe, evaluate, and approximate information with some degree of fuzziness, uncertainty, or incompleteness.

In Chapter 3 Stipaničev and Efstathiou describe fuzzy reasoning in planning decision making and control, focusing on applications in robotics, vision, and man–machine communication, based on natural language. Fuzzy dynamic controllers were used for the control of various systems, from large-scale industrial processes as, for example, cement kilns, water purification and treatment plants, heat exchangers, and sinter plants, to smaller scale laboratory and experimental systems comprising steam engines, marine auto pilots, diesel engines, pH neutralization, and water level control, among others.

In Chapter 4, Pedrycz, Diamond, and McLeod present a novel fuzzy cognitive structure: Fuzzy set theory and neural networks are combined to produce a robust system for representing and handling uncertainty. The system concept is implemented in a three-chip set which incorporates fault tolerance and a cellular automata based built-in self-test. VLSI design trade-offs are explored and details of the implementation are presented. The structure resembles that of a referential cognitive system. An artificial neural network exploits pre- and postprocessing stages based upon fuzzy set theory.

The basic idea is reasoning by analogy. Applications include pattern recognition, approximate reasoning based on fuzzy premises, image processing dealing with the restoration of blurred or distorted images, and so forth.

1.4 CRISP ASSOCIATIONS AND MASSIVELY PARALLEL PROCESSING

Intelligent behavior requires enormous computational power. A massively parallel computing architecture is the most plausible way to deliver such a power. Parallelism, rather than raw speed of computing elements, seems to be the way that the brain gets such jobs done. According to Souček and Souček [1], massively parallel architectures present the basis for brainlike, sixth generation computers. According to Fahlman, Hinton, and Sejnowski [6], massively parallel architectures could be classified by the type of signals that are passed among the computing elements into three classes: message-passing, marker-passing, and value-passing systems.

Message-passing systems are the most powerful family. They pass around messages of arbitrary complexity and perform complex operations on these messages. For a detailed description of message-passing concurrent systems and intelligent real-time systems, see Souček [2].

Marker-passing systems pass around single-bit markers. Each processor has the capability to store a few distinct marker bits and perform single Boolean operations on stored and marker bits arriving from other elements.

Value-passing systems pass around continuous quantities or numbers and perform simple arithmetic operations on these values.

Two architectures recently received special attention: associative memories/processors and cellular processors.

Associative or content-addressable memories (CAM) have been considered by computer designers for a long time. The advantage of such structures for speeding up search operations is unquestionable. In the past the state of technology allowed only very small CAM capacities. It is only now that the emerging state of the art in hardware integration enables the realization of such memories with reasonable bit capacities and cost/bit ratios.

In Chapter 5, Grosspietsch describes a novel associative processor/memory system. Its main idea is the systematic extension of the functionality of CAM by the following architectural features: combination of RAM and CAM access modes; extension of the CAM memory cell by a simple functional building block for the execution of 1-bit Boolean operations; extension of the memory structure by adder elements, whereby each of these elements is associated with a group of memory cells.

Cellular systems have a form of a uniform array of identical cells in an *n*-dimensional space. Each cell communicates only with its nearest neighbors. Cellular automata can be characterized by four basic properties: The cellular geometry, the neighborhood specification, the number of states per cell, and the computational rule under which the cellular automaton computes its successor state.

In Chapter 6, Katona presents the latest advances in cellular processing. These machines offer relatively high flexibility with a simple machine architecture. Relations between various cellular array architectures and cellular algorithms are discussed, including the problem of cellular programming and algorithm partitioning. For the mathematical theory of partitioning, see Chapter 7, prepared by Zimmermann.

In Chapters 8 and 9, Evans presents new parallel matrix strategies known as quadrant interlocking and quadrant iterative interlocking.

REFERENCES

[1] B. Souček, *Neural and Massively Parallel Computers: The Sixth Generation*, Wiley, New York, 1988.

[2] B. Souček, *Neural and Concurrent Real—Time Systems: The Sixth Generation*, Wiley, New York, 1989.

[3] B. Souček and IRIS Group, *Neural and Intelligent Systems Integration Fifth and Sixth Generation Integrated Reasoning Information Systems*, Wiley, New York, 1991.

[4] B. Souček and IRIS Group, *Dynamic, Genetic and Chaotic Programming, The Sixth Generation*, Wiley, New York, 1992.

[5] B. Souček and IRIS Group, *Fast Learning and Invariant Object Recognition*, Wiley, New York, 1992.

[6] S. E. Fahlman, G. E. Hinton, and T. J. Sejnowski, *Massively Parallel Architectures for AI:NETL, THIJTLE and BOLTZMANN Machines*.

CHAPTER 2 ————————————————

The Holographic Neural Method

JOHN G. SUTHERLAND

2.1 INTRODUCTION

A new concept of information is presented in this chapter. The manner by which systems may be constructed to emulate the predominant features of intelligent operation applying this conceptual basis are developed. To establish a frame of reference, the term ''holographic neural technology'' has been assigned to this new paradigm of intelligence. Some analogies for the neural process described may be made to the current understanding of the term ''holographic,'' particularly in its similarity to a class of mathematics found within electrodynamic field theory, and in the apparent *enfolding* of information observed within optical holograms. Some degree of similarity to the constitutive equations may also be found within the construction of Hilbert spaces as applied to quantum mechanical theory. These concepts described herein proceed considerably beyond the conventional meaning of *holographic* in relation to optical mediums and, in fact, require a form of complex manipulation not directly achievable through the dynamic interaction of electromagnetic fields.

The concept of learning and expression of information, represented in the form of analog stimulus–response associations, and an understanding of the manner by which the holographic neural process is able to generalize about these learned associations is fundamentally important. The holographic method principally derives its efficiency of operation in the ability to superimpose multiple stimulus–response associations (or, more precisely, analog mappings) on to the identically same correlation set representative of synaptic connections within the neuron cell.

One may consider information represented within a *data field* as comprised of a set of values bounded within an analog range. This set of values may reflect conditions or states measured within an external field or environment. The basis of stimulus–response association is to associate one set of analog measurements (stimulus field) to another group of measurements, in a manner that the presence of the first field invokes the issuance of the second. The mathematical basis for

Fuzzy, Holographic, and Parallel Intelligence, By Branko Souček and the IRIS Group.
ISBN 0-471-54772-7 © 1992 John Wiley & Sons, Inc.

holographic neural technology permits such stimulus–response associations to be mapped directly onto a correlation set comprised of complex numbers. The mechanism for holographic storage displays a capacity to achieve high information densities in the sense that large numbers of stimulus–response associations may be superimposed upon the identically same set of complex values. Individual associations are encoded or learned deterministically during one noniterative transformation. The holographic process generalizes in a manner whereby an analog stimulus pattern, of a determined closeness to any of the prior learned stimulus patterns, in transformation through the correlation set, regenerates the closest associated analog response with a high level of accuracy.

The holographic neural process may be constructed to perform a function analogous to pattern recognition, although pattern templates are effectively enfolded onto the same storage space, thus reducing memory requirements to only the amount of storage needed for a single pattern prototype. The complex valued response generated within the holographic neural process indicates both a degree of confidence (magnitude of the response vector) and an associated component of analog information (phase angle). Analog stimulus–response associations or mappings as learned and expressed within the holographic neural process are presented to neuron cells as arrays of such complex valued numbers. The holographic neuron cell displays both the capability to learn associations on a single encoding transformation and within the individual neuron cell.

One of the more standard approaches in pattern recognition (i.e., linear search) uses a convention whereby several pattern templates, whether in original or compressed form (i.e., frequency domain), must be stored and individually compared against the input reference pattern. These standard methods generally tend to require large amounts of memory and are computationally intensive and rather limited in their generalization capabilities. The linear search, for instance, indicates only a level of closeness for all stored pattern prototypes as compared against the input reference. Scaling problems are often encountered whereby a slight distortion of the input pattern incurs a large increase in the computed pattern variance (poor generalization properties).

The holographic neural theory is fundamentally different from the standard connectionist models in artificial neural system (ANS) theory. Within the holographic neural model the individual neuron cell follows a nonconnectionist mode of operation, whereby learning and subsequently expression of associations operates in a deterministic fashion within the individual neuron cell. The holographic model provides a vast increase in capabilities for neural based applications, in which the operational features exhibited by much larger connectionist networks may be effectively compressed into a single cell. The holographic process displays no restriction with respect to the generally applied concept of linear nonseparability. In other words, there exists no limitation in terms to the numbers of analog stimulus–response patterns and to the accuracy to which the associated mappings may be formed within individual neuron cells given a finite dimensionality in the **stimulus** input vector. For instance, Figure 2.11 page 92 illustrates the response recall accuracy for one cell having 20 scalar elements within the stimulus field; whereby 2,500 random stimulus–response patterns have been encoded subsequently displaying <2% average error in the analog response recall. Theoretical and empirical study indicate conclusively that both the number and accuracies of these mappings enfolded within single cells may be increased without bound.

To establish a coarse frame of reference within the current electronics industry, consider the following. The holographic cell operates intrinsically in an analog manner, and possesses a structure roughly analogous to the nonpassive transistor (Fig. 2.1). The holographic cell functions in a far more sophisticated manner, having an input signal defined within a multidimensional state space and permitting the dynamical characteristics of the device to be trained or specified over its input state space. Single cell units may be incorporated into multicellular systems to establish a connectionist structure operating within the holographic domain. Such "networks" operate in an enhanced capacity whereby stimulus–response associations propagate through, or establish recurrent loops among structured arrays of cells.

In operation, analog input states to the holographic based control element are transformed in a deterministic manner through the cell in accordance with the stimulus–response state mappings previously learned. In constructing arrays of such cells, response signals are generated through these state space mappings, and may further induce within subsequent layers of cells, both the modification of control mappings (encoding) and subsequent production of responses on decoding. One may envisage a circuit configuration somewhat similar in structure to analog devices based on the electronic transistor—each cell displaying a capability to change or modify its dynamical input–output characteristics, and having both input and output fields defined within a multidimensional control space. Potential applications, which may be constructed from this type of elementary device, may extend considerably beyond the current field of nonpassive electronics. One may further describe the operational characteristics of the holographic cell within the context of a content addressable memory. Such memory cells, in addition, possess the highly desirable capability for a deterministically modifiable property of generalization.

The holographic neural process has been integrated within a general purpose applications development system (HNeT)† as described in the following sections.

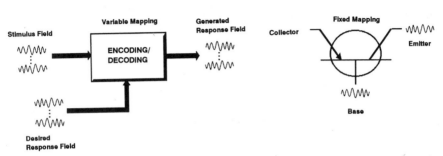

Figure 2.1 *Illustration of a logarithmic neural cell in comparison to discreet transistor devices.*

†HNeT © 1991 AND Corporation.

The HNeT system may allocate up to 32K holographic cells (memory limited) and permits one to establish data/signal flow between such cells in any desired configuration. This utility also facilitates a wide range of options in both the operational features of neural cells (i.e. generalization traits, memory profiles, neural plasticity, attenuation of learning, etc) and manipulation of data fields (i.e. production of higher order terms, confidence profiling, data extraction, sigmoidal redistribution, etc) These and other functions provide a high level of flexibility and control over the mapping characteristics of individual cells. Dynamic link libraries used in the configuration and execution of HNeT provides direct integration of the neural engine into the users application program.

2.2   THEORY OF OPERATION

2.2.1   Representation of Information

One element of information within the holographic neural paradigm is represented by a complex number operating within two degrees of freedom; that is, phase and magnitude (Fig. 2.2). Information as represented in this somewhat novel manner and, fundamentally important to an understanding of the holographic neural process, assigns analog information content to the component of phase orientation. The associated vector magnitude indicates a confidence level in that information (phase) value. Confidence or magnitude values for these complex numbers are typically bounded within a probabilistic range (i.e., 0.0 to 1.0). All information elements within the stimulus or response fields of the holographic system are therefore described by sets of complex numbers bounded within the unit circle.

Complex transformations such as the vector multiply take advantage of properties occurring within Riemann spaces—for instance, the manner in which multiply operations induce a vector rotation. It is important in this respect to note that transforms on complex values operate in a fundamentally different manner than do multidimensional Euclidian spaces. Following investigation of the process one comes to the realization that most characteristics of operation (i.e., learning or the enfolding of stimulus–response mappings onto a correlation set, response recall, properties of generalization, and ancillary features governing the properties of non-disturbance exhibited on learning, characteristics of dynamic memory, etc.) may

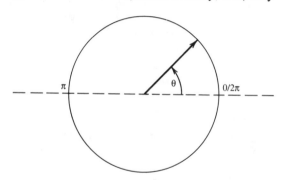

Figure 2.2 *Representation of an information element.*

be attributed to the properties inherent within complex manipulation as defined within the generalized Riemann domain. As stated previously, stimulus [S] and response [R] data fields within the holographic neural process are represented by arrays of complex values. Using the complex exponential convention, these data fields may be represented qualitatively as

$$[S] = \{\lambda_1 e^{i\theta_1}, \lambda_2 e^{i\theta_2}, \lambda_3 e^{i\theta_3}, \cdots , \lambda_N e^{i\theta_N}\} \tag{2.1a}$$

and
$$[R] = \{\gamma_1 e^{i\phi_1}, \gamma_2 e^{i\phi_2}, \gamma_3 e^{i\phi_3}, \cdots , \gamma_M e^{i\phi_M}\} \tag{2.1b}$$

External signals and response actions are most often represented within a real number domain; therefore, conversion of external real number values to the internal phase or information domain is required. Optimally this is performed by a sigmoidal preprocessing operation. Figure 2.3 illustrates the transformation characteristics. The real number domain extending along the horizontal axis is essentially unbounded ($-\infty$ to $+\infty$). The phase axis used within the holographic domain and extending along the vertical is circular however in this conceptual framework, bounded at the $0/2\pi$ orientation. The sigmoid function performs a transformation of real data sets, as experienced and measured within the external environment, to corresponding sets of phase angle orientations representing analog information within the holographic neural system. The sigmoidal transform also exhibits some highly optimal properties pertaining to symmetry considerations discussed in more detail in Section 2.2.6. The general form of mapping from scalar to complex may be illustrated qualitatively by

$$s_k \rightarrow \lambda_k e^{i\theta_k} \tag{2.2}$$

The magnitude value (λ_k) associated with each scalar value (s_k) in the input data field must be assigned some level of confidence. Assignation of confidence values facilitates control over dominance of the corresponding information component in its efficacy of operation within the encoding and decoding (response recall) processes. One must understand the concept of signal confidence (magnitude) from the vantage point that all input phase values are weighed in accordance to their magnitude in both the encoding of a stimulus–response association and the decoding or expression of a response. For instance, a phase element with an assigned magnitude of 0.0 will have no weighting or influence within the encoding or response recall of stimulus–response associations. Conversely, a confidence level of 1.0 will establish an influence of equal weighting to all other information ele-

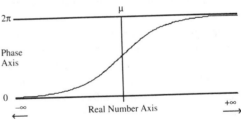

Figure 2.3 *Sigmoidal transform.*

ments within the data field, providing, of course, these elements also possesses a unity confidence level. One would normally assign unity magnitude values to all complex numbers within an input data field, although the effective weighing of these phase elements may be modified to any value extending within the probabilistic bound. This facility of modifiable confidence over information sets may be used to establish a confidence profile over segregate regions of the stimulus data fields.

Restricting confidence levels to within a probabilistic bound incorporates intrinsically the case rules of fuzzy logic within system operation. This is displayed, for example, in the computed confidence level for input events that combine to form higher order product terms or "statistics" (see Section 2.2.8, pertaining to higher order systems). This confidence level of the higher order terms is modified in accordance with standard probabilistic rules as indicated below, where p_i issues the measure of confidence in element i

$$P = \prod_i p_i \tag{2.3}$$

During the decoding operation, confidence values generated in the response recall are again of significant importance. The confidence (or magnitude) within the response presents a proportionate measure of recognition, indicating the degree of closeness of the input stimulus pattern to a prior learned stimulus state. By performing encoding–decoding transforms within phase space and using the conventions discussed earlier for information representation, this response magnitude is again bounded within a probabilistic range (0.0 to 1.0). A generated magnitude approaching 0 indicates a low level of confidence in recognition for the response recall; conversely 1.0 indicates a high level of confidence in recognition. This feature of operation may be used to determine whether the generated response information (phase) is the result of recognized or nonrecognized stimulus input. The magnitude or confidence in response recall operates, in a sense, as an analog switch turning ON the neural elements output for a recognition and OFF for non-recognition. Within both feed forward and recurrent multicellular configurations, association trains evoked within the system may either attenuate or decay away, depending upon their degree of expressed confidence on the response recall.

In the operation of protracted learning over large sets of disparate stimulus-response associations, the neural cell will eventually approach a state of saturation. Saturation results in the system's inability to further enfold analog mappings without significant distortion to those prior mapped states located within a prescribed distance of the new stimulus loci. This distortion of prior mapped states is predominantly a characteristic where the mapping relationship between the stimulus and response fields is overcomplex for the number of synaptic inputs or "dimensionality" of the neuron cell. A further characteristic of saturation encoding produces, over the extent of the input space, a statistical mean of unity in the generated confidence (vector magnitude) for response recall. This effectively eliminates the ability to provide discrimination between recognition and nonrecognition responses. This saturation effect on generated confidence levels becomes somewhat self-evident in that the overlapping regions of enfolded mappings produce effectively a recognition response over the majority of the input space.

2.2.2 Sigmoidal Preprocessing

Consider the following set of scalar values defining a stimulus field:

$$S = \{s_1, s_2, s_3, s_4, \cdots, s_N\} \tag{2.4}$$

The stimulus field may represent any measurable quantity; say, pixel intensities within a digitized image. A sigmoidal transformation, as discussed briefly in the previous section, transforms the above data field from the external real-valued domain to the neural system's internal complex number domain. Each element of information within this complex domain contains a representation of both the analog information value, representative in this case of pixel intensities, and an associated confidence level. One example of a transformation from the external to internal information domain may be illustrated by the following relationship:

$$s_k \rightarrow \lambda_k e^{i\theta_k} \tag{2.5a}$$

$$\theta_k \rightarrow 2\pi(1 + e^{(\mu - s_k)/\sigma})^{-1} \tag{2.5b}$$

where μ is mean of distribution over s; $k = 1$ to N, σ is variance of distribution, and λ_k is the assigned confidence level.

The above transformation maps the above raw input data set Eq. (2.4) to a corresponding set of complex values, illustrated as follows:

$$[S] = \{\lambda_1 e^{i\theta_1}, \lambda_2 e^{i\theta_2}, \lambda_3 e^{i\theta_3}, \cdots, \lambda_N e^{i\theta_N}\} \tag{2.6}$$

The above transformation is again performed by a nonlinear function of a generalized sigmoidal form. A class of functions may be used to perform this real valued scalar to phase transformation provided a limited number of constraints have been met. These constraints limit the mapping operation principally to the set of single valued continuous functions in which the limits of a real valued scalar range extending over an unbounded range (i.e., $-\infty$ to $+\infty$) are mapped to a bounded range extending over 2π. It has been found that the generalized sigmoid form performs this mapping ideally for purposes of establishing a symmetrical state over raw input data fields initially displaying distributions statistically representative of the Gaussian form.

Ideal symmetry, in the context of the holographic neural process, refers to a uniform distribution of complex elements oriented about the origin of the Argand plane. This state of ideal symmetry, particularly with respect to stimulus data fields, establishes the optimal condition for high encoding densities. Properties exhibited by the sigmoidal preprocessing on input real valued sets function inherently in a manner whereby normal or Gaussian distributions, occurring most often in real world systems, are mapped to a highly symmetrical distribution within the Argand plane. Algorithms thus may be constructed whereby this optimal mapping presents itself over a wide range of statistical distributions in terms of mean and variance for the real valued input population. The holographic neural process is however quite robust, in the sense that, close to optimal encoding densities may also be achieved for complex valued distributions displaying even a considerable degree of asymmetry about the origin.

From Figure 2.3 one observes that the limits of the external real valued range (i.e., $\pm\infty$) define a point of discontinuity at the $0/2\pi$ phase orientation. This discontinuity may be used to establish a fixed point of reference on the complex plane, immutable in the sense that external real number values approaching $\pm$ infinity (or the external boundary limit) asymptotically approach this fixed boundary on the complex plane. Information, as represented within the holographic systems internal phase domain, is therefore bounded along a fixed axis and unable to cross this boundary discontinuity. Similarly, the mean of the stimulus data distribution is generally centered about the opposite pole of the phase plane (π). This establishes an internal representation for information in which the conversion remains not strictly a one to one mapping, but a function of the initial data distribution. The sigmoidal adjustment based on the mean and variance of distribution in [S] as described by Eqs. (2.5a,b) normalizes input pattern distributions, to compensate for globally ambient conditions, that is variations in lighting intensity, volume, and so forth.

It is interesting to note also that some varieties of physiological receptor neurons (i.e., retinal rods and cones) preprocess input stimulus signals in a similar sigmoidal relationship. This preprocess operation is again a fundamental diversion from most standard ANS paradigms, whose operation employs a sigmoidal transform at the cells postprocessing stage. In summary, the holographic system requires a mapping of information between the external real valued number domain to the internal complex domain, and functions optimally in a Gaussian environment, having normally distributed stimuli mapped to normally distributed response fields.

2.2.3 Encoding (Learning)

The learning process realizes a holographic effect in its ability to enfold multiple stimulus–response associations onto the identically same correlation set [X] comprised of complex numbers. These numbers require a relatively low degree of numeric resolution (i.e., 8–16 bit dynamic range) to facilitate very high encoding or mapping densities. The encoding process is executed, at its most fundamental level, by a complex valued matrix product over the stimulus and response data fields. Evaluating one element within the correlation set (i.e., $x_{k,j}$) maps an association of stimulus element k to response element j, evaluating the following complex valued multiply and accumulate ($+ =$):

$$x_{k,j} + = \bar{s}_k \cdot r_j \tag{2.7}$$

Using complex exponential notation, elements of the stimulus and desired response fields are represented by

$$r_j = \gamma_j e^{i\phi_j} \tag{2.8a}$$

$$s_k = \lambda_k e^{i\theta_k} \tag{2.8b}$$

The above complex product in Eq. (2.7) may be rewritten in complex exponential notation as:

$$x_{k,j} + = \lambda_k \gamma_j e^{i(\phi_j - \theta_k)} \tag{2.9}$$

One may construct sets of stimulus and response fields extending over a given time frame where the information element index is along the horizontal and time incremented along the vertical:

$$[S] = \underset{\downarrow}{\text{time}} \begin{bmatrix} \lambda_{1,t_1} e^{i\theta_{1,t_1}} & \lambda_{2,t_1} e^{i\theta_{2,t_1}} & \cdot & \cdot \\ \lambda_{1,t_2} e^{i\theta_{1,t_2}} & \lambda_{2,t_2} e^{i\theta_{2,t_2}} & \cdot & \cdot \\ \cdot & \cdot & \cdot & \cdot \\ \cdot & \cdot & \cdot & \cdot \\ \cdot & \cdot & \cdot & \cdot \end{bmatrix} \tag{2.10a}$$

(element index →)

$$[R] = \underset{\downarrow}{\text{time}} \begin{bmatrix} \gamma_{1,t_1} e^{i\phi_{1,t_1}} & \gamma_{2,t_1} e^{i\phi_{2,t_1}} & \cdot & \cdot \\ \gamma_{1,t_2} e^{i\phi_{1,t_2}} & \gamma_{2,t_2} e^{i\phi_{2,t_2}} & \cdot & \cdot \\ \cdot & \cdot & \cdot & \cdot \\ \cdot & \cdot & \cdot & \cdot \\ \cdot & \cdot & \cdot & \cdot \end{bmatrix} \tag{2.10b}$$

The encoding process for multiple patterns as indicated above may be represented in a more canonical form by the following matrix formulation:

$$[X] + = [\bar{S}]^T \cdot [R] \tag{2.11}$$

In the above operation, the entire suite of stimulus–response associations are encoded within a matrix product solution over two complex valued data sets. Evaluating the above relation within a somewhat simpler problem domain, the formulations below assume only one element in the response field (i.e., one neuron cell). The resulting correlation set may then be presented in the following complex exponential form:

$$[X] = \begin{bmatrix} \displaystyle\sum_t^p \lambda_{1,t} \gamma_{1,t} e^{i(\phi_t - \theta_{1,t})} \\ \displaystyle\sum_t^p \lambda_{2,t} \gamma_{2,t} e^{i(\phi_t - \theta_{2,t})} \\ \cdot\ \cdot\ \cdot \\ \cdot\ \cdot\ \cdot \end{bmatrix} \tag{2.12}$$

The above encoding process effectively collapses or enfolds the dimensional aspect of time while retaining content of information. Information content in the system is preserved in the sense that one may express a prior learned response value upon exposure of [X] to the associated stimulus pattern (see description pertaining to decoding). This encoding method directly follows the principal of nondisturbance in that stimulus–response mappings, which have previously been learned, are minimally influenced by subsequently learned mappings. The property of nondisturbance permits a suite of patterns to be encoded in a linear sequence, having each association mapped into the correlation substrate on only a single learning trial. One may also interleave the encoding (learning) and decoding (response recall) functions without experiencing any degradation in performance. Neural networks based on gradient descent methods exhibit far more restrictive nondisturbance capabilities, in that several iterations about a suite of patterns are generally required to train the system, and have applications generally restricted to a far more limited pattern classification domain.

The above method presents the holographic encoding process in its most elementary form, whereby learning is not influenced by prior memory or knowledge accumulated within the system. An enhanced encoding method and its implications are further described in Section 2.2.5. The enhanced process operates in a manner whereby learning is directly influenced by prior learned memory (i.e., analog stimulus–response mappings previously enfolded within the correlation set). Enhanced encoding displays many highly desirable characteristics such as the creation of exact analog mappings on a single encoding transform, automatic control over attention, the capacity for reinforcement learning, increased storage densities, and stability of operation over a wider range of input data field distributions.

2.2.4 Decoding (Response Recall)

Decoding or *response recall* operates in manner whereby stimulus fields are transformed through all of the stimulus–response mappings enfolded within the correlation set [X] in a concurrent manner toward generation of the associated response [R]. Elements within the generated response field are again of complex form possessing both phase and magnitude components. In the event that the new stimulus field resembles any of the prior learned stimulus patterns, the neural cell generates the associated response phase values at a high level of accuracy, producing a confidence value approaching unity (magnitude ~ 1.0). The decoding transform may be illustrated in canonical form by the following complex inner product:

$$[R] = \frac{1}{c} [S]^* \cdot [X] \qquad (2.13)$$

where $[S]^*$ is the new stimulus field exposed to the neuron for issuance of the response recall. This input stimulus field may be represented by the following linear matrix:

$$[S]* = [\lambda_1^* e^{i\theta_1^*}, \lambda_2^* e^{i\theta_2^*}, \lambda_3^* e^{i\theta_3^*}, \cdots] \qquad (2.14)$$

The normalization coefficient (c) in Eq. (2.13) is desirably a function of only the stimulus field. Optimal characteristics of operation are exhibited using the following relation in normalizing the generated response magnitudes to within a meaningful probabilistic bound (i.e., 0.0 to 1.0).

$$c = \sum_{k=1}^{N} \lambda_k^* \qquad (2.15)$$

One may investigate the error characteristics exhibited on response recall by constructing sets of complex vectors of random orientation (i.e., random statistical testing). These error characteristics may be evaluated as a function of encoding densities, and it will be observed that as the number of patterns learned increases, the average error on response recall (or difference between the encoded and generated response on decoding) increases in a proportionate manner. This response recall error is sufficiently low in proportion to encoding densities, however, that very large numbers of stimulus–response mappings may be enfolded prior to the accumulation of significant analog recall error. The neural system's ability to enfold information is illustrated in a somewhat more expansive fashion, through numerically deconvolving the vector components embedded within the generated response values [R] in Eq. (2.13). This illustration requires a nominal understanding of the manner by which vectors transform within the generalized complex number domain.

Each response term generated within Eq. (2.13) above may be deconvolved into constituent parts whereby each part is itself a complex vector generated by a stimulus [S] transformation through one of the stimulus–response mappings previously enfolded within the correlation set [X]. The following presents a series expansion, expressed in complex exponential form, for one response value in [R] (assuming again that we are modeling a single neuron cell having one axonal process). Combining Eqs. (2.14) for the new stimulus [S]*, (2.12) for the correlation set, and the canonical form for the decoding transform (2.13), the following solution for the generated response value is obtained:

$$r = \frac{1}{c} \sum_{k}^{N} \lambda_k^* e^{i\theta_k^*} \sum_{t}^{T} \lambda_{k,t} \gamma_t e^{i(\phi_t - \theta_{k,t})} \qquad (2.16)$$

This solution may be rewritten in the following equivalent form:

$$r = \frac{1}{c} \sum_{t}^{T} \gamma_t e^{i\phi_t} \sum_{k}^{N} \lambda_k^* \lambda_{k,t} e^{i(\theta_k^* - \theta_{k,t})} \qquad (2.17)$$

The above represents a sequence of separate response components summed over time slices ($t = 1$ to T). Each of these deconvolved response vectors (see Eq. 2.18

below) corresponds to a response component produced by the inner product transform of a new stimulus field $[S]^*$ transform through a mapping encoded within the correlation set at some previous time t. Further rewriting the above Eq. (2.17) in a more compact form, each of the constituent response vectors generated over the prior encoded associations $t = 1$ to T may be represented numerically as follows:

$$r = \frac{1}{c} [\Lambda_1 e^{i\phi_1^*} + \Lambda_2 e^{i\phi_2^*} + \cdots + \Lambda_T e^{i\phi_T^*}] \tag{2.18}$$

where Λ_t is the magnitude or confidence level for one of the prior described vector terms convolved within the response. Each vector term $(\Lambda_t e^{i\phi_T^*})$ again corresponds to a new stimulus $[S]^*$ transform through a stimulus–response mapping enfolded into the correlation set at time t. Resubstituting Eq. (2.17) into the above, each of the constituent terms within the deconvolved response may be evaluated deterministically, where

$$\Lambda_t e^{i\phi_t^*} = \gamma_t e^{i\phi_t} \sum_k^N \lambda_k^* \lambda_{k,t} e^{i(\theta_k^* - \theta_{k,t})} \tag{2.19}$$

Following from the above, the magnitude and phase component of the above convolved response terms may be evaluated deterministically given the suite of stimulus–response associations encoded, whereby

$$\Lambda_t = \frac{\gamma_t}{c} \left[\left[\sum_k^N \lambda_k^* \lambda_{k,t} \cos(\theta_k^* - \theta_{k,t}) \right]^2 + \left[\sum_k^N \lambda_k^* \lambda_{k,t} \sin(\theta_k^* - \theta_{k,t}) \right]^2 \right]^{1/2}$$

$$\tag{2.20}$$

$$\phi_t^* = \tan^{-1} \left[\frac{\sum_k^N \lambda_k^* \lambda_{k,t} \sin(\theta_k^* - \theta_{k,t} + \phi_t)}{\sum_k^N \lambda_k^* \lambda_{k,t} \cos(\theta_k^* - \theta_{k,t} + \phi_t)} \right] \tag{2.21}$$

remembering to adjust ϕ_t^* to the correct phase quadrant.

Each of the terms on the RHS of Eq. (2.18) contain a magnitude or confidence statistically proportional to the degree to which the new stimulus pattern $[S]^*$ falls close to a stimulus mapping prior encoded at time t. In other words, the prior encoded stimulus patterns displaying the greatest similarity to the new input pattern $[S]^*$ produce the more dominant vector terms measured by Λ_t as defined by Eq. (2.20) within the generated response. Figure 2.4 illustrates a vector summation of these convolved response terms and the relative dominance of each of the terms. The properties of transformation within a Riemann domain exhibit a unique char-

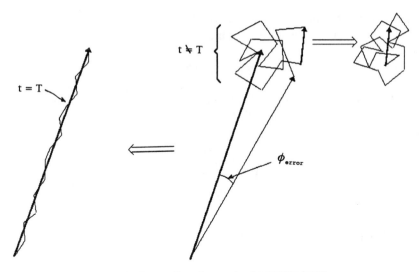

Figure 2.4 *Summation of convolved response terms.*

acteristic, whereby phase rotation operations (i.e., complex multiplies) impart a rotation within each of the vector terms enfolded within a complex summation. The holographic process realizes this unique property, whereby a subset of the convolved response terms derived from the enfolded mappings effectively line up producing a predominant recognition response (for $t = T$ in Fig. 2.4). Conversely the remaining terms in Eq. (2.18) generated from a stimulus transform through disassociated mappings learned at $t \neq T$ manifest a far smaller dominance or magnitude. These disassociated response terms (for $t \neq T$) are similarly summed, however, and follow a path characteristic of random walks in the ideal symmetric case (see Fig. 2.4). The net response vector, therefore, exhibits a small component of error, or fuzziness in recall, within the generated response (ϕ_{error}). The above random walk characteristics exhibited for the disassociated mappings, occur optimally for the systems having data field distributions that are reasonably symmetric, as defined in Section 2.2.1. It is the above random walk characteristic that establishes the condition by which multiple mappings may be enfolded onto the identically same correlation set.

A simple limit theorem may be constructed to evaluate the properties observed of the holographic neural method, by observing the asymptotic conditions for a new stimulus input pattern in its approach to a prior learned stimulus state. One may apply a limit argument using a random error factor ϵ_r, this factor again diminishing as the information elements within the new stimulus field $[S]^*$ approaches a stimulus pattern encoded at time T. Establishing the following numerical relationship:

$$e^{i\theta_k^*} = e^{i(\theta_{k,t} + \epsilon_r)} \tag{2.22}$$

over all stimulus elements $k = 1$ to N

where ϵ_r is the random error quantity. As the phase elements within the stimulus field $[S]^*$ tend toward the encoded stimulus pattern (T),

$$\epsilon_r \to 0 \qquad \text{over all } k$$

Substituting Eq. (2.22) into the phase and magnitude relationships for the response, [20] and [21], one finds that:

$$\Lambda_T \to \frac{\gamma_T \displaystyle\sum_{k}^{N} \lambda_k^* \lambda_{k,T}}{\displaystyle\sum_{k}^{N} \lambda_k^*} \tag{2.23}$$

whereby for λ_k, $\lambda_{k,T}$, $\gamma_T \cong 1$ over all k

Then

$$\boxed{\Lambda_T \to 1.0}$$

Similarly, for the generated phase orientation, the following asymptotic approach is observed on reduction of ϵ_r:

$$\boxed{\phi_T^* \to \phi_T}$$

The above value of confidence Λ_T presents again the magnitude expressed for the decoding transformation of a new stimulus field through a stimulus–response mapping prior encoded at time T, and presents the most dominant response vector generated from this new stimulus $[S]^*$. Similarly, the generated response phase angle in the above limit ($\epsilon_r \to 0.0$) approaches the prior learned analog response value for the mapping encoded at time T (i.e., ϕ_T).

To repeat, the remainder of the terms convolved within the response (i.e., $t \neq T$) characterizes a deterministic "error" or fuzziness within the generated response (ϕ_{error} in Fig. 2.4). The statistical variance on the magnitude for this error term is proportional to the total number of distinct and separate stimulus–response mappings enfolded within the correlation set. It is this fuzziness that places a limit on the encoding capacity or number of distinct associations that may be accurately mapped within the neuron cell. One may provide an upper estimate for any multidimensional orthogonal coordinate system, whereby the average magnitude resulting from a sum of P random walks, assuming unit steps is:

$$\sqrt{P}$$

Substituting this relationship into Eq. (2.20), one may evaluate an estimate for the average error within the response recall assuming ideal characteristics of random walks the set of dis-associated response terms displays an average magnitude approximating:

$$|r_{t \neq T}| = \left| \frac{1}{C} \sum_{t \neq T}^{P} \Lambda_t e^{i\phi_t^*} \right| \cong \sqrt{\frac{P}{N}} \qquad (2.24)$$

for γ_t, $\lambda_{k,t} \cong 1$ over all k and t

For purposes of estimating operational characteristics of a particular cell configuration, one may derive for the average response recall error, understanding the above mathematical relationship imposed by conditions of symmetry. This estimate assumes randomly generated patterns (illustrates the most limiting storage capacity within the enhanced encoding process Section 2.2.5). Recall error given the number of synaptic inputs or *dimensionality* of the cell (N) and number of patterns encoded (P) may be approximated by:

$$\phi_{\text{error}} = \frac{1}{\pi\sqrt{8}} \tan^{-1}\left[\sqrt{\frac{P}{N}} \right] \qquad (2.25)$$

The response recall ''error'' is in fact deterministic in its expression of the response contribution from the set of nonsimilar stimulus loci, and increases in a square root relation to the total number of stimulus–response associations encoded. Reiterating, stimulus patterns used in generation of response recall will invoke responses over the plurality of encoded stimulus–response mappings, each of the constituent responses issuing a proportionate degree of dominance or confidence within the net response value (Λ_T in Eq. 2.18).

A series of further enhancements on the above basic operational premise may be used to increase the accuracy of the holographic process considerably beyond that indicated by the error relation (2.25). For instance one may eliminate the pattern storage restriction by expanding the input stimulus field to higher order product terms in explicitly generating higher order ''statistics'' from the input data field (see Section 2.2.8). Employing this stimulus field expansion process, a raw input field of say 10 elements may be expanded to a virtually unbounded set of unique higher order product terms. For these stimulus fields comprised of unique higher order terms, the error relation given by Eq. (2.25) remains still a valid upper bound on error, however, with N now representing the total number of higher order terms generated at the preprocessing stage. The expansion of stimulus fields to higher order statistics thereby increases the dimensionality of the cell permitting a proportionally larger number of mappings to be enfolded within the neuron cell, and concurrently reducing the regions of generalization surrounding the stimulus loci. The above input stimulus field expansion, therefore, facilitates a means by which a virtually unbounded number of distinct analog stimulus–response mappings may be enfolded within a state space defined within a finite degree of freedom. Linear nonseparability therefore does not impose a constraints within the holographic neural process.

Enhancements such as that outlined above, and other fundamentally important aspects exhibited by the holographic neural process are listed below. These properties of the process

- Enhanced encoding
- Dynamic memory
- Higher order systems
- Commutative property

are defined within the sections following.

2.2.5 Enhanced Encoding

Operational characteristics of the holographic method are significantly enhanced employing a process whereby learning is a function of memory previously enfolded within the cell (i.e., prior stimulus–response association mapped within the correlation set). This enhanced encoding process may be used to map out effectively the entire input state space to a set of desired response values or control actions. The number of separate mappings that may be encoded, and the topological form of these mappings may be deterministically controlled through selection of higher order statistics generated at a preprocessing stage to the neural cell (see Section 2.2.8 pertaining to higher order systems).

Within the basic encoding system of Section 2.2.3, multiple stimulus–response associations are enfolded onto the correlation set, each association encoded at a preestablished level of confidence. Learning progresses independently from knowledge previously accumulated, and no control is afforded over *attention* or the degree to which encoding influences the stimulus–response mapping substrate (physical storage medium containing the correlation set). Within this basic encoding process, operation is nonoptimal in the sense that many similar stimulus–response associations will tend to significantly distort or influence all the mappings enfolded within the correlation set. Asymmetries may arise within these enfolded mappings to the extent that all generated responses tend toward a heavily reinforced response. These undesirable characteristics or limitations are not exhibited within the enhanced encoding process which effectively eliminates instabilities within the neural system resulting from a training set containing a heavily reinforced response (i.e., many stimulus patterns associated with the same response value). Magnitudes or confidence levels generated in the response recall, are more stably bounded within a probabilistic range (0.0 to 1.0) over the extent of the input space. The enhanced encoding process also displays an ability to generate a more sharply defined separation or "topological fold" in the mapping region between proximally located stimulus regions or loci (see Fig. 2.5). The response recall error as observed within the enhanced encoding process is substantially reduced over the basic encoding process of Section 2.2.3. As well, error on response recall may

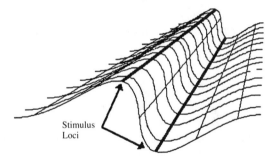

Figure 2.5 *Topological fold near proximally located regions of the input space.*

be effectively eliminated using relatively few reinforcement learning trials over the training set (typically <4).

By allowing encoding to proceed as a function of accumulated memory, the rate of learning (or attention) is automatically controlled by the degree to which similar stimulus–response associations or mappings have previously been learned. Only novel associations will maximally influence this mapping substrate. Conversely, encoding of previously learned associations will introduce a negligible effect on the correlation mapping. Affected is a mechanism that controls automatically the level of attention, defined in a manner whereby learning progresses maximally for novel stimulus–response associations. This enhanced method is in addition extremely powerful in its ability to construct a topology capable of mapping patterns of arbitrary complexity and their related set of permutations over time in scale, translation, rotation, and so forth to desired responses.

The enhanced learning process may be subdivided into essentially three stages of operation. The initial stage executes a decoding operation whereby the new stimulus set $[S]^*$ is transformed through the correlation set in the generation of a response. The second stage evaluates a vector difference (R_{dif}) between the generated and the desired response for this new stimulus input. The final step performs an encoding, whereby the new stimulus field is mapped to the above computed difference vector. These operational steps are illustrated below, assuming one complex value within the response field (i.e., one neuron cell).

1. Decode a stimulus field through the neuron cell to produce a (complex) response value R' that is,

$$R' = \frac{1}{c} [S] \cdot [X] \qquad (2.26a)$$

2. A vector difference R_{dif} between the above generated response and the desired response R for this stimulus–response association is evaluated simply, as follows:

$$R_{\mathrm{dif}} = R - R' \qquad (2.26b)$$

3. The correlation mapping is derived from the stimulus field $[S]$ and the above difference vector and encoded into the neural element, following the canonical form presented in Eq. (2.11):

$$[X] + = [\bar{S}]^T R_{\text{dif}} \qquad (2.26c)$$

The above process realizes an encoding method whereby the new stimulus field is mapped exactly to the desired analog response R following only one encoding pass, and irrespective of prior enfolded memory. Subsequent encodings will accumulate a distortion of this mapping at a gradual rate and proportional to the closeness of new stimulus states to the prior mapped $[S]$. A general formulation for the above learning procedure may be derived by combining the above steps, Eqs. (2.26a) to (2.26c), neglecting cross-product terms in the matrix solution:

$$[X] + = [\bar{S}]^T \cdot \left([R] - \frac{1}{c} [S] \cdot [X] \right) \qquad (2.27)$$

or reexpressing in an equivalent form:

$$[X] + = \underset{\substack{\text{basic} \\ \text{encoding}}}{[\bar{S}]^T [R]} - \underset{\substack{\text{enhancement} \\ \text{term}}}{[H] \cdot [X]} \qquad (2.28)$$

where $[H]$ represents a Hermitian form of $[S]$, that is,

$$[H] = \frac{1}{c} [\bar{S}]^T \cdot [S] \qquad (2.29)$$

The optimal mapping is achieved at the point where $[X]$ converges to a stable locus defined at

$$[X] = [H]^{-1} \cdot [X]_{\text{basic}} \qquad (2.30)$$

where $[X]_{\text{basic}}$ is the correlation set produced within the basic holographic encoding scheme presented by Eq. (2.11). A close to exact mapping over a large set of analog stimulus–response associations may again be achieved with relatively few reinforcement learning trials using the enhanced encoding process as presented by Eq. (2.27). Evaluating the complex matrix inverse $[H]^{-1}$ as per Eq. (2.30), however, requires both the entire suite of stimulus patterns to be present, and is considerably more computationally intensive requiring on the order of n^3 operations using Gauss–Jordan elimination methods. The inverse matrix approach does not, therefore, present a practicable real-time solution for neural based systems.

The matrix solution indicated in Eq. (2.27) presents a generalized form of the iterative learning process and represents one reinforcement learning trial over the complete suite of stimulus–response associations contained in $[S]$ and $[R]$. Reiterating, the enhanced encoding procedure may be performed over multiple reinforcement learning trials to achieve a rapid convergence to the set of desired stimulus–response analog mappings. From the test results illustrated in Section 2.7, one will observe that the analog error produced during response recall achieves low values (i.e., $<5\%$ absolute analog scale) following generally only one to four reinforcement learning trials for high encoding densities (i.e., where the number of random associations learned approaches the dimensionality of the cell). For lower encoding densities or associations that embody some degree or form or structure (i.e., patterns that are not random) the response recall error may be greatly reduced over the relation presented in Eq. (2.25). To further clarify the above operation, indices of the complex matrix formulation for the stimulus field $[S]$, response field $[R]$, and correlation matrix $[X]$ used within the above solutions (2.27–2.30) are presented in an expanded matrix notation.

$$[S] = \begin{array}{c} \text{synaptic element index} \rightarrow \\ \downarrow \text{Time index} \left[\begin{array}{cccc} s_{1,t_1} & s_{2,t_1} & s_{3,t_1} & \cdot\ \cdot \\ s_{1,t_2} & s_{2,t_2} & s_{3,t_2} & \cdot\ \cdot \\ s_{1,t_3} & s_{2,t_3} & s_{3,t_3} & \cdot\ \cdot \\ \cdot & \cdot & \cdot\ \cdot & \\ \cdot & \cdot & \cdot\ \cdot & \cdot\ \cdot \end{array} \right] \end{array} \qquad (2.31a)$$

$$[R] = \begin{array}{c} \text{response element index} \rightarrow \\ \downarrow \text{Time index} \left[\begin{array}{cccc} r_{1,t_1} & r_{2,t_1} & r_{3,t_1} & \cdot\ \cdot \\ r_{1,t_2} & r_{2,t_2} & r_{3,t_2} & \cdot\ \cdot \\ r_{1,t_3} & r_{2,t_3} & r_{3,t_3} & \cdot\ \cdot \\ \cdot & \cdot & \cdot\ \cdot & \\ \cdot & \cdot & \cdot\ \cdot & \cdot\ \cdot \end{array} \right] \end{array} \qquad (2.31b)$$

$$[X] = \begin{array}{c} \text{response index} \rightarrow \\ \downarrow \text{Synaptic index} \left[\begin{array}{cccc} x_{1,1} & x_{2,1} & x_{3,1} & \cdot\ \cdot \\ x_{1,2} & x_{2,2} & x_{3,2} & \cdot\ \cdot \\ x_{1,3} & x_{2,3} & x_{3,3} & \cdot\ \cdot \\ \cdot & \cdot & \cdot\ \cdot & \\ \cdot & \cdot & \cdot\ \cdot & \cdot\ \cdot \end{array} \right] \end{array} \qquad (2.31c)$$

Where each element within the above stimulus and response field is again defined by a complex value bounded typically within the unit circle.

The above formulations illustrate a method for the encoding of multiple pattern associations extending over a given time interval. In a practical application the encoding process would normally generate and enfold onto the correlation set a single stimulus–response mapping at each time increment to effect the real-time learning characteristics observed within biological systems. The recursion of the response difference terms (R_{dif} in Eq. 2.26b) is somewhat analogous to the back-propagation of error terms used in conventional gradient approaches; however, the holographic neural process displays far more efficient properties of convergence, or the ability to construct a mapping topology within a single cell, conforming far more exactly to the set of desired analog stimulus–response associations.

The underlying processes occurring within the holographic neural system on reinforcement learning (i.e., on the construction of a topology displaying the above convergence properties), may be illustrated in the following manner. One may consider two distinct stimulus patterns that are largely identical, however, varying between each other over a limited region. During the encoding process one may associate these two highly similar stimulus patterns to different analog responses. This is illustrated vectorially by the following relationship where the desired response vector for stimulus 1 is represented by:

$$R_1 = e^{i\phi_1} \tag{2.32a}$$

Similarly, the desired response vector for stimulus 2:

$$R_2 = e^{i\phi_2} \tag{2.32b}$$

again where $\phi_1 \neq \phi_2$.

Following encoding of stimulus–response pattern 1, decoding a response from stimulus pattern 2 will generate a vector close to R_1. As a first approximation, the difference vector (R_{dif}) encoded within the second pass of the learning process (i.e., encoding pattern 2) approximates the difference between R_1 and R_2. Illustrated vectorially in Figure 2.6, where:

$$R_{dif} \cong R_{1,2} = \beta e^{i(\phi_{1,2})} \tag{2.33a}$$

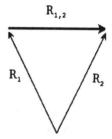

Figure 2.6   *Computed vector difference on enhanced encoding.*

and

$$\beta \cong 2 \sin\left(\frac{\phi_1 - \phi_2}{2}\right) \tag{2.33b}$$

For the reverse order in which stimulus–response pattern 2 has been encoded, followed by an encoding of pattern 1, the conjugate difference vector is generated $(R_{2,1})$. The following illustrates the mapping generated within correlation element x_k for an encoding pattern 1 given 2 mapped prior:

$$x_k + = e^{i\theta_{k,1}} \beta e^{i(\phi_{1,2})} \tag{2.34}$$

Similarly, for a further encoding of pattern 2 given 1 mapped prior,

$$x_k + = e^{i\theta_{k,2}} \beta e^{-i(\phi_{1,2})} \tag{2.35}$$

where $e^{i\theta_{k,t}}$ corresponds to element k within the stimulus field for pattern t and $e^{i\phi_{1,2}}$ is the phase orientation of difference vector $R_{1,2}$.

In other words, the vector difference for the first situation $(R_{1,2})$ is approximately equivalent to the conjugate difference vector produced for the reverse encoding order (i.e., $R_{2,1}$). For regions that are isometric between the above two stimulus patterns, the net contribution within the correlation matrix elements x_k over one learning trial largely cancels out—that is, for $\theta_{k,1} \cong \theta_{k,2}$ (isometric regions over k):

$$\left| \sum_{t=1,2} X_{k,t} \right| \to 0 \tag{2.36}$$

where $x_{k,t}$ are the correlation values for element k and stimulus pattern t.

In actuality, during multiple reinforcement learning trials, the mapping of stimulus patterns $t = 1, 2$ over isometric regions k converge to an interpolation between the two vector orientations R_1 and R_2. These response vector components derived from a decode operation over the isometric stimulus regions k in patterns 1 and 2 are denoted below by r_1 and r_2, respectively. Convergence to an interpolation between the two desired response mappings $(R_1$ and $R_2)$ is illustrated graphically in Figure 2.7 over three reinforcement learning trials, again where:

$$r_1 = x_k \cdot s_{k,1} \tag{2.37a}$$

$$r_2 = x_k \cdot s_{k,2} \tag{2.37b}$$

For regions of the stimulus field, however, which are nonisometric over the different response classifications, these vector differences inherently amplify the as-

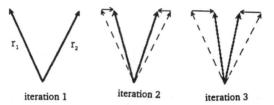

iteration 1   iteration 2   iteration 3

Figure 2.7 *Mapping convergence for isometric regions ($s_{k,1} \cong s_{k,2}$).*

sociated mapping within the correlation set. For dissimilar regions within the stimulus field (i.e., $\theta_{k,1} \neq \theta_{k,2}$), one learning trial accumulates a vector addition within the correlation value (x_k), on the order of:

$$\left| \sum_{t=1,2} X_{k,t} \right| = 2\beta \sin\left(\frac{\theta_{k,1} - \theta_{k,2}}{2} \right) \qquad (2.38)$$

The convergence process occurring within the correlation mapping for nonisometric regions over multiple learning trials is again somewhat complex; however, for illustrative purposes it is presented in vector form in Figure 2.8.

To repeat, the enhanced learning process inherently attenuates mappings within the correlation set [X] corresponding to regions in the stimulus fields that are isometric but mapped to separate or distinct response values. Over these regions, the process establishes a mapping that generates an interpolation between the desired response phase orientations. Conversely, for nonisometric (dissimilar) regions of the stimulus field, the corresponding correlation elements in [X] are amplified as illustrated in Figure 2.8. The above affects a correlation mapping, which converges stably to most classes of stimulus–response associations and displays an ability to amplify the discriminating features of the stimulus pattern prototypes through the mapping topology formed within [X]. Again, relatively few numbers of reinforcement learning trials (typically one to four) are required to substantially reduce response recall error over large sets of stimulus–response associations.

The accuracy of mapping generated for higher order systems (expanding the stimulus field to higher order terms; see Section 2.2.8) is similarly enhanced through reinforcement learning as illustrated above. From test results presented in Section 2.7 one may observe that a stimulus field of 20 inputs expanded to fourth

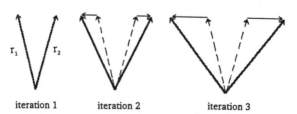

iteration 1   iteration 2   iteration 3

Figure 2.8 *Mapping convergence for nonisometric regions ($s_{k,1} \neq s_{k,2}$).*

order product terms or "statistics" is easily capable of encoding 2400 randomly generated stimulus–response associations. Following three reinforcement learning trials at this encoding density, average error within the response recall is less than $\pm 2\%$ of the analog output range (see Fig. 2.54 in Section 2.7.3). These empirical results illustrate the holographic neural system's ability to converge to a near perfect analog response recall, following relatively few retraining trials. Mapped regions within the control state space are not strictly hyperspheroid but have a topological form controlled by the order of statistics generated and shaped by the suite of stimulus–response associations encoded.

The enhanced encoding process increases operational stability within the holographic neural system to the degree that learned associations displaying highly nonsymmetric distributions incur a minimal influence upon prior enfolded mapping. These nonsymmetric conditions impose a highly limiting constraint upon the unenhanced encoding method of Section 2.2.3, whereby the enfolded mappings tend to become highly distorted through asymmetries present within the suite of stimulus–response prototypes. A very important aspect of the enhanced encoding method is with regard to the reinforcement learning of similar stimulus–response associations. Affected is a mechanism by which the correlation elements in $[X]$ are modified at a diminishing rate due to the fact that these associations are mapped out to ever increasing levels of accuracy (i.e., R_{dif} in Eq. 2.26b tends toward 0.0). Automatic control over *attention* is facilitated in this manner, whereby novel stimulus–response associations maximally influence the mapping substrate (correlation set) during learning; conversely, prior learned associations exhibit little or no influence within this mapping topology. Again, within the basic or nonenhanced learning system (i.e., learning is NOT a function of encoded information) all stimulus–response associations are encoded with equal weighting, affording no means for automatic control of attention, and similarly, facilitating no mechanism for reinforcement learning.

One example of an application that may be realized using the enhanced encoding process is the capability to encode a virtually unbounded set of stimulus–response associations for a three-dimensional visual object, this object being subjected to a continuous range of translations in rotation and scale. The enhanced encoding process is similarly capable of mapping related objects (different orientations and images of a cup for instance) to an associated response. In other words, the holographic process exhibits the capacity to construct a deterministic mapping over a wide class of similar objects creating in the above example, an abstraction or mapped generalization of the visual form of "cupness." These enhanced generalization properties are, of course, not strictly limited to the visual sensory mode of vision but extend to any form of data or stimulus–response association, potentially relating higher levels of abstraction.

2.2.6 Symmetry Considerations

Symmetry of data field distributions is of fundamental importance within the holographic neural process. The ability to superimpose multiple stimulus–response associations onto the identically same set of complex correlation elements is derived from the manner in which complex vectors are summed within a reasonably symmetric system. Assuming this azimuthally symmetric distribution of vectors, the net displacement over the inner product evaluated during both the encoding and decoding processes tend to grow in a manner analogous to a random walk. Diffusion in a liquid medium operates on a similar principle of Brownian movement. In general, the summation of N random steps of unity magnitude over any higher dimensional orthogonal space exhibits a distribution centered about the origin of walk, establishing a mean of the radial distribution approaching

$$\sqrt{N}$$

It is the principle of azimuthal symmetry that fundamentally enables the superposition, or enfolding, of information within the holographic based neuron cell. Symmetry as referred throughout this text is again defined by a uniform probabilisitic distribution of complex vectors oriented about the origin on the complex plane. Figure 2.9 graphically illustrates this concept of symmetry over a data set. To illustrate once again this concept of enfolding information, a state of azimuthal symmetry ensures that stimulus patterns that are distinct from previously learned stimulus patterns produce a vector response that approaches a sum over random walks. The average magnitude for these random walks establishes the mean confidence level for nonrecognition responses. Conversely, for stimulus input patterns that have been previously learned, a decode operation produces a magnitude or confidence level in response recall close to unity. Consider, for example, a neuron cell of $N = 1000$ synaptic inputs (small by biological standards) having encoded $P = 250$ patterns. On exposing the holographic cell to previously learned stimulus fields, response vectors with magnitudes probabilistically centered about 1.0 are generated on response recall. Unlearned stimulus input patterns, however, generate a characteristic random accumulation of displacements, producing a response recall possessing a magnitude centered about, in the above case,

$$\sqrt{\frac{P}{N}} = 0.5 \qquad (2.39)$$

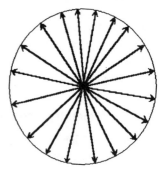

Figure 2.9 *Symmetrical distribution over the phase axis.*

This magnitude, as stated previously, presents a measure of confidence in the generated response and may be employed appropriately in several ways to flag or trigger a valid response for recognition. Systems operating within a high state of symmetry facilitate optimum discrimination between recognition and nonrecognition responses. This aspect of azimuthal symmetry within the data field distributions is achieved in two principal ways:

1. Through the use of sigmoid transforms to map normal (Gaussian) distributions from the external real number domain to the internal information or phase domain as indicated previously in the text.

2. Through expansion of the input data field to higher order product terms or statistics. Both processes are elaborated below in further detail.

As mentioned in Section 2.2.2, the sigmoid function or sigmoidal forms (i.e., tan or hyperbolic tan (2θ)) may be used in transforming an essentially unbounded real valued range to a closed range extending about the complex plane. The transformed information elements (complex vectors) are optimally distributed uniformly about the origin, forming an azimuthally symmetric distribution. This mapping of normal or Gaussian distribution to symmetric form in phase space is illustrated by the density distribution plots presented in Figure 2.10.

One may desire to construct a real valued to complex mapping further capable of compensating for a range of statistical distributions lying between Gaussian and uniform distributions. Such a functional interpolation between sigmoidal and linear mapping requires a measure of the initial symmetry for the data field. This measure of symmetry (Sym), may be evaluated simply from a vector summation over the complex valued data field, as follows:

$$\text{Sym} = \frac{\sum\limits_{k}^{N} \lambda_k e^{i\phi_k^*}}{\sum\limits_{k}^{N} \lambda_k^*} \tag{2.40}$$

In the event that the input field is highly symmetric, the magnitude of the above vector summation approaches a lower bound of 0.0 for any data field of reasonable

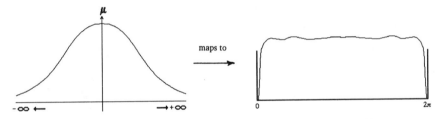

Figure 2.10 *Mapping from normal to symmetric distribution densities.*

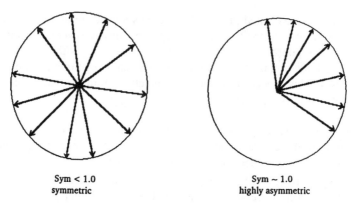

Sym < 1.0
symmetric

Sym ~ 1.0
highly asymmetric

Figure 2.11   *Symmetric versus asymmetric distributions.*

size. Conversely, for nonsymmetric distributions the vector summation will generate a magnitude approaching unity. This concept is illustrated graphically in Figure 2.11. Summation (2.40) produces a measure of symmetry bounded between 0.0 and 1.0, as well as a value for the mean phase orientation within the data distribution. Both of these statistical measures may be factored within the sigmoidal transform to modify parameters, in the optimization of symmetrization over a wider range of input distribution states.

A further and possibly more effective means of obtaining a highly symmetrical state over a wide class of input data distributions is through expansion of the input field to higher order combinatorial product terms. These higher order "statistics," as referred to in this text, represent the generation of Mth order product terms over elements within the raw stimulus data field, allowing for repeating factors. The generations of a higher order product term is illustrated simply in the following:

$$\prod_{m}^{M} \lambda_m e^{i\theta_m} \tag{2.41}$$

where M indicates the "order" of the above product solution. The number of combinations of unique Mth order product terms that can be generated from a data field of size N is defined by the following factorial relationship:

$$\frac{(N + M - 1)!}{(N - 1)! \, M!} \tag{2.42}$$

In this manner stimulus input fields of relatively small size may be expanded to extremely large data sets. A property inherent within the complex domain indicates that as one expands any set of values to higher order terms, the distribution of the resultant data set asymptotically approaches a near optimally symmetric state, irrespective of the initial data set distribution. Symmetry may be attained over the

$$\begin{bmatrix} 0\,0\,0\,1 \\ 0\,1\,0\,0 \\ 0\,0\,0\,0 \\ 0\,0\,0\,0 \end{bmatrix} \rightarrow \begin{bmatrix} 0\,0\,1\,0 \\ 1\,0\,0\,0 \\ 0\,0\,1\,0 \\ 0\,1\,0\,0 \end{bmatrix} \rightarrow \cdots \cdots \begin{bmatrix} 0\,1\,0\,0 \\ 1\,1\,0\,1 \\ 0\,1\,1\,0 \\ 0\,1\,0\,1 \end{bmatrix}$$

Figure 2.12 *Approach to a symmetrical state.*

vast majority of initial data distributions, with the exceptional case excluded (i.e., singular state in which all information elements are oriented along the positive real axis).

This data set expansion to higher order terms is illustrated in Figure 2.12 for a restricted binary system where information is defined at only two locations on the phase plane (i.e., 0 and π). The first frame indicates a highly asymmetrical distribution where 12.5% of the input elements are defined at 1 (or π). Following a generation of second order terms, the set distribution has been altered such that 25% of elements are now at the zero phase orientation. Following three iterations (i.e., eighth order terms) the data distribution is virtually symmetric about the imaginary axis (i.e., 50% zeros). This expansion to higher order terms operates in a similarly effective manner for symmetrizing data distributions whose elements are defined along a continuous (analog) range.

2.2.7 Dynamic Memory

Within the holographic neural process, each stimulus–response association maps out a generalization in the sense that stimulus input states of a determined closeness to a learned stimulus state are concurrently mapped to the desired analog response. If one were to apply dynamic decay to the correlation set $[X]$, which may contain a large number of such mapped generalizations, characteristics of memory are observed whereby the confidence of prior encoded mappings decay out over time. Correspondingly, an increase in the degree of deterministic "error" or fuzziness occurs within the recall response, expressed for these attenuated mappings. Mappings may be decayed out in essentially an analog manner and overwritten by subsequent encodings of stimulus–response associations. The following illustrates mathematically one form of memory attenuation applying a first order decay to elements within the correlation set $\{x_k \in [X]\}$:

$$x_k = \frac{1}{c} \int_{t_0}^{T} \lambda_{k,t} \gamma_t e^{i(\phi_t - \theta_{k,t})} e^{(t-T)/\tau} \, dt \tag{2.43}$$

where τ is the decay constant and T represents the current time frame.

In the above formulation, long term memory is characterized by a slow decay rate (long time constant τ), and short term by a proportionally faster rate of decay. In one practical implementation, memory may be controlled by setting an upper threshold level for the average magnitude of complex values stored within the correlation set. This threshold level effectively determines the point at which memory decay is initiated. The upper limit on memory (i.e., permanent memory) is established at the point where this confidence level expressed for nonlearned stimulus patterns is at a statistical mean of 1.0. At a point of saturation encoding, the magnitude of complex values within the correlation set approaches a mean bounded below:

$$|x_{k,j}| \cong \sqrt{N} \qquad (2.44)$$

where N is the number of elements within the stimulus field.

Dynamic memory decay as implemented within the HNeT development system functions in a similar manner, whereby as average vector magnitudes within the correlations set $[X]$ exceeds a pre-established threshold limit, scaling is applied to readjust average magnitudes below the threshold. This feature of dynamic memory control renders the holographic neural process numerically stable in the sense that, for correlation set values approaching the limit of numeric resolution, long term memory decay is invoked avoiding numerical errors incurred by data truncation or "clipping" at the range boundary. Numbers of relatively low resolution (i.e., 16 bits) are required to represent the phase and magnitude (or real and imaginary) components of complex values stored in the correlation set still allowing for high encoding densities over long term memory profiles.

The above threshold limit establishes the mean magnitude (or confidence) for responses generated over untrained regions of the input space. Low values (~ 0.0) initiate memory decay at proportionately low pattern storage densities. Correspondingly, short term memory profiles display a reduced level of fuzziness in the expressed response recall for recognized inputs (confidence = 1.0); however, a far more limited capacity in the storage of distinct stimulus–response mappings owing to the attenuation of memory. Within the HNeT development system, the lower threshold bound on short term memory has been set to 0.0.

In the limit of long term memory, the correlation set magnitudes stabilize somewhat below the theoretical upper bound as presented by Eq. (2.44), and irrespective of the number of enfolded mappings. What this manifestly means is that within the holographic neuron an unbounded number of arbitrarily constructed stimulus–response associations may be encoded onto a correlation set of limited finite resolution, without need for any form of memory decay or renormalization. Having established a profile of permanent memory the holographic cell displays, therefore, an *unbounded* capacity to encode stimulus–response mappings, however exhibiting a degree of fuzziness within response recall in proportion to the complexity of the environment projected within the suit of associations. Correspondingly, the confidence levels within the long term memory characteristic expressed for non-recognition stimulus are increased over the long term memory characteristic, thereby providing a smaller band for recognition discrimination (see Fig. 2.13). Employing the above modifiable features of memory decay, one may configure a neural network whereby distinct groups of neuron cells possess a range of memory profiles extending from immediate short term to long term or permanent memory.

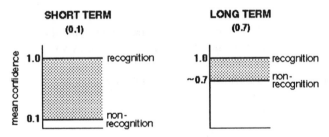

Figure 2.13 *Short-term versus long-term memory characteristic.*

2.2.8 Higher Order Systems

Conventional ANS models are reasonably restricted in terms of the numbers of associations that may be accurately encoded into a neural network. Within the holographic process, limitations on the mapping accuracy are largely overcome through a preprocessing operation involving the generation of high order product terms from the raw stimulus input set $[S]$. The response recall error relationship presented in Eq. (2.25), relates an upper error bound in a functional relationship to the encoding density and the size of stimulus field. This relationship remains valid for the situation in which the stimulus field is expanded to a higher dimensionality describing higher order relationships over a smaller initial data set. The error relationship Eq. (2.25) remains valid in this higher dimensionality, providing the generated product terms form uniquely defined sets, allowing for repeating factors. Within this context "unique sets" are defined by all the combinatorial groups over elements of the initial data set, providing no two product groups have been constructed from the identically same subset of raw input elements, irrespective of commutative order or conjugation.

In one limited example, the input data field may be expanded to a Hermitian matrix form in generating a complete set of second order terms. This Hermitian form may be obtained by representing a set in $[S]$ as a $1 \times N$ linear matrix, and evaluating the following outer product:

$$[H] = [\bar{S}]^T \cdot [S] \tag{2.45}$$

A matrix of the following form is thus generated:

$$[H] = \begin{bmatrix} 1 & \lambda_1 \lambda_2 e^{i(\theta_1 - \theta_2)} & \cdot & \cdot \\ \lambda_2 \lambda_1 e^{i(\theta_2 - \theta_1)} & 1 & & \cdot & \cdot \\ \cdot & \cdot & & \cdot & \cdot \\ \cdot & \cdot & & \cdot & \cdot \end{bmatrix} \tag{2.46}$$

The above form is skew symmetric, therefore a redundancy exists in that the lower diagonal forms a set of terms not unique to the matrix upper diagonal. From simulation one may verify that the same encoding densities are attained using the entire matrix expansion versus only the upper or lower diagonals. The number of unique terms generated from the above Hermitian expansion are:

$$\frac{N}{2}(N - 1) \tag{2.47}$$

The process may be further generalized whereby multiple data fields, for instance, represented by linear matrix $[A]$, forming a set of M elements disjoint to data field $[B]$ having N elements, are expanded as an outer product solution. The expansion may involve, but does not necessarily require, the conjugate transform of any subset of elements within either data set. One possibility is the following second order outer product expansion:

$$[H] = [A]^T [B] \tag{2.48}$$

For stimulus data fields expanded as above and providing that all product terms are unique, the upper limit on "error" within a response recall (decode operation) follows the relationship defined by Eq. (2.25) now realizing that the stimulus field contains $M \times N$ distinct complex elements. One may expand the process still further to facilitate mapping of higher ($>$2nd) order terms into the neuron cell. An input data field expanded to fourth order statistics, for example, may be generated by the following product solution for a higher order term k:

$$s_k = \prod_{m=1}^{4} \lambda_{r(k,m)} \, e^{i\theta_{r(k,m)}} \tag{2.49}$$

where $r(\ )$ is some arbitrary function that selects the input data element as a function of k and the product term m.

The above product solution performs both a phase rotation over the group of data elements and evaluates a net confidence level for the higher order term. The extraction of terms (i.e., $r(k, n)$ in 2.49) from the initial raw stimulus data set may be applied in a pseudorandom manner to obtain an even distribution of statistical measures. Again, this production of higher order terms in certain classes of applications may be optimally applied such that a uniform distribution is obtained over the total possible higher order product set. Each higher order product term forms essentially an "anded" condition over the input elements, thereby evaluating the net confidence value (magnitude) for that generated term. The evaluation of confidence levels for these higher order terms, therefore, maintains probabilistic consistency and follows precursive concepts of fuzzy logic. The above may be illustrated more explicitly as follows, where again the confidence for an information element m is represented simply by the magnitude component, i.e.,

$$\lambda_m \tag{2.50}$$

Any data element of low confidence will therefore attenuate the net confidence within the subset of associated higher order product terms. For instance, in a fourth order product, as indicated previously, any values of λ_1 to λ_4, being of low confidence, attenuate the net confidence values for the resultant s_k:

$$|s_k| = \lambda_1 \cdot \lambda_2 \cdot \lambda_3 \cdot \lambda_4 \qquad (2.51)$$

These higher order expansion terms may be incorporated within both the encoding and decoding operations to form the following generalized sigma–pi form

$$\text{encoding} \qquad x_k = \sum_t^P \gamma_t e_{i\phi_t} \prod_{m=1}^M \lambda_{r(k,m)} e^{-i\theta_{r(k,m)}} \qquad (2.52)$$

$$\text{decoding} \qquad r = \frac{1}{c} \sum_k^N x_k \prod_{m=1}^M \lambda^*_{r(k,m)} e^{i\theta^*_{r(k,m)}} \qquad (2.53)$$

Reiterating, the number of phase elements within the above product terms (M) defines the order of the statistic. The response recall error characteristic for any statistic of order >0 follows the relationship defined in Eq. (2.25), providing that the expanded set forms unique product groups, as defined earlier in this text. The limit imposed by this uniqueness criterion establishes a theoretical upper limit for the total number of higher order terms that may be generated for a given data set and order of statistics. This limit correspondingly establishes an upper limit for the storage density of the neural cell (assuming static data fields). The number of unique higher order terms may be extremely large for initial data fields of relatively small size. The following relation, well known within combination theory, determines the number of unique statistics based on an initial data field size N and order of statistic M, again allowing for repeating factors (i.e., element i taken multiple times):

$$\frac{(N + M - 1)!}{(N - 1)! \, M!} \qquad (2.54)$$

Table 2.1 lists values for the above combinatorial relationship for input data fields ranging from 1 to 20 elements. Implications of the above are extremely important in that the generation of higher order terms provides a mechanism whereby extremely large numbers of stimulus–response mappings may be enfolded onto one correlation set (i.e., one neuron cell), given a small initial stimulus set. For instance, consider a relatively small stimulus field comprised of 20 values and expanding up to 10th order statistics. In this particular case, greater than 3.0×10^7 unique higher order product terms may be generated, permitting a proportionate number of distinct mappings to be enfolded onto the neuron cell. Thirty million randomly placed analog mappings confined within a state space bound by 20 degrees of freedom, defines a system not limited in any respect by linear nonseparability concerns.

TABLE 2.1 Number of Terms as Function of Order of Statistic

		Order of Statistic								
	1	2	3	4	5	6	7	8	9	10
1	1	1	1	1	1	1	1	1	1	1
2	2	3	4	5	6	7	8	9	10	11
3	3	6	10	15	21	28	36	45	55	66
4	4	10	20	35	56	84	120	165	220	286
5	5	15	35	70	126	210	330	495	715	1001
6	6	21	56	126	252	462	792	1287	2002	3003
7	7	28	84	210	462	924	1716	3003	5005	8008
8	8	36	120	330	792	1716	3432	6435	11440	19448
9	9	45	165	495	1287	3003	6435	12870	24310	43758
10	10	55	220	715	2002	5005	11440	24310	48620	92378
11	11	66	286	1001	3003	8008	19448	43758	92378	184756
12	12	78	364	1365	4368	12376	31824	75582	167960	352716
13	13	91	455	1820	6188	18564	50388	125970	293930	646646
14	14	105	560	2380	8568	27132	77520	203490	497420	1144066
15	15	120	680	3060	11628	38760	116280	319770	817190	1961256
16	16	136	816	3876	15504	54264	170544	490314	1307504	3268760
17	17	153	969	4845	20349	74613	245157	735471	2042975	5311735
18	18	171	1140	5985	26334	100947	346104	1081575	3124550	8436285
19	19	190	1330	7315	33649	134596	480700	1562275	4686825	13123110
20	20	210	1540	8855	42504	177100	657800	2220075	6906900	20030010

(Row labels 1–20 denote Size of Stimulus Field.)

A further characteristic observed is that the region of generalization about the mapped locus point reduces in size as one increases the order of terms generated (see Fig. 2.14). Modifying the statistical nature of the data expansion thus facilitates a large degree of control over both the mapping or generalization characteristics within the neuron cell. Expansion of stimulus data fields to higher order terms performs a function somewhat analogous to hidden layers within gradient descent methods. For such models, hidden layers are believed to extract higher order statistics isometric between pattern templates categorized within a given class. The fundamental problem encountered within such models is that one cannot analytically determine which higher order statistics have been interpreted. Corre-

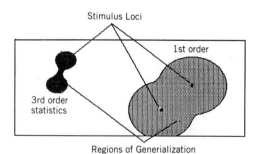

Figure 2.14 *The variation of mapped regions as a function of the order of statistic.*

spondingly, if the patterns vary by statistics other than those presumed to have been interpreted, pattern associations may not be correctly classified. Deterministic control of higher order statistics defining the mapping and generalization characteristics, as defined for the holographic process, is not possible within gradient descent or standard error back propagation techniques.

One may further modify in a deterministic manner the mapping characteristics within an individual neuron cell to suit the requirements of an application. For instance, in application toward vision systems, a high capacity to discern between images may be required in the central region of the visual field, while the periphery displays a lower storage capacity or mapping "resolution." Visual systems may be explicitly modified such that the central portion generates a significantly larger set of higher order statistics, facilitating a more dense stimulus–response mapping topology. The HNeT development system provides the flexibility to both separate out regions of the stimulus field and permits a high level of customization in the design of mapping characteristics through an extensive library of cell preprocessing options (Table 2-3 Pg 54).

2.2.9 Commutative Property

Neuron cells based on the holographic principle display a property referred to in this text as "commutativity." What this means is that neuron cells may be connected together through summing their response outputs (see Fig. 2.15) while maintaining operational characteristics in proportion to the net stimulus size. In other words, groups of cells connected in this manner display operational characteristics identical to a single cell possessing the sum total of all synaptic inputs over the group of distinct and separate neuron cells. Information storage capacity increases in an exponential relationship to the number of cells connected in this manner. This commutative property may be illustrated in a general form by the following mathematical equality:

$$[X]' \, [S]' = \sum_{r}^{N} [X]_r \, [S]_r \qquad (2.55)$$

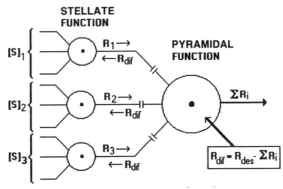

Figure 2.15 *A compound cell structure realizing the commutative properties of holographic cells.*

The above linear matrices may be represented in the following form:

$$[X]' = \{[X_1], [X_2], [X_3], \cdots, [X_N]\} \tag{2.56a}$$

$$[S]' = \{[S_1], [S_2], [S_3], \cdots, [S_N]\} \tag{2.56b}$$

Within a practicable general purpose neural development system this property may utilized in the construction of compound cell structures. One example of a compound cell structure may be constructed from multiple cells of type STEL-LATE as defined within the HNeT applications development system, executing the enhanced encoding/decoding process described herein, and each having their response fields providing the input to a PYRAMIDAL cell, internally configured as a complex vector summation unit. This configuration assumes that pyramidal cells perform essentially a complex summation of the generated response outputs over a group of connected stellate cells.

Cell structures configured in this manner function in a highly integrated manner as indicated above by Figure 2.15. Recursion of vector difference terms (R_{dif}) across STELLATE and PYRAMIDAL cell boundaries are required to facilitate the enhanced encoding process within this compound cell structure. The desired responses over all STELLATE cells are defined by the response fed into the connecting PYRAMIDAL cell. A CORTEX1 function as defined within the HNeT system internally configures the above compound structure of PYRAMIDAL and STELLATE cells.

For a practical example, consider a system comprised of 64 neuron cells, each possessing 16K synaptic inputs. Individually each cell can encode up to 32K random stimulus–response associations displaying a reasonable degree of accuracy on response recall ($\sim 2\%$ analog response error following three learning trials). The total number of synaptic inputs over the entire system however, is, 1 million, and through combining multiple cells within a structure as illustrated in Figure 2.15, a proportionate number of independent stimulus–response mappings ($\sim 500,000$) may be enfolded onto the neural structure, indicating similarly low error characteristics on response recall.

To repeat, the PYRAMIDAL cell within the HNeT system has been designed to accommodate the commutative property. A typical structure is illustrated, as follows, for a series of connected STELLATE cells, whereby the generated or decoded vector responses are summed over cells $i = 1$ to N:

$$R_{sum} = \sum_{i}^{N} R_i \tag{2.57}$$

A vector difference (R_{dif}) between the above vector summation term and the desired response vector R is evaluated within the summing unit (PYRAMIDAL cell) producing:

$$R_{dif} = R - R_{sum} \tag{2.58}$$

This vector difference is transmitted back to each of the originating STELLATE cells on an encode execution pass within the neural engine. The above compound cell structure, therefore, requires a bidirectional transfer of information along the synaptic connections established between STELLATE cells and the PYRAMIDAL cell, as illustrated again in Figure 2.15. The CORTEX1 function within the HNeT system internally allocates the above structure consisting of multiple neuron cells (this number determined by the number of stimulus input fields to the cortex cell) is connected together in the above manner effectively forming a "superneuronal" structure operating within the enhanced learning mode, as described in Section 2.2.5.

2.3 STRUCTURE OF THE NEURAL ENGINE

The HNeT operating kernel permits one to structure the neural engine as a virtual array of cells. A general purpose neural computing system of this type allows the applications developer to structure a wide range of cell configurations as well as to establish the associated data flow paths between such an array of cells. A device of similar operation may be constructed in a nonvirtual manner, whereby the cells are specifically hardwired within a physical embodiment for optimization over a more restricted class of neural configurations. The HNeT system is structured such that critical sections of the neural operating kernel are resident within the neural microprocessor on-chip RAM, having data storage structures allocated for the configuration of virtual cells located in the slower off-chip memory. Off chip memory access within the HNeT system is also required in the storage and retrieval of data fields and correlation sets. Refer to Table 2.2 for a general layout of the HNeT memory map.

The users' application program, resident within a host processor, facilitates ini-

TABLE 2.2 The HNeT Memory Map

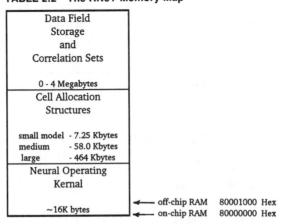

tial configuration of the neural engine as stated above, functions for transfer of complex valued data sets between the host and neural coprocessor, as well as instruction sets to establish control over execution cycles within this neural engine. Within HNeT the neural coprocessor and host processes communicate via a high speed serial port but otherwise function independently, accessing both executable code and data from their own local memory. Figure 2.16 presents a functional block diagram for this hardware structure forming the basis for the HNeT system.

The following provides a brief description of one possible hardware embodiment to establish a conceptual basis for future generation computing systems, using as a principle of operation the holographic neural process. This "neurocomputer," as it shall be referred to subsequently in this text, is intended to be general purpose in operation, as facilitated by a highly flexible reprogramming utility. The programming convention employed, however, is significantly different from conventional programming methodologies, as is illustrated within the sections following.

The neurocomputer hardware platform may be comprised of one or a plurality of processing nodes arranged in a manner by which data may be transferred between nodes. A single processing node within this hardware embodiment contains the following significant features:

A processing means to execute complex based transformations that comprise the encoding, enhanced encoding, decoding, and supplementary preprocessing operations. This processor may be general purpose in nature in order that it may execute the variety of complex vector manipulations, as described under previous sections relating theory of operation. Ideally, a hardware embodiment capable of executing in-parallel vector operations could be incorporated into the design. The holographic neural process is of inherently an analog nature, however, either analog or digital processing means may be effectively used.

A data storage means by which the stimulus data and associated response data fields may be addressably stored. Similarly, a data storage means by which correlation set data may be addressably stored, that is, the correlation substrate. The data storage means will also be required to store configuration information identifying the cells functional category and features, and related parameters of operation. Such operational parameters may identify the data flow structure (i.e., synaptic interconnection map) established between the plurality of cells configured within the neural processor as well as other features specific to the cell type (i.e., order of statistics generated, memory profile, etc.)

Memory interface unit for providing access to the processor for addressably accessing the data storage means in retrieval of stimulus–response data sets, correlation data, and cell allocation parameters.

Establishing a parallel processor hardware configuration requiring the means to communicate stimulus–response data fields to other similar processing nodes within the neurocomputing system. Communication may, of course, be performed via either a serial or parallel data transfer protocol.

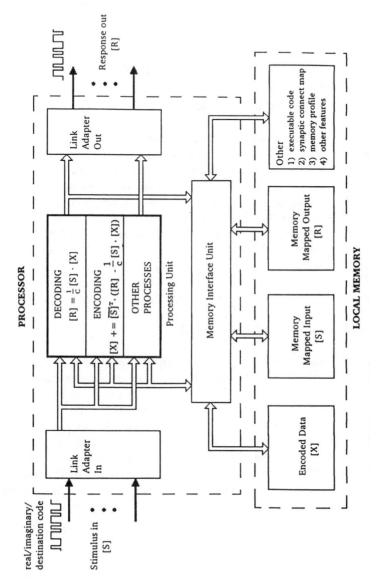

Figure 2.16 *A possible hardware embodiment for a neural processing node.*

In the specific hardware embodiment illustrated in Figure 2.16 two principle components are indicated within the processing node, that is, the single chip neural processor of Figure 2.16 and the external memory storage unit, that is, RAM, ROM, magnetic, or optical storage media. The single chip neural processor may be accommodated by devices containing the following generally desirable features:

- Central (neural) processing unit
- On-chip high speed random access memory (RAM)
- External memory interface
- Interprocessor high speed communication

The above embodies a single chip device capable of configuring neural cells in a virtual mode whereby the arrangement of what are essentially "functional blocks" may be software configurable. These functional blocks allocate virtual cells having the capacity to replicate the operations of the encoding, enhanced encoding, and decoding described within the theory neural process. Additional cells may be configured within the neural processor in the performance of supplementary tasks such as generation of higher order statistics, sigmoidal redistribution of data fields, conjugation of complex elements, conversion from real valued to complex values number domains, extraction or appending of data fields, and other aspects of operation indicated under Section 2.2. Similarly, parameters of operation specific to each cell may be modified, exhibiting control over memory profiles and the modification of neural plasticity as described further in this chapter. In one sense the above tasks are structured principally through matrix operations over data fields.

A data field as defined herein refers essentially to a set of complex values. The size of the data field, of course, indicates the number of complex values, or information elements, within that field. For purposes of extracting and appending sections of these data fields, the fields may be arranged as two-dimensional arrays or matrices of complex values (see Fig. 2.17). The complex valued elements of the stimulus and response fields may be stored and communicated in either their real/imaginary or phase/magnitude syntax. For purposes of illustration, it will be assumed that the real/imaginary representation is taken and it has been found that this representation lends itself to higher computational efficiency. Phase and mag-

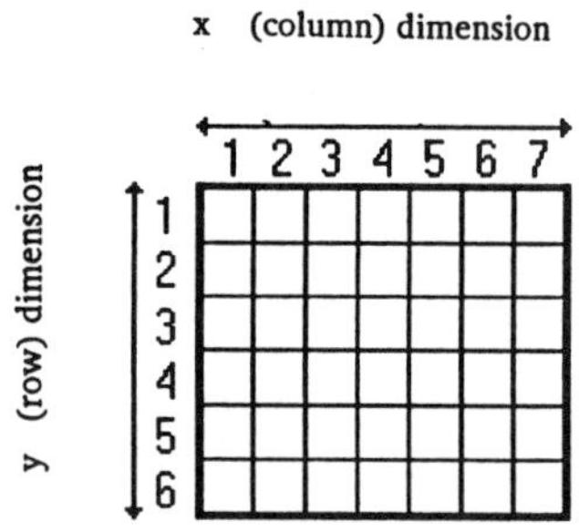

Figure 2.17   Matrix formulation of a data field.

nitude components may be expressed through conversion of an analog pulse modulated signal (as in real neurons). However, using the binary representation required within digital computers one must descretize the analog range in a suitable manner. For the phase component having limits established at the $0-2\pi$ regions, this range may, for instance, be descretized to a 0 to 255 binary representation within the HNeT system, permitting a $\pm 0.25\%$ numerical error along the analog range. Similarly, for the magnitude typically bounded within the 0.0–1.0 probabilistically relevant range, the unity representation may be scaled to a 0 to 128 binary representation. One element of information within either the stimulus or response fields could therefore be represented in two bytes. In assigning a higher level of numerical resolution within these data sets and internal operations of the neural engine a negligible increase in recall accuracy or storage density is attained. The nature by which the holographic process overlaps control mappings onto the correlation substrate inherently produces a measurable, albeit small, component of "fuzziness" in response recall. This fuzziness generally overshadows any increase in the response recall accuracy resulting from the use of a finer level of numeric resolution within the numeric process.

Data elements of the stimulus or response fields may be transmitted to or from external processor nodes or between the memory unit and neural processing unit via either the memory interface unit or serial data links as illustrated in Figure 2.16.

Encoding Operation. In execution of encoding, elements of the stimulus input field may be read into the neural processor unit either via one of the serial communication means, or accessed from the external memory means providing facility for memory mapped input. Similarly, the element or plurality of elements within a response data field is read into the neural processor by similar addressable access. For purposes of computational efficiency, it is generally preferable that the correlation set $[X]$ stored within the external memory unit be represented in the real/imaginary syntax. (The reader may wish to investigate algorithmic variations of the holographic process to verify this assumption.) In a similar vein, the central processor retrieves correlation values $\{x_{i,j} \in [X]\}$ by addressable access to external memory. The neural processor executes the steps in operation of the encoding transform as defined in Eqs. (2.27–2.30) under Section 2.2.5, that is;

$$[X] + = [\bar{S}]^T \cdot \left([R]_{\text{des}} - \frac{1}{c} [S] \cdot [X] \right)$$

with $[S]$ being the new stimulus set and $[R]_{\text{des}}$, the associated or desired response set.

The above transform enfolds the learned analog stimulus to response mapping onto the existing correlation set $[X]$. The encoded element or elements of the correlation set $[X]$ are stored back into the external memory, this storage substrate performing a somewhat analogous function to the synaptic processes of the biological equivalent.

Decoding Operation. In the decoding process, the elements of the stimulus input field may again be read into the neural processor unit either via interprocessor communication means or accessed from the external memory means thus providing a facility for memory mapped input. Complex values representing the correlation set $\{x_{i,j} \in [X]\}$ are similarly accessed from the external memory. The decoding unit performs the process steps in operation of the response recall by execution of the following transformation as defined by Eq. (2.11) under Section 2.2.3:

$$[R] = \frac{1}{c} [S] \cdot [X]$$

Note that for the functional block description presented in Figure 2.16, one hardware exemplar may be a conventional system exhibiting much of the functionality of a general purpose processor, whose operations within the above matrix evaluation are largely performed in a sequential manner. A preferred embodiment would employ parallel processing hardware to more efficiently evaluate bulk of matrix product terms. Response recall $[R]$ may be transferred to external processing nodes via a plurality of data transfer links or through external memory for memory mapped output.

Supplementary Operations. A third function block, as described in Figure 2.16 within the neural processing unit, is related to supplementary features of the holographic process. This functional unit accesses and stores stimulus–response data in a similar manner to that described for the encoding/decoding processes. These supplementary processes include operations related to generation of higher order statistics, sigmoidal processing, outerproduct, normalization of magnitude components, complex conjugation, etc. This functional group should optimally include all of the supplementary operations described under the sections pertaining to theory of operation.

A plurality of processing nodes may be interconnected via serial or parallel communication means to form an array of neural elements executing optimally in an asychronous fashion. One possible parallel configuration is illustrated in Figure 2.18, this embodiment comprised of 16 processing nodes of similar type. Each processing node within such a neurocomputing device may be a replication of the hardware embodiment presented within Figure 2.16. The interprocessor communication arrangement presented is a four-dimensional Boolean hypercube. Within this structure, each neural processing node addressably accesses its own local memory and establishes bidirectional communication links directly with the neural processors of the four nearest nodes. A data field transfer from any node to any other therefore requires on average two link transfers to establish communication. This illustrates the general hardware configuration for an advanced hardware pro-

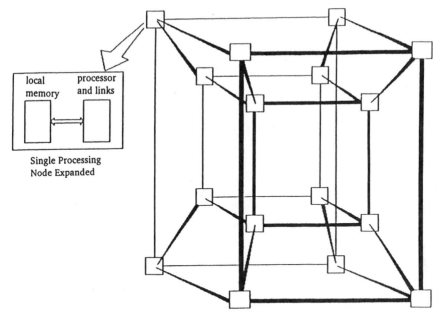

local   processor
memory   and links

Single Processing
Node Expanded

Figure 2.18   *Illustration of a hypercube parallel processing structure.*

totype the author has developed (NC 2000) operating from the holographic principle.

The neural engine functions in essentially two modes of operation, that is,

1. Allocation of cells and data flow paths defining the structure of the neural configuration
2. Neural engine execution

The execution phase (2) consists principally of porting input data fields to the neural engine, initiation of the execution cycle, and reading generated response values back to the host processor. During the execution phase, the host processor functions principally as the interface for system console, I/O servers, and controller over the peripheral sensing and control devices. The bulk of tasks performed by the host resident application program is normally related to the processing or conversion of data read from peripheral devices, and porting of these data fields to the neural engine. During an execution cycle, the neural engine and the host processor resident application function optimally in a concurrent manner, maximizing usage of both the neural and host processing facilities. The HNeT system is in fact structured in this manner, permitting the host system to retrieve and process data during concurrent operation of the neural engine.

Although the preferred embodiment as well as the operation has been specifically described in relation to the figures, it should be understood that variation in this embodiment could readily be accommodated without departing from the fundamental concepts encompassing such artificial neural devices as revealed within this chapter.

2.3.1   Cell Types

Given the above hardware platform, a configuration of "virtual cells" may be allocated separately within each neural processing node. The cell types available within the HNeT system have been segregated into two categories these being:

- Adjunct operator cells
- Cortical cells

Cells within each of these categories have a general structure possessing one or more input fields and one output data field as illustrated by Figures 2.23 and 2.25.

> *Adjunct Operator cells* permit one to structure a wide range of data manipulation operations and complex vector transforms over data fields, storing the result within the cell's output field. These cells perform a range of preprocessing operations over the data fields read into the neural engine. For instance, expanding a data field to higher order statistics (STAT), extracting a portion of a data field (EXTRACT), performing a complex conjugate transform over data field elements (CONJUGATE), and a number of similar complex valued matrix transform operations. (An illustrative but not comprehensive list of possible operator cell functions is provided in Table 2.3.)
>
> *Cortical cells* are illustrated here by two exemplary cells, CORTEX1 and 2. This category of cell perform the encoding/decoding processes within the neural engine, storing stimulus–response mappings onto one or more correlation sets. Holographic neural cells both function and are structured in a highly generic manner. Each cell is capable of receiving one or more stimulus input fields (each field comprised of a set of complex values), and can concurrently learn (encode) and express (decode) a response field associated to that input stimulus. This generic structure for neural cells, combined with the flexibility to structure data flow between cells in any manner. (An illustrative list of possible cortical cell types are provided in Table 2.4.)

A class of adjunct operator cells operate primarily as storage buffers for data fields read into the neural engine from the host processor. Other cells within the neural configuration (cortical or operator cell types) may access data fields stored within these buffer cells.

In general, the output data field of any cell type may provide input to any other cell subsequently configured within the neural engine. A pseudo-coding format within HNeT has been adopted, as illustrated in the following examples, whereby configuration calls for allocating the cells within the neural engine return a label to the cells output data field. For instance, one may configure an input cell receiv-

---

†Holographic-based artificial neural devices are patent-pending AND Corporation.

ing a 10 × 20 data array from the host application program. This cell is allocated within the neural engine using the following configuration call:

```
A = buffer(10,20);
```

The above label A may be used within the parameter list of subsequent configuration calls allocating cells within the neural engine. Cells subsequently allocated and referencing label A within their parameters list use the BUFFER cells data field as input. Below is an example for the operator cell STAT which expands its input data field to higher order terms. This operator cell reads the data field referenced by label A, and returns a label to its output field (B), containing for instance 200 higher order terms as illustrated below. Again, the STAT operator cell accesses data field (A) stored within the BUFFER cell by reference to the label returned i.e.

```
B = stat(200, A, ENDLIST);
```

In this manner, an arrangement of cells and data flow paths within the neural engine are constructed from a series of configuration cells. Using combinations of feed forward and recurrent data flow paths, arrays of cells may be structured in nearly any manner. One may, for instance, fan out a cell's output data field to any number of subsequent cells. Recurrent data flow paths may be established, whereby data fields generated within higher layers may be fed recursively to the input fields of cells located within lower layers of the neural configuration. Expanding further, the general purpose neural based system may configure operator cells which combine subsets of output data fields within a single cell (i.e., fan in structure). These various structures for data flow (i.e., fan in, fan out, recurrent flow) are illustrated above in Figure 2.19.

A subset of the adjunct operator functions provided within the HNeT system allow one to perform operations over defined windows within the data fields transferred between cells, thus permitting a greater level of control over manipulation of data. Operations involving the appending or extraction of window regions within data fields may correspond to sections of data defined over a physical domain. Figure 2.20 illustrates an example of the EXTRACT_WND function used to con-

Figure 2.19 *Illustration of possible data flow assignments between cells within a multicellular neural configuration.*

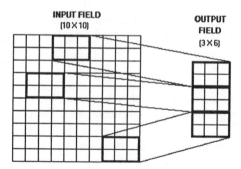

Figure 2.20 *Extraction of data elements from within defined windows of a data field.*

figure a cell which extracts window regions from its input data field (see Table 2.3 presenting a representative list of window based operations).

Using this matrix format for data fields each axis may represent physical parameters such as frequency/time as in an auditory input, or the x/y pixel position within a visual field (see Fig. 2.21). Manipulation of data sets within this two-dimensional format permits one to design separate neural configurations operating over different regions within a visual field, spectral frequencies, etc. The user may therefore construct several distinct neural configurations within the neural engine, each configuration dedicated to separate regions or aspects of the raw input data fields.

The convention used in cell allocation simplifies the design effort and allows

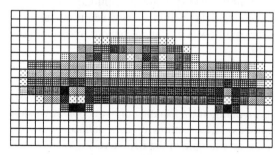

Example of a pixelized visual input

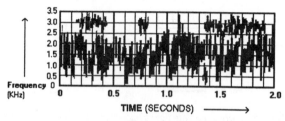

Example of an auditory input

Figure 2.21 *Examples of data fields containing visual or auditory data.*

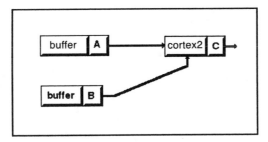

Figure 2.22 *A simple neural configuration.*

one to construct highly powerful networks, requiring relatively few function calls to allocate the internal structure of cells within the neural engine. The following provides an illustration of a neural configuration established through three function calls, this neural configuration consisting of two BUFFER cells and a CORTEX2 cell. In this example, BUFFER cell (A) receives a stimulus field of size 10 by 2 and cell (B) receives a desired response field of size 1 by 4. These two cells provide the data field input to the respective stimulus and desired response input fields of the cortical cell. The CORTEX2 cell internally expands the input stimulus field to 1000 statistics. This data field expansion initiates with 1st order terms and follows a linear progression through the exhaustive set of unique higher order products until 1000 values have been generated. The neural configuration is illustrated by Figure 2.22 and the cell allocation function calls required to establish this configuration within the neural engine are presented as follows:

```
A = receptor(10,2);
B = buffer(1,4);
C = cortex2(1000, B, A, ENDLIST);
```

This simple configuration may be used to encode or generate a highly complex topological mapping of the stimulus field containing 20 analog values to a response field comprised of 4 analog values. One may subsequently express these associations during decoding cycles of the neural engine. The encoding capacity within this configuration is essentially unbounded; however, the system is capable of accurately constructing its input–output mapping to only certain level of complexity (i.e., up to 1000 arbitrary mappings). Many useful and highly advanced applications may be fulfilled using only a very simple neural configuration of the type illustrated above.

2.3.1.1 Adjunct Operator Cells. These cells access one or more input data fields as illustrated in Figure 2.23. The adjunct operator cells function in a manner whereby they receive input data fields, perform a defined operation on that data field, and store the generated result in the cells output field. The primary function of this class of cells are the manipulation and/or preprocessing of data fields prior to input into a cortical cell for encoding and decoding of stimulus–response asso-

Figure 2.23 *Structure of the adjunct operator cell.*

ciations. Access to correlation sets are limited to the cortical category of cells. A list of possible adjunct operator cell types is presented in Table 2.3.

The general functions that may be performed within this class of cells are grouped as follows:

1. Extracting or Appending Data Fields

One may configure an operator cell to extract subsets of complex elements from existing data fields. Elements from these data fields may be extracted in either a predefined or pseudo-random manner, that is, EXTRACT/EX-TRACT_RND. Extracted values may also be defined over a linear array or within a window region of the input data field, that is, EXTRACT_WND. Similarly, any number of data fields may be appended into a single field via the use of the APPEND function.

2. Data Field Transformation

This functional group performs complex vector transformations over data fields. Transformation operations include generation of higher order terms (STAT); complex vector conjugation (CONJUGATE); matrix transpose operation (TRANSPOSE); and formation of outer product from two input fields (OUTERPROD), these illustrating a limited variety of possible data field transforms. Also included within the HNeT system is a cell performing a sigmoidal transform over its input data field (SIGMOID), where the phase orientations of the elements contained therein are redistributed to optimize properties of azimuthal symmetry.

3. Modification of Confidence Values

This class of functions may perform operations on the confidence levels (magnitudes) of the complex elements within a data field. These operator cells facilitate user control over confidence levels established within infor-mation or data fields. Confidence levels may be redistributed about a specified mean (NORMALIZE) or undergo a non-linear sigmoidal mapping about a confidence threshold (the THRESHOLD cell).

4. Window Based Operations

As defined previously, window cells permit the user to define multiple windows within an input data field and perform complex vector transforms or data extraction for elements located within that window. Transform opera-

TABLE 2.3   List of Possible Adjunct Operator Cells

Name	Description
APPEND	Appends multiple data fields and stores the result as a 1 by N linear matrix.
BUFFER	Operates as a storage buffer for data read in from the host processor. The buffer is assigned by the user as a two dimensional data field. This data field is subsequently read into other cells within the neural configuration.
CONJUGATE	Generates the complex conjugate of values read in from a data field.
EXTRACT	Extracts values from a data field in a linear sequence. The output is stored as a 1 by N linear matrix.
NORMALIZE	Normalizes magnitudes of values read in from a data field about a mean confidence level.
OUTERPROD	Reads two data fields as linear matrices and generates the outer product solution $[A]^T \cdot [B]$.
RECURSE	Copies the data field from any cell allocated downstream to this cell's output data field, permitting recurrent data flow.
REDUCE	Outputs a data matrix of reduced dimension by averaging adjacent elements read in from a data field.
RESIZE	Reassigns the dimension of a data field stored as a linear matrix.
SIGMOID	Redistributes phase orientations of values read from a data field to a symmetric distribution using a sigmoidal mapping.
STAT	Reads values from multiple data fields and expands the set to higher order terms as described by Eq. (2.49). Stores the result as a 1 by N linear matrix.
THRESHOLD	Performs a non-linear scaling on magnitudes (confidence level) for values read in from a data field.
TRANSPOSE	Geneates the transpose matrix of a data field.
Window Based Cells	
AVERAGE__WND	Evaluates vector averages for N windows assigned within a data field. Stores the result as a 1 by N linear matrix.
EXTRACT__WND	Extracts values from window regions assigned within a data field. Stores result as a 1 by N linear matrix.
PRODUCT__WND	Evaluates complex product over N windows assigned withina data field. Stores the result as a 1 by N linear matrix.

tions may include but are not exclusively limited to generation of higher order terms, vector product, and averaging.

5. Data Field Buffering

These cells operate essentially as buffers for data field transmissions. The BUFFER cell remains dormant during an execution cycle and performs only the allocation of memory for storage of input data fields read from the host application program. The RECURSE cell copies a data output field generated by the designated source cell to its own output data field. The source cell may be any cell allocated within the neural configuration. Recurrent data fields are transferred on the following cycle of execution, as illustrated in

Figure 2.24. In this configuration, the output field of the CORTEX1 cell (E) forms a recurrent data flow to the RECURSE cell (A). During the execution cycle at tn the neural engine generates an output field (E) from stimulus data read into cells A and B. On the initiation of the next execution cycle (t_{n+1}), the RECURSE cell copies data field (E) onto its output data field. The operator and cortical cells are then executed in the sequence by which they appear within the configuration code. In this example the SIGMOID cell (C), STAT cell (D), and CORTEX1 cell (E). A new data output field for the cortical cell (E) is produced at the termination of the next execution cycle (t_{n+1}). Recurrent data flow within any neural configuration is facilitated in a manner similar to the above.

Within a general purpose architecture, as described previously, any of the above operator cell functions may be implemented on any data field within the neural configuration, permitting maximum flexibility in construction of design. Again, adjunct operator functions are generally configured to perform preprocessing operations on data fields prior to input to cortical cells.

2.3.1.2 Cortical Cells. These cells (Table 2.4) perform the principal function within the neural engine, that is, encoding (learning) and decoding (response recall) of analog stimulus–response associations. Cortical cells possess a structure somewhat different from the adjunct operator cell group. Cortical cells have one or more stimulus input data fields and an associated desired response input field. The desired response input field is read only during an encode execution cycle of the neural engine. These cells generate a mapping of the input stimulus fields to the set of values contained within the desired response input field. By means of holographic encoding, a plurality of such stimulus–response mappings is superimposed or *enfolded* onto the identically same correlation set. The cortical cell generates as output a single data field, this field containing the generated outputs for the response recall (i.e., decoding). The structure for this category of cells is indicated in Figure 2.25. A variety of composite cortical cell types may be configured combining the unitary STELLATE and PYRAMIDAL cells with various adjunct operator cells into one functional unit.

For instance, the composite cell CORTEX1 establishes a compound cell structure built upon of unitary cells only of type STELLATE and PYRAMIDAL. The compound cell structure forms what has been referred to as a superneuronal struc-

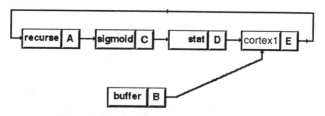

Figure 2.24 *A recurrent neural configuration.*

TABLE 2.4 List of Cortical Cells

Name	Description
STELLATE	Executes the encode/decode function for the holographic neural process both generating in generation of the correlation set [x] and response recall.
PYRAMIDAL	Ancillary cell permits the outputs from multiple STELLATE cells to be summed realizing the "commutative" property described in Eq. (2.55) and Figure 2.15.
CORTEX1	Compound cell structure composed of the above STELLATE and PYRAMIDAL cells arranged in a connective structure as illustrated in Figure 2.26.
CORTEX2	Compound cell structure composed of a STAT operator cell, STELLATE and PYRAMIDAL cells as defined above. The internal structure is illustrated in Figure 2.26.

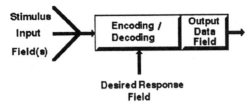

Figure 2.25 *Structure of the neural cell.*

ture (see Section 2.2.9 pertaining to the commutative property) whereby the generated response fields from multiple cells of type STELLATE performing the holographic based encoding/decoding process are fed into a single PYRAMIDAL cell executing the vectorial addition over corresponding elements within the generated response output fields (see Fig. 2.15). This compound cell structure permits multiple stimulus fields to be fed into a single cell and allows this cell structure to operate as an integrated unit. A second example of a composite neural cell is illustrated by the CORTEX2 cell which again configures a compound structure similar to the above, however providing the option to expand the stimulus input field up to any order and number of higher order terms or "statistics." The CORTEX2 cell configures a structure that executes the sigma-pi encoding/decoding process as indicated in Eqs. (2.52) and (2.53). The STAT cell forms a coarse analogy to reticular and granule cells located at the pre-cortical efferent pathways to somatosensory regions of the cerebral cortex Figure 2.27. The cell structures configured by both the CORTEX1 and 2 functions are illustrated graphically in Figure 2.26 and mimic a certain class of structures found within the cerebral cortex.

For the preceding illustration of composite neural cell types, the enhanced encoding process may be employed whereby learning is a function of the memory previously enfolded within the cell's correlation set. This enhanced encoding process facilitates automatic control over attention, whereby only new stimulus re-

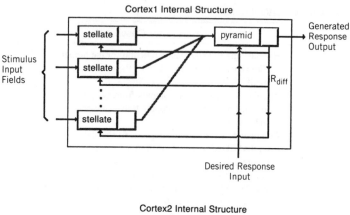

Cortex1 Internal Structure

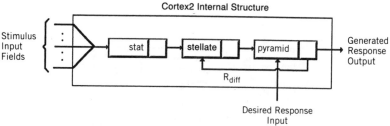

Cortex2 Internal Structure

Figure 2.26 *Internal structure of the cortex1 and 2 cells.*

sponse associations influence the mapping substrate (memory means storing the correlation set). This process also permits reinforcement learning whereby the analog error on response recall may be substantially eliminated over few (typically <4) reinforcement learning trials.

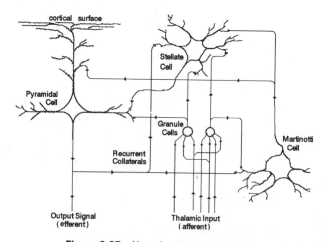

Figure 2.27 *Neural pathways within the cerebral cortex.*

2.3.2 Memory

Memory embodies the stimulus–response associations or "mappings" enfolded within the correlation set, allocated for cells belonging only to the cortical group. These correlation sets may be comprised of arrays of complex numbers requiring only a reasonably low level of dynamic resolution (i.e., possibly as low as $-127 \rightarrow +128$ integer using an 8 bit binary representation along the real and imaginary axis).

The HNeT development system in actuality stores one correlation element in 64 bytes storage using a 4 byte floating point representation for each of the real and imaginary axis. The size of the correlation set for a cortical cell having N elements in its stimulus input field and M elements in the response field is $N \times M$. In reading or retrieving correlation sets using the memory file transfer functions (see sections following), correlation values are retrieved within the HNeT system by row and column in the general format illustrated by Figure 2.28. Retrieving the first row, therefore, presents the correlation set associating the stimulus field to the first element in the response field. The correlation set is thus arranged as a two dimensional matrix, in this example, the stimulus input field having 10 elements, and 5 elements in the response. The neural engine allocates storage space for these correlation sets in RAM memory above the neural operating kernel and cell allocation structures. A compound cell structure such as that configured by the CORTEX1 function may contain several STELLATE cells and thus allocate a proportionate number of correlation sets. The number of STELLATE cells within this structure is established by the number of stimulus input fields defined within the CORTEX1 function parameter list (see Fig. 2.26). These correlation sets may be read either from or loaded into the neural engine kernel using appropriate data transfer schemes.

Cortical cells permit a modifiable memory profile whereby the user may specify characteristics extending from long term to short term memory. Modification of memory profile is facilitated by a SETMEM function, see Table 2.5. The default value specified on configuration of cortical cells is the limit of long term or permanent memory where response recall, on a cell having reached saturation encoding, generates a statistical mean of 1.0 in the magnitude component of complex elements within the response recall. Random statistical tests indicate that the correlation set magnitudes approach asymptotically, and stabilize somewhat below the theoretical limit presented in Eq. (2.44). This asymptotic maxima defines ef-

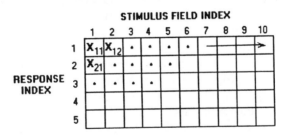

Figure 2.28 Matrix formulation of the correlation set.

fectively the upper limit of numeric resolution required for permanent memory. This limit remains again bounded irrespective of the number of distinct stimulus–response associations encoded. Implications being that no restriction exists in the number of unattenuated stimulus–response mappings which may be encoded or enfolded into the holographic cortical cell. A degree of fuzziness is displayed during response recall due to the nature by which densely populated mappings influence their proximal regions. The number of synaptic inputs (i.e., order and size of stimulus field) establishes characteristics of the mapping topology, defining the cells capacity to map out discrete sets of stimulus–response associations. The coefficient of memory used within the HNeT system has been normalized to a value of 0.0 for short term and 1.0 for the upper limit of long term or permanent memory.

2.3.3 Neural Engine Execution

Following configuration of the neural engine, using the pseudo-coding format as indicated in the previous sections, the second portion of the host application program is implemented. This comprises the execution stage of the prior structured neural engine. The basic steps performed during this execution phase are

- Write stimulus data fields into the neural coprocessor engine,
- Command an execution cycle,
- Read generated response recall back from the neural engine.

These are the general steps required for one execution cycle. One may enable an iterative series of execution cycles within the neural engine for real time applications. One such application may be in the construction of control systems capable of learning and subsequently expressing temporally varying stimulus–response or ''spatio-temporal'' patterns. The user may also configure iterative processing among recurrent data flow loops to facilitate applications in associative reasoning (see Section 2.6.3).

One execution cycle is performed by enabling an EXECUTE command within the HNeT system. This executive command provides an option to enable decode only or both decode/encode functions within one execution cycle. During an execute cycle, the neural engine resolves all cells in the order by which they have been allocated during configuration of the neural engine. The speed of execution may be measured in terms of ''connections per second'' where one connection refers to the correlation element or synaptic connection established between one element within a stimulus input field and one element within the associated response field. The neural processor described in the example of an embodiment presented in Figure 2.16 is capable of performing up to 10 Million connections/second using commercially available RISC microprocessors.

Additional modules have been included within the HNeT development system to facilitate modification of parameters influencing both the learning and expression processes. Such parameters of execution may be modified at run time between cycles of execution. Two examples of the type of functions provided within the

TABLE 2.5   List of Executive Functions

Function	Description
EXECUTE	Initiates an execution cycle within the neural engine. The neural engine may perform both encode/decode or decode only on one pass.
OPTIMIZE	Controls neural plasticity (eliminates connections) to optimize the global mapping accuracy within cortical cells (see Section 2.5).
SETEXE	Enables/disables specific groups of cells within the neural configuration.
SETNORM	Modifies the mean confidence parameter within the NORMALIZE cell.
SETMEM	Modifys the dynamic memory profile within cortical cells. Default is permant memory.
SETLRN	Holographic cortical cells produce exact stimulus to response mappings by default in one encoding operation. This function sets damping parameters on the rate of learning.
SYSCLR	Clears the entire configuration of cells within the neural engine.

HNeT system for such dynamic modification of parameters are SETMEM and OPTIMIZE. The SETMEM function facilitates user control over the dynamic memory profiles within cells of the cortical group. The OPTIMIZE function facilitates limited control over neural "plasticity" whereby the user may interactively eliminate those connections to cortical cells which indicate little or no contribution within the correlation mapping (see Table 2.5).

2.3.4   Data Transfer between Host and Neural Engine

A range of data transfer functions has been provided within the HNeT development system for porting data fields between the host application program and cells allocated within the neural engine. An illustrative list is provided in Table 2.6. Data

TABLE 2.6   List of Data and Memory Transfer Functions

Function	Description
INDATA	Converts a real valued data stream to the neural engines internal COMPLEX format and ports this data to the designated cell. The conversion is performed as a simple linear transformation.
INSIG	Measures the mean and standard deviation of the real valued input stream and dynamically adjusts a sigmoidal function to map this input to a symmetric distribution in the COMPLEX format. Permits the user to port unprocessed floating point data into the neural engine.
OUTDATA	Reads a data output stream from any cell within the neural configuration.
INMEM	Reads a correlation set from any cortical cell within the neural configuration to the host application.
OUTMEM	Transfers a correlation set from the host application to a specified cortical cell.
LOADMEM	Loads all correlation sets for the current neural configuration from a disk file to the neural engine.
SAVEMEM	Saves all correlation sets within the current neural configuration to a disk file. Configuration information is also saved for verification on subsequent reloading.

sets as measured within real world applications are generally represented by a real number system. Data conversion must, therefore, be accommodated during the transfer operation between host application and the neural engine performing its operations within the complex number domain. Data transfer functions provided within HNeT allow values expressed in either real floating point or a COMPLEX format to be ported to the neural engine from the host application. These functions perform the automatic conversion of real valued data sets into a floating point COMPLEX data type. Typically, BUFFER cells are those used to receive data fields from the host application.

Supplied also are functions for saving correlation files for the entire neural configuration to disk and correspondingly load these files from disk storage to the neural engine. These functions allow one to interactively, from the application program, change or reload memory enfolded within cortical cells during learning. Headers within the file storage format contain cell configuration information, allowing the neural engine to verify that the correlation file to be loaded is in fact compatible with the configuration currently allocated within the neural engine. One may also transfer the correlation sets directly between the user's application program and the neural engine using the INMEM/OUTMEM functions. This facility is useful in the event that the user wishes to monitor or modify the correlation sets within the neural engine.

2.4 CELL CONFIGURATION TYPES

The following sections illustrate some general programming structures that may be used in configuration of the neural engine. As stated previously, operation of the neural engine is structured in two parts, that is, configuration code for setting up the neural engine, followed by the execution code performing tasks related to transferring data between host and the neural engine, and initiating the execution cycles for both encode/decode operations.

2.4.1 Feed Forward Neural Configuration

Design features for the HNeT operating kernel allow a largely unrestricted level of flexibility in establishing the data flow paths interconnecting various cells allocated within the neural engine. A feedforward configuration at nearly any defined level of complexity may be built up from the set of HNeT library function calls used in cell allocation. The structure of a feedforward neural configuration is of a form indicated in Figure 2.29 in which BUFFER cells are generally the first allocated within the neural engine. The second stage in the design of a neural configuration is generally concerned with the allocation of adjunct operator cells for performing various preprocessing operations on these input data fields. Subsequent layers within the configuration are comprised of cortical cells, receiving stimulus and response fields from previous or lower layers within the neural configuration. Multilayered structures of cells may be structured, whereby the output or response

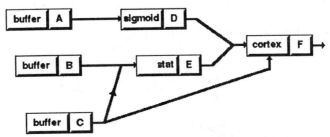

Figure 2.29   *Illustration of a feedforward configuration.*

fields from cortical cells may be fed into subsequent layers of cortical or adjunct operator cells. Figure 2.29 illustrates a feedforward configuration of this type which preprocesses stimulus data along a series of cells and transfers the desired response values to a CORTEX cell. The holographic process accommodates an operation by which both the encoding (learning) and decoding (response) operations may be performed concurrently within a single execution cycle. The configuration code required to allocate this neural configuration is as follows:

```
A = buffer(15, 12);
B = buffer(5, 5);
C = buffer(2, 1);
D = sigmoid(A);
E = stat(500, C, B, ENDLIST);
F = cortex(C, D, E, ENDLIST);
```

2.4.2   Recurrent Neural Configuration

A recurrent data flow structure defines a neural configuration in which the data output fields generated at higher layers within the array of cells are fed back as input fields to cells within the same or lower layers. The HNeT development system described in this text facilitates recurrent data flows by use of a RECURSE cell. Any number of recurrent loops may be formed within a neural configuration, limited only by available memory and the cell allocation resource. The configuration code to establish the recurrent configuration illustrated in Figure 2.30 is presented below. The START/ENDCNF statements permit the compiler to perform a two pass compilation over the cells located between these keywords in order that the data field labels establishing the recurrent data flow paths may be resolved.

```
STARTCNF
A = buffer(15, 12);
B = recurse(5, 5, F);
C = buffer(5, 5);
D = sigmoid(A);
E = stat(500, B, C, ENDLIST);
F = cortex(C, D, E, ENDLIST);
ENDCNF
```

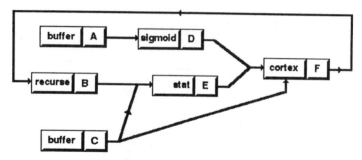

Figure 2.30 *Illustration of a recurrent configuration.*

2.4.3 Compound Cell Structures

A particular structure of cells may be required many times within a neural config-uration, this structure possibly consisting of multiple cells of both the adjunct op-erator and/or cortical cell category. It may be useful in this case to construct a function call which internally allocates the desired compound cell structure. This desirable feature allows the user to construct his own function call in the allocation of any arbitrarily defined compound structure, while conforming to the general calling format used within the HNeT configuration library functions. A configu-ration call structured in this manner receives input data fields labels through its parameter list, returning a label to the output data field, thus:

```
output_label = user_cell(parm1, ...parmN; input_label1,.
.,input_labelN);
```

For instance, the following function establishes a cell structure in which input data are loaded from the output data fields of two cells, the conjugate evaluated for one data field (label__A) and then both input sets expanded to higher order terms. A function of this type may have the following format within its parameter list:

```
A = user_func1(number, label_A, label_B)
```

This user defined function returns a single label to the output data field (A). The label returned corresponds to the output field for the final cell within the structure allocated by the user-defined function, in this case being a STAT cell, therefore complying with the established function call protocol. The above example requires the use of two implicit operator cells to perform the required functions, and the configuration code to allocate this user-defined compound cell structure may be as follows:

```
int user_funct1(number, label_A, label_B)
{
int A, B;
A = reflect (0.0, 100.0, label_A);
B = stat(number, A, label_B, ... ENDLIST);
return(B);
}
```

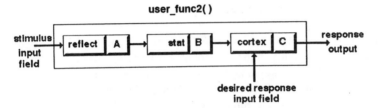

Figure 2.31 *Illustration of a compound neural cell structure.*

An example of a compound neural cell structure is illustrated in Fig. 2.31 whereby a stimulus data field is read in (stimulus), a complex conjugation applied to 50% of the elements of the stimulus field (A) and the set expanded to higher order statistics (B). This function again allocates a compound structure operating in a similar manner to a neural cell in generating a mapping of the data fields by the label (stimulus) to a response field (des_resp). The above compound composite cell structure is configured by the following sequence of function calls:

```
int user_func2(des_resp, stimulus)
{
int A, B, C;
A = reflect(0.0, 50.0, stimulus);
B = stat(1000, A, ENDLIST);
C = cortex(des_resp, B, ENDLIST);
return(C);
}
```

2.5 CONSIDERATIONS IN APPLICATION DESIGN

Neural networks are most often applied toward applications that fall within the domain of pattern classification. This is by far the simplest type of application, and the holographic neural processing may be easily constructed to exhibit quite advanced capabilities in pattern classification, requiring the resources of limited numbers of cells. Fundamental considerations one must take into account in designing a neural based application are as follows:

Symmetry Considerations.   Symmetry refers to a state whereby complex vectors are uniformly distributed about the Argand plane. Stimulus data fields should optimally be presented to the neural cell in a form that is representative of a high state of symmetry. The neural system is capable of classifying associations that display largely asymmetrical distributions; however, the encoding densities and accuracies attained on response recall (decoding) can increase substantially for the class of inputs that assumes a reasonably symmetrical or uniform distribution. One should not confuse the concept of symmetry with the generally applied concept of "orthogonality," as pertaining to a specific state or interrelationship between the stimulus pattern prototypes. Within the holographic process, attaining a state of "orthogonality" between stimulus patterns is not a limiting constraint, as applied in a manner toward certain classes of prior-art models (i.e., linear matrix methods).

The SIGMOID operator cell or INSIG function of the HNeT development system is applied principally in the redistribution of phase elements within data fields to achieve a high state of symmetry. This operation performs a sigmoidal redistribution on the input data field in the translation of input sets to a uniform distribution of elements about the complex origin. Within this data field translation, the end points of the external real valued boundary remain fixed, defining a point of reference for $+/-$ infinity within the complex plane $(0/2\pi)$.

A second means of attaining a high state of symmetry is to expand the stimulus input data field to higher order terms using the STAT operator cell. This data field expansion is again performed in phase space, taking advantage of an inherent property of complex fields, whereby the orientation of phase distributions asymptotically approaches an ideal symmetrical state. The following three cell allocation functions may be used in conjunction to configure a preprocessing structure that is capable of attaining a very high level of symmetry over nearly any input data distribution.

```
A = buffer(10, 10):
B = sigmoid(A);
C = stat(1000,B,ENDLIST);
```

These preprocessing steps are generally applied at the front end of the configuration to process data fed into the stimulus fields of cortical cells.

Cell Connectivity.   In addition to permitting cells of diverse types to be connected in any manner through their data transfer paths, the HNeT system permits the user to extract distinct regions from within data fields. Data fields again refer to two dimensional arrays or matrices of complex elements, each of these elements expressing an analog information component (phase) and confidence (magnitude). The neural applications designer may wish to allocate a number of distinct neural configurations operating over separate and distinct regions within input data fields. For instance, HNeT library functions permit the user to either to allocate cells which extract data in a pseudorandom manner or to specify windows within data fields. One of many possible examples may be in application toward real-time speech recognition. A configuration may be designed whereby the order and number of input statistics generated from the input data steam is reduced along the time axis (see Figure 2.32). Window based operator functions may be used to segregate regions in the above format to facilitate separate preprocessing configurations over a dynamic input data stream.

The general structure of a neural configuration is defined principally by its cell interconnectivity. These neural structures are generally comprised of input cells allocated at the initial layer, having their outputs fed into adjunct operator cell types. Within subsequent layers an arrangement of cortical cells may be constructed to perform multileveled associative reasoning, whereby the response gen-

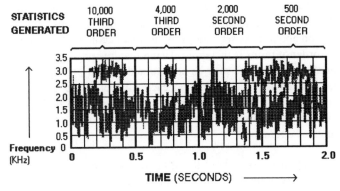

Figure 2.32   Segmentation of an audio input steam.

erated from cells in lower layers further induces associated responses within subsequent layers of cells. In the illustration in Figure 2.33 a response generated from cell A induces a further associated response recall from cells B and C. In this manner, the cells form a coarse analogy to the far simpler mode of operation exhibited by transistor-like elements, where cells within lower layers, through generation of a confidence value in the response, moderate the activity of cortical cells further downstream. One may also, using the HNeT system, construct systems whereby data fields are routed through the configuration in a recurrent manner. The recurrent associator example illustrated in Section 2.7 is an example of this.

Generalization Characteristics.   The STAT cell provides explicit control in the generation of data sets constructed from higher order statistics, also allowing multiple data fields to be appended at the cells input. The order and size of these higher order data sets establish the characteristics by which subsequent cortical cells generalize. Higher order terms produce stimulus mappings that define narrower regions of generalization about the stimulus locus. Such higher order data sets permit a more densely packed mapping topology, whereby there exists a greater

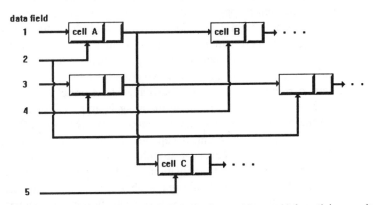

Figure 2.33   A structure of neural cells executing multilayered inferential reasoning.

number of distinct stimulus–response mappings that may be enfolded within the cortical cell for a given dimensionality within the initial stimulus field. The regions of generalization about these separate stimulus loci become, again, more restricted in size as the order of terms is increased. Using features provided within the HNeT system, neural configurations may be constructed forming groups of cells operating over customized statistics, allowing each distinct group of cortical cells to display diverse generalization characteristics. This control of higher order expansion terms in the preprocess stage facilitates a deterministic control over the following aspects of operation.

1. Generalization regions about the stimulus loci are modifiable and becomes more narrowly defined as the order of the statistic generated increases. This modification of the mapping characteristics is illustrated by Figure 2.14.

2. The number of stimulus–response associations that may be mapped onto the correlation substrate increases in proportion to the increased dimensionality and the order of terms generated. Correspondingly, the analog error produced on response recall is reduced in proportion to the order and dimensionality.

3. Such higher order data fields permit a greater level of discrimination between the confidence level produced on recognition (unity) and the background level produced for a nonrecognition response (< 1.0), assuming a given encoding or mapping density. The increased level of discrimination over confidence values allows the neural system to more reliably distinguish between recognition and nonrecognition responses.

Feature Extraction.   Distinct classes of stimulus patterns as visualized within a state space framework, may be located within a close proximity, or as more generally termed "clustered." It may be desirable in some applications to construct a neural system capable of associating these highly isometric sets into separate classifications or response categories. Feature extraction depends upon two fundamental aspects of the holographic process. These aspects are defined by the higher order relationships derived from the initial input data set and the inherent ability within the generated mapping topology for convergence to a nearly exact mapping as illustrated in Section 2.2.5. For a separation of two patterns into distinct response categories, these patterns displaying a high level of isometry, statistics of sufficiently high order are required whose generalization region is bounded reasonably within the distance separating the two stimulus loci.

Reinforcement learning operates on a somewhat abstract principle whereby the dominance of regions within the correlation mapping is amplified or attenuated, depending upon the nature of the associations encoded (see Section 2.2.5). The degree to which reinforcement learning is capable of amplifying the region pertaining to nonisometric conditions over the stimulus–response pattern set is deterministic, albeit highly complex in its evaluation, and largely dependent upon the data in question. At this point one should practically rely on quantitative or statistical studies for estimates of the feature extraction capabilities. In summary, the regions of nonsimilarity over a given suite of patterns define those aspects that permit the holographic system to generate distinct mappings to distinguishing sets of analog responses.

Memory Profile. As illustrated in Section 2.2.7, one has control over the dynamic memory characteristics within the neural cell. This capability is of particular importance in real-time learning or control systems where attenuation may be desirable over the stimulus–response control states. Significant differences are displayed in the response recall characteristics for short term versus long term memory profiles. Short term memory possesses a reduced capacity to accurately map out large numbers of stimulus–response associations owing to the attenuation of these mappings over time. Short term memory, however, facilitates a more accurate mapping for the more recently learned stimulus–response associations and, as well, displays a larger discrimination band in the generated confidence level (magnitude) for recognized versus nonrecognized input. Conversely, long term or permanent memory can potentially exhibit an unbounded capacity for encoding stimulus–response associations; however, the response recall tends to exhibit a greater level of recall error (dependent primarily on the number and complexity of the stimulus–response mappings enfolded). In the limit of saturation encoding (i.e., number of distinct enfolded mappings $\gg$ dimensionality of the input field to a cortical cell) the generated confidence level approaches a mean of unity over the entire input space affording a highly reduced discrimination between recognition and nonrecognition.

Neural Plasticity. An efficient implementation of neural plasticity may be achieved in permitting individual elements within the correlation sets (synaptic connects) to be eliminated. To illustrate the utility of such a feature one must understand the following inherent characteristic within the holographic process. Each complex element within the correlation set produces effectively a complex convolution over time, each corresponding magnitude indicting the degree of correlation between the related stimulus and the response field element for the suite of associations encoded, providing an illustration for the basic encoding process, that is,

$$x = \sum_t \lambda_t \gamma_t e^{i(\phi_t - \theta_t)} \qquad (2.59)$$

This process is somewhat analogous in its functionality to a Fourier time series. A large magnitude in x indicates a high level of correlation in that synaptic connect over the suite of associations learned; conversely, a low magnitude presents a proportionately low level of mapping correlation. In this manner, the user may monitor the magnitudes over individual correlation elements to allow a heuristic decision as to whether that particular synaptic connect should be disabled or remain intact (i.e., one may establish the cutoff at a fixed threshold value of magnitude $|x|$). If one employs this concept of neural plasticity, the network may be allowed to self-optimize in its synaptic connection map to achieve an optimal mapping over a minimum number of synaptic interconnects. One may, in fact, employ this process to construct "equations of state" defining the relationship between associated fields, given sufficient empirical data by allowing the system to identify itself and extract the significant higher order relationships. This optimizing feature is automated through the OPTIMIZE function.

The first stage, naturally, in designing any application is the specification of functional requirements. The type of application you may wish to design can fall into one of several categories (i.e., classification or pattern recognition, signal processing, process control, expert systems, data compression, simulation, forecasting, etc.). Each group of applications requires a somewhat specialized neural configuration. A general purpose neural development system should provide a high level of flexibility to accommodate nearly any type of configuration. The following indicates some general classes of applications and illustrates various neural configurations that may be designed to suit using the HNeT system.

2.5.1   Pattern Classification System

Within the realm of pattern classification, the neural system designer must decide how to represent classification within the cortical response field. The simplest means of classification would be to employ a binary scheme in the response field, having phase orientations situated along the positive real axis (0) to represent one group and an orientation along the negative real axis (π) for the second classification group. This classification is, of course, quite limited and does not take advantage of the inherent analog nature of the holographic neural process. One should also note that, in addition to phase information, the response indicates a confidence level (magnitude) whereby the network is capable of identifying new stimuli which fall within an established generalization region of previously learned stimulus loci. The neural system responds to recognized stimuli generating close to unity confidence (magnitude) within the response value, and conversely non-recognized stimuli are presented with a low magnitude (< 1.0) in the response recall.

For a slightly more advanced scheme, the phase plane for the response may be divided into an arbitrary number of phase regions, permitting a single neural cell to generate a proportionate number of separate classifications. One may employ multiple values in the response field permitting each cell to identify a base N value (where N is the number of phase regions). Considering a system in which the response plane has been segregated into 8 phase regions of equivalent size (see Fig. 2.34), each output within the response field would therefore indicate a number base 8 value. Three response values descritized in manner as illustrated above would be capable of classifying up to 512 separate categories. In designing an application as above, some investigation into the mapping topology is required to determine the optimum threshold on magnitude (confidence) used in flagging a recognition response, and prevent the neural system from classifying incorrectly. The threshold level establishes essentially a trade off between the neural systems ability to generalize, and its immunity from incorrect classification. Features within

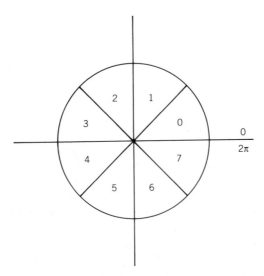

Figure 2.34 *Division of a response into separate phase regions.*

preprocessing stages, such as generation of higher order terms, may be modified explicitly to achieve optimum characteristics of classification within a given problem domain.

2.5.2 Analog Control System

Far more sophisticated applications may be realized using holographic neural technology within analog control regimes. One example has been constructed indicating the analog control of a satellite navigational system whereby one CORTEX2 cell having three values in its response field is configured to control pitch, yaw, and roll in response to ground topographies. Current ANS methods do not lend themselves particularly well to analog control applications because of the nature by which most operate in a binary mode, and are configured to operate in either a classification or a heteroassociative manner. The holographic system, again, operates inherently within an analog domain and is ideally suited to a wide range of analog control applications. The design of preprocessing stages is similar in most respects to the neural configuration for classification applications. The principal difference is in the manner in which the response field is structured.

Within analog control regimes a response is defined along a continuous range extending over defined and bounded limits. A principle consideration within this field of application is that analog control signals are most generally defined by sets of real valued numbers. Again, the phase values manipulated within the neural engine are, however, defined over a closed range extending about 2π. On translation of the internal phase data representation to the external real number system, the $0/2\pi$ discontinuity establishes the external real valued boundary (or $+/-$ infinity in the event of a sigmoidal mapping). In practical application, phase values oriented near the $0/2\pi$ discontinuity boundary may express a small degree of response recall error. This recall error (ϕ_{error}) may cause the generated output to flip over the discontinuity boundary (see Fig. 2.35). Response values close to the discontinuity boundary and exhibiting sufficient recall error may, therefore, induce a spastic behavior, whereby response values effectively oscillate between the max and min boundary limits of the external real number domain. In some sense, this behavior may be considered analogous to the neurological induction of muscle spasms, as experienced following excessive physical stress or activity. The above problem, inherent to the use of a phase representation for information, can be resolved in several manners, the most direct being to establish a region or distribution of valid response values at a defined margin from the $0/2\pi$ discontinuity boundary. The appropriate margin may be determined from the relationship governing confidence level and phase error in the recall response considering both the encoding densities attained for a given application and preprocessing structure of the neural configuration.

One may evaluate a relationship describing the variation in distribution of confidence (magnitude) as a function of the response recall error from either empirical study or theoretical estimates. Such estimates may be used to establish the desired distribution of response states and the confidence threshold value at which a response action is activated. For example, assume that the confidence threshold for a recognition response is set as 0.5. Empirical analysis over a data set may establish that, at this confidence level, the variance in response recall error is approximately 5% of the phase range. To reduce the above spastic behavior in the analog response recall, one may map response phase components to a cardiod distribution, as illustrated by Figure 2.36.

A second manner of resolving the phase discontinuity problem is to translate desired response values to a distribution of confidence levels centered about the

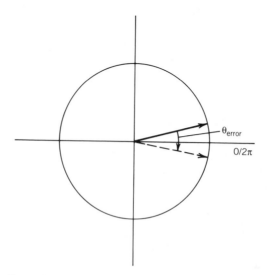

Figure 2.35 *Traversing the phase discontinuity boundary during response recall.*

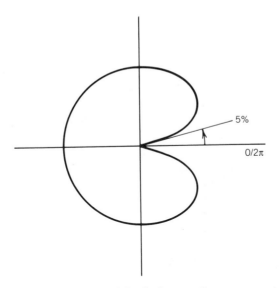

Figure 2.36   *A cardiod distribution over the response set.*

complex origin, in which case the output is mapped directly to a bounded real valued range.

Still more sophisticated applications may be realized because of the manner in which the holographic system follows ideally the nondisturbance principle. Following from this principle of nondisturbance, one may map temporally varying associations onto the neural system, whereby the input states of a current time step (i.e., time t) are mapped to the next incremental time step ($t + 1$). In this manner a neural configuration may be constructed quite easily to both learn and express a control sequence of spatio-temporal patterns. Figure 2.37 illustrates a possible neural configuration which may be applied toward learning and expressing such spatio-temporal patterns. This capability may be applied toward applications within the field of robotic control, again, where the neural system is employed in the learning and recall of potentially very large numbers of movement sequences hav-

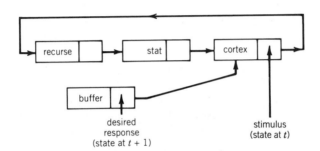

Figure 2.37   *Neural configuration for learning spacio-temporal patterns.*

ing mappings enfolded, relating current position and rate of change to effector response.

The generalization and characteristics permit the user to construct spatio-temporally based control systems which exhibit high stability of operation. Stability, in this sense, presents a control system capable of setting into motion a spatio-temporal movement sequence and displays a high immunity to distortion or variation from its initial starting state. Similarly, cortical cell expression displays the inherent ability to stably converge to prior learned spatio-temporal pattern following an disturbance due, for instance, to a path obstruction. Control systems of this type operate in a feedback manner, whereby the current state vector is fed back into the neural system to produce the next incremental movement along the time sequence. Within this control scheme, one may usefully apply other time dependent factors (e.g., rate, acceleration) or possibly other forms of sensory modalities (e.g., vision) over the time sequence of input state vectors to be encoded. Given the level of deterministic control and mapping density permitted within cortical holographic cells, the number of movement sequences is essentially unrestricted.

2.5.3 Expert Systems

The current mainstream of artificial intelligence applications are based on heuristic techniques. Heuristics is a term used to define the concept of rule based programming. In general, the approach applying multiple decision or "inference" rules against input state conditions in order to issue a seemingly intelligent response. Heuristics was initially employed within the field of game playing (i.e., chess) and displayed particularly impressive results. Rule based programming has become largely the basis of AI research and has since found more practical applications within the field of expert systems. The principle drawback with the heuristic approach is that decision or inference rules must be constructed and applied in a largely sequential fashion, prior to arriving at a given decision or outcome. For expert systems operating within applications involving some degree of complexity, the number of rules and thus search time required increase dramatically, limiting the capabilities achievable within this approach.

A simple analogy between the holographic neural process and functional aspects of the heuristic technique shall be made using the generally applied concept of a decision tree. The form of the decision tree is represented in Figure 2.38. The top event is defined as one possible outcome, and the branching network below describes the Boolean relationship that arrives at this top event. The Boolean tree describes all conditioning inputs leading to the top decision event in the form of AND and OR relationships (illustrating the simplest case with no chaining rules). Such capabilities may be directly achieved using a single cortical cell. More advanced expert systems achieve associative reasoning capabilities typically through a combination of forward or backward chaining rules and methods for allowing such systems to construct their own knowledge base using "expert" training supervisors. Sophisticated applications of this type may be achieved through struc-

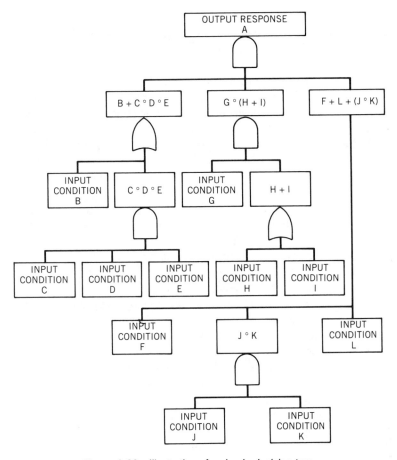

Figure 2.38 *Illustration of a simple decision tree.*

turing holographic based neural cells, and the flexibility to configure multiple layers or recurrent structures. In the example given by Fig. 2.38,

```
Event A is true IF  [B + (C ◦ D ◦ E)]+
                    [G ◦ (H + I)] +
                    [F + L(J ◦ K)]
```

Applying a Boolean cutset reduction to the decision tree given in the above example yields the following result:

```
1.    B ◦ G ◦ H ◦ F +
2.    C ◦ D ◦ E ◦ G ◦ H ◦ F +
3.    B ◦ G ◦ I ◦ F +
4.    C ◦ D ◦ E ◦ G ◦ I ◦ F +
5.    B ◦ G ◦ H ◦ L +
.     "  "   "
.     "  "   "
12.   C ◦ D ◦ E ◦ G ◦ I ◦ J ◦ K
```

Each of the above minimal cutsets (1 to 12) consists of a series of "anded" conditions, in other words, states occurring simultaneously in time, which lead to the top event or decision. Assuming that each of the input states may in some way be represented by a series of numbers, the above cutsets or "input scenarios" may be enfolded into a neural element in the form of stimulus–response associations, the response being the decision or top event in the logic tree. The holographic neural process provides an enormous capacity of storage of stimulus–response associations and is capable of generalizing about these associations. This holographic neural methodology facilitates a means for construction of extremely large and complex rule based systems. Again, large numbers of syntactical associations or rules may be enfolded within the cortical cell, presented effectively as a sequence of minimal cutsets. Expression (decoding) operates in a manner that the highest correlated response or decision is arrived at in an inherently parallel manner. Employing this method, the generated output intrinsically generates a level of confidence (magnitude) within the response decision.

To illustrate a powerful concept of associative reasoning within holographic neuron cells, both learning and expression may be applied within a recurrent structure, whereby a plurality of stimulus-response associations are enfolded onto the same group of cortical cells. Each frame of stimulus-response assocation is temporally connected, relating for instance visual objects associated in some manner through syntactical content. During an iterative decoding operation within this recurrent structure, associations are expressed or unfolded from the cell, in this case generating a time sequence of visual objects connected in some manner through either syntactical content or temporal proximity during learning. The LINASSOC demonstration program is provided within HNeT to illustrate this concept (see Section 2.6.3). Consider the following case, in which a series of patterns providing a syntactical representation for an external state (for instance, representative of visual images A to F as indicated below) are encoded onto a recurrent neural structure:

	Stimulus	Associated to	Response
State	A	→	B
	D	→	E
	B	→	F
	E	→	A

Establishing a recurrent loop within the neural configuration provides the ability to regenerate on each execution cycle, one association pair within the sequence of associations. For instance, from the above set of associations, state D is indirectly associated to F. Following learning of the above association pairs, one may expose the recurrent neural system to an input state, say B. On multiple execution cycles, the neural engine will re-express the stimulus–response associations in their temporally connected order, that is,

Execution cycle	1	D → E
	2	E → A
	3	A → B
	4	B → F

The above capability has direct implications within expert or automated reasoning systems operating, again, in a manner analogous to an inference engine. The advantage naturally is that vast numbers of inference rules may be enfolded onto the same cortical cell, and these input states effectively processed through all of the enfolded inferences in a parallel manner. The above simplified example may be extended to more sophisticated systems in which a much wider range of association rules or inferences are enfolded onto arrays of such cells.

2.5.4 Fourier Type Analysis/Data Compression

Do the following formulations look familiar?

$$f(x) = \sum_{n=-\infty}^{+\infty} c_n e^{in\theta/L} \qquad (2.60a)$$

where

$$c_n = \frac{1}{2L} \int_{-L}^{L} f(x) e^{-in\theta/L} \, dx \qquad (2.60b)$$

These equations present a complex notation for the well known Fourier series. The holographic neural process is in fact an extension of Fourier analysis. On comparing the above to the holographic neural process, one realizes that Eq. (2.60b) is similar to the basic encoding process and that Eq. (2.60a) is analogous to decoding. The $f(x)$ term in the Fourier scheme, however, is expressed generally as a single real valued function, and the values expressed therein are mapped to higher order frequencies of the sinusoidal:

$$\cos \theta + i \sin \theta \qquad (2.61)$$

In conceptualizing the operational basis of the above Fourier series, the point of view taken is that these weightings of the sinusoidal function may be superposed, allowing one to reconstruct any continuous function from a summation of the higher order harmonics. In taking a different perspective such as that realized within the holographic neural process, the capabilities of such Fourier-type analyses may be expanded dramatically. One may construct an analogous Fourier operation within the HNeT system using a STELLATE cell having one element defined within its input field and mapping the cell to higher order harmonics of the sinusoidal Eq. (2.61). For a comparative evaluation, the following illustrates a Fourier analysis over a two-dimensional field using harmonics up to 100th order. Two degrees of freedom within the input field define the x and y coordinates of the pixel location (i.e., a 2d Fourier transform). The visual image reconverted back into the spacial domain is seen in Figure 2.39. Constructing an analogous operation using a holographic cell, using 40th order statistics, the image reconverted back into the spatial domain is presented as Figure 2.40.

The holographic neural process displays the ability to construct a nearly exact

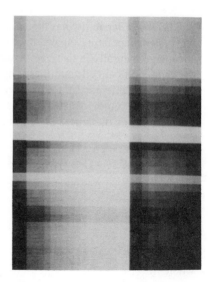

Figure 2.39 *A Fourier Churchill.*

frequency domain representation of the image as illustrated by the spacial reconstruction. One may employ this process, therefore, within any application that benefits from the use of Fourier-type transformations. Such applications may be in the field of spectral analysis or in data compression through the conversion time or spacial domains to frequency. The holographic method may potentially be applied in a similar manner toward data compression of spatio-temporal pattern sequences, which are largely continuous in nature (i.e., visual or auditory data streams).

Figure 2.40 *A logarithmic neural Churchill.*

2.5.5 Simulation/Forecasting

Generation of higher order statistics permit the designer to construct a neural system whereby the extent of the input space defining a particular stimulus field is mapped out to a continuum of desired response values or functions. Applications may be extended to analysis or simulation, whereby neurons can function as nodes within a finite element analysis, receiving input conditions from proximally located nodes within a mesh structure (see Fig. 2.41*a*).

As in standard finite elements analysis schemes, a node (or cell) may read its input state conditions from a number of adjacent nodes over current or previous time steps. One principle advantage may be realized in that the neural system is capable of generating highly complex input/output state functions by allowing it to "learn" the set of parametric conditions from either simulation or model mockup. The holographic process may permit the entire input/output state conditions for one node to be mapped onto a group of neural cells. The HNeT system

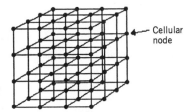

Cellular node

Figure 2.41a *A mesh configuration for finite element analysis.*

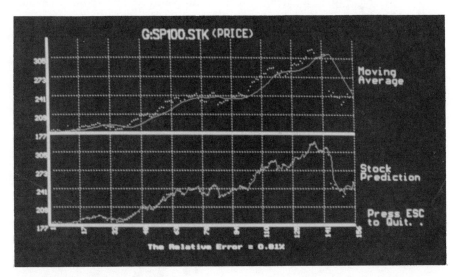

Figure 2.41b *Display illustrating a stock forecasting application. The top plot indicates 12 week moving average. The bottom plot is the neural system forecast given 12 weeks prior history following two learning trials.*

can accommodate a plurality of such cells providing the capability to interconnect these cells in various mesh geometries.

This technique of analysis or simulation may be usefully applied toward applications in forecasting, whereby the state conditions within each node of the mesh structure have been mapped out along time or rate dependent variables. Applications may be within the areas of weather forecasting, financial technical analysis (see Fig. 2.41*b*), thermohydraulic analysis, stress analysis, and so forth.

2.5.6   Content Addressable Memory

The holographic neural process ideally embodies the concept of content addressable memory. Multiple pattern associations, at nearly arbitrary levels of complexity, may be enfolded onto a neural cell. Encoded responses or "outputs" may subsequently be generated or accessed from the cell via content of input. Input fields may be representative of addressing schemes or "syntax," and are transformed in an inherently parallel manner through all of the content "addresses" enfolded within the cell. In response to an address or stimulus signal, the cell regenerates the associated output data field, indicating also the degree of confidence in that output association. The holographic process can be structured to operate directly within the context of content addressable memory, whereby input–output associations enfolded within a given memory "cell" are expressed directly through content of input.

Realizing this capability, one may construct expert or automated reasoning systems (Section 2.5.5) along an associative network, in which each neuron cell functions, in an analog sense, as one unit of content addressable memory. Expressed associations may propagate along several neural pathways either within feedforward configuration or within a recurrent structure. Such neural based systems may be configured to form, for instance, the operational kernel of an inference engine for applications within expert or diagnostic systems.

The holographic neural based process facilitates reasoning by association in the above manner, functioning within a content addressable manner. An illustration of a simple content addressable memory scheme operating within a recurrent loop structure is shown in the recurrent associative memory example presented under Section 2.6.3.

2.6   Example Applications within HNeT

The HNeT system is provided with a series of example applications to illustrate the manner by which neural configurations are structured. These example programs illustrate the programming convention used in configuration of the neural engine, interfacing the application program to the neural engine and execution.

2.6.1   Control System (Robotics/Navigation)

The following illustrates one possible application within the domain of analog control for navigational and/or robotic systems. This particular example of an analog control system has been applied to the field of navigation control (Fig. 2.42). The stimulus field is obtained from simulated ground topographies, these (sensor) inputs encoded or mapped to an arbitrarily assigned set of axial and positional coordinates corresponding to pitch, yaw, and roll within a satellite. A single CORTEX2 cell is used in the mapping of each of the three stated coordinate axes. The simulation encodes a plurality of ground topographies to satellite control movement in sequence, where each mapping of topographical input data to positional response of the satellite is enfolded within the cortical cells correlation set.

The configuration for this neural application is more explicitly illustrated in Figure 2.43 below. Raw stimulus data is comprised of a 48 × 48 data field representing the ground elevations. This input field is reduced to an 8 × 8 field and a SIGMOID cell allocated to redistribute phase elements using the transform described in Eq. (2.5). Sufficient levels of symmetry are achieved over most classes of distributions using this preprocessing transform, particularly for cases where distributions are of approximately Gaussian form (as in most naturally occurring distributions). The data field from the SIGMOID cell is then fed into a CORTEX2 cell stimulus field. This cell has been configured to expand its input stimulus field to 200 higher order statistics. This application encodes 40 distinct control mappings over 2 reinforcement learning trials. The error on response recall at this encoding density is < 1.0% of the analog range.

Similar concepts may be applied to any type of control system, particularly for the case in which the input field is highly complex. Holographic neural based control may, for instance, be similarly applied to automatic guidance, robotic control, multivariable process control, or process monitoring applications.

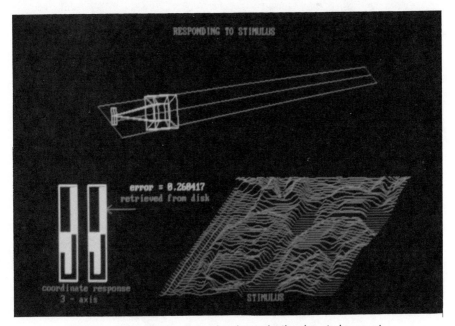

Figure 2.42 Display illustrating the navigational control concept.

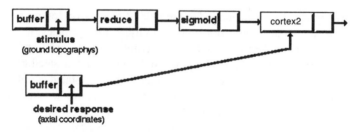

Figure 2.43 Neural configuration for the satellite navigation demonstration.

2.6.2 Automatic Targeting and Recognition (Visual)

This second application illustrates the neural system capabilities in visual targeting and recognition (Fig. 2.44) using two CORTEX2 cells, and having stimulus fields of 250 and 500 synaptic inputs respectively. During the training session, the system indexes through the suite of visual images, encoding each in sequence and displaying the image on a CRT. The user teaches the neural system the associated targeting movements by positioning the cross hairs to an arbitrary object within each visual frame and specifying an ASCII tag to associate with that object. Training on each object is performed only once (no reinforcement learning). During the decoding (response recall) process, images are randomly retrieved from the visual data base and processed through the neural system in the generation of both tar-

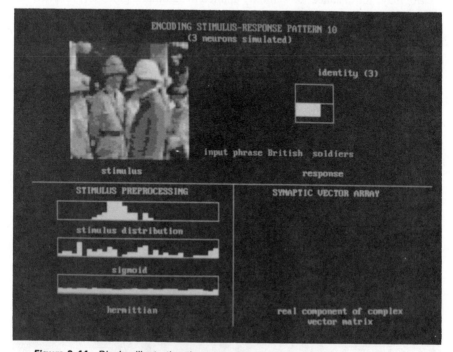

Figure 2.44 Display illustrating the automatic targeting and recognition concept.

geting and identification responses. One CORTEX2 cell is used to encode the coarse positional orientation of the object and the second for fine targeting and identification. Different aspects of operation are utilized within each of the coarse and fine targeting subsystems as described following.

Coarse Targeting Subsystem.   The neural configuration for the coarse targeting subsystem is presented in Figure 2.45. This portion of the neural configuration receives a 64 × 64 pixel array as the raw stimulus field. A REDUCE operator cell averages the input visual field down to an 8 × 8 pixel field. The output from this adjunct operator cell is processed through a SIGMOID cell redistributing the phase elements to a high state of symmetry. The output field from the SIGMOID cell is subsequently fed into the stimulus field of the CORTEX2 cell internally expanding its input field to 250 higher order statistics. This expanded stimulus field is associated to the x/y targeting position for the visual object, as provided by the user. In this subsystem, then, the entire visual frame provides the stimulus field and the encoded response is associated to the value indicating the approximate position of the object within the visual frame. On decoding, this neural configuration operates, therefore, in a peripheral capacity to provide approximate targeting of the object. The second subsystem is then actuated to perform fine targeting and identification (recall of ASCII tag) functions.

Fine Targeting and Identification Subsystem.   This subsystem is, again, comprised of a CORTEX2 cell and executes fine targeting of the object and identification. Targeting within this configuration is performed in a fundamentally different manner from the coarse targeting system described above. In this system, the magnitude component of the generated response recall vector is used to determine if the cell recognizes any object on which the window has been positioned. For an object that has been previously learned, the expressed magnitude (confidence level) on response recall (decoding) approximates unity, while nonrecognized objects express a much reduced magnitude. The fine targeting system employs this confidence feature (i.e., generated magnitude) by scanning a window over the visual input field and monitoring the magnitude of the expressed response. For a response recall magnitude indicating a high confidence level (i.e., close to unity), the probability is high that the cell is targeted precisely upon an object it has previously learned. The phase components for these generated response vec-

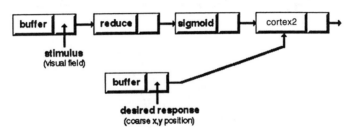

Figure 2.45 *Configuration for the coarse targeting subsystem.*

tors indicate the analog response value or aspect of information used in the identification of the object. Within this rather simple neural configuration illustrating a basic ATR application, the neuron performs both tasks of targeting and identification. The configuration for this subsystem is illustrated in Figure 2.46. The stimulus field is obtained from an 8 × 8 window placed within the 64 × 64 visual frame. The second stage of preprocessing redistributes the phase elements via the SIGMOID operator cell in a similar manner to the coarse targeting subsystem. The output data field from this cell is then expanded to 500 higher order statistics within the CORTEX2 cell. On target identification (response recall), this subsystem uses the coarse targeting subsystem to obtain an approximate location for the object, and then scans along a 9 × 9 axis about that position to determine the exact location of the object. The response phase angles generated from the cortical cell are separated into four phase regions of equal size. This permits each response element (of which there are three) to generate effectively a base 4 numeric digit. This cell may then be used in the targeting and identification of 64 classes or distinct groups of images.

In some senses, the coarse targeting subsystem functions as the peripheral vision, and the second subsystem emulates aspects of the central region (fovea centralis) within the biological retina. It is expected that in expanding this rather simple neural configuration to larger sizes and/or higher order systems, considerably greater numbers of images may be learned. Response testing using dynamically varying visual frames indicates that highly ideal generalization over visual data is readily attained using the holographic neural process. High speed of operation is exhibited by the capacity to enfold a plurality of visual inputs to targeting/identification associated responses onto the identically same correlation set over one learning trial. Generalization properties exhibited within the holographic process are realized, whereby multiple representations of an image over wide ranges of scale and rotational translation may be encoded to the same response association. The neural cells essentially build up a mapping of the object, in all of its visual orientations, to the associated response. Identification may then proceed, irrespective of the orientation of the object to be identified. This capability, although normally intractable, is straightforward to implement within the holographic neural system using relatively few neural cells.

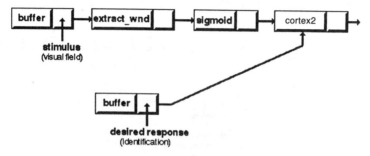

Figure 2.46 *Configuration for the fine targeting and identification subsystem.*

2.6.3 Recurrent Associative Memory

This example of a type of recurrent structure illustrates a simple exercise in associative reasoning. Such methods may be applicable to expert systems or control applications. Associative reasoning may be performed by configuring recurrent loops within the neural configuration where associations encoded within the cell essentially unfold as data fields flow recursively through the network. Configuring holographic cells within a recurrent loop is, in a very coarse sense, analogous to the Hopfield net or Bi-directional Associative Memory models. The operational characteristics of this recurrent configuration, based on holographic principles, however, indicate capabilities far in advance of either of the above prior art methods.

The holographic network is capable of enfolding associations in the sense that input of one pattern prototype will induce the issuance of the second, thus subsequently inducing the issuance of a third, and so on. Patterns generated within a recurrent data flow may express a linear sequence of associations, each pattern association connected through its encoding within one temporal frame (i.e., associations are linked by their proximity in time). This process of linear association may be considered to be somewhat analogous to the associative reasoning processes in animal cognition, where a thought train may be expressed through a sequence of associations initially learned over time. For example, the image of a fork may invoke the impression of plate, subsequently invoking an impression response in association to a kitchen table or food, for instance. In this manner, the holographic system courses through a sequence of sensory impressions, each of which has been formed by images temporally connected.

This feature is characteristic only of the holographic process because of the manner in which highly accurate responses are generated on a single pass decoding transformation. An illustration has been constructed to emulate this characteristic of linear association. The example constructed consists of a CORTEX1 cell arranged within a recurrent structure, as illustrated in Figure 2.47. The response field from this set of neural cells is averaged down to a 8×8 array and fed back into the stimulus input field for the CORTEX1 cell. During encoding, a sequence of 20 related visual images are exposed to the network as stimulus–response pairs; however, these associations being somewhat arbitrary. These association pairs are encoded in a manner that supplying the stimulus field with one pattern will evoke a response in the generation of the prior associated output image.

During the decoding (or expression) portion of this example application, one of the visual images selected by the user is provided as the initial stimulus to the array of neuron cells. The user also has the option of applying a variable degree of random distortion to this initial input pattern. One each subsequent execution cycle, the cortex cells express an association along a linear sequence. The associations enfolded within the cell are thereby regenerated as a sequence of visual patterns, expressed in their temporally connected order. One example of this, provided with the HNeT system, enfolds two disconnected trains of visual associations within the neural cell, each consisting of 10 visual images. Depending on

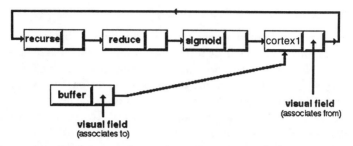

Figure 2.47 *Configuration for the recurrent associator demonstration.*

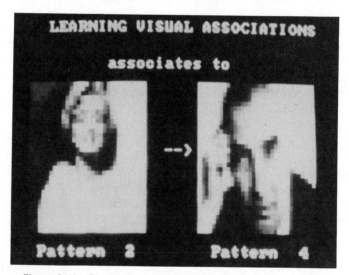

Figure 2.48 *Display illustrating the recurrent associator concept.*

which initial pattern one presents to the neural engine, the system will course through one of the two sequences of visual associations (Fig. 2.48).

Applying the above concepts within an expert system application, one may view the input field not as visual images but input state conditions. For instance, an input field consisting of, say, 1000 values, may store the input state conditions to a diagnostic system. The holographic system may enfold a vast number of scenarios for those state conditions and associated diagnostic responses onto the neural system. In this manner, the expert system need not parse through a logical or heuristic tree structure. The holographic process permits all input/output scenarios to be enfolded onto the same correlation elements, and one stimulus pass through the neural system will generate the closest associated response.

2.7 SIMULATION RESULTS

The following presents an analysis of error characteristics within the holographic neural process for randomly generated pattern associations (i.e., random statistical tests). The results from these analyses provide a useful guide in determining the suitability and accuracy of a particular neural configuration for an application. It should be noted that these error analyses present a worst case scenario (i.e., random associations) in evaluating the operational accuracy within the holographic system.

Various aspects of the holographic neural process that have been analyzed may be grouped into three general categories. These analyses are related to the determination of average response recall errors, as a function of stimulus–response pattern storage densities, stimulus distortion (i.e., in the evaluation of generalization properties), and response recall accuracy occurring within higher order systems. Test routines have been provided within the HNeT system (test1 to test3.c) allowing one to perform similar error evaluation analyses. Presented in the following sections is a general discussion of these response recall error characteristics and a graphical presentation of results.

2.7.1 Storage Density

Error results indicated below in Figure 2.49 are based on the simulation of one cortical cell with 1024 synaptic inputs, encoding up to 512 randomly generated stimulus–response associations using a uniform distribution between 0 and 2π. These patterns are trained over one to three reinforcement learning trials. The mean analog error within the response recall, having 512 patterns encoded over three reinforcement learning trials, is 2.1% of full scale, or 5 levels within a descritized phase range extending over 256 levels. Within conventional linear search methods, the number of bytes required to distinctly store the above suite of patterns is 512 K. The holographic process, however, permits the above quantity of stimulus–

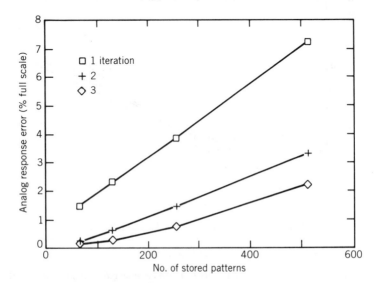

Figure 2.49 *Response recall error versus number of learned associations for a single neural cell (cortex) with 1024 synaptic inputs.*

response data to be enfolded onto 1024 complex vectors for a total storage requirement of 8 KBytes (assuming floating point storage of phase and magnitude variables).

One important feature of the holographic neural process relates to an intrinsic property whereby the storage capacity for random pattern associations is directly proportional to the number of synaptic inputs or dimensionality of the cell. Appreciating this aspect of operation, one can conceivably store several thousands of separate analog stimulus–response associations (or generalizations) onto one cortical cell of relatively modest size (2–4 thousand synaptic inputs). Empirical testing employing random statistical methods has been performed on neurons with up to 32K synaptic inputs, and has verified this invariance in the capacity to store large numbers of stimulus–response associations while exhibiting low error levels in the response recall. The test result below illustrates the response error relationship as a function of pattern storage density for various sizes of neuron cells ranging from 512 to 8K synaptic inputs. The pattern storage density in Figure 2.50 is indicated as a ratio of the stimulus field size.

2.7.2 Generalization Properties

The property of generalization is crucial within neural systems. Ideally, the input stimulus pattern should be capable of undergoing large degrees of distortion with minimal deviation in the generated response output. The holographic model displays ideal properties of generalization, through realization of the properties inherent within vector transformations over a multivalued complex space (i.e. Riemannian manifold). Generalization is achieved in the sense that, following one

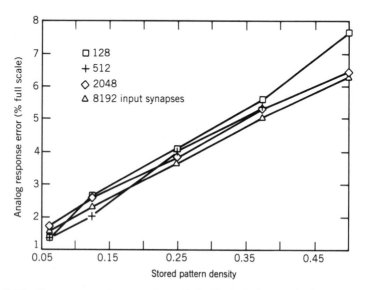

Figure 2.50 *Response recall error versus cell size for a single neural cell (cortex1) on one learning trial.*

encoding transform, a large region adjacent to the input stimulus state is concurrently mapped onto the desired response outputs. Figures 2.51 and 2.52 illustrate this property, whereby varying degrees of distortion are applied to a prior encoded stimulus pattern, and average deviation from the desired response following a response recall (decoding) is evaluated.

These test results indicate the response error characteristics over a full range of stimulus pattern distortions. Results for one neuron having 1024 synaptic inputs are shown, encoding 256 random stimulus–response associations. Following the learning process, each stimulus pattern is randomly deformed up to 100% of full distortion. That is, complex values within the stimulus field are rotated randomly up to 100% of the 2π phase range. Average analog error on response recall is then evaluated over the training sets (response error is measured as the relative difference between the desired and expressed response phase values). Results below indicate the response recall error for up to two reinforcement learning trials.

Similar tests have been performed to evaluate the response error as a function of pattern storage density. Figure 2.52 displays response error for one neuron having 1024 synaptic inputs at storage densities ranging from 64 to 512 randomly generated stimulus–response pairs. Test results have been compiled for one reinforcement learning trial.

Results indicate a large immunity to high stimulus distortion levels and at high pattern storage densities. Accuracy of response recall following stimulus distortion indicates that generalizations have been formed, in the sense that each stimulus–response pair maps a wide region within the input state space to the desired response. Figure 2.52 illustrates somewhat the characteristics of this generalization. Process or analog control systems may realize this ideal property in the construc-

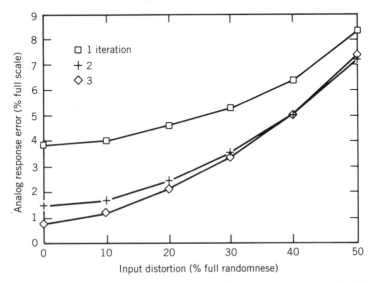

Figure 2.51 *Response recall error versus input distortion for a single neural cell (cortex1) with 1024 synaptic inputs.*

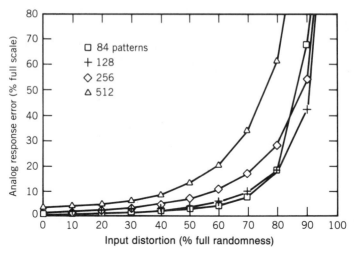

Figure 2.52 *Response recall error versus input distortion for a single neural cell (cortex) with 1024 synaptic inputs—two learning trials.*

tion of systems highly immune to input noise and control instabilities. Vision recognition systems may be used to response correctly to images following high levels of distortion or image translation in terms of rotation or scale. Pattern recognition may be significantly enhanced in many areas related to diagnostics, expert systems, and others. One may construct adaptive systems able to learn large numbers of control points within arbitrarily complex structures, while maintaining a high level of both accuracy and generalization within its control space.

2.7.3 Higher Order Systems

A principle requirement for neural system models in the ability to encode sets of stimulus–response associations that define a linearly nonseparable structure within their state space mappings. Conventional gradient descent methods achieve this capability, principally through the addition of hidden, internal layers of neuron cells (Section 2.2.8). Within the holographic process, higher order terms are defined at the input stage, expanding input stimulus sets explicitly to higher order relationships. These features of operation permit the neural system designer a high level of deterministic control over mapping characteristics and facilitate a means by which the number of encoded mappings may far exceed the dimensionality of the initial stimulus field, thus avoiding restrictions imposed on pattern storage densities. The following simulations illustrate the above concept whereby a stimulus field of 20 elements has been expanded up to a higher order dimensionality and recall error evaluated over randomly generated stimulus–response pairs.

Again, the simulation results were obtained for a raw stimulus field composed of 20 values, expanded to second and fourth order terms. The size of these expanded stimulus fields are 190 and 4,845 higher order values respectively. Test

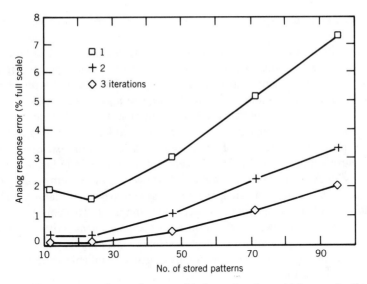

Figure 2.53 *Response recall error for second order system for a single neural cell (cortex2) with 20 stimulus values.*

results indicating the response recall error for these randomly generated pattern associations are illustrated in Figures 2.53 and 2.54, respectively.

As illustrated in Figure 2.54, recall of 2,422 randomly generated stimulus–response associations confined within a region of 20 degrees of freedom, defines an ability to learn mappings which are densely populated within the input space.

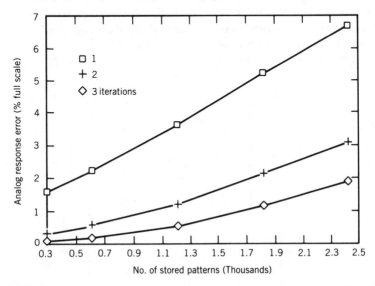

Figure 2.54 *Response recall error for fourth order terms for a single neural cell (cortex2) with 20 stimulus values.*

Test results indicate response recall errors for up to three reinforcement learning trials.

This ability to learn large numbers of arbitrarily complex input patterns is necessary for control applications where the number of sensory inputs is relatively small or the control scheme may be highly complex. For instance, within a robotic system using a limited number of control axes, one may expand sensory feedback stimuli to potentially tens of thousands of higher order terms. Generation of higher order statistics, in this manner, permits the system to learn very large numbers of stimulus–response control operations for complex process or spacio-temporal robotic control applications. Regions of generalization inherently become more restricted as higher order terms are produced. However, by allowing one to modify the higher order terms generated, the neural system designer attains a high level of control over both the mapping and generalization traits. This concept governing explicit control over higher order terms and mapping characteristics is a fundamental diversion from gradient descent models in which higher order ''statistics'' are captured in a generally nondeterministic or uncontrollable manner, similarly producing inexplicable results.

2.8 SUMMARY

One may regard the holographic neural process as a new control paradigm. This representation may be illustrated in a conventional manner (Fig. 2.55) in which the rudimentary cell receives both a multivariable control signal and a training input. Such cells are capable of generating an appropriate response to input as conditioned through previous training. These operational features are well suited to conventional control concepts may be readily employed within a wide range of applications, some of which have been only briefly discussed within this chapter.

In providing an analogy current state space control theory, the holographic cell permits a largely unrestricted mapping of multivariable input states to desired out-

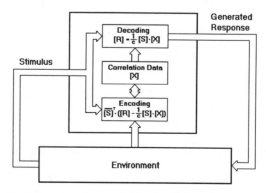

Figure 2.55 *Illustration of environmental feedback through a neural control element.*

put states. The mapping scheme requires no linear dependence between these input to output states. Stability is achieved through a high immunity to input distortion in that large variations in the input state need only induce minimal distortion in the generated control output, this immunity to noise is demonstrated without mechanisms of feedback. On a more abstract level, such input-output or mappings define an area of generalization extending over a hyper-ellipsoidal region in the N-dimensional input space. One may manipulate both the geometry and size of these generalization regions through explicitly defining the quantity and order of statistics formed from the input. This state space comparison is not directly applicable to conventional control theory in that the mathematics is not defined in terms of multi-dimensional Euclidian spaces but phase orientations within a multidimensional complex space or Riemannian manifold.

The concept of enfolding is introduced whereby input-output or stimulus-response mappings are superposed onto the same set of values stored within the holographic cell. The cell issues a response action as a deterministic transformation of stimulus through all of the mappings enfolded within the cell. The response comprised of a summation of vectors each component of which results deterministically from the stimulus transformation through one of the enfolded mappings, and each whose degree of dominance or magnitude convolved within the net response is proportional to the degree of closeness to the input state.

In understanding the operational characteristics exhibited by the holographic process, one may envisage a control system capable of dynamic learning through modification of its internal state space mappings and the concurrent expression of a response. Learning is directly influenced through automatic control in attention and possess the capability for dynamic memory profiles. Such a system may be structured to operate within an environmental feedback capacity, in essence, receiving stimulus from the external environment and transforming this information through the accumulated mappings enfolded within the system. A resultant response action influences the environment and may directly or indirectly modify the external stimulus fed back into the control element. Concurrently, learning modifies the stimulus-response state space mapping within the system as influenced by the external environment. Given the unrestricted capacity within holographic cells for the enfolding of unattenuated mappings, this internal structure may embody to a limited degree an abstract representation of the external environment and the systems influence within this environment. Even within a relatively simple framework, recurrent systems of this type may preclude a fully reductionist analysis and appear to evolve control capabilities of significant complexity.

REFERENCES

A. Afifi and R. Bergman, *Basic Neuroscience*, Urban & Schwarzenberg, Baltimore, Maryland 1980.

E. Prugovecki, *Quantum Mechanics in Hilbert Space*, Academic Press, New York, 1981.

J. Sutherland, *Holographic Model of Memory, Learning and Expression*, Internat. J. Neur. Syst., 1 (3), 256–267, (1990).

J. Sutherland, *A Transputer Based Implementation of Holographic Neural Technology, Transputing '91*, 2, 657–675, (1991).

L. Yarolavski, *Methods of Digital Holography*, Plenum Press, New York, 1980.

CHAPTER 3 _____

Fuzzy Reasoning in Planning, Decision Making, and Control: Intelligent Robots, Vision, Natural Language

DARKO STIPANIČEV
JANET EFSTATHIOU

3.1 INTRODUCTION

A quarter of century ago Lotfi Zadeh introduced a mathematical theory known as fuzzy set theory suitable for dealing with problems and situations that are in their nature ambiguous and not precisely defined. On the other side, in the past couple of decades robotics has been established and developed as a well defined and widely practically applied field of mechanical and electrical science. At first sight it seems that there are no connecting points between terms as ambiguous, imprecise, vague, or fuzzy and the mathematically well defined field of robotics. This chapter will try to emphasize the possible connections between them.

Let us start with a few notations concerning robustness and its importance, particularly in the field of robotics. In this context robustness means the ability to respond without program modification to slightly perturbed or to somewhat in-exactly specified situations [1]. The expression "slightly perturbed situation" needs a more detailed explanation. For example, in an assembly line equipped with in-dustrial manipulators it would be highly desirable for each step to perform its function in spite of inevitable inaccuracies of the positions of objects coming down the line. Standard programs for assembly line robots, like, "rotate 14.3 degrees clockwise, raise 10.3 cm," certainly do not possess this property. But an example of desirable robust robot behavior would be the situation in which an industrial manipulator carries loads whose weights alter from sample to sample. Even more complex situations, where it is possible to find more ambiguity and fuzziness, are connected with robot action in an unknown environment. A typical example would

Fuzzy, Holographic, and Parallel Intelligence, By Branko Souček and the IRIS Group.
ISBN 0-471-54772-7 © 1992 John Wiley & Sons, Inc.

be the activity of a mobile, unmanned robot in unknown space. Such a robot is usually a sensor-guided robot, the machine that exhibits a connection of perception and action, and perception is usually connected with a considerable degree of inprecision.

A lot of vagueness, ambiguity, and fuzziness is present in all of these examples, so that all methods capable of dealing with and solving problems in such situations can find a lot of applications. Of course, the fuzzy set theory is not an exception. This chapter will be a kind of survey, the review of applications of fuzzy set theory in different subfields of robotics.

Four main areas of application of fuzzy set theory in robotics could be distinguished:

1. Control of robot dynamics
2. Interpretation of information received from a robot's sensors
3. Robot motion planning and control
4. Modes of communication with robots using natural language

Before proceeding with particular applications, a short introduction to fuzzy set theory will be presented. Fuzzy set theory is nothing but a generalization of classical set theory. In classical set theory, an object (element) from the universal set may or may not be a member of a particular set of object classes, because the characteristic function of an element in a set in classical set theory is binary: either 0 or 1. This law of excluded middle (*tertius non datur*) limits the applicability of classical set theory. In many practical applications the membership of an object in a class is not binary: Classes of fat men, pretty persons, or elongate objects are some classes whose membership cannot be represented satisfactorily by only 0 and 1.

Zadeh observed that allowing the characteristic function of elements of a set to take a value in the interval [0, 1] will dramatically extend the applicability of the set theory. He introduced concept of fuzzy set (A) as a subject of universal set (Ω), such that the characteristic function $f_A(x)$, $x \in \Omega$ takes any value in the interval [0, 1].

The union, intersection, and complementation of fuzzy sets A and B are defined as fuzzy sets, too, and their membership functions are calculated by formulas:

$$f_{A \cup B}(x) = \max\left(f_A(x), f_B(x)\right) \tag{3.1}$$

$$f_{A \cap B}(x) = \min\left(f_A(x), f_B(x)\right) \tag{3.2}$$

$$f_{\overline{A}}(x) = 1 - f_A(x) \tag{3.3}$$

Since its introduction, fuzzy set theory has been studied and applied in diverse fields. In this report its applications in robotics are considered. Let us start with its first application area, the control of robot dynamics.

3.2 CONTROL OF ROBOT DYNAMICS

Fuzzy dynamic controllers have been used for the management of various systems, from large scale industrial processes, such as cement kilns, water purification and treatment, heat exchangers, and sinter plants, to smaller scale laboratory and experimental systems, such as the famous Mamdani's steam engine, marine auto pilots, diesel engines, processes of pH-neutralization, and water level control [2]. Recently a whole range of consumer goods run by fuzzy controllers, such as washing machines, vacuum cleaners, air conditioners, TV sets, video cameras, dishwashers, and microwave ovens, have been introduced on the market, announced as intelligent household appliances [3]. The results of these applications have shown that fuzzy controllers perform either better or at least as well as optimally tuned PID controllers. The main advantages of the fuzzy approach to the control are as follows:

It does not require a detailed mathematical model of the controlled process to formulate the control algorithm

It has more robust and adaptive capability

It is capable to operate for a large range of inputs

It is cheaper

The properties of fuzzy controllers, robustness and adaptivity, are particularly interesting in their application in the field of robotics. Let us use as an example a robot system with revolute and prismatic joints [4].

Such robots are widely used for numerous tasks in industry because they are fast acting and they approach the flexibility of use normally ascribed to the human arm. Industry has successfully mastered the techniques of manufacturing such robot arms, but it is now at the stage where their dynamic performances are often called into question.

The problem is that the moment of inertia of the arm, links about their main control axes (rotation, shoulder and arm) can exhibit pronounced changes with the change in disposition of the robot, as well as the load carried at its tip. This results in highly complex dynamics [5].

Model-reference adaptive control (MRAC) is the usual approach to the control of such systems. The disadvantage of MRAC is that it generally requires a detailed knowledge of the required system dynamics and assumes that

1. These are linear
2. The dynamics of the actual system differs from the model only with respect to values of its coefficients

Contrary to this approach, the fuzzy control approach is based either on only appropriate knowledge of the system behavior, which need not be linear (in the case of a nonlearning rule based fuzzy controller), or on very simple incremental system model (in the case of a learning, self-organizing, rule based fuzzy controller). The joint feature of both fuzzy control approaches to the control of robot dynamics is the existence of a knowledge base or, more precisely, the existence of a rule base where rules about control procedures are stored. Because of that, a fuzzy controller is a special case of *production system*, where fuzzy set theory has been used for representation of knowledge (control rules) and for doing inferences with the knowledge. Figure 3.1 shows situation schematically.

The main idea of fuzzy controller is quite simple: Knowledge about the control procedure is stored in a rule base as a collection of "if . . . then" rules. A typical example of such rules is

If error is *small positive* and change-in-error is *small positive* or *zero*, then control most be *small negative*

Error, change-in-error, and control normally take values in real universes. Fuzzy set theory connects these real universes (subsets of real numbers) and linguistic terms such as small positive, zero, and small negative.

For each robot movement a controller considers at each sampling instant the error between required and actual angles, as well as the change-in-error. The con-

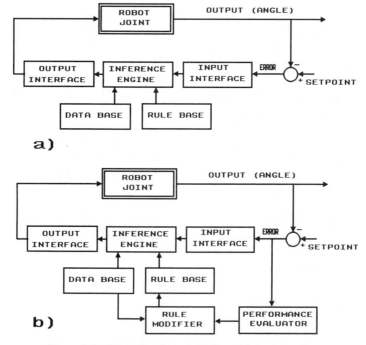

Figure 3.1 *Block diagrams of rule based fuzzy controllers:*
a. Simple nonlearning rule based fuzzy controller.
b. Self-organizing rule based fuzzy controller.

troller feeds these two quantities into a rule base through the inference engine and decides, by use of fuzzy logic, which of several rules may be used to provide a contribution to a controller output and what this output (control action) should be. This control action is then applied through output interface. The main difference between a nonlearning and a learning fuzzy controller is that for the first one all control rules must be known and defined at the beginning of the control session, whereas for the other one, a self-learning fuzzy controller is capable of creating its own rule base during on-line operation. Also, a self-learning fuzzy controller has the property to adapt itself and tune its rule base if the system is changed. To do this self-organizing, a fuzzy controller needs quite simple performance evaluators, which is another collection of "if . . . then . . ." rules created using a simple incremental model of the controlled system. A typical example of such rules is

If error is x and change-in-error is y, then control should be reinforced by z

where values x, y, and z could be also expressed linguistically.

It is interesting that such a simple idea applied in the field of robotics in a number of cases gave better results than mathematically well defined and *precisely* described controllers.

Both nonlearning and learning fuzzy controllers have been applied to control the robot dynamics. The first example that will be presented here is the fuzzy control of one link manipulator servo system [6]. The nonlearning fuzzy controller was applied and the control procedure was defined by six general proposed rules:

1. If e is *LP* and $\dot{e}$ is any, then u is *LP*
2. If e is *SP* and $\dot{e}$ is *SP* or *ZE*, then u is *SP*
3. If e is *ZE* and $\dot{e}$ is *SP*, then u is *ZE*
4. If e is *ZE* and $\dot{e}$ is *SN*, then u is *SN*
5. If e is *SN* and $\dot{e}$ is *SN*, then u is *SN*
6. If e is *LN* and $\dot{e}$ is *any* then u is *LN*

where e is error (output from shaft encoder − set point), $\dot{e}$ is change in error ($\dot{e} = e(nT) - e[(n-1)T]$), u is output from servo drive unit and *LP*, *SP*, *ZE*, *SN*, and *LN* mean large positive, small positive, zero, small negative, and large negative. Two quantizations of variables were used: one for coarse control when the output is distant from the set point and one for fine control when the output is close to the set point. For example, for an incremental type of shaft encoder having a resolution of 1000 for coarse control, the real universe of error from −1000 to 1000 was quantized into eleven levels (−5, −4, −3, −2, −1, 0, 1, 2, 3, 4, 5). The breaking point between coarse and fine control was an error value less than 100, and then error values from −100 to 100 were quantized into nine levels (−4, −3, −2, −1, 0, 1, 3, 4). The same was done for change-in-error and control. Figure 3.2 shows a block diagram of the system layout.

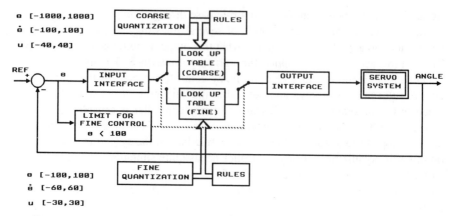

Figure 3.2 A block diagram of a servo rule based fuzzy controller according to [6].

Linguistic terms *LP*, *SP*, *ZE*, *SN*, and *LN* were defined by appropriate fuzzy sets. Figure 3.3 shows fuzzy set membership functions for fine quantization.

Control procedure was the classical fuzzy control graphically represented in Figure 3.4. The real error and change-in-error were quantized and applied to each rule. The control contribution of each rule was calculated using a min method, and overall control was evaluated by a max procedure. The real-time quantized control was calculated by a center of gravity method. For values marked on Figure 3.4 $(e_0 = \dot{e}_0 = 3)$, $u_0 = (0.6 \cdot 2 + 1.0 \cdot 3 + 0.6 \cdot 4)/(0.6 + 1.0 + 0.6) = 3$. The next procedure was inverse mapping from quantized u_0 to real control value from interval $[u_{\min}, u_{\max}]$.

For comparison, two other control algorithms were implemented, the conventional digital PI controller and the model-reference adaptive controller (MRAC), and then applied for servomotor control. The fuzzy controller gave better results than the PI controller. In was comparable to MRAC from the point of view of its

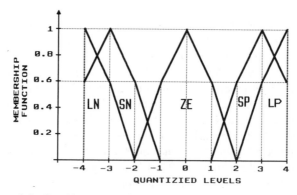

Figure 3.3 Graphic representation of fuzzy sets membership functions.

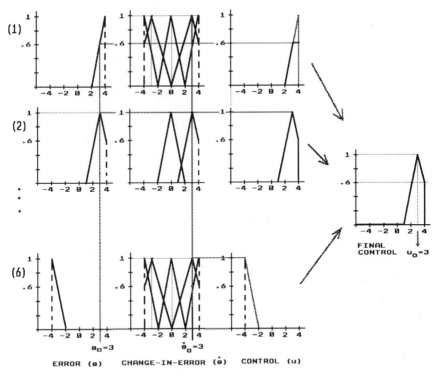

Figure 3.4 *Graphic representation of fuzzy rule based control procedures.*

sensitivity to disturbance (changing of mechanical time constant); yet its dynamic response was better (less overshoot and shorter settling time).

Another group of researchers [7] made a modification on a fuzzy controller layout and put the fuzzy controller in parallel with a feedforward gain passage, so mixed fuzzy control was obtained. Figure 3.5 shows the system layout.

The fuzzy controller was responsible for only dynamic regulation. Static per-

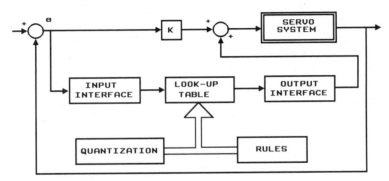

Figure 3.5 *A mixed fuzzy controller according to [7].*

formances were satisfied by position feedback. Because of that, the problems of oscillation and static error that could occur in conventional fuzzy controllers were overcome. Simulation results have shown better dynamic response performances and static behavior than that of optimally tuned PID and common fuzzy controllers.

Another specific use of fuzzy set theory in control of robot dynamics is the tuning of conventional robot servo systems [8]. The position and velocity gains K_p and K_v are tuned by fuzzy interface autotuning system using a rule based, common fuzzy controller with two sets of rules that correspond to human tuning procedures.

In the following, the application of a fuzzy controller in controlling robot dynamics differs from previous approaches in the sense that a learning, self-organizing type of fuzzy controller was used and real life experiments were performed [4, 9].

The principles of a self-organizing fuzzy controller (SOC) applied in this case could be summarized as follows: In the main control loop there is a common fuzzy controller. For a specific error value (any change-in-error value) one of few control rules is chosen, and subsequently the specific control action is evaluated. The learning part monitors the controller's performances with reference to an incremental performance criterion and decides if it is necessary to reinforce some of the existing rules or even create a new rule in the rule base. The performance table is derived from linguistic rules of the form:

If error E is x, and change-of-error ΔE is y, then process output U should be really different by p units

where quantity p could be a positive or negative value. Now a simple incremental model is assumed, consisting of a gain (which is usually unity for linear processes) and a process time-delay of m samples.

In each sampling instant, the reinforcement p is taken from the performance table, and the control rule (or rules) responsible for control action m sampling instants in the past are changed from $(\Delta E_m, E_m, U_m)$ in $(\Delta E_m, E_m, U_m + P)$. The robot used in these experiments with SOC is shown schematically in Figure 3.6. The robot has the 1m reach and a lifting capacity of 1.5 kg. An SOC algorithm was applied in a Pascal-like process control language of a DEC computer.

Each robot joint (rotation, shoulder, arm) was controlled with a separate self-organizing fuzzy controller. Nonlinear gains for input and output variables were used. The system has shown better performances than an optimally tuned PID controller, particularly in the tracking procedure. The maximum deviation from the nominal squared trajectory was twice as big for the PID control than for the SOC. The final conclusions were that a self-organizing fuzzy controller

a. Could cope with the transient aspect of the robot response
b. Could deal with changing system properties (unlike the PID controller)

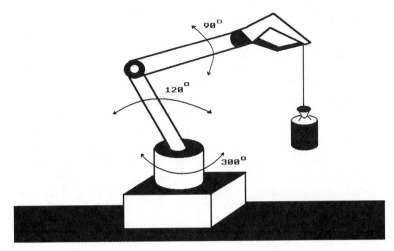

Figure 3.6 *A schematic drawing of a revolute joint robot arm used in experiments with SOC, according to [4, 9].*

  c. Could learn fast so that the controller could adapt itself to changing process characteristics, such as robot loading

  d. Could work in cooperation with another separate SOC in the face of cross-coupling effects

We also did a lot of simulation trials of robot dynamic control with different forms of self-organizing controllers and found that, in the synthesis of self-organizing controllers, one of the most difficult parts was the tuning of controller parameters [10]. SOC has many parameters that have to be defined and tuned in order to obtain satisfactory system response and convergence of self-organization of control rules. The most important parameters of SOC are

- Input and output scaling factors
- Delay in rule modification m
- Performance index (PI) table

but these parameters

- Definition of fuzzy values in control rules
- Definition of inference procedure
- Definition of defuzzyfication method

also have an influence on closed loop behavior.

A lot of simulations and experimental trials have been made to compare different inference and defuzzification methods and to find the influence of fuzzy values definition on controller performances, but a general procedure has not been found. In order to overcome the problem with the tuning of scaling factors, we have proposed a self-tuning procedure [10]. Our idea was to try to summarize the influence of different tuning parameters on a system response in the form of tuning rules, and then to use this approximate knowledge in the tuning procedure.

Three main difficulties were met during the simulations of a self-tuning, self-organizing fuzzy procedure for the control of robot dynamics with a nonlinear model of a PUMA 560 manipulator.

The first problem was due to the unstable characteristic of the system because the final position was in an unstable space sector. The use of high values for the gains allowed the process stabilization but the convergence was very hard. With low values of gains, several learning experiences were needed to obtain stability. Afterward, convergence was possible. This problem could have been solved by including an "a priori" knowledge in the control rule base to avoid instability, instead of starting the learning phase without rules, as we did. That starting rule base could approximate the behavior of a conventional controller. Equations $\Delta U \cong E + \Delta E$ or $\Delta U \cong E + \Delta E + \Delta E^2$ could be used in the case of the three term controller.

The second difficulty was that several steps in the same direction of change (increase or decrease) were needed to observe the effects of these changes in gains. In fact, the relationships linking the ratios and the gain have several local minima due to the nonlinearities of the controller and the process.

The third problem was that it was necessary to start with scaling factors, which at least would have led to a stable closed loop and to the convergence of the control strategy. Our self-tuning strategy was good for the improvement of response characteristics but not for finding the starting combination of scaling factors.

Although our study was primarily related to the project aiming at the use of fuzzy models of human behavior and their transpose to robotics applications, we believe that such control principles could be quite useful also for the real control of robot dynamics. Experimental results previously reported have demonstrated the advantages of self-organizing fuzzy control for robot dynamics control. We believe that in the future more applications of fuzzy controllers and particularly self-organizing fuzzy controllers to control robot dynamics will be encountered.

Another group of fuzzy controller applications to control robot dynamics is in the field of *sensor-guided robot manipulators*. The sensor-guided robot requires, according to the nonlinear characteristics of a certain interaction process between the robot effector and the object, a robust control algorithm for the sensory control loop. Here we will suppose first that the values obtained from the robot sensors are precisely known and that they could be unambiguously interpreted. Fuzzy set theory is used only in the control loop. Palm [11] has classified the total task in sensor-guided robots in two parts: the motion task and the reaction task, schematically shown in Figure 3.7.

The motion task is controlled on the servo level, whereas the relation task has to be controlled on the sensor level. The values obtained from sensors are, together with values described from the reaction task, considered as inputs to a controller.

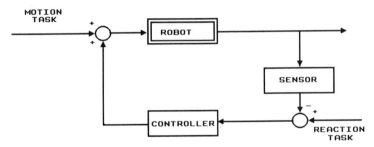

Figure 3.7 *A block diagram of sensor-guided robot control.*

The controller produces a control law. That control law is responsible for the correction of the planned trajectory obtained in the pure execution of the motion task. The controller in the external feedback loop requires a quite high robustness because of nonlinear effects, like the loss of contact between the effector and the object, or dry friction. Fuzzy control is an example of such a control procedure.

Palm has used the ordinary, common fuzzy controller. Control rules were derived classifying the phase plane of error and change-in-error into six ambiguous regions, as shown in Figure 3.8. Following the principle of suboptimal control, the line $e + \dot{e} = 0$ serves as the switching line of the control variable sign.

The linguistic interpretation of fuzzy sets for error, change-in-error, and control were positive big *(PB)*, positive small *(PS)*, negative big *(NB)*, and negative small *(NS)*. Each fuzzy set was linearly quantized into 22 levels. Shapes of membership functions are shown in Figure 3.9.

The general control procedure, obtained heuristically, could be summarized as follows:

1. If region F then $u = NB$
2. If region A or D then $u = NS$
3. If region B or C then $u = PS$
4. If region E then $u = PB$

where regions A, B, . . . , f are defined on Figure 3.8.

The inference mechanism was quite simple, a conventional max–min procedure and the center of gravity method for defuzzification. Experiments were performed with a tactile sensor, with the controller programmed in Prolog and implemented on a PDP-11-like machine. The sensor, mounted at the robot's hand, measured the reactions between the robot effector and the object. The task was to keep a constant distance from the object during the tracking procedure.

The advantages of the fuzzy controller, in contrast to a conventional PD-controller, were better tracking capabilities and less error, and the main disadvantage was a relatively fast alternation of control output.

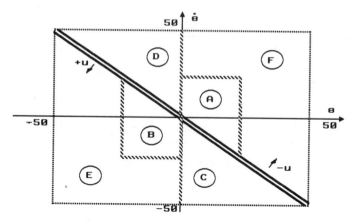

Figure 3.8 *A phase plain of sensor-guided fuzzy robot control, according to [11].*

In this section we have shown how fuzzy set theory was used and how it could be used for the control of robot dynamics. Although all of the described applications were laboratory experiments, we suppose that the newly introduced fuzzy hardware (fuzzy integrated controllers and fuzzy microprocessors) will give additional spur to the practical application of fuzzy control principles. The conventional control of robot dynamics will be no exception, but from our point of view, fuzzy control principles will find a better field of application in sensor-guided robots. This kind of robot control has been partly discussed in the present section, but only for the case in which the sensory information is precisely known and when it is not necessary to analyze or interpret it. The following section deals with the cases when additional analysis of sensory data are required, showing how fuzzy set theory could be employed for such tasks.

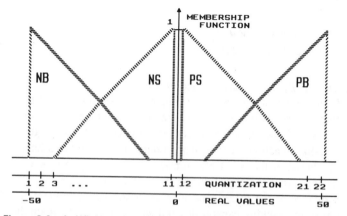

Figure 3.9 *A definition of fuzzy sets in sensor-guided fuzzy robot control.*

3.3 ANALYSIS AND INTERPRETATION OF ROBOT SENSOR INFORMATION

According to R. Palm [11], the new generation of sensor-guided robots (robots of the third generation) must have ''intelligent connection of perception and action.'' An academic discussion could be opened in connection with the meaning of the word ''intelligent.''

A unique approach does not exist and lot of definitions of intelligence have been given, but it is possible the exact answer could never be made because the intelligence itself is a fuzzy feature. Here we are dealing with robots, and in this context an intelligent robot is treated as a machine capable of solving problems. The problem is generally defined as a situation for which a person or machine does not have a ready answer, a ready response. Problem solving involves

The sensing and identification of the problem

The formulation of the problem

The utilization of relevant information

The generation and evaluation of solutions (hypotheses) [12]

In robotics, problems are always connected with some kind of *motion*: motion of a robot hand to reach an object, motion of a robot grasper to take an object, or motion of a robot itself if it is a mobile robot. The functional decomposition of intelligent robot tasks could be done according to Figure 3.10.

Fuzzy set theory has already found a lot of applications in almost all parts of this functional decomposition. New trends in sensor technology and particularly the development of fuzzy sensors and fuzzy transducers [13, 14] will probably find a lot of applications in robotics, but let us here discuss techniques already applied.

Gupta et al. [15] have emphasized that in systems of natural perception, where natural sensors are used for perception of images, temperature, sounds, and fragrance, the process of ''feeling'' or ''recognizing objects'' entirely depends upon the perception of certain attributes, rather than the measurement of their physical characteristics in absolute terms. In natural systems ''perception'' plays the same role as ''measurement'' in artificial systems. In the development of an intelligent system it is proposed, therefore, to make use of ''perceptions'' by employing some sort of *perceptor* rather than taking absolute quantitative measurements by means of precise and conventional measuring devices. Fuzzy reasoning could easily find application in such systems.

As a typical example let us use the perception of distance for an adaptive arc welding industrial robot [16]. An industrial robot with nine servo controlled axes is equipped with a noncontact distance sensor, which scans seam motion in the plane perpendicular to the trajectory to be welded. The sensor consists of an infrared pulse laser mounted on scanning platform together with a CCD (charge coupled device) line camera. The laser sensor measures distance between the CCD

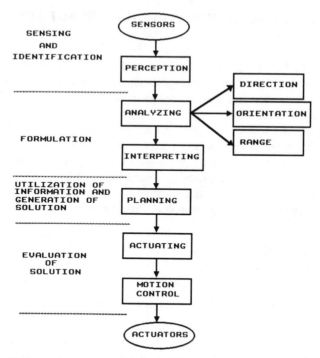

Figure 3.10   *Functional decomposition of intelligent robot tasks.*

receiver and the surface to be welded, as Figure 3.11 shows. For every scanning motion a snap of the cross section is registered.

If such distance sensor is to be used, it is necessary to find

1. How to estimate measured distances
2. How to estimate actual trajectory deviation from the pretaught one on the bases of registrations in 1

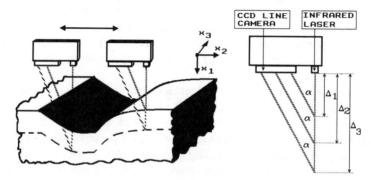

Figure 3.11   *Laser distance sensor.*

Every laser emission is registered via its reflective image on the line CCD camera. By a definite constant angle between the falling and reflecting laser beam (α), the distance Δ from receiver to measured surface is given as a serial number of the CCD camera lines. Unfortunately the image is rather a spot than a point, and consequently the registered value is not a single value but a set or values. This unsharp measuring calls for a fuzzy estimate.

The idea of ith level fuzzy set was used; ith level fuzzy set was defined as

$$F^{(i)}(X_i) = \{\mu^{(i)} | \mu^{(i)}: X_i \rightarrow L_i\} \tag{3.4}$$

where L_i is an argument of the previous level. For example, for a vertical distance X_1, $L_1 = [0, 1]$, for a cross-deviation X_2 of welding seam $L_2 = X_1$, and for a longitudinal deviation X_3 of the welding seam, $L_3 = X_2$ were used. As an information carrier of fuzzy set its power was taken. Based on the relative power of the longitudinal deviation for fixed prediction interval length, the proximity was determined and expressed in linguistic terms: very close, medium, far, and very far, and for every proximity estimate, the corresponding fuzzy action was assigned to eliminate deviation. Figure 3.12 shows fuzzy sets for one step of this procedure.

Another quite important problem in modern sensor-guided robotics is a problem of robot vision, as a special case of the more general problem of computer vision. Computer vision has a wide range of potential applications, so that the past two decades have seen a growing interest in building systems able not only to "see" using a camera as an eye, but also to understand the image. In the next section, a fuzzy vision transducer will be introduced, designed for tasks of robot motion planning and control. Here the process of image understanding or scene analysis

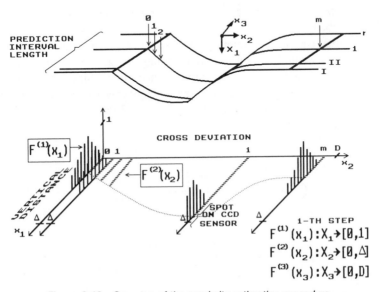

Figure 3.12 *One step of the proximity estimation procedure.*

based on fuzzy set theory will be described. This process involves the extraction of the description of the scene in terms of the objects presenting the image and the spatial relationships among them. The goal is to obtain the three-dimensional information about the scene from its two-dimensional projection, the image.

There are lots of difficulties caused by complexity and imprecision, which makes the process of scene analysis quite difficult [17]. A scene analysis procedure usually has two distinct phases:

1. segmentation or feature selection
2. interpretation or classification

In segmentation, the image array is partitioned into disjoint regions, each region satisfying a predicate based on some property of intensity value. During the interpretation, the domain knowledge is applied to extract some specific information from the segmentated image.

For a variety of inspections and manipulation tasks in robotics, the recognition of objects by means of computer vision is quite important. A typical example is the safety inspection in nuclear power plants by robot vehicles. Such a system [18] has to

- Verify the position of values and dampers
- Measure oil and liquid levels in sight meters
- Read instruments and gauges
- Detect and locate steam/water leaks
- Verify the integrity of security locks, and so forth

As an example of fuzzy set theory application in this domain, the edge perception will be described.

Perception of edges is an example of segmentation processes suitable for object recognition. This could be done by transforming the gray-level image from the absolute intensity domain to the perception domain using fuzzy set theory, since it deals with a set of phenomena that may ambiguously belong to a set. That is also a feature or natural human perception. Figure 3.13 gives the functional block diagram of such a system [15].

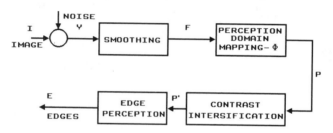

Figure 3.13 *A functional block diagram of an edge perception system.*

I is the original, gray-level digital image in a spatial-intensity domain, which could be mathematically represented by a matrix $\mathbf{I} = [i_{m,n}]$. The image Y, corrupted by noise, still in a spatial-intensity domain, is a matrix $\mathbf{Y} = [y_{m,n}]$. If we take the histogram of this noisy image, the distinct regions of the various intensity levels may not be readily identifiable. In order to reduce the effect of noise, a simple averaging scheme is taken over a window W of size $q \times q$. Thus, the smoothed pixel in the image can be defined as an average pixel intensity over the window W. The smoothed image is $\mathbf{F} = [f_{m,n}]$, where $f_{m,n}$ is the intensity value of the pixel (m, n). The next procedure is domain mapping from a spatial-intensity domain to a spatial-perception domain using the mapping function ϕ. The transformed image is $\mathbf{p} = [p_{m,n}]$, where $p_{m,n} \in [0, 1]$. The mapping function decimates the entire intensity region into a number of distinct regions assigning alternatively the low $\in [0, 0.5)$ and high $\in [0.5, 1]$ perception values. Thus, mapping from $f_{m,n}$ to $p_{m,n}$ may be considered as an aggregate phenomenon of perceiving the intensity levels of the gray digital image. This aggregation or granularity is one of the important attributes found in human perception, thinking, and decision making. The calculation procedure is quite simple. First the histogram for intensity levels from an image is determined. Generally an image is composed of k intensity levels L_1, $L_2, \ldots, L_k$ in intensity range $[x_m, x_M]$ as Figure 3.14 shows.

These intensity levels are distinctly identified at their peaks for values $x_1, \ldots$ x_k, and maximum uncertainty is at valleys $x_{c1}, \ldots, x_{ck}$. The reason is that, for example, the intensity value x_{c1} may belong to either intensity level L_1 or intensity level L_2, so the uncertainty is maximal. The multiregion mapping $\phi(x_1)$ is defined so that the whole range of intensity values $[x_n, x_M]$ is mapped in two distinct intensity levels: low and high. Crossover points from low to high and high to low are intensity values with maximum uncertainty $x_{c1}, x_{c2}, \ldots, x_{ck}$. Now to each

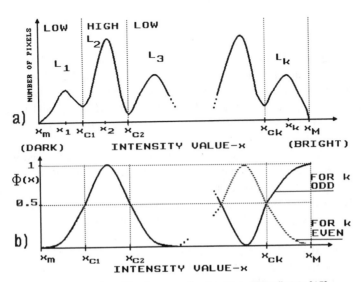

Figure 3.14 *A multiregion mapping function, according to [15].*

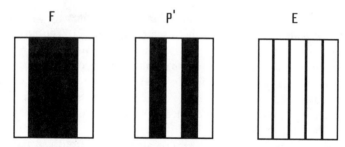

Figure 3.15 *A simple example of edge perception with three distinct intensity levels.*

pixel from smoothed image $f_{m,n}$ which has some intensity value x, a number $\phi_{m,n}$ = $\phi(f_{m,n})$ from interval $[0, 1]$ is assigned. The transformed image $\mathbf{P} = [\phi_{m,n}]$ is nothing but a fuzzy matrix. Value 1 corresponds to completely bright and 0 to completely dark. The next step would be the *contrast intensification*, an operation well known in fuzzy set theory. Its task is to reduce the entropy and to make some kind of focusing and reduction of the fuzziness. As a result of this operation bright becomes very bright and dark becomes very dark.

The resulting image $\mathbf{P}' = [p'_{m,n}]$ is composed of regions with two distinct brightnesses. A simple example of this is shown in Figure 3.15.

The next step would be edge perception. Most of the pixels in the image $\mathbf{P}'$ are either in the low or high perception range, but at the edge of this region are pixels with perception levels near to 0.5. In order to detect these boundaries, a max–min operation is performed over a window W of size $q \times q$ using the operation known as EDG[·]. An example of this operation is

$$E = [e_{m,n}] = \text{EDG}[\mathbf{P}'] = \left| \left\{ p'_{m,n} - \min_{(i,j) \in W} p'_{i,j} \right\} \right| \tag{3.5}$$

where for $(i, j) \in W$, $(i, j) \neq (m, n)$.

Finally the edge locus could be defined as all pixels (m, n) for which $e_{m,n}$ belongs to a certain interval $[\alpha_1, \alpha_2]$, where $\alpha_i \in [0.1]$ are the values that bound the degree of perception. For example, primary edges could be defined as $e_{m,n}$ from interval $(0.75, 1]$, secondary edges for $e_{m,n} \in [0.5, 0.75]$ and no edge for $e_{m,n} \in [0, 0.25]$. The size of the window W determines the width of the edges in perception domain.

When the edges are determined and located (position is determined with pixel position (m, n)), the recognition process could be started using specific knowledge. An example will be the knowledge about spectral, spatial, and relational properties of objects. In [18] a frame based system was used for the presentation of such knowledge. The knowledge for slider recognition could be

```
# 1   NAME: SLIDER     No. of subobjects = 2
              Name of subobject:  HANDLE
              Name of subobject:  SLOT
```

Intrarelational property: Slot is right-of-handle
Spatial property: undefined
Spectral property: undefined
#2   NAME: HANDLE   No. of subobjects = 0
Intrarelational property: no
Spatial property: min relative size: 20%
                    max relative size: 60%
                    shape: rectangular
Spectral property: The object is darker than background

Although in [18] the nonfuzzy techniques were used for object recognition, the fuzzy set theory could make the system even more versatile by expressing object properties with linguistic values modeled by fuzzy sets. For example, the linguistic expression of the size could be small, quite small, very big, and so forth, and to each of them an appropriate fuzzy set could be assigned according to Figure 3.16.

The other applications of interpretation of information obtained from robot sensors, also based on fuzzy set theory, are as follows:

- filtering and editing sensor data in space flights for space shuttle rendezvous problem [19]
- moving mark recognition [20]
- information fusion in computer vision [21], and so forth

Some examples from the next section deal with these tasks, as well. In addition, a good review with extensive bibliography covering publications concerning fuzzy set theory application in more general problems of pattern recognition could be found in [22].

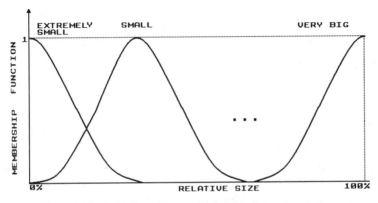

Figure 3.16 *Definition of fuzzy sets for object size descriptions.*

3.4 ROBOT MOTION PLANNING AND CONTROL

After the object has been perceived and recognized, the motion of the robot has to be planned and executed, that is, the motion of a robot hand toward the object to be reached or picked or the motion of the whole mobile robot avoiding obstacles. In both cases, the planning procedure is usually based on the construction of an internal robot model of the real world. The problem is that the complexity of the environment in which the robot has to act cannot be fully represented in the model. A lot of uncertainty and fuzziness is present in such robotic systems either because of inadequacy of robot receptors and effectors, or because of impossibility to represent objects, locate objects, or perform actions on objects with sufficient accuracy. Because of that it is not possible to construct a precise functional mapping between the state space of the model and the state space of the external world. Fuzzy set theory gives the methodology to handle such kinds of problem. Our approach based on fuzzy relations [23] will be discussed here.

The starting point was the work of Averkin and Dulin [24]. They used fuzzy mapping as a bridge between the state space of the internal model and the state space of the external world, so the first fuzzy mapping and fuzzy relations will be introduced shortly.

The binary fuzzy relation R^* is the relation that may hold between the elements of any two crisp sets X and Y to any degree between 0 and 1. Formally, it is a set of ordered pairs $R^* = ((x, y), R(x, y))$, where (x, y) is an element of the Cartesian product $X \times Y$ while $R(x, y)$ is its characteristic function. Transition from a binary fuzzy relation to an n-ary fuzzy relation is straight.

If X and Y are discrete sets, $X = \{x_i | i \in I\}$ and $Y = \{y_j | j \in J\}$, where I and J are index sets, then R^* is a discrete fuzzy relation and it can be completely given by its fuzzy matrix $\mathbf{R}^*$ with components

$$r_{ij} = R(x_i, y_j), \qquad i \in I, \quad j \in J \tag{3.6}$$

This fuzzy matrix may be concrete if X and Y are finite sets; otherwise it would be only conceptual.

Let us suppose that we have a fuzzy relation R^* from X to Y and fuzzy relation P^* from Y to Z. The composition o of fuzzy relations R^* and P^* is also a fuzzy relation S^*, but from X to Z whose membership function, for each pair (x, z) could be obtained by equation

$$S(x, z) = \sup_{y \in Y} \min (R(x, y), P(y, z)) \tag{3.7}$$

$S(x, z)$ could be seen as the strength of a set of chains linking x and z. The strength of such a chain is that of the weakest link, and because of that the operation min is used. But between x and z there are more chains through different y, consequently the strength of the relation between x and z is that of the strongest one (operation supremum over all y from Y).

The composition of finite fuzzy relations can be viewed as a matrix product. With $\mathbf{R}* = [r_{ij}]$, $\mathbf{P}* = [p_{jk}]$, $\mathbf{S}* = [s_{ik}]$, and $\mathbf{S}* = \mathbf{R}* \circ \mathbf{P}*$ we have

$$s_{ik} = \sum_j r_{ij} \otimes p_{jk} \tag{3.8}$$

where Σ is in fact operation max and $\otimes$ operation min. The composition (3.3) or (3.4) is usually called sup-min composition.

Let $A*$ and $B*$ be fuzzy sets defined on X and Y, respectively. $A*$ implies $B*$ ($A* \rightarrow B*$) or, expressed in words, "If $A*$ then $B*$" is a fuzzy conditional proposition. A mathematical operation for translating this proposition into a fuzzy relation $R*$ in $X \times Y$ is called the fuzzy implication operator. There are many possible definitions of this operator, but in control applications Mamdani min definition is most frequent:

$$R(x, y) = \min (A(x), B(y)), \quad x \in X, \quad y \in Y \tag{3.9}$$

Fuzzy relational models are the appropriate way to represent the uncertainty of the external world. They can be used in cases when it is not possible to construct a precise functional mapping between the state space of the internal model and the state space of the external world. The values of membership functions of fuzzy modeling relations may be seen as degrees of similarity between the world and the model, or as degrees of precision of the real world description. Fuzzy modeling relation $R*$ is a binary fuzzy relation between the world state space W and the model state space M. For example, $R*$ could be seen as a fuzzy matrix whose columns correspond to the robot's world state space, let us say, to the discrete values of the passageway width through which the mobile robot must pass. The rows of fuzzy matrix $R*$ correspond to the robot's internal model state space as, for example, elements symbolically expressed in words: "very wide" (VW), "wide" (W), "narrow" (N), and so forth. Table 3.1 is a typical simple example. The elements in this table express degrees to which the elements of the world state space W belong, to the elements of the model state space M, and vice versa.

Each row of Table 3.1 defines a membership function of fuzzy set m_i^* from the model state space whose support set is the real world state space W. The situation is more-or-less identical for each column in Table 3.1, which defines a member-

TABLE 3.1 Fuzzy Modeling Relation *RI* * for Passageway Width (values of *W* are in meters)

PASSAGEWAY WIDTH		WORLD (WI)			
		0.5	1	1.5	2
MODEL (MI)	VERY WIDTH (UW)	0	0.1	0.25	1
	WIDE (W)	0	0.3	0.5	1
	NARROW (N)	1	0.7	0	0

ship function of the fuzzy set w_j^* from the world state space whose support set is the state space of the model M. A typical example is the fuzzy set "wide" whose membership function is fuzzy vector [0 0.3 0.5 1]. This fuzzy vector says that, for example, the real value 1.5 belongs to the concept expressed with "wide" degree 0.5. Also, the real value 1.5 m could be seen as fuzzy set "1.5 m" defined on the model state space with fuzzy vector [0.25 0.5 0], which means that, for example, the symbolic value "very wide" belongs to the fuzzy set "1.5 m" with degree the 0.25. The elements of the real world are not fuzzy in the real world state space, but they become fuzzy in the model world state space, and vice versa.

It is important that using this approach we can construct the internal model representation of the real world with various levels of abstraction. The level of abstraction is directly connected with the cardinality of the model state space M. At the lowest level of abstraction, the state space of the model is the same as the state space of the world ($M = W$). A case apart represents the nonfuzzy, functional model when modeling relation is Boolean and one-to-one. The real abstraction begins when state spaces M and W are no more sets with the same elements. The special case with Boolean but not one-to-one mapping is the quantization of real line. For example, the element symbolically expressed with "0.5" or I or #1 may stay for all real values between 0. and 0.5.

If we introduce more elements in the model state space M, for example, the terms "very very wide" or "not so wide," the level of abstraction diminishes, but if we reduce the cardinality of the set M the level of abstraction increases. The model state space with only two elements, "wide" and "narrow," is more abstract than the one given in Table 3.1.

It is important to notice that, in the case when model state space M has more elements than world state space W, we have a situation contrary to abstraction; we have some kind of interpolation.

Let us now suppose that we have a fuzzy modeling relation for both inputs and outputs of the robot control system. Table 3.1 could serve as an example of relational models of input information "passageway width" and Table 3.2 for output information "robot velocity."

The task of the control system is to plan the robot velocity according to the specific input information about passageway width. Let us suppose that the velocity could be adjusted only in discrete steps from Table 3.2 and that information about passageway width is also discrete shown in Table 3.1.

TABLE 3.2   Fuzzy Modeling Relation RO* for Robot Velocity (values of W are in meters per second)

ROBOT VELOCITY		WORLD (WO)				
		0.2	0.5	0.8	1	1.5
MODEL (MO)	HIGH (H)	0	0	0.2	0.8	1
	MEDIUM (M)	0.2	0.7	1	0.8	0.1
	LOW (L)	1	0.9	0.2	0	0

The final result of the planning procedure, which is the input information to low level controller, must be one and only one element coming from the robot velocity world state space. This means that finally each controller that acts in the real world must be a deterministic controller. But on the model level it is not necessary to have a deterministic procedure. Moreover, a nondeterministic, fuzzy procedure is closer to the description of the control procedure that humans use during control. Let us suppose that we are using human knowledge for passageway width—a robot velocity planning task. The planning procedure could be expressed with production rules like these:

If passageway width is very wide, than velocity could be high

or

If passageway width is wide, then velocity could be high, too

or

If passageway width is narrow, then velocity could be low

Conventional procedure is to express these rules with fuzzy condition propositions connected with union ($VW* \rightarrow H* \cup W* \rightarrow H* \cup N* \rightarrow L*$) where $VW*$, $H*$, $W*$, $N*$ and $L*$ are fuzzy vectors obtained as rows of Table 3.1 and 3.2. To transform these rules in fuzzy relation between the real world state space of passageway width and real world state space of robot velocity, a fuzzy implications operator must be used. For example, if we define a fuzzy implication with Eq. (3.10) and union with max, the result is Table 3.3. The final step is interpretation, and that means changing Table 3.3. into a Boolean table, where in each row one and only one nonzero element exactly equal to 1.

Using the theory of fuzzy relations, let us now show how this procedure could be interpreted. The production rules are relations between the model state space of passageway width and the model state space of the robot velocity. For the production rules this relation is a Boolean one, given in Table 3.4.

As elements of fuzzy modeling, relations of control algorithms could be seen as degrees of strength between input and output world state space; the natural way of obtaining this relation is by composing fuzzy relations $RI*$, $RP*$, and $RO*$.

TABLE 3.3 Fuzzy Relation of Control Algorithm

CONTROL ALGORITHM		WO				
		0.2	0.5	0.8	1	1.5
WI	0.5	1	0.9	0.2	0	0
	1	0.7	0.7	0.2	0.3	0.3
	1.5	0	0	0.2	0.5	0.5
	2	0	0	0.2	0.8	1

TABLE 3.4   Production Rules as Relation RP*

PLANNING RULES		MO		
		HIGH	MEDIUM	LOW
MI	VERY WIDTH (VW)	1	0	0
	WIDE (W)	1	0	0
	NARROW (N)	0	0	1

Boolean relation $P*$ from Table 3.4 is also only a special case of fuzzy relations:

$$RC* = RI* \circ RP* \circ RO* \qquad (3.10)$$

It's interesting that the results obtained by Eq. (3.10), where composition $\circ$ is given by Eq. (3.7), or more preciously by Eq. (3.8), completely coincide with Table 3.3, which is obtained by fuzzy implication operator, Eq. (3.9), and the definition of union with max. This equality could be proved.

This approach, which uses the composition of relations instead of fuzzy implication, has one additional degree of freedom. That degree of freedom is that, in production rules, instead of a Boolean relation there is a real fuzzy relation. Examples would be as follows:

If passageway width is very wide, then velocity could be high with degree 1, medium with degree 0.8, or low with degree 0.2

or

The velocity could be high if passageway width is very wide with degree 1, wide with degree 0.9, or narrow with degree 0.1

The existing fuzzy control algorithms are usually based on a fuzzy implication, which leads to Boolean relations. The proposed fuzzy approach is a novelty and it is suitable for the cases when it is not possible to obtain consensus about control actions.

Practical applications of these ideas concerning fuzzy modeling relations could be motion planning and control of a mobile robot. An example would be an unmanned submersible, which must act in relatively unknown underwater surroundings.

The typical decomposition of a robot's tasks are planning, navigation, and piloting [25]. For each of these tasks, fuzzy modeling relations with different levels of abstraction could be used. At the highest but least precise and detailed level is the *planner*, which operates on incomplete information. The level of abstraction is here the highest one. Real world is described just roughly, with an approximate model. The next level is *navigator*, which utilizes a more detailed map to evaluate an obstacle-free local path satisfying some performance criteria. With the path description the pilot provides motion control avoiding obstacles. It requires the most precise information and the least possible abstract model state space. This operation of decreasing the level of abstraction of internal model state space could be called *zooming of abstraction*. It could be defined as a procedure that increases the cardinality of the model state space. Complementary to this procedure could be *zooming of fuzziness* when values of fuzzy relation membership are changed so that fuzziness diminishes (values are clear to 1 and 0). The third procedure could be *zooming of precision*, defined as a procedure that increases the cardinality of the world state space. For example, the world state space of the passageway width is more precise then the one shown in Table 3.1 if it has more then five elements for widths between 0 and 2 m.

These three procedures could be used together to obtain a more-or-less precise picture of the external, real world for different tasks of mobile robot motion planning and control.

Let us explain how fuzzy set theory could be used in mobile robot motion, planing, and control *on the pilot level*, when the robot is equipped with the vision sensor. The image represents a limited range of space in front of the mobile robot. For free obstacle motion control, it is necessary to evaluate the boundaries dividing the floor and the objects. For this task a simple differentiation of camera signal could be used [25]. Distances and positions of objects and walls are defined according to their x, y position in the image, taking into account the camera height and the tilt angle. Figure 3.17 shows a simplified image together with definition of most important quantities. W is the width and L is the distance between the robot and the obstacles.

The main planning objective on the pilot level is to find a permissible route without obstacles. The widest permissible path is determined by W and P, where $W = \max_i (W_i)$, and P is the coordinate that represents the direction of the robot motion. For the case shown in Figure 3.17 the widest path is W_2. If the robot is too close to the object or the robot diameter is bigger than W_2, the pilot will conclude that there is no passageway in front of the robot. Consequently the robot will start turning around to find a passage in a new direction.

When there is an acceptable passageway, a minimum distance between the ro-

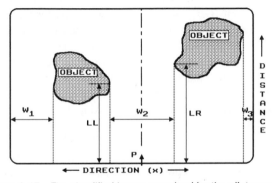

Figure 3.17 *The simplified image perceived by the pilot camera.*

bot and the obstacles is calculated, taking into account the robot width *WR*. For this calculation equation $L = \min(LL, LR)$ is used. After that a simple fuzzy algorithm could be applied for direction and velocity control. In [25] direction control was obtained by changing the speed of the left and the right wheel according to these equations:

$$U_L(k) = U_L(k-1) + G \Delta U + aT \tag{3.11}$$

$$U_R(k) = U_R(k-1) + G \Delta U + aT \tag{3.12}$$

U_L and U_R are left and right reference wheel speed commands, G is the direction control gain, ΔU is the direction control rate, a is the acceleration control input, and T is the sampling period. Conventional feedback loop was used to stabilize real speeds V_L and V_R to their reference values U_L and U_R. The control variables determined by fuzzy controller were g, ΔU, and a. Three types of control rules were defined:

$$R_1: (\Delta V = \Delta V_i \text{ and } P = P_i) \rightarrow \Delta U = \Delta U_i \tag{3.13}$$

$$R_2: (\text{sgn}(\Delta V)) = S_i \text{ and } L = L_i) \rightarrow G = G_i \tag{3.14}$$

$$R_3: (V = V_i \text{ and } W = W_i) \rightarrow U = U_i \tag{3.15}$$

where ΔU and G were defined previously; ΔV is the speed difference between the left and right wheels at the sampling instant $k - 1$; p is the permissible passageway direction; $\text{sgn}(\Delta V)$ is the sign of ΔV; L is the distance from the robot to the nearest obstacle; V is the average speed command of the left and right wheels at sampling instant $k - 1$; W is the permissible passageway width; and U is the reference speed. ΔV_i, P_i, ΔU_i, S_i, L_i, G_i, V_i, W_i and U_i are linguistic values of variables mathematically defined by fuzzy sets; 49 rules of type R_1, eight rules of type R_2, and 16 rules of type R_3 were defined. Real worlds of ΔV, P, and ΔU were quantized into 13 levels $(-6, -5, \cdots, 6)$ and their corresponding model world into seven levels (negative big (*NB*), negative medium (*NM*), negative small (*NS*), zero (*ZO*), and the same for positive). The real world of G was quantizied into seven levels $(1, 2, \cdots, 7)$ and its model world into four levels (zero (*GZ*), small (*GS*), medium (*GM*), bit (*GB*)), and the same was done for the model worlds of *LL*, *LR*, *W*, and *U* (*Z*, *S*, *M*, *B*), but their real worlds were quantized into nine levels $(0, 1, 2, \cdots, 8)$. Rules are given in Table 3.5.

Max–min composition was used, the implication was defined by min operator, and the center of gravity method was applied for the interpretation of the resulting fuzzy sets. G and ΔU from Eqs. (3.11) and (3.12) were directly derived from the rules. Acceleration control a was calculated by using this simple equation:

$$a = (U - V)/(m \cdot T) \tag{3.16}$$

where constant $m \in [1, 5]$ was chosen on the basis of the surrounding situations and acceleration characteristics of the robot.

TABLE 3.5 Fuzzy Control Rules for Mobile Robot Steering and Speed Control According to [25]

		ΔV						
		NB	NM	NS	ZO	PS	PM	PB
p	NB	ZO	NS	NS	NM	NM	NB	NB
	NM	PS	ZO	NS	NS	NM	NM	NB
	NS	PS	PS	ZO	NS	NS	NM	NM
	ZO	PM	PS	PS	ZO	NS	NS	NM
	PS	PM	PM	PS	PS	ZO	NS	NS
	PM	PB	PM	PM	PS	PS	ZO	NS
	PB	PB	PB	PM	PM	PS	PS	ZO
		ΔU						

		LL				LR			
		Z	S	M	B	Z	S	M	B
sgn (ΔV)	PO	GZ	GZ	GS	GS	GB	GB	GM	GM
	NE	GB	GB	GM	GS	GZ	GZ	GS	GS
		G							

		V			
		Z	S	M	B
W	Z	Z	Z	Z	Z
	S	S	S	S	S
	M	M	M	M	B
	B	M	M	M	B
		U			

The reported simulation and experiment results were quite successful, and the only problem was not connected with the fuzzy control, as one might expect, but with the vision system. The reflected glares on the floor due to the lamps on the ceiling were occasionally mistaken for obstacles, and sometimes strong surrounding reflections influenced the detection of boundaries.

In [26, 27] the same problem of motion planning and control on pilot level was solved in a different way. The rules were defined as a prescription of motion execution command to the actuator controller, taking into account that the present state would be changed to the desired one in a specified time. It was necessary to construct the robot environment representation, and robot self-representation was constructed.

The pilot used a "self-concentrated" reference frame for environment representation, where the location of each object in relation to the robot was defined by two polar coordinates: distance and angle. The robot self-representation contained two locomotion parameters, velocity and acceleration, and one steering parameter, angle of steering.

The control rules were defined as order triplets of present state, final state, and acceleration command. Rules were obtained from verbal description of analytical systems models and constraints derived from an optimal criterion of minimum time control. That means "bang-bang" change of acceleration. Two types of rules were used: acceleration–deceleration (braking) rules and steering rules. Acceleration–deceleration rules were of the form:

$$\begin{pmatrix} \text{present velocity} \\ \text{final velocity} \\ \text{goal distance} \end{pmatrix} \rightarrow \text{acceleration or deceleration}$$

Similarly, steering rules were of the form:

$$\begin{pmatrix} \text{present velocity} \\ \text{goal distance} \\ \text{goal angle} \end{pmatrix} \rightarrow \text{steering angle}$$

A typical example of acceleration–deceleration rules for static objects when the final robot velocity is zero, because the object velocity is zero, is this:

If robot velocity is *medium fast*, and object (goal) distance is *close* then acceleration–deceleration is *hard brake*

If several rules are triggered, a strategy of minimum time locomotion would be used. For example, for acceleration control that means to choose the highest value of acceleration. To illustrate this procedure, let us suppose that the obtained acceleration command is $ACC = \{0.8/HB, 0.8/B, 0.6/SU\}$, where HB is hard brake, B is brake, and SU is speed up. First a certainty level α is defined and than maximum acceleration is chosen, whose membership value is higher than that certainty level α. For higher certainty level, $\alpha = 0.7$, it is "brake," and for lower, $\alpha = 0.5$, it is "speed up." The certainty level could be treated as a kind of hazard measure. If it is low, the behavior is more hazardous, which means that the obstacle will be reached in shorter time, but in that case it might happen that the robot doesn't stop in time. The authors have concluded that the main disadvantage of a knowledge-based approach to robot motion planning and control is the difficulty in analyzing the controllability of the system and the stability of the control loop. Also, a large number of max–min operations must be computed and this is not possible in real time without special fuzzy hardware.

Let us now explain how a fuzzy approach could be used in motion planning and control of the robot hand in the case of "eye-hand coordination." The main idea is to control the motion of the robot hand using information obtained from vision sensor, the robot eye. The control task stated as "perceive and follow point light source in two-dimensional space'' will be considered, but first let us describe principles of the fuzzy eye [14].

As a rule the process of vision has three stages:

1. the optical stage when an image of the outside world is projected on the retina
2. the transduction stage when the light-sensitive visual cells absorb photons and respond by generating electrical signals
3. the physiological stage when these primary signals are analyzed [28]

The idea of the fuzzy vision is primarily connected with the second and the third stage. Fuzzy vision sensor (fuzzy eye) is conceived as an array of light-sensitive elements (photo detectors) arranged in a way that a quite simple analysis of electric signals generated by them is sufficient to detect the position of the light source. This vision signal is used as input information to the controller, whose task is to control the actuator. Generally, the geometry of an eye is quite different for the eye that requires an image of a point source of light and the eye of the extended bright field that normally is encountered by diurnal animals. The idea of the fuzzy vision based control is here introduced and explained in the first case where the main control task is to see and then to follow a point source of light. A typical example is a lamp or a small luminescent object on a dark background. To simplify the presentation, a one-dimensional case will be considered. The control task is to see and to point by an actuator at the light source positioned on the circle. Figure 3.18 shows situation schematically. In the center of the circle is the vision sensor and actuator, the pointing device. The final goal is to position the pointing device in the direction of the light source.

Since nature is an unlimited source of ideas, the inspiration for the fuzzy eye comes from nature, too. In the animal kingdom, two types of eye are encountered. The first one is a well known lens eye characteristic of vertebrate animals, and the second one is a compound eye characteristic of invertebrate animals or, more precisely, insects. A man-made copy of a lens eye is a conventional video camera. Here we are proposing a fuzzy eye as a man-made copy of a compound eye or, to be more precise, of an apposition compound eye [28]. Figure 3.19 shows the cross section of the apposition compound eye and the fuzzy eye.

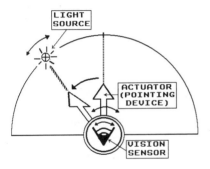

Figure 3.18 *A light source following based on the principle of eye-hand coordination.*

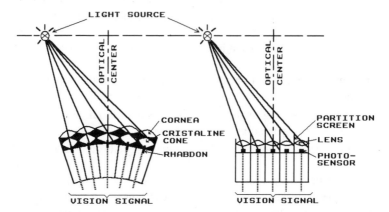

Figure 3.19 *Cross sections of the apposition compound eye (left) and the fuzzy eye (right).*

The apposition compound eye consists of sections called ommatidea. In each ommatidea light passes through the cornea, which acts as a lens, and the crystalline cone, exciting a light-sensitive sensor called rhabdon. In the rhabdon, light is converted into a vision signal. The amount of light that the rhabdon receives is biggest when the light passes through the optical axis of the rhabdon. As the light source moves away from the optical axis, the amount of light the rhabdon received decreases rapidly. Ommatidea are arranged so that each one "covers" one part of the space. When the light source is positioned in its part of the space, the vision signal of that ommatidea will be biggest, but other ommatidea in its vicinity will be excited, too. As a result the vision signal received from a set of ommatidea carries information about the position of the light source. A real compound eye is an array of ommatidea, so it can detect a light source in two dimensions, and binocular vision with two compound eyes could be used to detect the light in three-dimensional space.

The organization of the fuzzy eye is quite similar, as Figure 3.19 shows, but the fuzzy eye has an additional feature, which we describe below.

Light sensors are photo detectors constructed in such a way that lenses are incapsulated together with the sensitive element. The sensitivity of such sensors also decreases with angular distance from the photo detector center line (optical axis), similar to the sensitivity of the rhabdon. Even the shapes of sensitivity curves of both natural and man-made light sensors are qualitatively quite similar. They are both "bell-like" curves shown on Figure 3.20. The angular distance between the light source and the sensor optical center is plotted on x-axis and the relative sensor sensitivity on y-axis.

The fuzzy eye has one additional feature as a result of introducing the partition screens between photo sensors. These screens have a strong influence on the vision signal. Changing the screen height, we can manipulate the shape of the obtained vision signal and assign more-or-less importance to certain photo sensors.

The vision signal carries information about a light source position. Usually this position is determined according to the optical center of the eye. For the case

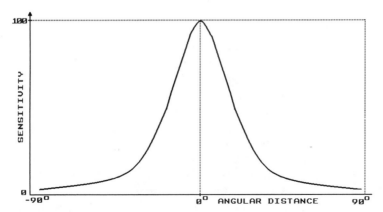

Figure 3.20 *Sensitivity of photo sensors as a function of angular distance from the sensor's optical center.*

shown in Figure 3.19, the intensity of the signal produced by the sensor in the left corner is the biggest, and the last three sensors on the right are not affected by the light. After we normalize, the vision signal could be expressed by a vector, for example [1   0.5   0   0   0]. Numbers represent the relative intensity of each sensor signal normalized according to the highest value. This vector carries information about the light source position, and it could be seen and analyzed as a fuzzy vector. That is the reason why we have used the expression "fuzzy eye." Fuzzy vectors could be used as an input to the controller that controls the velocity and the position of the actuator.

Figure 3.21 shows two typical examples. The first one shows vision signal of

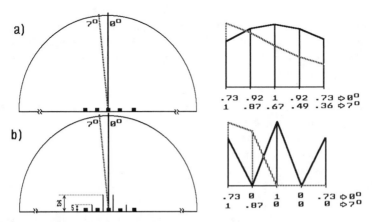

Figure 3.21 *Fuzzy eye geometry and the fuzzy vision signal for a light source position at the optical center and seven degrees left:*
a) Without partition screens.
b) For partition screens 0, 5, 25, 5, 0 mm high, looking from left to right.

a fuzzy eye without partition screen and the second one a vision signal of a fuzzy eye for certain combinations of screen height. Light was positioned at the optical center and seven degrees left of the optical center.

According to Figure 3.18, our final goal is to position the actuator (pointing device) in the direction of the light source. The actuator and the fuzzy eye have independent motors, so each one is able to rotate independently. When the light turns on, the fuzzy eye produces the vision signal in the form of a fuzzy vector. From the shape of this vector it is possible to determine the approximate position of the light. This information is used as an input to the rule based fuzzy control algorithm, which gives the direction and velocity of fuzzy eye rotation. The eye will stop rotating when its optical center line intersects the light. The pointing device starts to rotate at the same time as the fuzzy eye, but the control algorithm takes care that the eye is positioned first. Then final precise adjustment of the pointing device position is made using the precise information of the fuzzy eye location.

In this section few examples of robot motion planning and control using fuzzy set theory were described. Planning procedure is usually based on internal models representative of the robot surroundings, and fuzzy models are quite appropriate for internal model construction if the robot surroundings are not precisely known. Our next task is to show how the fuzzy technique could be used in communication with robots by means of words and sentences of natural languages.

3.5 COMMUNICATION WITH ROBOTS USING NATURAL LANGUAGE

Giving instructions to robots using natural language is one of the challenging tasks of modern robotics. The procedure consists of three main parts: sensing, recognizing, and understanding natural language. In this chapter our interest focuses on the third and the most complicated part: making the robot understand commands given in natural language and having it act according to the instructions given therein. We will suppose that words are received and correctly recognized, but that their meaning is not yet understood. Fifteen years ago Gougen [1] wrote a visionary article about fuzzy robot planning and control using natural language. He emphasized that rigid syntactic foundation is not necessary for natural language understanding. That is a rather robust affair because the words of most natural languages have inherent fuzziness. No rigid boundaries could be drawn for their use. He gave a simple example of colors: There is a linear continuum of hues between red and yellow, and at no point there is a clear separation. Even the intermediate value "orange" doesn't help, because the boundaries of orange are equally unclear.

In connection with natural language communication with robots by means of instructions about robot motion, Gougen has proposed to map the words of a natural language by a semantic interpreter into an "intermediate representation language" (IRL). In its simplest form, an IRL consists of a sequence of fuzzy vectors, each vector containing *fuzzy length*, a fuzzy set defined on a interval of path lengths [0, L], and *fuzzy direction*, a fuzzy set defined on circle unit, represented with degrees from 0° to 360°. A subset of natural language words is used to express the appropriate kind of hints (H) which are in IRL a selection of fuzzy vectors. Gougen claims that such hints, and even a very simple one, can be sufficient for robot guidance through a very complex maze, but no simulation or experiment results are presented.

A couple of years latter Zadeh [29] introduced and more correctly defined *meaning representation language for natural language (PRUF)*. His main assumption was that impression intrinsic in natural language is, for the most part, "possibilistic" in nature rather than probabilistic. So each proposition translates into a procedure P, which returns a possibility distribution Π. P is the meaning of the proposition, and Π is the information conveyed by proposition.

Let us use, for example, a simple proposition with an object description:

The blue box which is quite small and very close.

In PRUF the representation of this proposition is this:

$$(\text{Object (category} = \text{box)}$$
$$(n \text{ (color)} = \text{blue)}$$
$$(n \text{ (size)} = \text{quite small)}$$
$$(n \text{ (distance)} = \text{very close))}.$$

where n is a fuzzy descriptor. Thus n(color) is a fuzzy set characterized by possibility distribution over perceived colors of box, n(size) descriptor contains the linguistic modifier "quite," which modifies the possibility distribution associated with the fuzzy linguistic value "small" and similar to that n(distance) with a modifier "very."

Although there is a close connection between the concept of a possibility distribution and that of fuzzy set, there is also a difference between them, especially in interpretation. The reader can find complete discussion in [29, 30].

A simple proposition is defined as p: X is F, where X is a variable taking values in a universe U, and F is a fuzzy set defined in U, which induces a possibility distribution Π_x numerically equal to F. Linguistically F is expressed by words of a natural language. For example, a proposition in linguistic form could be: "*Relative size is small*," where *relative size* is a variable defined in an interval [0%, 100%] and *small* is a fuzzy set whose possibility distribution could be defined by Figure 3.16.

In PRUF there are also four types of *translation rules:*

(I) Modification Rules

$$p : x \text{ is } mF$$

where m is the modifier (not, very, quite, extremely, etc.) that modifies possibility distributions, for example, not corresponds to the complement $(1 - \Pi)$, or very to the second power (Π^2).

Example: Relative size is *very small*.

(II) Translation Rules

$$p = q * r$$

where g, q, r are propositions and $*$ denotes the operation composition, for example, conjunction (and), disjunction (or), implication (if $\cdot$ $\cdot$ $\cdot$ then $\cdot$ $\cdot$ $\cdot$), and so forth

Example: q Object is close
  r Speed is very small
  p If object is close then speed is very small

(III) Quantifier Rule

$$p : QN \text{ is } F$$

where Q is a fuzzy quantifier (most, many, few, some, almost all, etc.)

Example: Almost all boxes are black.

(IV) Qualification Rules

$$P : p \text{ is } \gamma$$

where γ might be a truth value $- \tau$ (true, not true, very true, more or less true, not very true, etc.), a probability value $- \lambda$ (probable, not very probable or likely, not very likely, etc.) or a possibility value $- \omega$ (quite possible, almost impossible, etc.)

Example: Object is very close is not very true.
  Object is very close is quite likely.
  Object is very close is very possible.

In conclusion, we quote Zadeh, "PRUF bears the same relation to fuzzy logic that predicate calculus does to two-valued logic. Thus it serves to translate a set of premises expressed in natural language into expressions in PRUF to which the rules of inferences may be applied, yielding other expressions in PRUF, which upon retranslation become the conclusion inferred from the original premises" [30, p. 4].

As an example of giving instructions to robots in terms of natural language using fuzzy set theory, a work of Uragami et al. [31] will be presented. A three legged "Inchworm robot" moved in real space under control of a program expressed in terms of natural language. Four types of fuzzy-linguistic instructions were used:

1. Go about n steps
2. Go to x
3. Go about n steps to x
4. Turn to the right (left)

with two supplementary instructions, which give initial values to the system

5. Head east/west/north/south.
6. Start from x.

References of the real world were given in virtual space by a data structure map, which contains the robot's actual position and gives information of the robot's immediate surrounding. An example of a town map and a data structure map is given in Figure 3.22.

Fuzzy linguistic instructions were transformed into machine instructions using the max method. For example, the linguistic value "about n steps" is defined as "normalize a fuzzy set having the membership value equal to 1 for steps whose value equals n." Figure 3.23 shows a fuzzy set "about 15 steps."

If robot is at position x with "head east" and has to execute instructions, "Go about 15 steps," it will stop near the church because for the church (C) the value $\mu_{about15}(X_c)$ is maximum. Machine instructions for degrees below a certain threshold are not chosen. For example, for the threshold shown in Figure 3.23 intersection 1 is abandoned. If there is no solution, back tracking to the previous instruction occurs and the machine instruction with the second highest degree is executed. For example, if we go back to the instruction "go about 15 steps" for the second time the robot will stop near the restaurant $R1$.

The second type of instructions is "go to x." If x is not specified, the nearest x is chosen. For example, if the robot starts from x and has to execute "go to

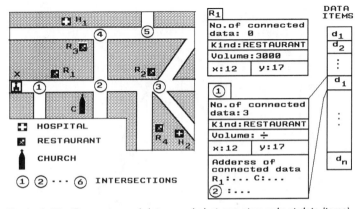

Figure 3.22 *Town map and data map (robot can stop only at data items).*

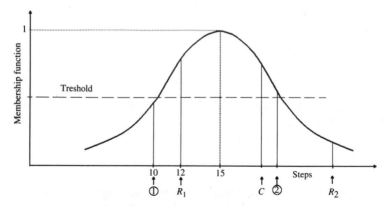

Figure 3.23 *Membership function of the fuzzy set "about 15 steps."*

restaurant,'' it will stop at R_1, but if specific instruction is given ''go to R_2,'' it will go to R_2.

The third type of instructions is ''go about n steps to x.'' Now again a figure like Figure 3.23 is used. For example, for the instruction ''go about 15 steps to restaurant,'' the robot will stop near the restaurant R_1.

In object size description, three linguistic values were used: ''large,'' ''middle,'' and ''small,'' defined with adequate fuzzy sets. An example is shown in Figure 3.24. If x is again the starting point and the instruction is ''go to small restaurant,'' the robot will stop near R_2 because the membership value of fuzzy set ''small'' is maximum at point R_2.

The last type of instruction is ''turn to the right (left).'' The membership function of direction is shown in Figure 3.25. Again the maximum principle is used, so it the robot is on intersection 3 and instruction is ''turn to the right,'' it will go

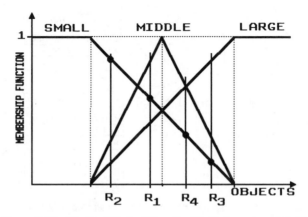

Figure 3.24 *Membership functions for object size values definition.*

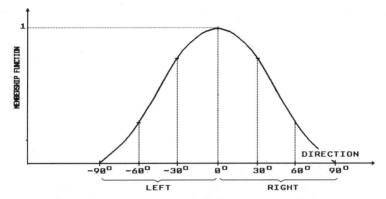

Figure 3.25 *Membership function of a fuzzy set for direction.*

to house H_2, and not to restaurant R_4, because for the street leading to H_2 the direction angle is smaller and degree from Figure 3.25 is higher.

Uragami and his collaborators reported a number of successful simulation trials. Their conclusion was that by using fuzzy linguistic instructions as commands, people will be able to handle robots more easily, especially in situations where it is necessary to handle a robot from a remote place. Typical examples are explorations under water and in outer space.

Another interesting example of communication between a person and robot by using natural language words is the control of a robot gripping force reported in [32]. The commercial fuzzy inference controller was used and a force feedback loop was arranged according to Figure 3.26. When gripping an object, the experimenter made a judgment of the attributes of the object. Then using natural language expressions he communicated this judgment to a fuzzy inference controller. Words as "heavy," "fragile," and "slippery" were used. Then by a conventional fuzzy control algorithm, based on control rules, the appropriate gripping force was determined. An example of a gripping force rule is

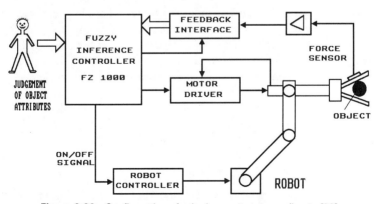

Figure 3.26 *Configuration of gripping system according to [32].*

If the object is *heavy*, *slippery*, and *nonfragile* then the desired level of gripping force is *high*.

The fuzzy controller was also used to keep the desired gripping force. For this task, the feedback signal from strain gauges was employed together with control rules of the form:

If error between desired force and real force is *positive small* and change-of-error is *positive big*, then open the hand *slightly slower*.

The third task of the fuzzy controller was to send start and stop signals to the robot controller, and to issue the instruction to open the hand at the end of the operation. Robot dynamics was controlled by a conventional controller.

This last application can be treated as a particular case of the idea of fuzzy transducer [13] where human sensor could be used to determine variable values. Results of human observations expressed in natural language, together with signals measured conventionally, form a basis for an intelligent measuring system and could be used for control purposes, too.

We believe that in the future more applications like this will be registered, because fuzzy reasoning is particularly suitable for the representation of meanings in natural languages.

3.6 CONCLUSION

In this chapter is was shown that fuzzy reasoning has already produced some interesting applications in the field of robotics. The control of robot dynamics, analysis, and interpretation of information obtained from robot sensors, particularly visual information, planning, and control of robot motion and communication with robots using natural languages are the areas where most theoretical and experimental work has been done, but the range of applications in other fields is growing steadily.

Fuzzy set theory gave to robotics more flexibility, robustness, and adaptability, and these are characteristics of human problem solving. Fuzzy set theory gave simple but powerful practical methodology for transfer of human knowledge, especially heuristic knowledge based on intuition and experience, to artificial robot systems, providing them with at least some primitive features of human intelligence.

REFERENCES

[1] J. A. Gougen, "On Fuzzy Robot Planning," in C. A. Zadeh, et al. Eds., *Fuzzy Sets and Their Application to Cognitive and Decision Processes*, Academic Press, New York, 1974.

[2] J. Mayers and Y. S. Sherif, Application of fuzzy set theory, *IEEE Trans. SMC*, 15(1), 175–189 (1985).

[3] K. Self, Designing with fuzzy logic, *IEEE Spectrum*, 42–44 (November 1990).

[4] H. Scharf, N. Mandič, and E. H. Mamdani, A self-organizing algorithm for the control of a robot arm, *Internat. J. Robotics and Automation*, 1(1), 33–41 (1986).

[5] G. Lee, Robot arm kinematics, dynamics and control, *IEEE Computer*, 15(part 12), 62–80 (1982).

[6] Y. F. Li and C. C. Lav, Development of fuzzy algorithms for servo systems, *IEEE Control Syst. Mag.*, 4, 65–72 (1989).

[7] C. Ken, L. Jin n-Ya, and Z. Y. Xiang, Fuzzy control of robot manipulator, *Proc. 1988 IEEE Internat. Conf. on Systems, Man, and Cybernetics*, Vol. 2, 1210–1212 (1988).

[8] M. Arfo, Auto-tuning system for robots, *Proc. Internat. Workshop on Fuzzy System Applications, IIZUCA-88*, 263 (1988).

[9] R. Tanscheit and E. M. Scharf, Experiments with the use of a rule-based self-organizing controller for robotics applications, *Fuzzy Sets and Systems*, 26, 195–214 (1988).

[10] D. Stipaničev, M. De Neyer and R. Gorez, Self-tuning self-organising fuzzy robot control, *Proc. IFAC Symp. on Robot Control SYROCO '91*, Vienna (September 1991).

[11] R. Palm, Fuzzy controller for a sensor guided robot manipulator, *Fuzzy Sets and Systems*, 31, 133–149 (1989).

[12] R. P. Sobek and R. G. Chatila, Integrated planning and execution control for an autonomous mobile robot, *Artificial Intelligence in Eng.*, 3(2), 103–113 (1988).

[13] J. Božičević and D. Stipaničev, Development of fuzzy transducer, *Proc. IMECO 88 Word Conference*, Austin, Tex. (1988).

[14] D. Stipaničev, Fuzzy vision and fuzzy control, *Proc. 13th IMACS World Congress*, (July 22–26 1991).

[15] M. M. Gupta, G. I. Knopf, and P. N. Nikiforuk, "Edge Perception Using Fuzzy Logic," in M. M. Gupta and T. Yamakawa, Eds., *Fuzzy Computing: Theory, Hardware and Applications*, North Holland, Amsterdam, 1988, pp. 35–51.

[16] D. Lakov, Adaptive robot under fuzzy control, *Fuzzy Sets and Systems*, 17, 1–8 (1985).

[17] D. Jain and S. Haynes, "Imprecision in Computer Vision," in P. A. Wang, Ed., *Advances in Fuzzy Sets, Possibility Theory and Applications*, Plenum Press, New York, 1983, pp. 217–236.

[18] M. M. Trivedi, C. X. Chen, and S. B. Marapane, A vision system for robot inspection and manipulation, *IEEE Computer*, 22, 91–96 (June 1989).

[19] R. N. Lea and L. B. Johnson, Fuzzy sets and autonomous navigation, *Proc. SPIE Conf. on Application of Artificial Intelligence*, 786, 448–452 (1987).

[20] K. Hirota, Y. Arai, and S. Hachisu, Moving mark recognition and moving object manipulation in fuzzy controlled robot, *Control Theory and Advanced Technol.*, 2(3), 399–418 (1986).

[21] H. Tahani and J. Keller, Information fusion in computer vision, *IEEE Trans. SMC*, 20(3), 733–741 (1990).

[22] W. Pedrycz, Fuzzy set theory in pattern recognition: methodology and methods, *Internat. Workshop of Fuzzy System Applications, IIZUKA-88 (tutorials)*, 51–64 (1988).

[23] D. Stipaničev, Fuzzy relational models for intelligent control, *Proc. IMACS Annals on Computing and Applied Mathematics MIM-S^2*, 90, IV.B.2.1–2.5 (1990).

[24] A. N. Averkin and S. K. Dulin, Fuzzy modelling relations for robots, *Proc. IFAC Symp. on Artificial Intelligence*, 331–336 (1983).

[25] T. Takeuchi, Y. Nagai, and N. Enomoto, Fuzzy control of a mobile robot for obstacle avoidance, *Information Sci.*, 45, 231–248 (1988).

[26] J. C. Isik, and A. M. Meystel, Pilot level of a hierarchical controller for an unmanned mobile robot, *IEEE J. Robotics and Automation*, 4(3), 241–255 (1988).

[27] C. Isik, Inference engine for fuzzy rule based control. *Internat. J. Approximate Reasoning*, 2, 177–187 (1988).

[28] J. N. Lythgoe, *The Ecology of Vision*, Clarendon Press, Oxford, 1979.

[29] L. A. Zadeh, "PRUF—A Meaning Representation Language for Natural Language," *Intern. J. Man–Machine Studies* 10, 395–460 (1978).

[30] L. A. Zadeh, Fuzzy sets as a basis for a theory of possibility, *Fuzzy Sets and Systems*, 1, 3–28 (1978).

[31] M. Uragami, M. Mizumoto, and K. Tanaka, Fuzzy robot control, *J. Cybernetics*, 6, 39–64 (1976).

[32] T. Ishida, Sensory information control system, *Proc. Int. Workshop of Fuzzy System Applications*, IIZUKA-88, 261–262 (1988).

CHAPTER 4 ─────────────────

A Fuzzy Cognitive Structure: Foundations, Applications, and VLSI Implementation

W. PEDRYCZ

J. DIAMOND

R.D. MCLEOD

4.1 INTRODUCTION

This chapter deals with the VLSI implementation of a fuzzy cognitive system. Aspects of fuzzy set theory and neural networks are combined to produce a robust system for representing and handling uncertainty. A novel architecture for digital neural networks is introduced and analyzed. The system concept is implemented in a three-chip set which incorporates fault tolerance and a cellular automata based built-in self-test. VLSI design trade-offs are explored and details of the implementation are presented.

Specifically, an artificial neural network that exploits pre- and postprocessing stages, based upon fuzzy set theory, will be discussed. The structure resembles that of a referential cognitive system. This will be followed by a brief introduction to VLSI implementation strategies with the focus being primarily upon digital realizations. This section will discuss some of the problems common to implementing VLSI with particular attention to testing and reliability issues particular to artificial neural and fuzzy logic types of systems. The final section will overview the three-chip set prototype designed and fabricated during this project. The chapter is self-contained: The reader will be familiarized with essentials of fuzzy set theory, fundamentals of VLSI design, and basic ideas of test and fault tolerance.

Recent progress in the development of fuzzy set theory has been centered around areas such as fuzzy controllers, expert systems, digital signal and image processing systems, and robotics [1, 2]. With this progress has come an increase in system complexity, meaning that some software driven systems are very slow.

Fuzzy, Holographic, and Parallel Intelligence, By Branko Souček and the IRIS Group.
ISBN 0-471-54772-7 © 1992 John Wiley & Sons, Inc.

Concurrently, hardware development has advanced to the scale of very large scale integration (VLSI) on a single chip. Moreover, a great deal of research has been conducted on massively parallel computing schemes involving neural networks. The learning capabilities of these networks have been rigorously documented in numerous case studies (involving, for example, speech and pattern recognition) [3, 4].

It is also evident that fuzzy sets form a well suited tool for modeling processes of knowledge representation, especially for adjusting the relevant cognitive perspective of a system [5, 6].

The merger of these technologies would obviously be of great interest, and some research has been done in this field, particularly [7]. Most of this research has been centered around using fuzzy controllers as algorithms for control purposes realized in an uncertain environment.

The aim of this chapter is to consider a fuzzy cognitive scheme and to discuss its implementation and applications. A software version of this scheme has already been implemented for signal classification purposes [8]. A preliminary discussion of the hardware has been presented in [9] and is considerably modified and expanded upon here. It will be pointed out how the proposed scheme can be used in autonomous systems.

In the next section, the underlying system theory is discussed, followed by a discussion of the neural net (with emphasis on learning strategies). In Section 4.4, various areas of application are examined, further exhibiting the system's general structure. This is followed by a discussion of structured VLSI design. Next, the hardware implementation is discussed, with a detailed examination of obstacles presented by the theoretical system in effective realization. The interactive software environment is considered, followed by a system update and a discussion of future areas of research.

4.2 MAIN STRUCTURE OF THE SYSTEM

In a very concise setting, the cognitive system can be visualized as a three stage structure. Its main components are presented as Figure 4.1. The system is a three stage structure consisting of the following components:

- Matching (in the input space)
- Transformation (of the matched input space to the output space)
- Inverse matching (in the output space)

Below we discuss how the system works. The structure possesses a referential character, since it does not work with directly input information. The input data (called the objective) being a vector in an "n"-dimensional unit hypercube is compared to a prototype description in the input space. This results in a vector of degrees of equality, reflecting a degree of "similarity" observed between these two vectors and having the same dimension as the object in the input space.

To reduce the dimensionality of the problem, a certain aggregation may be

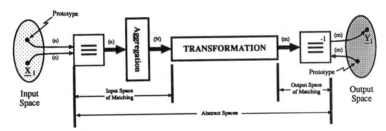

Figure 4.1 *Structure of the fuzzy cognitive system.*

desirable (this is represented by the block denoted by "Aggregation" in Fig. 4.1, where $n' \ll n$); however, it is not necessary to make the structure workable.

At the second stage of processing, the vector of the degrees of equality in the input space of matching (Fig. 4.1) is transformed to the relevant vector in the output space of matching. Finally, knowing the prototype description in the output space and having these degrees of equality, a relevant vector in the output space is calculated within the process of inverse matching [6].

In its essence, the processing in the reference scheme is carried out as follows: First it converts the original problem defined in a relevant *physical* space into its equivalent form in a corresponding *abstract* space (e.g., unit hypercube). This is accomplished by imposing appropriate matching mechanisms. Afterward, the result of the matching is mapped from the (abstract) input space of matching into the (abstract) output space of matching. Definitely, in this space the degrees of matching can be magnified or reduced in comparison to the results in the input space. This process is determined by properties of the mapping realized by the mapping block.* Finally, the results are converted into the physical output space by completing the inverse matching.

In the simplest and self-evident case, this structure may be applied to a classification problem. At the matching stage, the features of the pattern and the prototype are compared, while at the level of inverse matching, a vector of class membership is calculated. In this context, the transformation layer is related to determination of relationships between the features and classes distinguished in the recognition problem.

The matching, in a broad sense of the word, is a process of comparison of successive coordinates of two objects (patterns). Usually, one of the objects is viewed as the prototype (reference). Denote by $A = [a_1 a_2 \cdots a_n]$, and $X = [x_1 x_2 \cdots x_n]$ the objects matched, where lower case letters represent corresponding coordinates to be matched, $a_i, x_i, \in [0, 1]$. The matching procedure returns a vector of results of comparison realized coordinatewise, $a_i \equiv x_i$, where $\equiv$ stands for the matching operator [6]. It is considered of the form:

$$a_i \equiv x_i = \frac{[(a_i \to x_i) \wedge (x_i \to a_i)] + \{[(1 - a_i) \to (1 - x_i)] \wedge [(1 - x_i) \to (1 - a_i)]\}}{2} \quad (4.1)$$

---

*It is worthwhile to mention that in models of reasoning, by analogy, we can usually find a simplified version in which the transformation block realizes a trivial identity mapping.

where → and ∧ are implication and the logical "and" conjunction, respectively. For implementation purposes, it is convenient to treat → as the Gödelian implication, and model ∧ by the min operator, namely,

$$
x_i \rightarrow a_i = \begin{cases} 1, & \text{if } x_i \leq a_i \\ a_i, & \text{if } x_i > a_i \end{cases} \tag{4.2}
$$

therefore,

$$
(x_i \rightarrow a_i) \wedge (a_i \rightarrow x_i) = \min \left[(x_i \rightarrow a_i), (a_i \rightarrow x_i) \right] \tag{4.3}
$$

Further simplification is possible due to the fact that

$$
(x_i \rightarrow a_i) \wedge (a_i \rightarrow x_i) = \begin{cases} x_i \wedge a_i, & \text{if } x_i \neq a_i \\ 1, & \text{if } x_i = a_i \end{cases} \tag{4.4}
$$

$$
[(1 - x_i) \rightarrow (1 - a_i)] \wedge [(1 - a_i) \rightarrow (1 - x_i)]
$$
$$
= \begin{cases} 1 - (x_i \vee a_i), & \text{if } x_i \neq a_i \\ 1, & \text{if } x_i = a_i \end{cases} \tag{4.5}
$$

where ∨ is the maximum operator.

The matching block converts data from the physical space, in which the objects are characterized, into an abstract space representing degrees of matching achieved at the input space. These values are then compressed, arranged into a vector form, and sent to the inputs of the transformation block.

The transformation block's main role is to calculate the degrees of equality being the elements in the output space of matching. Hence it operates on the domain of the input space of matching, whereas its codomain is viewed as the output space of matching. The transformation block is implemented as a neural network with "n" inputs and "m" outputs. For the sake of simplicity, the basic network being implemented is a one-layer one with a threshold element,* that is,

$$
y_i = T \left(\sum_{i=1}^{n} w_{ij} x_i \right), \quad j = 1, 2, 3, \cdots, m \tag{4.6}
$$

where

$$
T(z) = \begin{cases} z, & \text{if } z \in [0, 1] \\ 1, & \text{if } z > 1 \\ 0, & \text{if } z < 0 \end{cases} \tag{4.7}
$$

---

*If necessary, the mapping can be implemented as a multilayer structure. It does not change, however, the essence of the overall architecture presented here.

At the final stage of processing, the vector of degrees of equality (the elements of the abstract space) is transformed by an inverse matching process into the values of the physical output space.

There are two mechanisms of parallelism that could be easily implemented in the overall structure. The first one deals with the neural network itself, where computations are performed in parallel. The second form is related to parallel structures, where each basic system (calculation of equality vector–transformation–inverse problem) is responsible for each class recognized. Thus the speed of the entire system does not depend on the number of classes in the problem at hand.

The reference structure has some evident advantages essential for autonomous systems. First, because of this pairwise comparison (prototype–new object) we get much more data to estimate the weights of the neural network. Second, and more interesting, the result of comparison—expressed as an interval valued fuzzy set—reflects a quality of matching: the broader the interval, the less precise the result of matching. Thus the proposed structure is self-flagging and expresses precision of results produced by the system.

4.3 LEARNING STAGE IN THE COGNITIVE STRUCTURE

Before the cognitive structure can be effectively utilized, a learning stage must be completed.

Consider the learning set at our disposal. This set consists of pairs of input–output vectors, say $(\mathbf{x_i}, \mathbf{y_i})$, $i = 1, 2, \cdots, N$, defined in the abstract input and output spaces of matching. The values of these pairs determine all connections of the neural network. As we have indicated in the previous section, the learning phase requires calculation of connections and the prototypes. A relevant illustration is contained in Figure 4.2.

1. Learning of weights (connections) of the network. In this phase, objects (elements) of the learning set are presented to the system. Thus we are faced with a supervised style of learning. Having N inputs and corresponding outputs, we form all possible pairs, say $(\mathbf{x_i}, \mathbf{y_i})$ and $(\mathbf{x_j}, \mathbf{y_j})$. Thus we get the vectors in the input and output spaces expressing results of matching in both spaces,

$$v_{ij} = f(\mathbf{x_i} \equiv \mathbf{x_j}) \tag{4.8}$$

and

$$w_{ij} = \mathbf{y_i} \equiv \mathbf{y_j} \tag{4.9}$$

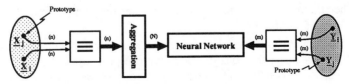

Figure 4.2 Learning phase.

Observe that the function $f: [0, 1]^n \rightarrow [0, 1]^{n'}$ forms the role of aggregating function over the original vectors, yielding the resulting quantities $\mathbf{x}_i \equiv \mathbf{x}_j$. Usually $n' \ll n$, especially if the original dimensions are quite high and some compression is necessary. If one keeps the same original dimensions, then f is simply an identity function, and this form of processing is irrelevant. Having N objects (viz., inputs–outputs), the weights of the network are determined on the basis of $N(N + 1)/2$ possible pairs (since the equality index forms a symmetrical function of its arguments, namely having comparison of the jth and the ith object already done there is no need to compare the ith and the jth one). Additionally, N particular pairs such that $(\mathbf{x}_1 \equiv \mathbf{x}_1, \mathbf{y}_1 \equiv \mathbf{y}_1), (\mathbf{x}_2 \equiv \mathbf{x}_2, \mathbf{y}_2 \equiv \mathbf{y}_2), \cdots, (\mathbf{x}_N \equiv \mathbf{x}_N, \mathbf{y}_N \equiv \mathbf{y}_N)$, yield exactly N inputs and outputs of the reference space equal identically to 1. More precisely we derive,

$$\binom{N}{2} + N = \frac{N(N - 1)}{2} + N = \frac{N(N + 1)}{2}. \tag{4.10}$$

Notice that the number of data processed in the reference scheme becomes larger than the number of original data (namely $N(N + 1)/2$ versus N). An advantage of this scheme becomes evident. For example, for N equal to 20 for the reference model, we get around 10 times more, or 210 pieces of data. The weights of the network are calculated following some of the well known learning schemes used in neural net modeling, [4].

2. Having the weights of the neural network already determined, we must establish the prototypes that play a primordial role, due to the referential structure of the system. We will start with a simple however often found case, which is common for classification tasks. Recall that in classification problems we are faced with a finite set of classes that a given pattern is assigned. Simply, in the learning set, one has a natural way to distinguish some cluster in the output space, where each cluster corresponds to an individual class. Usually the dimension of the output space, called the class space, is significantly lower in comparison to the dimension of the input space. The problem of prototype determination is reduced to the indication of such an input vector among the family of inputs–outputs for which the relevant output equals the given class. Denote by χ the family of inputs induced by a certain class $\tilde{\mathbf{y}}$ (i.e., belonging to this class),

$$\chi = \{\mathbf{x}_i | \mathbf{y}_i = \tilde{\mathbf{y}}\}, \text{ card } (\chi) = \tilde{N} \tag{4.11}$$

Then the prototype of this class is viewed as one coming from this set. It is selected accordingly:

Pick the first element of χ and treat it as a potential prototype denoted by $\mathbf{x}'$. Calculate the equality index with respect to all elements of χ, and derive the equality index resulting from the output of the neural network.

Calculate the following performance index:

$$V(x') = \sum_{j=1}^{m} \sum_{x_i \in \chi} F_j(x_i \equiv x') \qquad (4.12)$$

where $\mathbf{F}(\mathbf{x_i} \equiv \mathbf{x'}) = [F_1(\mathbf{x_i} \equiv \mathbf{x'}), F_2(\mathbf{x_i} \equiv \mathbf{x'}), \cdots, F_m(\mathbf{x_i} \equiv \mathbf{x'})]$ denotes a vector of equality values at the output of the network ($\mathbf{F}$). The above sum is taken over all $\mathbf{x_i}$ as well as all coordinates of the output reference space. The higher the value $V(\mathbf{x'})$, the better choice of $\mathbf{x'}$ as the prototype of the class characterized by $\tilde{\mathbf{y}}$.

Repeat the above computations for all remaining elements of χ. The prototype $\mathbf{x'}$ is selected on the basis of the maximal value of $V(\mathbf{x'})$.

3. For problems in which the number of distinct fuzzy sets $\mathbf{y_i}$ in the learning set becomes greater, and no clusters could be distinguished, a choice of the prototypes is performed in a different fashion. Let us establish several fuzzy sets $\mathbf{y}^1, \mathbf{y}^2, \cdots, \mathbf{y}^p$, which are treated as centers. For example, one could be interested in fuzzy sets possessing the following membership functions:*

$$\begin{array}{c} [1000 \cdot \cdot \cdot 00] \\ [0100 \cdot \cdot \cdot 00] \\ \cdot \cdot \cdot \\ [0000 \cdot \cdot \cdot 01] \end{array} \qquad (4.13)$$

Then the prototype $\mathbf{x}^1, l = 1, 2, \cdots, p$ is obtained as follows:

Take $\mathbf{x_i}, i = 1, 2, \cdots, n$ as a potential candidate to be the prototype of $\mathbf{y}^l, l = 1, 2, \cdots, p$. Calculate the equality index for $\mathbf{x_i}$ and remaining $\mathbf{x_j}, j = 1, 2, \cdots, N$ and obtain the output of the neural network driven by $\mathbf{x_i} \equiv \mathbf{x_j}$, namely,

$$\sum_{j=1}^{N} \mathbf{F}(\mathbf{x_i} \equiv \mathbf{x_j}) \qquad (4.14)$$

Usually we should include a weighting vector indicating the degree to which $\mathbf{y_j}$ is equal to the prototype $\mathbf{y}^1$ we are interested in. Denote this by ω_j

$$\omega_j = \mathbf{y}^1 \equiv \mathbf{y_j} \qquad (4.15)$$

where ω_j is an m-dimensional vector ω_j: $[0, 1]^m \rightarrow [0, 1]^m$. Then the original sum as stated above is replaced by the scalar product of $\mathbf{F}(\mathbf{x_i} \equiv \mathbf{x_j})$ and ω_j,

$$\sum_{j=1}^{N} [\mathbf{F}(\mathbf{x_i} \equiv \mathbf{x_j})]^T \omega_j \qquad (4.16)$$

*Note that in pattern classification these vectors have an evident interpretation as vectors of class membership.

In other words (4.16) can be expressed as:

$$\sum_{k=1}^{m} \sum_{j=1}^{N} [F_k(\mathbf{x_i} \equiv \mathbf{x_j})]\omega_{jk} \qquad (4.17)$$

where ω_{jk} stands for the kth coordinate of ω_j. The prototype of the lth class is selected by maximizing $V(\mathbf{x_i})$ over the entire set. Then the process is repeated for the remaining classes, $l = 1, 2, \cdots, p$.

In the following section, we will point out several examples towards which the fuzzy cognitive system could be directly applied.

4.4 APPLICATIONAL AREAS OF THE COGNITIVE SYSTEM

In this section, we will summarize some direct areas of application of the discussed system. Generally speaking, we can state that the main idea used here is to be viewed as a form of reasoning by analogy [10, 11]. Roughly speaking, this type of reasoning is concisely specified as follows:

$$(A/B)_C$$
$$(A'/B' = ?)_C \qquad (4.18)$$

where in these two situations, A and B are associated while A' and $B'(?)$ have to be related as well. B' is determined on the basis of the given situation A' and should satisfy links provided by A and B being tied in a certain case (of course this process is worked out in a given context C). This makes the scheme of reasoning very general and allows us to cope with a variety of particular reasoning formulas. Now we will investigate some of them:

- **Pattern Recognition:** In classification problems, one deals with an input space called a feature space in which all patterns being classified are described and an output space (called class membership space) in which membership of the patterns is defined. Usually the feature space is created individually with respect to a problem at hand. Moreover, a suitable perception perspective is established with the aid of linguistic labels (information granules), [12]. For some other related issues refer to [13]. Then the reference space is built on the basis of equality indices computed for the feature vectors and vectors of class membership. Classification is performed with respect to all classes distinguished in the problem. Interval valued results of classification refer closely to a level of confidence attached to them.
- **Inference Scheme of Modus Ponens with Fuzzy Premises:** This scheme of reasoning is often studied in the realm of approximate reasoning. Recall that it works with fuzzy premises collected along the line.

$$A'$$
$$\frac{\text{if } A_i \text{ then } B_i, \ i = 1, 2, \cdots, N}{B' = ?} \tag{4.19}$$

where A_i, B_i, A' are fuzzy premises (fuzzy sets or relations) defined in appropriate universes of discourse while B' is the fuzzy conclusion to be inferred. Usually the above scheme is called a fuzzy modus ponens where, contrary to a classic scheme of reasoning, A' is not necessarily one of the fuzzy premises standing in the rules. The above scheme is applied in the fuzzy controller or some rule-based expert systems. The input space is created by fuzzy sets expressing condition parts, while the output space is created by fuzzy sets of the condition parts.

- **Image Processing:** In this area of application, see also [14] a family of pairs of input and output images is considered. Each pattern is described as a vector containing numbers from [0, 1] scale, and representing a grade of brightness of each pixel. Input images are blurred versions of some output image. Then the cognitive system produces for any input, possibly distorted image, its enhanced version bearing into account a finite set of prototypes (example images). Now the output of the system being in general, a certain subinterval of [0, 1] refers to two images formed on the basis of the prototype image. They create envelopes of the prototype and provide complete information concerning the possible image that could result from the input image.

The following section briefly describes VLSI design environment including some aspects of the technology and an overview of design tools, as well as several of the testing issues we tried to address with our design example.

4.5 INTRODUCTION TO STRUCTURED VLSI DESIGN

4.5.1 Structured VLSI Design

The process of design is long and complex. It involves numerous trade-offs on the part of the designer, including an analysis of technologies, methodologies, approaches and strategies. In general, the concerns of the designer may be summarized as

- Performance
- Size (area) of die
- Time to design
- Price
- Ease of testability

These items are very intertwined, and selecting the best design alternatives is not a simple procedure. The flow of design is normally quite consistent, regardless of the project specifics.

Present design techniques often involve a *top-down* (high level of abstraction to low level), *bottom-up* (low level of abstraction to high level), or *middle-out* (some hybrid of the previous two). Design is a dynamic process in which it is not unusual to change the project requirements mid-way through design. A consistent routine of design followed by simulation is adopted. As each level is completed, a subsequent level of abstraction is started.

Ideally, a system will be developed in which a product may be manufactured from a fuzzy problem description. Several compilers would take the design to less abstract stages until a physical layout is produced and sent for fabrication. VLSI design aids attempt to reduce complexity of the silicon design process.

This section attempts to deal with these design concerns, and in so doing, give the reader an appreciation for the some of the aspects of structured design.

Design Domains.   Three domains, or levels of design may be used in the development process. Each has dramatic effects on performance, design time and portability.

- *Behavioral:* An abstract description of *how* the device should perform is given. Structural and physical levels are then generated from this information.
- *Structural:* A concrete description of device connectivity is given to the system. Physical representations are created from this information.
- *Physical:* Device physics are used in design at the silicon level.

Usually a design will begin at the behavioral level. If very complex behavior is encountered, it may be advantageous to have the system developed based on this information (called synthesis). The resulting layout will probably have poor performance (since it is extensively automated), but design time will be greatly reduced. This domain is extremely portable between technologies, since no demands on the physical domain are presented, only functional information.

If the behavior is not unreasonably complex, it may be advantageous to design some of the system at structural (circuit) level. This involves specific knowledge of the computing architectures required for the development, but it gives the designer the ability to create much more efficient designs at a small design time expense. Design at this level is also quite portable between technologies, since mostly connectivity information is presented.

Alternatively, maximum performance may be required, in which case a physical layout is generated directly. This domain is extremely time intensive, and is therefore normally automated. At one time, this was the *only* option open to the designer. The physical domain's lack of portability is a great downfall. If a designer spends a great deal of time designing a physical layout in a 5-μm CMOS technology, it is extremely difficult to redesign the system for advanced technologies as they become available.

Usually some part of the design is attempted in all three design domains, with some parts synthesized from behavioral descriptions, a large number of structural designs with a few circuits designed at a physical level for high performance.

Structured Design Strategies. When very large circuits are developed, it would be unreasonable to employ an ad-hoc strategy, randomly placing random blocks. To manage the kinds of extreme complexity found in VLSI circuits, it is prudent to develop structured strategies to cope with tens of thousands of circuits.

A valid analogy to this procedure is that of software development. When thousands of lines of code are developed, it is necessary to take a few precautions to prevent drowning in complexity. In general, four criteria may be used to this end:

1. Hierarchy: Hierarchy involves the breaking down of complex modules into simpler, submodules.
2. Modularity: Design is greatly aided by creating *well formed* submodules. For example, a well formed cell may be constrained as to position, name, layer type, size and signal type of external connections.
3. Regularity: An example of regularity in IC design is a RAM, which uses an array of identical cells.
4. Locality: The exterior interface of a system should not require knowledge of specifics of that system's internal structure. By hiding information, the apparent complexity of the system is reduced.

4.5.2 Design Methodologies

Full Custom (Hand Crafted). Full custom VLSI design is a time consuming but very powerful method of circuit implementation. It involves the production of a formal description of the physical silicon layout. The transistors are placed as a unit or as individual layers with careful attention given to transistor sizing and positioning.

The full custom methodology will become more important as analog designs become integrated to a greater degree with digital systems. It is anticipated, however, that synthesis tools will also replace hand crafting in analog design much in the same manner that they have been used for digital design.

Gate Array. Gate array implementations are very popular because of their price, performance, and speed of design. A predefined topology is prefabricated and stockpiled by the vendor. Only the upper layers remain to be deposited, but these layers will configure the general transistor layout into an application specific integrated circuit (ASIC). Upper layers available may include single layer metal (and contacts) or double layer metal (and contacts, vias, etc.).

The ability to preprocess the wafer in a very general way (in the sense that the very specific design may be flexibly reconfigured) means that great expense is saved in generating masks for many different wafers, and a great deal of processing time is saved when the actual design is finalized and ready for implementation (since most of the processing has *already* occurred).

Standard Cell. This intermediate or compromise form takes design time approaching that of gate array combined with performance approaching that of full

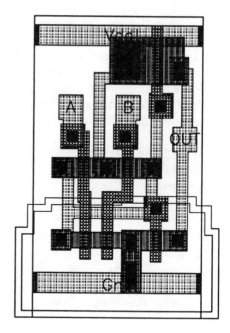

Figure 4.3 *Two-input AND standard cell.*

custom designs to create a very attractive alternative. Each of the *standard cells* is hand crafted and interconnected with other standard cells in either a manual or autorouting environment. A two-input AND gate standard cell is presented as Figure 4.3.

This system is more flexible than gate arrays but less so than full custom. Cells may be placed *anywhere* on the die, but transistors are fixed within the cells. All of the cells on the die are used in the design, so the waste of gate array implementations is removed.

Since all masks must be made, the implementation is more expensive but with potentially better performance than gate arrays. Although design time is greatly reduced over handcrafting, performance is not as impressive.

Several standards should be adopted to increase performance and decrease design time. These include fixed height with variable width, and fixed positions for wells, power, and ground rails. Typically, these cells are abutted to reduce size, and these constraints aid in routing and distribution of required signals. Since a full mask set must be developed, special purpose functional blocks (such as RAMs, ROMs, or PLAs) may be placed on the chip to work with the standard cells.

Alternatives. Several alternatives to compete with chip fabrication have appeared in recent years. These technologies have the advantage of being field programmable, that is, no fabrication house is required and so many designs may be tried before a chip is finalized. Another huge advantage is price. Since these parts are sold in large numbers and all are identical, they are relatively inexpensive to produce. These technologies are attractive for low volume requirements or prototyping. Since schematic capture environments are used to configure the devices, design time is short as well.

Reprogrammable FPGAs Logic Cell Arrays (LCAs) (by Xilinx*) are clusters of logical blocks, such as the one shown in Figure 4.4*a*. Any function of *n* inputs or less (usually *n* = 5) may be calculated in this block, and many of these blocks are contained on a single chip with reconfigurable routing between the blocks. Figure 4.4*b* shows how the configurable logic blocks connect to form a chip. Each pad can be configured as input or output (power and ground pads are reserved), and a maximum of about 10,000 usable gates may be configured on a chip.

Another attractive feature of this technology is the ability to quickly reconfigure the complete system. This means that if one ASIC is in operation and a different operation is required, it can be reconfigured and changed an unlimited number of times.

Problems with this technology include relatively lower speed and gate count. Larger gate counts are promised for the near future.†

One Time Programmable FPGAs Fused or anti-fuse Field Programmable Gate Arrays offer higher densities than LCAs, approaching the densities of full gate arrays. They require more area than gate arrays because of their built-in programmability.

Fuseable links (or often anti-fuses) are used for permanent configurability. Because the fuse (or anti-fuse) is permanent, much of the routing resources required for the LCAs can be avoided. These elements are also quite small and reliable. When a large voltage (i.e., $3 \rightarrow 4 \times V_{dd}$) is presented to the fuseable link, it either disconnects or connects (in the case of the antifuse) its two layers. Since these parts can be made nonvolatile and quite dense, they are very attractive to industrial applications.

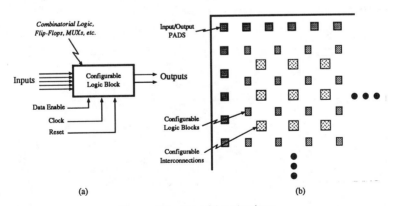

Figure 4.4 *The LCA technology.*

*Xilinx and LCAs are trademarks of Xilinx, Inc.
†A 20,000 gate part was recently announced.

4.5.3 Design Trade-offs

Utility. Using the right device for a given application can save money and turn-around time. A design is very dependent on budget constraints and performance requirements.

Since speed is rarely an issue in industrial control systems (any of the methodologies described will easily achieve the objectives), either of the alternative technologies presented above is attractive.

It should be noted that gate arrays often use the most advanced technology (i.e., reduced feature size) much earlier than standard cell implementations. This often compensates for performance differences that would occur using identical processes (same minimum device dimensions).

For microprocessor design, usually standard cell or full custom designs is used for high performance. Gate arrays are used occasionally in microprocessor design since their design time is short, with sometimes nominal performance degradation. Other methodologies are unequipped to handle these types of computing structures efficiently, and so a great deal of silicon area is wasted when this is attempted. Furthermore, high speed computation makes many demands on the technology, indicating that only handcrafting will yield maximum performance.

For an intermediate application like peripheral communication or *glue* logic, a gate array would work quite nicely. These parts are relatively inexpensive for medium volume runs, yet yield adequate performance.

LCAs and other FPGAs are ideal for prototyping applications, in which it may be required to produce many versions of a design until the final version is ready for a more intricate implementation. These are also ideal for very rapid product launches or low volume applications.

Methodological Comparison. The design methodologies presented in the previous sections are related in very abstract ways. Table 4.1 gives an overview of some of the information already presented.

Other considerations often required include startup cost and turnaround time.

TABLE 4.1 Design Methodologies Comparison (1990)

	SSI & MSI ICs	PLDs	PGAs	Gate Arrays	Custom ICs
Integration in Gates	100s	100s-2k	1k-10k	1k-100k	1k-500k
Speed	Fast	Med.-Fast[†]	Slow-Med.	Slow-Fast	Fast
Function Defined by User	No	Yes	Yes	Yes	Yes
Time to Customize	-	Seconds	Seconds	Weeks	Months
User-programmable	No	Yes	Yes	No	No
% of Wafer Preprocessed	0%	100%	100%	80%	0%

High speed PALs †

TABLE 4.2 Typical Minimum Costs (1990 $US) for Establishing Design Platforms

Parameter	PCBs	PLDs	PGAs	Gate Array	Standard Cell	Full Custom
Processing to Prototyping Samples	500	10-500	50-1000	50,000†	100,000†	100,000†
Design Software on Personal Computer	3,000	2,000-5,000	2,000-5000	5,000-25,000	——††	——††
Design Software on Major Workstation	150,000	——	10,000	50,000-200,000	50,000-200,000	50,000-250,000

High cost is associated with making the masks.†
Insufficient design platform.††

TABLE 4.3 Typical Turnaround Times for Samples to Be Delivered by Foundries (extremely liberal)

Year	Gate Array	Standard Cell	Full Custom
1984	6-8 Weeks	12-16 Weeks	18 Months
1986	3-4 Weeks	8-12 Weeks	10 Months
1988	1 Week	6-10 Weeks	15 Weeks

Tables 4.2 and 4.3 indicate these relationships. Many of the costs are dropping, as are delivery times, in direct relationship to the advancements in computer aided design software and hardware. In recent years, standard cell technology has become competitive in terms of design time with gate array design. Schematic capture has advanced to allow more automatic place and route capabilities than the simple last layer metals of gate arrays.

Figure 4.5 indicates relative prices for each of the methodologies. It is difficult to give accurate price quotes since these numbers are constantly decreasing. Relative figures remain approximately constant.

4.5.4 Overview of Alternative Technologies

While many, many technologies exist, the design methodologies of the previous section still apply. This section is a brief introduction to alternative technologies, that is, technologies other than *ordinary* CMOS, which have potential applications in VLSI.

BiCMOS The combination of bipolar's drive and high speed switching with CMOS's low power consumption/high densities yield a very powerful combination.

CMOS's greatest advantage is size. Since it is self-aligning and low power, the devices may be scaled very easily. This allows CMOS devices to be made much smaller than bipolar ones (which must dissipate substantially more heat), meaning

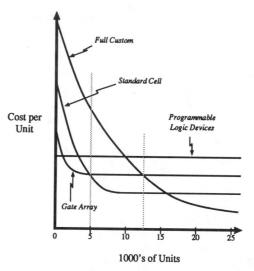

Figure 4.5 P:rice index for various design methodologies.

that the speed of CMOS is on par with TTL. TTL, however, uses much more power than CMOS, as does ECL in comparison to TTL. ECL's speed is much greater than CMOS, and so a balance must be struck by the designer with regards to power consumption, drive and speed.

One great advantage of BiCMOS is that companies may greatly increase performance of their CMOS chips without a great investment in new processing equipment (which is extremely expensive).

Gallium Arsenide (GaAs) One area of research that is becoming very important is the area of III–V compounds, and gallium arsenide in particular. One of the advantages of using these compounds is the higher mobility that silicon (or group IV elements in general). These devices have excellent characteristics for use in microwave circuits as well as light emitting applications.

GaAs was attempted for many years until recent advances in processing technology have made it realizable. An inherent difficulty with GaAs is the formation of an oxide or gate dielectric.

4.5.5 Integration of Design with Simulation and Testing

Simulation and testing are vital parts of design flow. Simulation has long been used to verify circuit operation, and while testing has always been important, a great deal of research has recently been conducted on including provisions for testing at the design stage.

With the advent of high-speed workstations, software packages have greatly reduced the time spent at the verification stage. Hierarchy in design is usually exploited at this stage, simulating each level before the next layer of abstraction may be designed. This technique is analogous to software debugging, where each subroutine is checked individually before being inserted into the higher level routine.

Testing, on the other hand, had long been seen as a *nuisance* to designers. The idea of *giving-up* silicon area for devices that play no part in main circuit operation is often resented. With the advent of VLSI, however, the inclusion of testability at the design stage has become a requirement. One reason for this is the huge cost of repairing systems when they fail in the field. Many design teams now utilize the skills of a test engineer throughout the design cycle. Software tools similar to those used for design entry and simulation are constantly being developed in an attempt to ease the testing stage. These tools range from test pattern generation to test point insertion.

Design is a dynamic process, involving many engineering trade-offs interspersed with simulation and testability. The next few sections deal with testability as an improvement to design.

4.6. DESIGN TOOLS

Improved fabrication techniques and decreasing device sizes have allowed the implementation of large complex systems on a single chip. The increased complexity of current commercial ICs is due in part to the availability of Computer Aided Design (CAD) tools, which free the designers from the lower level tasks, and let them deal with higher level tasks in IC design. In this section we will briefly introduce some of the available Design Tools; further details concerning some of the underlying algorithms these tools employ can be found in [15, 16].

Each of the tools used in the design of Integrated Circuits shares a common database. Interfacing to other tools using a different database is accomplished by translating design information to interchange formats, which are standard languages supported by most CAD tools vendors.

4.6.1 Design Entry

The most important tools used in an IC design environment are the design entry tools and their associated databases. These tools are used to create, edit, and maintain design information, whether it be layouts, connectivity, or behavioral information. In this section we discuss some of the different design entry programs, and the different database techniques that are employed with them.

Regardless of the design entry medium employed, a good user interface is a must for all programs. These programs are the ones that the designer will be using the most. Despite the capabilities of the programs, if the designer does not like the interface the programs are useless.

Layout Editors.   Layout editors are the programs used to enter, modify, and maintain layout geometries. While most drawing programs are capable of drawing the simple shapes which usually are used in IC design, most layout editors contain editing features specifically incorporated for IC design. The interaction with design rule checkers, and other tools is also important.

Schematic Capture.   Often it is not necessary for a designer to worry about mask geometries if sophisticated tools are available to generate layouts. Schematic capture can be used to enter connectivity information about a design. The designer enters a circuit description by placing symbols on the design, and connecting the ports of the symbols with wires. Typically the symbols used in a schematic are either gates of a standard cell library or transistors available in the IC technology. A schematic design of an ALU slice is shown in Figure 4.6.

A hierarchical design may be entered by creating symbols to represent lower level blocks, and connecting them in a similar manner to gates.

Once a schematic is entered, the connectivity information between components in the design is extracted by following the wires ports of the symbols. Simple design errors such as unconnected nets may be detected at this step. Schematic capture also allows designers to extract netlists without creating layouts. This allows functional simulation of designs during the design cycle.

Hardware Description Languages.   Instead of entering design information using interactive graphical systems associated with layout editors and schematic capture, it is often more convenient to enter design information in textual form. Hardware Description Languages (HDL) are used to describe design information of larger systems, using more abstract constructs than are allowed in schematic capture.

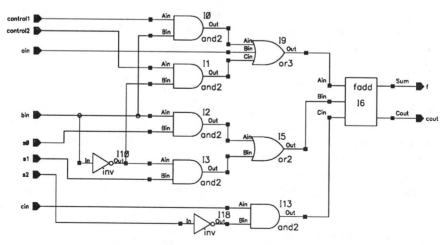

Figure 4.6 *ALU schematic.*

4.6.2 Future Design Tools

As IC designs get larger and more complex, the need for new design automation tools becomes more apparent. This final section summarizes some of the current areas of research for new design tools.

- High level behavioral synthesis tools are still an open area of research.
- Analog design tools. All the tools mentioned in the preceding are primarily for digital design. Tools are needed to aid in the design of analog circuits.
- Incorporation of fault tolerance and testing techniques into the synthesis of a circuit. Currently it is up to the designer to specify testing structures and fault tolerant techniques. New tools are being investigated that will incorporate these into designs.

4.7 REGULAR STRUCTURES

This section covers several basic regular structures. The main advantages offered by regular structures is in managing the design complexity as digital designs get larger. In particular, as complete systems are being integrated the use of regular structures becomes mandatory. For example, there is not a single major microprocessor built that does not use a variety of regular structures. Although there are a large number of regular structures and methodologies, here we will primarily discuss programmable logic arrays.

As opposed to *structured logic*, digital functions can be realized as *random logic*. The term random logic is used to describe circuits constructed in much the same manner as small scale ICs were assembled on a circuit board. Because of the variety of small scale chips and their use at irregular places on the circuit board they appeared disordered or random. Structured logic has some sense of order and regularity, often implemented as some type of array structure. The randomness associated with the logic is hidden within the overall orderly appearance of the array. One advantage of using a regular structure is in automating the layout. With the implementation constrained to a regular structure, tools may be simplified to placing only one of several predesigned cells to specific locations within the array. Another advantage is the use and reuse of expertly designed and exhaustively tested cells. A wide variety of texts and papers have been written on structured logic arrays; several general texts include [17–20].

4.7.1 Programmable Logic Arrays

PLAs or Programmable Logic Arrays are perhaps the most structured approach to logic function implementation. Recall that any logic function can be expressed as a sum of minterms. Usually this can then be further reduced or simplified by a variety of methods. The basis for PLA function implementation is sum of products. Additional factors concerning testability also play a major roll in PLA implementation, but for our purposes here, we will be concerned primarily with the implementation of the sum of products representation desired by the designer. As it is a sum of products, the implementation is more compact than a sum of minterms (ROM implementation).

A typical PLA consists of two major sections or planes. One is called the "AND" plane and the other is called the "OR" plane. The AND plane is responsible for generating the product terms while the OR plane sums the required terms. The basic organization is shown in Figure 4.7. The PLA when fabricated in CMOS is generally implemented NOR–NOR, and can be designed in a variety of dynamic or static families. Logically, the two level AND–OR can be easily seen to be equivalent to a two level NOR–NOR, as illustrated by the following example:

$$f = x_1 x_2 + x_3 x_4 = \overline{\overline{(\overline{x}_1 + \overline{x}_2)} + \overline{(\overline{x}_3 + \overline{x}_4)}}. \tag{4.20}$$

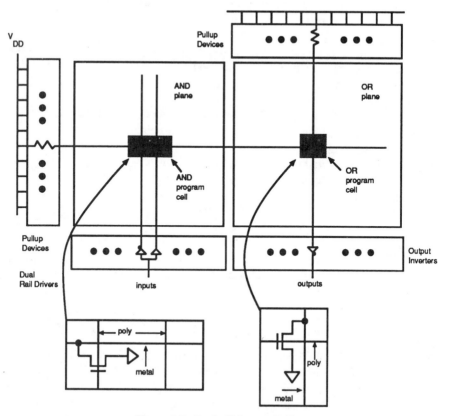

Figure 4.7   *Basic PLA organization.*

As such, the complement of the literals in the AND–OR expression are used in the NOR–NOR implementation in addition to an inversion as the final stage. With this basic notion, a PLA can be easily designed. The basic NOR–NOR design is outlined as follows:

- For each product in the original expression f, a transistor is placed on a corresponding product line activated by the literal's complement in the AND plane
- For each of the product terms required for f, a transistor is placed on a corresponding sum line in the OR plane
- The output is obtained by a final inversion

The inputs to the PLA have to be available in complemented and uncomplemented form. Usually the inputs are also latched. The outputs of the PLA are also usually latched. A wide variety of design styles are available when implementing a PLA. These include static, pseudo-nmos, clocked, domino, and so forth. Strategies may also include precharge and differential sensing, in a similar manner to RAM of ROM.

PLA Optimization. The first thing to note when discussing optimization is that we are concerned with two level logic and a very regular array structure. Principal concerns are in minimizing area and reducing delay. As such, reducing the number of actual product lines may be an optimization criteria.

PLA folding is also a very common technique for physically reducing the size of a PLA. Rows and/or columns are merged to reduce the sparsity of the transistors in the array. For example, if two product terms are disjoint and can be separated, it may be possible for a literal and its complement to share AND plane columns. A similar technique is available for the OR plane. With respect to all types of structured logic, the PLA is probably the most extensively investigated and studied. This is evidenced by the numerous papers devoted to automation, optimization, test, and layout over the past 10 years.

Finite State Machines. PLAs are widely used to implement FSMs (Finite State Machines). These are machines consisting of combinational logic and a feedback path containing memory to hold the machine's previous state. The basic PLA is readily modified by adding a feedback latch (memory element) between the output and input. Automation tools are available for taking a FSM's state transition diagram, generating the state table, minimizing the logic, and producing the PLA layout.

This section briefly discussed several structured logic design techniques. An IC designer most likely will not be required to design a RAM for his or her system but will probably require RAM as a system building block. Several manufacturers are now offering system level macros or modules that allow the incorporation of RAM relieving a digital designer from having to reinvent the wheel for his or her system.

4.8 INTEGRATED CIRCUIT FAULTS AND TESTING

Testing is a vital area of study and will only gain in importance as circuit complexity increases. In general, with shrinking device dimension and increased area come more faults, and it is these faults that testing attempts to isolate.

4.8.1 Fault Modeling

Simulating a circuit for each of the different possible faults is clearly impossible. Instead it is necessary to establish a model for the effects of the faults. This model can be used in simulation to determine how the circuit will be affected by the presence of faults. This simulation is vital when determining the effectiveness of test vectors and testing hardware.

Stuck-at Faults. The stuck-at fault model is the model most commonly used in industry. This model assumes that a fault in a circuit will cause one of the lines to be permanently stuck-at the logical 0 or 1 level. The stuck-at model discussed here is modeled at the gate level. This assumes that a fault within the gate causes the output of the gate to be fixed at either logic 0 or logic 1. An example of the stuck-at fault is shown in Figure 4.8. If the input vector **ABC** = 101 was applied, the output **F** would equal 0. If the NAND gate for inputs **AB** were to develop a fault that was stuck-at modeled as a constant output of 0, then **F** would be 1. In this case the output of the circuit is incorrect.

The stuck-at fault model is good for shorts to the power or ground lines. This rather limited subset of possible faults has raised concerns as to whether this model provides a practical representation of actual VLSI faults. A more realistic VLSI fault model may be one that includes open circuit faults.

Stuck-open Faults. Faults that cause open circuits are especially difficult to detect in CMOS VLSI devices. The occurrence of an open fault can cause both the pull-up and pull-down sections of a circuit to be nonconductive. In this case the previous value of the circuit is retained as a result of capacitance. This memory effect presents a significant challenge to fault detection.

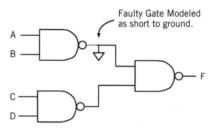

Figure 4.8 *The stuck-at model.*

The difficulty inherent in testing for stuck-open faults is further compounded as exhaustive testing for these faults has been shown to require $N * 2^{(N+1)}$ [2] test patterns. This represents a rather considerable increase over the 2^N vectors required to exhaustively test for stuck-at faults. The increase in test vectors arises from the necessity to first excite the circuit under test, then apply another test vector to detect the stuck-open fault. Thus two vectors are required to detect a stuck-open fault.

Delay Line Faults. The delay faults are termed *slow-to-rise* and *slow-to-fall*. Let $c_1, c_2, \cdots, c_q$ be the expected bit sequence for a line of a circuit, the delay faults yield the sequence $d_1, d_2, \cdots, d_q$ defined as follows:

$$slow\text{-}to\text{-}rise\ d_i = \begin{cases} 1 & \text{for } c_i = 1 \text{ and } c_{i-1} = 1 \\ 0 & \text{otherwise} \end{cases}$$

$$slow\text{-}to\text{-}fall\ d_i = \begin{cases} 0 & \text{for } c_i = 0 \text{ and } c_{i-1} = 0 \\ 1 & \text{otherwise} \end{cases}$$

A circuit with m lines has $2m$ potential single delay faults.

4.8.2 Conventional Test

Testing is done in order to discover faults in a digital circuit that may have been caused during fabrication or by wear-out in the field. Test patterns (or test vectors) are applied to a circuit in order to sensitize existing faults and propagate a faulty response to an observable output of the system, thus detecting the faults. Test generation techniques attempt to systematically derive a set of test vectors that exposes all possible faults in a logic circuit. The testing may be performed on special purpose hardware called *automatic test equipment* (ATE).

In this section the test generation techniques are presented, with a brief discussion of fault simulation and diagnosis.

Fault Simulation and Diagnosis

Fault Simulation Fault simulation determines the behavior of the circuit in the presence of each of the faults from a specified set. As a result of the large number of potential faults in any large circuit and the complexity of simulation algorithms, it is usually assumed that only a single fault can be present in the circuit at any given time. Fault coverage is defined as the ratio of the number of detected faults to the total number of simulated faults. This measure of test quality can be used for improving the test sequence, if necessary. Fault simulation is also used for building a dictionary (in a data base) of the *signatures* of the different faults for the purpose of fault location. Actual fault responses collected from the circuit under test are compared with the fault signatures in the database to find the closest match and thereby identify the most probable failure.

Fault Diagnosis   Upon detection of errors (during testing), the tester may perform fault-diagnosis to identify the faults in the circuit producing the errors. This information may enable the repair of the system, or be used in a redesign.

Fault diagnosis performs many additional tests, using different patterns to sensitize alternative paths and obtain various responses. The location of the fault is then determined by diagnostic decisions and comparisons between the expected responses and the obtained responses.

After the faulty unit has been repaired, the integrity of the repaired unit must be verified to ensure that it is fault-free. The complete system, including the repaired unit, then must be tested to ensure that the fault has been corrected.

Test Pattern Generation.   This section considers several basic techniques for test pattern generation.

Methods vary from algebraic to algorithmic. The Boolean difference method is an algebraic technique for determining test vectors. This technique finds all test vectors for each fault, but because of its complexity it is limited to small circuits. Both the D-algorithm and the PODEM algorithm use *path sensitization*. The basic idea of path sensitization is to select a path from the site of a potential fault to a primary output. Next the signal value on the fault line is propagated to the primary output along the path.

D-algorithm   In the D-algorithm and PODEM algorithm, a binary variable D and its complement $\overline{D}$ are used to represent the state of an error signal. D denotes a signal that is '1' in the fault-free circuit and '0' in the faulty and $\overline{D}$ denotes the complementary situation. The D-algorithm, first formulated by Roth (1966) [22], developed a five-valued $\{0, 1, X, D, \overline{D}\}$ calculus to carry out the path sensitization and line justification in a very formal manner. Initially a D or $\overline{D}$ is placed on the faulty line, and this value is back propagated to primary inputs. Path sensitization finds a path from the site of the fault to a primary output of the circuit. This will select a set of gates through which the effect of the fault is propagated until it reaches a circuit output line. *Line justification* attempts to assign values to the unspecified inputs of the circuit that produce the desired sensitized path. In D-calculus, the faulty line is first assigned a D or $\overline{D}$ depending on the fault on the line. The next step is to use D-calculus and circuit structure information to determine values on the other lines so that the D or $\overline{D}$ can be sensitized to the circuit outputs. Line justification is then carried out to justify the values assigned in the proceeding step. Both path sensitization and line justification may have to be carried out many times before the test vector is obtained (if one exists).

4.8.3 Design for Test

Ironically, the increase in IC complexity that complicates testing provides a potential solution to the testing problem. The increased densities of ICs makes it possible to include hardware to improve testability on the chip itself. This approach, referred to as Design for Testability (DFT), is not restricted to control of external pins but has access to internal nodes of the circuit. Furthermore, all testing hardware can be included on the chip, possibly removing the requirement of expensive test equipment. This approach is called Built-in Self-Test (BIST), and allows quick diagnoses in the field and even while the device is operating.

Two main considerations when evaluating the testability of a circuit are

- Controllability: ease at which internal nodes may be controlled from primary inputs
- Observability: ease at which internal nodes may be observed from primary outputs

Nodes of the circuit with low controllability and/or observability indicate areas where the testability should be improved.

Approaches to DFT.   Design for Testability methods are categorized as either *ad hoc* or *structured*.

Ad hoc methods consist of heuristic methods like circuit partitioning or adding extra test points. Circuit partitioning involves dividing a large circuit into smaller circuits that are easier to test. Extra lines, used for testing purposes only, are added to increase the controllability and observability of the partitions. Ad hoc methods are suitable for specific designs but are not generally applicable. Moreover, ad hoc methods are dependent on the skill and experience of the individual designer.

Structured DFT techniques were developed in large part to introduce a degree of standardization into the testing field. In addition, structured techniques improve the testability of sequential machines. Structured techniques approach the testability of designs by aiming for a high level of both controllability and observability through a design methodology. This usually involves a set of design rules that are followed from the initial stages of the design. The following sections will look at a few of the many approaches to structured DFT.

Built-In Self-Test.   A further extension of DFT is Built-In Self-Test. BIST includes hardware to evaluate test responses—in effect, it has the ability to test itself. Any BIST method has two elements:

- Method for generating the test inputs
- Strategy for evaluating the test response

In BIST these are all an integral part of the system under test.

Test Pattern Generation   For a BIST application it is necessary to generate the test patterns on the chip. A ROM could be employed to store a set of test vectors on the device. However, the large area required by these devices makes this approach impractical. The test vectors must be generated using circuitry that requires practical area overhead. One method would be to use a simple binary counter to cycle through all the possible inputs. This approach is good only for combinational circuitry where the current state has no affect on the next state and where the number of inputs is low enough to make the testing time reasonable. A method that requires low area overhead while still providing acceptable fault coverage is pseudorandom test vectors generated by on-chip circuitry such as a Linear Feedback Shift Register (LFSR).

Test Data Evaluation   There are many different methods to evaluating the test response data for BIST methods. Selection of a method depends on the area available for the necessary hardware and the amount of allowable sacrifice in fault coverage.

One method is parity checking, where the output data is reduced to a simple parity. Another method is *syndrome analysis* [23]. This method is used for exhaustive testing and consists of counting the number of 1s in the output stream. However, most of the VLSI implementation of test data evaluation hardware use a signature analysis method.

Combinational vs. Sequential Logic.   Test pattern generation methods are primarily used for combinational logic. Combinational logic is simply a collection of logic gate primitives whose output is dependent only on the current circuit inputs. There are no memory elements in combinational logic. Sequential machines consist of combinational logic and memory elements. The primary outputs of the circuit are functions of the state variables or both the state variables and the combinational logic.

Sequential logic is much more difficult to test than combinational logic. It is necessary to verify that the correct output is produced for an input in addition to the correct state transition taking place. Thus the circuit must be tested for all possible inputs and all initial states. To facilitate testing of sequential logic it is desirable to convert a sequential machine into strictly combinational logic. To do this it is necessary to break the feedback loop containing the memory elements. Figure 4.9 shows a general sequential machine modified so that the state variables

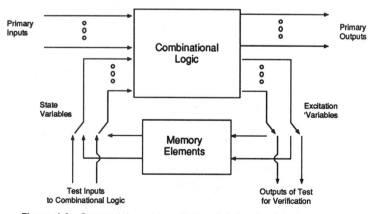

Figure 4.9 *Sequential machine with break in feedback loop for testing.*

can be controlled and the excitation variables observed. In this configuration it is possible to control and observe all the inputs and outputs to the combinational logic block.

Scan Design. *Scan design* replaces the flip-flops in a design with special flip-flops that can operate in two modes: operate and test. In the operate mode the flip-flop functions normally. In the test mode the flip-flops accept test vectors and output the excitation variables. The flip-flops are connected as a shift register to minimize routing and external pin overhead.

The scan design method used to improve the testability of a sequential machine is illustrated in Figure 4.10. The memory elements are replaced with flip-flops that

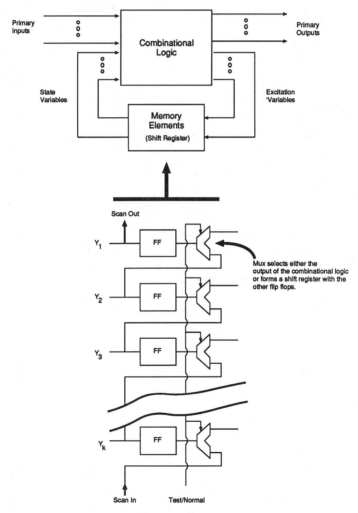

Figure 4.10 *General scan design approach.*

can operate individually or be connected as a shift register. In normal operation the memory system is in operate mode and functions as a collection of independent flip-flops. For testing, the memory system is placed in test mode and the flip-flops are connected as a shift register. It is possible to load a test vector into the flip-flops using the Scan-In line. The resulting excitation response from the combination unit can likewise be loaded into the flip-flops and shifted out via the Scan-Out line.

Signature Analysis. *Signature analysis* is an important and popular application of the Linear Feedback Shift Register (LFSR) [24]. Test data are presented to the LFSR, which divides them by the characteristic polynomial. The remainder of the division, called the signature, is used to check the operation of the circuit. This signature is compared with the signature of a correct circuit. Instead of comparing a large set of outputs produced by many test vectors, only one result, the signatures of the good circuit and the circuit under test need be compared.

The Signature Analyzer is connected to selected nodes of the circuit under test. It is usual to use modulo-2 addition between each of the registers to have a multiple input signature analyzer. An example of a multiple input shift register is shown in Figure 4.11.

Signature analysis can be applied externally to the outputs of an integrated circuit to reduce the magnitude of the comparison chore. However, the small amount of circuitry signature analysis requires allows the hardware to be included on the chip. This allows increased access to the internal nodes while reducing the verification task. The generation of test vectors can also be included on the chip, resulting in a device that contains all the necessary test hardware.

Boundary Scan. Design for Testability methods discussed to this point are generally applied to specific circuit blocks or modules. However, most designs are ultimately composed of many modules connected together on a printed circuit board. There are three major test problems to be addressed in a circuit composed of modules.

1. Confirm that each module is functioning properly
2. Check module interconnections
3. Correct interactions between modules—intended function performed

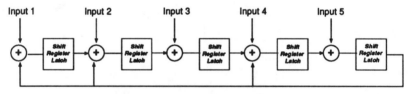

Figure 4.11 *Multiple input shift register.*

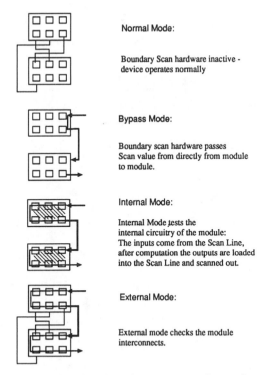

Normal Mode:

Boundary Scan hardware inactive - device operates normally

Bypass Mode:

Boundary scan hardware passes Scan value from directly from module to module.

Internal Mode:

Internal Mode tests the internal circuitry of the module: The inputs come from the Scan Line, after computation the outputs are loaded into the Scan Line and scanned out.

External Mode:

External mode checks the module interconnects.

Figure 4.12 *Major boundary scan operating modes.*

The boundary scan method was developed to address the first two points. Boundary scan consists of modified I/O hardware that incorporates a programmable shift register. The independent modules are then connected in a long shift register chain.

The boundary scan hardware performs four main operations. These operations are illustrated in Figure 4.12 and discussed below:

Normal: The boundary scan is invisible to the circuit. This is the normal operating mode.

Bypass: The boundary scan hardware passes values from module to module, bypassing the internal scan circuitry

Internal: This mode tests the internal circuitry of the modules. The input vectors are loaded in on the scan line and the outputs are scanned out

External: The interconnects of the modules are tested using the scan line. The external connections are excited by the pattern shifted along the scan line, the results are then loaded into the scan line and the result shifted out for test

The boundary scan method applied to a set of interconnected modules is shown in Figure 4.13.

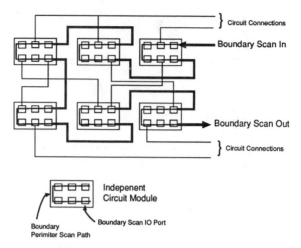

Figure 4.13 *Example of boundary scan applied to a set of interconnected modules.*

Concurrent Checking. The solutions discussed to this point are useful only when the circuit is being tested and do not address the problem of a failure occurring while the device is operating. A momentary error is difficult to detect since the error is not necessarily present when tested with the approaches described earlier. In certain critical applications the occurrence of the error must be detected while the device is operating so corrective measures can be undertaken. This class of testing is referred to as *concurrent checking*.

Numerous approaches to concurrent checking have been developed [25, 26, 27]. Error checking codes such as parity or Hamming codes can be used to check data path and storage element integrity. The encoded data can be checked during normal operation by on-chip circuitry which outputs a good/bad indication.

Duplication The most direct concurrent checking approach is duplication of the circuit and comparison of the two sets of outputs for discrepancies. This approach is shown in Figure 4.14.

With current devices demanding as much of the available die space as possible, this approach is often unacceptable. Duplication requires over twice the area of a nonredundant system. However, redundancy approaches are useful in fault tolerant applications.

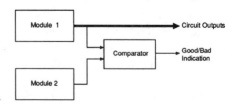

Figure 4.14 *Built-in self-test using duplication.*

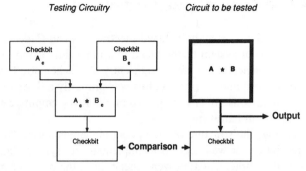

Figure 4.15 *Arithmetic checking.*

Arithmetic Coding   One class of information codes is well suited to checking of arithmetic circuitry, the *arithmetic code*. These codes allow arithmetic circuitry to be easily verified by the scheme shown in Figure 4.15. The output of an arbitrary operation * on operands *A* and *B* is encoded by a Checkbit generator. This is compared to the result of the same operation on the encoded operands.

Arithmetic coding has two major strengths:

- The checking hardware is isolated from the actual circuit
- The operands are generally mapped to a smaller range by the encoding function; the arithmetic logic for the checking section requires much less hardware than other methods such as duplication

DFT Caveats.   The increase in access to internal nodes has its price. Inclusion of scan design hardware increases the complexity of the device under test. Because of the additional hardware, the likelihood of failure in increased. The trade-off is that now at least it is easier to detect faults.

This section has discussed Design for Testability methodologies, where support for testing is incorporated into a device at the design level. Sequential logic presents a challenge to testing; methods based on the scan design principle were presented. The Linear Feedback Shift Register and its application to testing was examined. Boundary scan, built-in self-test, and concurrent checking were also discussed.

Another area of VLSI design that is receiving increased attention is that of fault tolerant design. At present many of the techniques that were originally developed for system level reliability are migrating down to the circuit level. This is particularly interesting and relevant to Wafer Scale Systems (WSI) where faults are inherent. The recent renewed activity in WSI has also brought self-timed computation back into popular research, perhaps vindicating those who have been diligently working in this area for some time now.

4.9 IMPLEMENTATION OF THE SYSTEM

The design tools used in this study included Electric [28] and Cadence [29]. Electric is primarily a layout system better suited to a more full custom design methodology whereas Cadence allows for design entry at a schematic level followed by automated placement and routing. As this was primarily a design space exploration project, several constraints were placed on the fuzzy cognitive system prior to its implementation in hardware.

Figure 4.16 shows the structure of the system implementation. The first major constraint is resolution. It was decided to implement the system digitally, since many aspects of the implementation were uncertain at the onset of research and digital prototyping was the most expeditious and reliable. Because of this constraint, it was necessary to assign some number of bits to the input, output, and intermediate blocks. A uniform resolution of four bits was decided upon. This decision was based primarily on implementation concerns such as area and preliminary system simulations with fixed-bit arithmetic. From a VLSI standpoint, it would be possible to prove the validity of design methodologies, while still implementing functional devices.

The second constraint was silicon area, and it was decided to break the system into three separate chips. This would ensure that if an alteration was required on one of the stages of operation, only that chip need be redesigned. VLSI limitations also enforced that the neural network would be a massive undertaking on its own, requiring a very large die size to fabricate even a simple network. The three-chip system consists of a matching chip with optional aggregation, a reconfigurable neural network chip, and an inverse matching chip. Northern Telecom's 3-μm double-level-metal CMOS process was used for all fabrication.

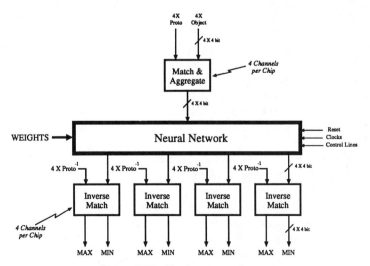

Figure 4.16 *Hardware overview.*

It was also decided that four sets of objectives/prototypes would be allowed as inputs (four independent channels) and that the output would have 16 discrete points of resolution (i.e., a vector of 16 sets of upper/lower bounds).

4.9.1 The Fault Tolerant Methodology

Fault tolerance is a technique used to ensure reliability of performance in a system [30, 31]. Normally some form of redundancy is used to maintain system integrity in the event of some failure, be it transient, intermittent, or permanent. The failure could take the form of a flaw in material processing when the device is fabricated or some unforeseen circumstances while in operation, such as an alpha strike or voltage surge.

In the constraints of the fuzzy cognitive system, three different techniques of fault tolerance were attempted (one for each chip designed).

On the first one, the matching chip, triple modular redundancy (TMR) with voting was used. In this scenario, with three processors each independently performs identical calculations. The output of these sections are then compared and a *two-out-of-three* approach taken. If one of the processing elements is faulty, the other two units would overrule it at the voting stage. In this way the system may suffer a fault in one unit without consequence to the resulting calculations. In this error-masking scheme, it may be advantageous to produce information when one of the processors is consistently found to be at fault. The information may then be used to judge how long the system will continue before total failure.

No attempt was made in the matching chip to indicate time-to-failure. Additionally, each redundant block would ideally be a unique hardware implementation, meaning that the same calculation is performed several times in different ways. Coded checking (such as residues) is one commonly used scheme. All of the redundant blocks are identical on this chip since time constraints on the design did not allow experimentation of this kind.

The second chip designed, used for inverse matching, utilizes a different scheme. In this case, duplex redundancy (DR) with error detection was used. Two identical blocks were used to compute the inverse matching output, and these results were compared. If they do not agree, one output line changes indicating that an error has been detected. At this stage, the user may choose to replace the part completely, or ignore the error flag and take the output as valid (a very dangerous decision). Regardless of the action, steps may be taken to ensure acceptable performance. The main reason for choosing this less acceptable form of fault tolerance is complexity considerations. The inverse matching operation is much more computationally demanding (and therefore more area intensive) than the matching operation. The DR scheme utilizes only $\frac{2}{3}$ of the area of the previous scheme, and furthermore the comparison equipment at the output is less complex in this technique.

The final scheme used for fault tolerance comes from the nature of parallel computations in a neural network. Fault tolerance of neural networks is a relatively new field of study, although a few attempts have been made [32].

It has long been known that biological systems degrade gracefully as neurons become faulty (i.e., brain damage). Since the computation is both highly parallel and distributed, a few bad neurons do not totally disable the complete system. In our system in which 16 neurons will feed 16 neurons, if one neuron produced an erroneous result it is then passed on to the next layer. At this point, a weighted summation is taken of all neurons on the previous layer and one of the 16 values in this summation is in error. In a worst case scenario, this means that the total is correct 15 parts out of 16. While this is tolerable, it reduces for larger networks. The built-in self-tolerance is a very attractive feature of neural networks.

The training process may also reduce the effect of faults by recovering from them intelligently. The working neuron's weights may be compensated to lessen the impact of the faulty areas. While it would also be advantageous to make fault tolerant neurons, the demands were found to be too area intensive for this application.

An interesting scenario for fault tolerance will be examined after the neural network system structure has been presented.

4.9.2   Built-In Self-Test

Built-in self-test (BIST) is a technique used to reduce the difficulty of testing [33]. Random test vectors are generated on-chip and presented to the circuit where the output is then compressed and compared to the known correct code. A signal is presented to the user indicating the success or failure of the test. BIST eliminates the need for bulky, expensive test equipment and is potentially much faster, since computations are accomplished on-chip.

The use of cellular automata (CA) for BIST has been well documented [34, 35]. There are however, more conventional alternatives primarily based upon the linear feedback shift register. As we are interested in experimental prototypes we felt a more experimental test scheme based upon CAs was justified. Under constrained conditions, CA structures will generate $2^n - 1$ possible nonzero combinations of an n-bit system in a pseudorandom order. CAs are a very good structure for VLSI since they require only localized connections, are simple to implement, and offer good fault coverage. The CAs implemented here are linear "1"-dimensional arrays with nearest neighbor connections.

The CAs in all chips were two-bits longer than actually required for the test, with the two outer bits ignored (and null boundary conditions). This overestimation approach was taken to increase fault coverage (the vectors used in the test are *more random*) at the expense of nominal silicon area.

The first two chips designed (matching and inverse matching) take advantage of redundant channels. The technique used involved creating pseudorandom numbers with the CA, propagating the same random number through each channel in parallel, and comparing the outputs. A discrepancy in any of the outputs sends a signal to the user, inviting further testing on individual channels.

The neural network chip also uses the pseudorandom numbers to cycle through a chain of neurons, comparing all neurons at the output (they should have identical responses). Discrepancies indicate further testing is required to isolate the damaged neuron.

4.9.3 Preprocessing: The Fuzzy Matching Operation

As previously discussed, in Section 4.2, the matching operation may be concisely expressed as Eq. (4.21). The expression $a \equiv b$ may be interpreted as *the degree to which a matches b*.

$$a \equiv b = Q = (a \wedge b) + M - (a \vee b), \quad a, b \in [0, M] \quad (4.21)$$

This equation may be implemented, as shown in Figure 4.17a. Aggregation would be included optionally. This function was implemented with a barrel-shift adder, which simply keeps a running total of inputs.

Four identical independent channels are implemented on the chip, and these are used as comparisons against each other in the BIST. This chip also uses triple modular redundancy with voting at the matching stage to ensure some fault tolerance. The completed implementation is presented as Figure 4.18.

A graphical description of the blocks in the design is presented as Figure 4.19. Some specifications of this chip are presented in Table 4.7.

4.9.4 Postprocessing: Inverse Matching

Also, as previously discussed, the inverse matching function of Eq. (4.22) may be implemented as shown in Figure 4.17b.

$$a = b \pm (Q - M), \quad a, b \in [0, M] \quad (4.22)$$

This block is obviously more complex than the matching operation, and it is justifiably more area intensive. Part of this complexity is derived from the function's dual output nature (it must generate the bounds of an interval).

Four identical independent channels are again implemented on the chip, and

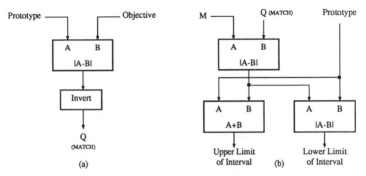

Figure 4.17 *Fuzzy matching/inverse matching implementations.*

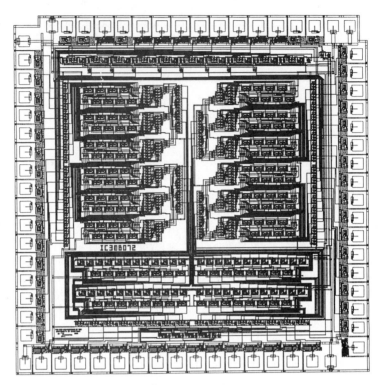

Figure 4.18 *Matching chip with aggregation.*

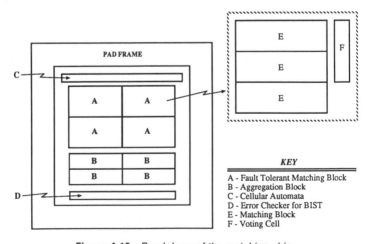

Figure 4.19 *Breakdown of the matching chip.*

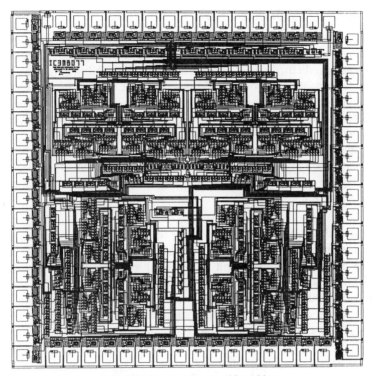

Figure 4.20 *Inverse matching chip.*

these are used as comparisons against each other in the BIST. This chip used duplex redundancy for error checking.

The completed implementation is presented as Figure 4.20. A graphical description of the blocks in the design is presented as Figure 4.21. Some specifications of this chip are presented in Table 4.7.

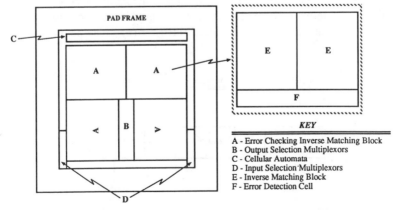

Figure 4.21 *Breakdown of the inverse matching chip.*

4.9.5 Neural Processing

The most complex part of the fuzzy cognitive system is the neural network. Many identical neurons transmit their information to many other identical neurons, and the immense parallelism is very difficult to implement in VLSI. The more neurons on a single chip, the less complex the neurons must be. The more serialized the computation, the smaller the neuron, and therefore more may be placed on a single chip. Each serialized neuron is now slower than a more parallel implementation.

In an attempt to find an optimized solution, a compromise was arrived at: Parallel computation would be performed with a distributed serial system. While each neuron performs a pipelined operation, many neurons perform in parallel, thereby maximizing the computing potential and distribution. A more complete comparison and can be found in [36].

Neural Architecture.   Since the number of available neurons on the chip was uncertain at the onset of this research, it was decided that the synapses and neuron would be designed as a single unit. Based on this fact, the term *neuron* may be used to infer both the neural and synaptic structures.

It was decided at an early stage to use a three-bit resolution for the weights since this was a complementary resolution to the four-bit activations. The large amounts of memory required made on-chip learning too area intensive for implementation. It would be necessary to develop a system architecture that would allow fast access to both weights and threshold values.

The basic conceptual architecture of Figure 4.22 was used to implement the neuron. A form of simplified bounded multiplication is performed at the synapse, and a running bounded accumulation is used at the neuron itself. At the thresholding stage, the neural output is forced through a piecewise linear thresholding function with variable slope. A threshold was used instead of a bias term, since it gives more control of the neural output. If a 4×4 full multiplier were used, few neurons could be placed on the chip. Since multiplication is extremely area intensive in VLSI, a simplified multiplication scheme was used, as shown in Table 4.4.

The simplification of multiplication/division by factors of 2 yields a tremendous simplification in terms of hardware complexity since it may be implemented by base-2 shifting. For example, the number $(0110)_2 = (6)_{10}$ may be multiplied by a

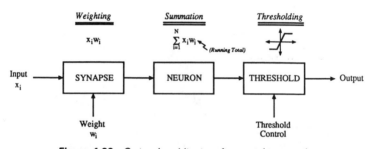

Figure 4.22   *General architecture for neural processing.*

TABLE
4.4 Simplified Synaptic Scheme

a_2	a_1	a_0	Multiplier
1	1	1	-2
1	1	0	-1
1	0	1	$-\frac{1}{2}$
1	0	0	-0
0	0	0	$+0$
0	0	1	$+\frac{1}{2}$
0	1	0	$+1$
0	1	1	$+2$

TABLE
4.5 Thresholding Scheme

a_2	a_1	a_0	Results
0	0	0	ZERO
0	0	1	$/2$
0	1	0	$\times 2$
0	1	1	$-\frac{1}{2}$MAX
1	0	0	$+\frac{1}{2}$MAX
1	0	1	$/4$
1	1	0	$\times 4$
1	1	1	MAX

factor 2 by shifting the bits once to the left, as $(1100)_2 = (12)_{10}$. The original number may be halved by shifting once to the right, as $(0011)_2 = (3)_{10}$.

At the thresholding stage, the neural output is forced through a piecewise linear thresholding function with variable slope. A three-bit resolution was used for threshold control, and the scheme implemented is presented as Table 4.5. Options are included to either totally disconnect the neuron (output ZERO) or turn the output always "on" (output MAX). The $\pm\frac{1}{2}$MAX option could be used to induce a more extreme, *hard limiting* output.

Another source of area saving may be found in the adder-tree associated with a fully parallel implementation. Some research regarding trade-offs in serializing the neural/synaptic operation is summarized in Table 4.6. Since it was desired that 16 neurons would be implemented on a chip, the most serialized network would be used (level 4). It should be noted that while the level 3 estimate in Table 4.6 indicates that 18 of these neurons could be placed on a chip, this does not account for interconnectivity, the pad frame area, or any equipment used for testability.

Network Architecture. While several engineers have attempted to implement digital neural networks in VLSI, most of the attempts have been very regimented; that is, a specific network was envisioned, and that precise network was implemented. The technique developed here greatly increased flexibility and processing speed while decreasing power consumption and size.

Most implementation attempts have utilized multiplexors at either the input or output of the neuron to allow serial processing in the neurons at each layer. This requires that a physical connection from each neuron on each layer to each neuron on the next layer be present. This high degree of interconnection greatly reduces neuron complexity, since much of the silicon area is now required for intercon-

TABLE 4.6 Trade-offs in Neural Pipelining

Levels Pipelined	Area of Neuron ($\mu m^2 \times 10^6$)	Clock Cycles per Neural Cycle	Neurons per Chip
0	21.29	1	4
2	8.44	4	11
3	5.36	8	18
4	4.76	16	26

nections. Large drivers must also be used for each of these lines, as they may be propagating distant signals. The solution is to use fairly large drivers, in the hope that signals that are required to travel only a short distance are over driven, while only the very longest lines are slightly underdriven. The result is mediocre performance, and medium size. If the network is to be reconfigured, the multiplexor block must be reconfigured and replaced in each neuron. While this increases size (the new multiplexors are inherently larger) and slows computation (more logic implies slower response), the major problem is that of reconfigurability for the designer. Furthermore, once fabricated, there is *no* reconfigurability whatsoever.

Another scheme that has been used [32] is the bus architecture. This technique allows any number of computational elements to use the bus, and even to access devices off-chip that are given access to the bus. The long lines require very large drivers for realistic speed. The single communication channel also becomes a bottleneck when communications become intensive. While a multibus structure alleviates some of this problem, a multitude of bus arbitrators and controllers becomes necessary. This, in turn, makes it difficult to design efficient structures in VLSI, Although a common bus architecture has much to offer neural network implementations if built around standard interfaces and high speed commercial processors.

In contrast to the fully parallel or bus systems, consider the architecture of Figure 4.23. In this configuration, each neuron is fed one value of the input vector. The neuron processes the datum and passes it to the next neuron in the chain (of the same layer), which in turn processes the piece of information. Each neuron maintains a running total for its cumulative weighted summation. This process continues until all neurons on the layer have processed each piece of information from the previous layer. The cyclic chain ensures that each neuron on the layer receives every piece of information. To add one neuron to a particular layer, the chain for that layer must be expanded by one "link." Note that neither the neuron itself nor any of its parts need be redesigned. The addition of a link increases

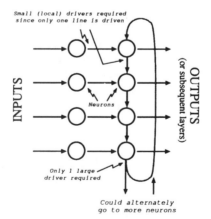

Figure 4.23 *A neural-slice feed-forward network.*

processing time by one *neural cycle*, that is, the number of clock cycles required to process one piece of information at one neuron.

Each neuron feeds only the "next neighbor," thereby using local connections. Only small drivers are needed for this, since the distance between two neurons may be specified at the *placement* stage of design. Speed is also improved because only a predictably small driver is required for the very short line. Only one line from each neuron to its nearest neighbor is required, thereby eliminating $(n^2 - n)$ lines from the fully parallel case.

Although this technique greatly reduces area, its greatest advantage is reconfigurability. Several chips may be interfaced together as required to create a network with *any number of neurons on a layer*. In addition, the scheme can be extended to bypassing defective neurons by a variety of techniques [37].

Iterative techniques may be used to cycle the chip upon itself. By collecting the data at each neuron until all data for the layer have been processed, the neuron is then ready to transmit its information to the subsequent layer of neurons. The information may then be transmitted to another chip or returned to its own inputs to process further layers. An infinite number of layers on a single chip may be created in this way. Alternately, several chips may be used to pipeline layers.

A chip was designed using the aforementioned design principles, and a metal layer representation is presented as Figure 4.24. A graphical description of the blocks in the design is presented as Figure 4.25. Some specifications of this chip are presented as Table 4.7. Padframe requirements forced serial loading and unloading of the shift register chain, although parallel off-chip communication is a trivial task given more compact pads.

At the time of implementation it was felt that there might be some advantage keeping the shift register as an autonomous entity. It seems more practical, upon reflection, to embed the shift register elements within each neuron. This would become more desirable if the number of neurons on a chip were increased. One disadvantage of this architecture is that the weights and threshold control lines must be available *as required* by the neuron. Since it is extremely area intensive to implement memory devices on-chip, pins must be reserved to load these values from off-chip as required. Fortunately, only one weight per neuron is required at any given time. Furthermore, the weights and threshold controls are not required at the same time.

4.9.6 Software Environment

The complex VLSI technology discussed in the previous section would cause an organizational nightmare if it was necessary for the user to manually route all the data each time the system was used. An interactive software environment is required to allow all data processing and manipulation to be transparent to the user. While the overwhelming majority of system operation is controlled by hardware (for speed), the user may decide specific operations and initiate the classification

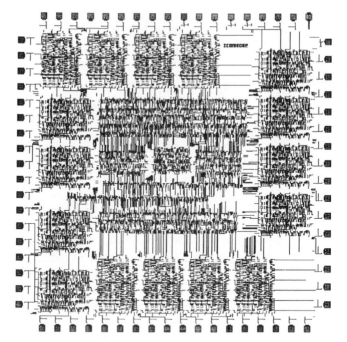

Figure 4.24   *Neural network chip.*

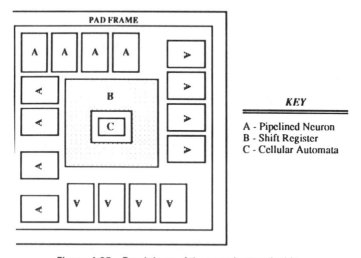

Figure 4.25   *Breakdown of the neural network chip.*

TABLE 4.7   Chip-Set Summary

	Matching	Neural Network	Inverse Matching
Chip Size in 3 μm Tech.	4503×4503	7200×7446	4503×4503
Number of Pins	68	70	68
Number of Input Pins	32	4[†]	32
Number of Output Pins	16	4[†]	32
Number of Pins for Weights	N/A	48[††]	N/A
Number of Pins for Thresholding	N/A	32[††]	N/A
Number of Dedicated Test Pins	5	3	5[††]

[†] Serial
[††] Multiplexed

process. For obvious reasons of architectural accessibility and universality, the system should be implemented as a special function board for a PC or workstation. Direct memory access should be used for downloading the data from memory to the board. The software interface should be a user-friendly windowing system for control and graphical interpretation of output. The software environment should encompass the following features:

- Preprocessing: graphical selection of membership functions and calculation of input vectors.
- Communication: allowing data to be down/uploaded to the special function board, as well as execution of system tests
- Output display: several output formats allowing the user to tailor the system for a specific application
- User interface: windowing, menu selection, and ergonomics

The complete cognitive system may then be viewed as presented in Figure 4.26. The software layer "shields" the user from the complexity of the hardware, al-

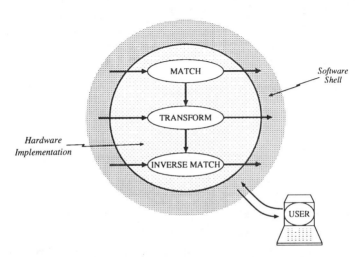

Figure 4.26   Software shell for the fuzzy cognitive system.

lowing nonhardware experts to examine and interpret the fuzzy system with a minimum of time and effort. Several aspects of this environment are under way, although a working system has not yet been completed.

4.10 SUMMARY

This chapter deals with a fuzzy cognitive system. A three layer structure was explored, consisting of a matching layer, neural network, and inverse matching layer. The basic fuzzy theory underlying the system was covered as well as the constraints imposed in VLSI implementation. VLSI, neural networks, and fuzzy set theory were combined to produce a system for real-time application. Fault tolerance was attempted and redundancies of the layouts were advantageously used for built-in self-test. The result of this eclectic merger should be a very robust chip set. Finally, the user interface was examined with emphasis on system overview.

The following points summarize all fundamental features of the fuzzy cognitive structure. Noticeable is the fact that all key requirements for autonomous systems are met there.

- Reliable learning
- Acceptance and handling of incomplete and/or imprecise input information (not realizable in standard architectures of neural networks)
- Focussed and flexible form of information processing (such as the specification of user defined prototypes)
- Self-flagging character of results obtained in the structure (explicit articulation of generalization capabilities)
- Parallelism in information processing
- VLSI implementation and fault tolerance of digital implementation

Future research of the cognitive system will be centered around the structure of the neural net, especially algorithms to reduce the time and area for the weighting factors. Multilayered neural nets are also under examination. An attempt will also be made to implement an 8-bit system.

ACKNOWLEDGMENTS

Support provided by the Natural Sciences and Engineering Research Council of Canada and the Canadian Microelectronics Corporation is highly appreciated. We would also like to thank D. Blight and J. Dickson for their contributions to the sections on VLSI.

REFERENCES

[1] Preprints, *II IFSA Congress*, 2 vols., Tokyo, August 1987.

[2] H. Togai, and H. Watanabe, Expert systems on a chip: An engine for real-time approximate reasoning, *IEEE Expert*, 1, 55–62 (1986).

[3] S. Grossberg, *Neural Networks and Natural Intelligence*, MIT Press, Cambridge, Mass., 1988.

[4] F. L. McClelland and D. E. Rumelhart, Eds., *Parallel Distributed Processing: Explorations in the Microstructure of Cognition*, 2 vols., MIT Press, Cambridge, Mass., 1986.

[5] W. A. Pedrycz, Fuzzy cognitive structure for pattern recognition, *Pattern Recognition Lett.*, 9, 305–313 (1985).

[6] W. Pedrycz, Direct and inverse problem in comparison of fuzzy data, *Fuzzy Sets and Syst.* 34, 223–235 (1990).

[7] C. Johnson, NASA unites neural nets, fuzzy logic, *Electronic Eng. Times*, 40–41 (May 23, 1988).

[8] G. Bortolan, R. Degani, K. Hirota, and W. Pedrycz, Classification of electrocardiographic signals with the aid of fuzzy pattern matching, *Proc. Internat. Workshop Applications of Fuzzy Sets*, IIZUKA-88, (1988).

[9] J. Diamond, R. McLeod, and W. Pedrycz, A fuzzy cognitive system: Foundations and VLSI implementation, *3rd IFSA Congress*, Jim Bezdek (ed.), 396–399 (1989).

[10] J. G. Carbonell, R. S. Michalski, and T. M. Mitchell, "Learning by Analogy: Formulating and Generalizing Plans from Past Experience," in *Machine Learning: An Artificial Intelligence Approach*, R. S. Michalski, J. G. Carbonell, T. M. Mitchell (eds.), Springer-Verlag, Berlin, 1984, pp. 137–159.

[11] R. E. Kling, Paradigm for reasoning by analogy, *Artificial Intelligence*, 2, 147–178 (1971).

[12] W. Pedrycz, Selected issues of frame of knowledge representation realized by means of linguistic labels, *J. Intelligent Systems* (to be published).

[13] J. Mantes, Methodologies in pattern recognition and image analysis—A brief survey, *Pattern Recognition*, 20, 1–6 (1987).

[14] A. Rosenfeld, Image pattern recognition, *Proc. IEEE*, 69, 596–605 (1981).

[15] W. Fichtner and M. Morf, *VLSI CAD Tools and Applications*, Kluwer Academic Pub., Norwell, Mass., 1987.

[16] J. D. Ullman, *Computational Aspects of VLSI*, Computer Science Press, Rockville, Md., 1984.

[17] L. A. Glasser and D. W. Dobberpuhl, *The Design and Analysis of VLSI Circuits*, Addison Wesley, Reading, Mass., 1985.

[18] N. Weste and K. Eshraghian, *Principles of CMOS VLSI Design: A Systems Perspective*, Addison Wesley, Reading, Mass., 1985.

[19] F. D. Fabricus, *Introduction to VLSI Design*, McGraw Hill, New York, 1990.

[20] R. L. Geiger, P. E. Allen, and N. R. Strader, *VLSI Design Techniques for Analog and Digital Circuits*, McGraw Hill, New York, 1990.

[21] J. A. Bate and D. M. Miller, "The Exhaustive Testing of Stuck-open Faults in CMOS Combinational Circuits," in *Developments in Integrated Circuit Testing*, Academic Press, New York, 1987.

[22] J. P. Roth, Diagnosis of automata failures: A calculus and a method, *IBM J. Research Dev.*, 10, 278–281.

[23] J. Savir, Syndrome-testable design of combinational circuits, *IEEE Trans. Computers*, C29(6), 442–451 (June 1980).

[24] H. J. Nadig, Signature analysis: Concepts, examples, and guidelines, *Hewlett-Packard J.*, 28(9), 15–21 (May 1977).

[25] I. L. Sayers, G. Russel, and D. J. Kinniment, "Concurrent Checking Techniques— A DFT Alternative," Dept. Electrical and Electronic Engineering, University of Newcastle, England, 1987.

[26] Janak H. Patel and Leona Y. Fung, Concurrent error detection in multiply and divide arrays, *IEEE Trans. Computers*, C-32 (4), 417–422 (April 1983).

[27] W. Kent Fuchs, Chien-Yi Roger Chen, and Jacob A. Abraham, Concurrent error detection in highly structured logic arrays, *IEEE J. Solid-State Circuits*, (4), 583–594 (August 1987).

[28] S. M. Rubin, *Computer Aids for VLSI Design*, Addison-Wesley, Reading, Mass., 1987.

[29] Cadence EDGE system. Version 2.1f1.

[30] D. A. Rennels, Fault-tolerant computing—Concepts and examples, *IEEE Trans. Computers*, C-33, [12], 1116–1129 (Dec. 1984).

[31] B. W. Johnson, *Design and Analysis of Fault-Tolerant Digital Systems*, Addison Wesley, Reading, Mass., 1989.

[32] L. C. Chu, and B. W. Wah, Fault tolerant neural networks with hybrid redundancy, *Internat. Joint Conf. on Neural Networks*, Vol. II, 639–649 (1990).

[33] T. W. Williams, VLSI testing, *IEEE Computer*, pp. 126–136 (October 1984).

[34] P. D. Hortensius, R. D. McLeod, W. Pries, D. M. Miller, and H. C. Card, Cellular automata-based pseudorandom number generators for built-in self-test, *IEEE Trans. Computer Aided Design of Integrated Circuits and Systems* 8, 842–859, (1989).

[35] B. W. Podaima, and R. D. McLeod, Weighted test pattern generation for built-in self-test using cellular automata, *3rd Technical Workshop on New Directions for Integrated Circuit Testing*, Halifax, October 1988, pp 195–205.

[36] J. Diamond, "VLSI Implementation of a Fuzzy Cognitive System," M.Sc. thesis, University of Manitoba, 1990.

[37] R. Negrini, M. G. Sami, and R. Stefenelli, *Fault Tolerance Through Reconfiguration in VLSI and WSI Array*, MIT Press, Cambridge, Mass., 1989.

CHAPTER 5 _____

Intelligent Systems by Means of Associative Processing

K. E. GROSSPIETSCH

5.1 INTRODUCTION

Systems with associative (i.e., content addressable) access to data and associative control of processing have been in the discussion of computer architecture research for a long time. Especially, systems where not only the memory is organized associatively (i.e., associative processor systems) promise to be a flexible tool that can be applied to a wide range of applications.

In this chapter, an innovative concept for the combination of content addressable memory and processors is outlined. Its main idea is the systematic extension of the functionality of a content addressable memory by architectural features such as, for example,

Combination of RAM and CAM access modes

Extension of the CAM memory cell by a simple functional building block for the execution of 1-bit Boolean operations

Extension of the memory structure by adder elements, whereby each of these elements is associated with a group of memory cells

The chapter first gives a general survey of the state of the art. Subsequently, the basic architectural features of the introduced approach are discussed. A machine instruction set for the system is introduced and illustrated by some simple programming examples. The advantages of the architecture for various application fields are shown.

In the practice of data processing we can observe a growing demand for more

Fuzzy, Holographic, and Parallel Intelligence, By Branko Souček and the IRIS Group.
ISBN 0-471-54772-7 © 1992 John Wiley & Sons, Inc.

and more ''intelligent'' hardware systems, that is, subsystems have to take over from the end user a growing spectrum of subtasks within the entire hardware system automatically. Well-known standard examples are management of intelligent data bases, picture processing, and pattern recognition in general. Additionally, for many applications computing systems are requested to be adaptive to changing external situations, that is, to show some learning behavior. If such extensions of functionality are realized only at the level of software, this usually causes unacceptable performance results. Alternatively, the additional functionality can be transferred into hardware outside the central host processor.

With respect to the applications mentioned, the following basic architectural features seem particularly important:

Massive parallelism of computing elements (important, e.g., for picture processing)

Means for the flexible, selective definition of activity patterns on the array of computing elements (e.g., for intelligent data base management)

Transfer of parallel data processing directly into memory (intelligent memory)

Avoidance of unnecessary data transfers between processor and memory (removal of the ''von Neumann bottleneck'')

In this context, as one interesting step toward smarter memories, systems for associative (meant here always as a synonym for content addressable) storage and processing of data can also gain rising importance: Content addressable memories (CAMs) have already been in the discussions of system developers for a long time. The advantage of such structures for speeding up search operations is unquestionable, but in the past the state of technology allowed only very small CAM capacities. It is only now that the emerging state of the art in hardware integration enables the realization of such memories with reasonable bit capacities and cost/bit ratio. Moreover, the extension of the principle of content addressing from storage of data to processing of data has been proven to imply many interesting features for various fields of parallel processing (e.g., image processing, CAD support).

In this chapter, an approach for a combined associative processor/memory system is outlined. First, Section 5.2 gives a survey of the state of the art in the field of associative memories and processor systems. Then, Section 5.3 discusses basic principles and the resulting hardware realization. Section 5.4 introduces a machine instruction set and illustrates its use by discussing some elementary macro routines. Subsequently, Section 5.5 shows the advantages of the architecture for various application areas, such as data base management, picture processing, Petri net emulation, or neural net emulation.

5.2 STATE OF THE ART OF ASSOCIATIVE SYSTEMS

5.2.1 Associative Memories

Classical CAM Model. In contrast with access via memory addresses in conventional random access memories (RAMs), in a CAM the content of a word cell is accessed by means of a comparison with a given search argument. So, functionally the word cells of a typical CAM consist of two parts:

- A search key field the contents of which by some associative logic can be compared with the search argument
- The data field built out of conventional RAM bit cells

If the search key field of a word cell i ($i = 0, \cdots, w - 1$) matches the search argument, a hit line emanating from the search key field activates the bit cells of the data field of word cell i (see Fig. 5.1). The length of the search key field is denoted by k and that of the data field by l; the entire word length is then $n = k + l$. For $l = 0$ we have the special case of a CAM where each bit slice has associative search logic. When a search pattern is compared with the search key fields, it is loaded into the search argument register SAR. The subsequent comparison is performed for each of the w word cells of the CAM concurrently; inside each word cell the comparison is presumed to be carried out bitwise in parallel. If the key field of a word cell i is equal to the given search argument, a "hit" signal is produced and is stored in cell i of the hit register HR (see Fig. 5.1).

The comparison with the contents of the SAR may be masked by means of a second input register, the mask register MR. If a bit j ($j = 0, \cdots, k - 1$) in this mask register is set to 1, in all bit cells of the corresponding bit slice j the comparison is not carried out; instead, in these cells a local hit signal is always generated. So, the mask register can be utilized to reduce the number of effective bits in the key field.

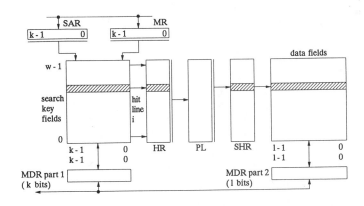

HR	hit register,
MDR	memory data register,
MR	mask register,
PL	priority logic,
SAR	search argument register,
SHR	selected hit register.

Shaded areas: the two parts of word cell i.

Figure 5.1. CAM architecture.

This memory structure allows multiple hits within the CAM. In the case of a write operation, into all word cells found via their search key fields, the same bit pattern can be written from the memory data register MDR (see Fig. 5.1). In the case of an associative read operation with more than one hit, the output of the words found has to be serialized. This is performed by some priority logic PL; this logic is presumed to select one out of the set of word cells found, for example, that one with the highest internal address i which is given by the bit position of the hit signal in register HR. If word cell i has been selected, this is noted by placing a 1 into bit cell i of the selected hit register SHR; all other bit cells of the SHR have the value 0 (see Fig. 5.1).

Functionally, the CAM bit cell, in addition to the normal RAM bit cell flip-flop, has to provide some comparison logic. In a gate level implementation, this could be achieved by using an $\overline{\text{EXOR}}$ gate for the comparison with the corresponding hit cell of the SAR and an OR gate for producing the hit signal in the case of masking by the MR. At transistor level, different solutions have been developed. They will be discussed in the next section.

Realization of CAM Bit Cells

Static CAM Cells. One way to build a CAM bit cell is to extend the classical static RAM flip-flop cell. Such an approach is shown in Figure 5.2: In addition to the six transistors of the flip-flop, we have three other transistors to implement the match logic. Writing a ''1'' (''0'') is performed as in a RAM: via the word line WORD the pass transistors T1 and T2 are opened; the bit line BIT is set to ''1'' (''0''), whereas the complementary line BIT is driven to the inverted signal of BIT. As a result, transistor T6 (T5) is conducting, and T5 (T6) is nonconducting, thus representing the storage of the written value.

The comparison logic is simply realized by two pass transistors T7 and T8. If the content of the cell is to be compared with a search bit s, the match line is first

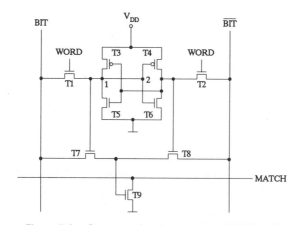

Figure 5.2. *Structure of a nine-transistor CAM bit cell.*

precharged to "HIGH". Then line BIT is set to the inverted search value $\bar{s}$ (and, correspondingly, $\overline{\text{BIT}}$ to s). If, for example, a 1 was stored in the flip-flop so that node 1 is "HIGH", transistor T7 propagates the value "0" from line BIT to the gate of T9. So, this transistor remains nonconducting, and the match line is not discharged to "Ground".

Any mismatch (i.e., coincidence of a signal 1 of line BIT with the value "HIGH" of node 1), however, opens T9 and causes discharging of the match line. A masking of the bit cell is performed by driving both bit lines to 0.

A similar approach simply uses four additional pass transistors to combine nodes 1 and 2 by negated EXORS (see Fig. 5.3). The output of these "EX-NORS" is wired to the match line. In this 10-transistor cell, a match against a stored bit is carried out by driving the line BIT to the noninverted search value s (and $\overline{\text{BIT}}$ to $\bar{s}$). Mismatch again leads to the discharge of the precharged sense line; masking is performed by applying 0s to both bit lines. On the basis of this circuit architecture, Kadota et al. [1] some years ago developed a CAM chip comprising 256 words of 32 bits; that is, the entire chip contained 8 k bit cells. To minimize access time, both bit and sense lines were laid out to have low resistance, to avoid RC delays. This was solved by double layer metallization techniques.

As another, comparative approach, Ogura et al. [2] developed a CAM chip of only 4-kbit capacity; it consists of 128 words of 32 bits. However, apart from retrieval functions, this chip can carry out also parallel writing in multiple words.

The mentioned chips were still research prototypes. In 1987, Advanced Micro Devices introduced a first commercial version of a VLSI CAM chip, the AM95C85. It comprised 1 k bits; the array of the chips could respond to an 8-bit key in about 10 μsec. In 1989 Advanced Micro Devices followed up with the 12-kbit AM99C10 chip. The chip uses a 48-bit wide key, which can be compared in parallel with 256 words. One of its intended application areas is address management in local area networks.

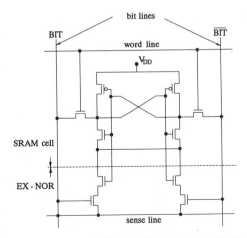

Figure 5.3. *Ten transistor CAM bit cell (according to Kadota et al. [1]).*

Dynamic CAM Cells.   There are also approaches to realize CAMs by extending dynamic RAM cells. Dynamic RAM techniques achieve larger bit capacities per chip because of smaller numbers of transistors per bit cell (1-transistor cell, 3-transistor cell). However, these techniques need refresh operations because of either leakage currents or destructive read operations. As several bit cells are simultaneously read in a CAM, a destructive read operation as used in conventional dynamic RAMs is not possible. Data must be stored in such a way that a mismatch cannot destroy it.

This can be accomplished by storing the data on the gates of two transistors. Such a bit cell was recently proposed by Wade and Sodini (see Fig. 5.4): The two transistors T4 and T5 operate as pass transistors, which are opened only if a write access is to be carried out in the bit cell. According to the bit pattern applied to the bit lines, the gate capacitances of the transistors T2 and T3 are charged or discharged. An internal ''don't care'' is stored by driving both bit lines low during the write operation; thereby the gate capacitances of both transistors are discharged.

Matching is performed by precharging the match line to ''HIGH'', and then driving the bit lines to the required logic levels. If a ''LOW'' signal is applied to the bit line of the branch where a high potential was stored, a current will flow through the corresponding transistor T2 or T3 and will discharge the match line. If, on the other hand, the bit line corresponding to a conducting transistor T2 or T3 remains HIGH, no current will flow; thus a hit is indicated. If a ''don't care'' was stored, both of these transistors are off and no discharge of the match line can occur.

Masking of the bit cell in a search operation is performed by driving both bit lines to HIGH; in this case again, no discharge of the match line can occur.

Refresh is organized in the following way: The bit lines are discharged to ground; then the potential of the match line of the word to be refreshed is raised to HIGH. If transistor T2 or T3 has stored a high potential on its gate, the potential

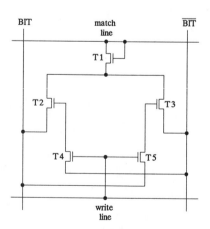

Figure 5.4.   *Dynamic CAM bit cell of Wade and Sodini [18].*

of the corresponding bit line will also rise. This potential read out is then written back into the selected cell.

Unorthodox Approaches

Orthogonal Memory. An approach that differs significantly from the classical CAM structure is the orthogonal memory recently proposed again by Kokubu et al. [3] after a similar structure had previously been realized by Batcher in the STARAN machine [4]. In the orthogonal memory there is no comparison logic within the bit cells. So, the bit cell is quite similar to that one of a RAM except that via two additional pass transistors, the contents of the cell can also be read out to the word line (see Fig. 5.5).

So, besides the normal random access mode, there is a second memory mode wherein an entire bit slice can be accessed concurrently. This bit slice can be compared outside the cell array bitwise in parallel with the search pattern. Thus, a word-parallel, bit-sequential associative search can be easily performed.

Associative Random Access Memory (ARAM). This approach was proposed by Tavangarian [5, 6]; it is also called "location addressable" associative memory. It is realized by a very simple change of the usual RAM decoder. In addition to the AND gates $G_0, \cdots, G_{w-1}$ we have the additional gates $A_0, \cdots, A_{2m-1}$ ($m = ldw$, being the length of the memory address), which combine the input address with some mask pattern coming from the mask register MR (see Fig. 5.6). If the contents of MR is zero, the extended decoder functions like a normal 1-out-of-w decoder. Otherwise, a multiaccess to all cells with addresses matching the unmasked bits of the input address is performed.

The corresponding memory array is, in the simplest approach, formed by exactly one bit slice. Associative processing is then based on the following rule: Storage of an m-bit pattern $b_0, \cdots, b_{m-1}$ in memory is performed by setting a

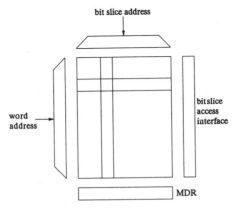

Figure 5.5. *Orthogonal memory.*

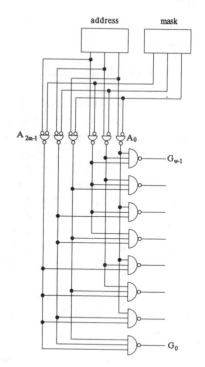

Figure 5.6. *Masked decoder of the ARAM (according to Tavangarian [5]).*

1 to the cell with the address $b_0 \cdots b_{m-1}$. Search for the pattern analogously is carried out by the check whether the corresponding bit cell stores a 1 or a 0.

Fault-Tolerant CAMs. The development of VLSI in general offers the possibility of greatly increasing the capacity of associative memory chips; the implementation of a CAM on a VLSI chip with large capacity or even on a single wafer would avoid the present limitations of CAM capacities, which are caused mainly by pin limitation problems.

With the use of larger CAMs, however, the question also arises of how to produce and operate them reliably. Here, the difference in memory structure, compared with usual random access memories (RAMs), means that well known fault tolerance solutions for RAMs cannot simply be transferred to CAMs. So far, very little systematic work has been done in the area of fault tolerant CAMs.

Fault Tolerance in Classical CAMs. Functionally, the effect of faults in a CAM may be classified into two large groups, that either (1) a given word that is to match a search argument is not found, or (2) a word that does not match the search argument is memorized as a hit. In general the second effect could be detected at the output interface of the CAM, if some appropriate logic is available. If the peripheral registers are fault-free, such a hit of a wrong word is caused either by faults in the storage part of the CAM bit cells or by faults in their comparison logic. The detection of these two possibilities could be carried out efficiently by some extra hardware. Here, Grosspietsch, Huber, and Müller proposed two additional architectural features [7] (see Fig. 5.7):

- An error detecting code for the storage part of the CAM bit cells
- Comparison logic between the search register SAR (masked by *MR*) and the output register MDR (this logic is the same as that used in the CAM bit cell array itself)

Thus, after a word is read out to the MDR, the comparison with the search argument in the SAR is repeated by an $\overline{\text{EXOR}}$ unit (see Fig. 5.7), which checks bitwise in parallel whether both contents are equal; this comparison can be masked again by the content of the mask register via the OR unit. If after a read operation the contents of an unmasked bit position in the SAR and in the MDR are not equal, a comparison error signal is generated (see Fig. 5.7).

By use of these two elements, for an associative memory access, instantaneous detection for a large class of memory malfunctions is achieved.

Moreover, to detect more complex faults that cannot be checked instantaneously during memory operation, additional detailed test procedures were described. Based on a detailed reliability model, different strategies to handle detected faults by

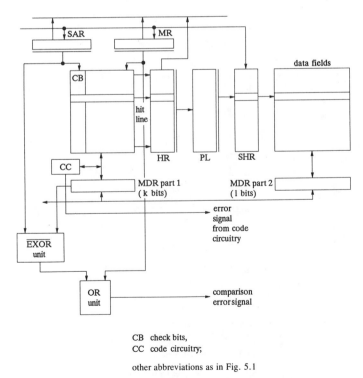

CB check bits,
CC code circuitry;

other abbreviations as in Fig. 5.1

Figure 5.7. *Fault-tolerant and easily testable CAM.*

means of reconfiguration, were compared and evaluated. The developed architecture was implemented by a prototype VLSI chip.

In a subsequent publication, Mazumder and Patel developed tests especially for pattern sensitive faults in dynamic CAMs [8].

Fault Tolerance in Orthogonal Memory Structures.   Faults in the basic components of the orthogonal memory (e.g., cells, decoders) do not differ from well known RAM faults. The question arises, however, how such faults can be detected and handled in the case of the bit slice mode, that is, writing or reading an entire bit slice.

For the detection of errors in a bit slice caused by internal cell faults, of course, the bit slice can be augmented by extra check bits of a coding scheme. Together with ''longitudinal'' check bits utilized for the word cell access mode, these ''transversal'' check bits enable a detailed location and correction of simple cell faults (see Fig. 5.8).

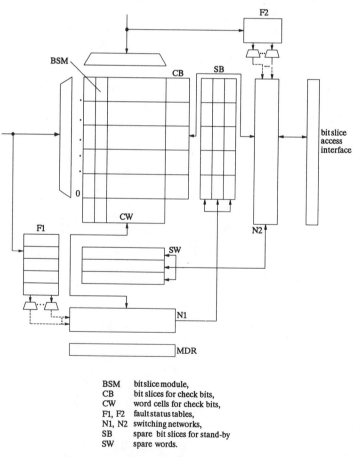

BSM	bit slice module,
CB	bit slices for check bits,
CW	word cells for check bits,
F1, F2	fault status tables,
N1, N2	switching networks,
SB	spare bit slices for stand-by
SW	spare words.

Figure 5.8.   Fault-tolerant orthogonal memory.

To increase the flexibility with regard to the number of tolerable faults, a combination of coding schemes with stand-by strategies appears reasonable. Therefore, in addition to a two-dimensional coding scheme, Grosspietsch [9] considered a standby technique to replace defective memory cells by intact ones. A dynamic switching scheme is proposed where the hardware structure of the basic cell array is left totally unchanged. Reconfiguration is performed by two networks situated at the word access interface and at the bit slice access interface, respectively (see Fig. 5.7). For every access in one of the two access modes, the corresponding network is dynamically switched dependent on fault status information held outside the memory array. This information is stored in two tables which—redundantly—store the fault status of the memory array.

A detailed discussion of this standby technique can also be found in the survey paper by Sarrazin and Malek [10]. With regard to implementation of the scheme, a VLSI chip that combines the necessary interface logic for one memory dimension was presented by Grosspietsch, Muhlack, Paap, and Wagner [11]; this chip structure might also be used as a building block for the two-dimensional reconfiguration scheme.

Fault-Tolerance in the Associative Random Access Memory. Unlike with classical CAMs, with this memory the following fault problems arise:

> The storage of a bit pattern is always fixed to a certain physical location given by the pattern. So, in case of a cell fault it is not sufficient to simply reload the fault-coincident bit from outside to some other cell. Instead, a reinterpretation of the physical memory address has to be performed in some way.

> Compared with the hardware needed for the cells of the memory bit slice, the decoder cannot be neglected any more as a source of failure. Most of the faults in the output gates of the decoder render only the associated memory cell inoperable whereas, for example, a stuck-at fault in an input gate A_0, $\cdots$, A_{2m-1} affects exactly half of the entire memory.

To treat faults the effect of which is confined to individual cells, a simple special checker/reconfiguration circuit was designed and implemented by Glaeser and Steinhausen [12].

5.2.2 Associative Processor Systems

Kohonen [13] defined the notion ''associative (content addressable) processor'' as follows:

> A content addressable processor (CAP) is
>
> 1. A content addressable memory in which more sophisticated data transformations can be performed on the contents of a number of cells selected according to their contents, or
> 2. A computer system that uses such memory as an essential component for storage or processing

In the following, according to this distinction, we shall try to classify the existing approaches.

Processor Systems Built around CAMs

Early Approaches   The use of such processor systems was already investigated in the early times of computer science in the fifties and sixties. Probably the most well known early approach for building an associative processor system was the STARAN computer developed by K. Batcher [4]. This system used a memory with access capabilities similar to those of Kokubu's orthogonal memory [3]: Apart from normal word access, also access to entire word slices was possible. Moreover, there were also access features between these two extremes: In a mixed mode, a regular diagonal pattern of bit groups was accessible throughout the memory. Good surveys about further approaches of that "early" time can be found in the book of Foster [14], and in the survey papers of Thurber and Wald [15], or of Yau and Fung [16]. These approaches could usually not be transferred to the market because of high hardware costs.

CAMs for Artificial Intelligence Applications.   Several approaches were recently reported to develop application-specific architectures of CAMs, for example, for the support of artificial intelligence features.

Kogge et al. [17] developed a CAM that is tailored to specific artificial intelligence applications. These applications employ the use of some form of if-then-rule-programming. Languages that mainly use production rules imply that data are compared against "if" parts until the arguments are satisfied. The "then" parts usually indicate how the database has to be changed. Other more deductive languages (e.g., Prolog) perform matches between a goal (the truth value of which is usually not known) and the "then" part of a rule.

A VLSI coprocessor together with a CAM was developed to work as a hardware accelerator for such tasks. A 10-transistor CAM bit cell is used which, with regard to needed cell area, is comparable to the cell of Wade and Sodini [18]. It turned out that for the applications considered, the flexible cascading of CAM chips is especially essential. This is necessary both in terms of using additional words and of increasing the word length. In the approach, the basic word length is 32 bits. Extensions of this data word length are implemented by using an additional counter field of five bits in each word. This field encodes 32 different positions in a larger extended data set. So, the efficient word length can be varied between 32 bits and $32 * 32 = 1024$ bits.

Several schemes were demonstrated for using this CAM-oriented architecture for tasks such as variable binding, heap processing, or clause filtering. The host processor of the system is a normal RISC-like processor. The merits of the architecture were demonstrated by several benchmark examples, partially showing very large processing speedups.

As another example of such work, Ng, Glover, and Chung [19] especially considered the problem of variable binding. In their approach, fact clauses as well as rule clauses are stored in a CAM. To maximize the speed of variable bindings, strategies were elaborated to replace in parallel the variable contents of all matching expressions with their bound value; this is performed directly when the match is detected, not only when the variables are transferred to a special "bindings stack" as in former architectures for functional languages. Different special CAM bit cells were investigated, and a special 10-transistor CAM cell resulted.

The so-called pattern addressable memory (PAM) by Robinson [20] also uses SIMD processor parallelism together with a memory that is content addressable via hardwired pattern matching. The basic bit cell is a simple 3-transistor dynamic RAM cell, together with a comparator element formed by six transistors. The prototype PAM chip comprises 1152 20-bit words, thus enabling (together with tag bits and additional markers) an effective chip capacity of about 32 k bits.

Another interesting approach for building processing logic around a CAM was presented by the GLiTCH ("Goes Like the Clapper, Hopefully") approach of Duller et al. [21]; it is mainly to support vision processing. A GLiTCH chip contains 64 processing elements, each with 68 bits local CAM. Operations in a processing element are performed bit-serially by means of a simple ALU. Routing of data from the local CAM bit cells to the ALUs is performed by using the hit line: A search pattern consisting of a 1 in one bit position and "don't cares" elsewhere, causes each CAM word which in that position also stores a 1, to send a hit signal 1 to its ALU, or 0 (i.e., nonhit) elsewhere. The hit is stored in a tag register of the ALU. The contents of this tag register can be shifted to other ALUs. So, operations between data fields in adjacent or distant processing elements can be programmed. This is achieved by means of a 32-bit wide interchip data communication path. Transfer between this path and the local chips is controlled by programmable logic assigned to each CAM chip.

Associative Mass Memory Systems.   With regard to the storage of large amounts of data, in addition to the hardware costs of the mentioned CAM approaches there are two other essential limitations:

- The memory must be loaded before it can be used for search operation
- The fixed size of the array also implies a fixed comparison length, and special efforts are necessary to change such a format if once selected

Therefore, it was also proposed to perform the desired search operation directly at the interface between main memory and slower background mass memory media like disk or tape. Such methods employ the concept of "logic per track" that is, comparison circuits are added to the read/write heads of disks or comparable media, and the checking for equivalence with search patterns is carried out "on the fly" when a stream of mass data is transferred toward the main memory. On the basis of this concept, a number of "search engines" was developed. One of the major research developments was the SURE ("Such–Rechner") system developed at the University of Braunschweig. A recent paper by Zeidler [22] describes this system, within a general survey of existing approaches.

Very recently Lun Lee and Lochovsky [23] described an approach for a text retrieval machine HYTREM for large data bases, which employs associative processing. It uses a signature file that compresses the text pattern of a large data base; typically this file comprises about 10 to 20 percent of the size of the entire data base. HYTREM contains two major subsystems: a signature processor, which compares a preprocessed search pattern against the signature file, and a pattern matcher, which has to eliminate false hits caused by considering only the compressed data.

Another high speed search machine was developed by Yamada et al. [24] (see Fig. 5.9). Besides processing logic, it uses a special 8-k CAM. The CAM has a

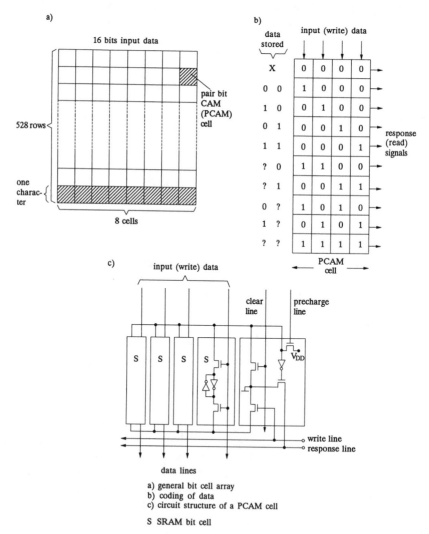

a) general bit cell array
b) coding of data
c) circuit structure of a PCAM cell

S SRAM bit cell

Figure 5.9. *Pair bit CAM cell (according to Yamada et al. [24]).*

capacity of 528 characters in a 16-bit character code. The CAM cell for storing one character consists of eight pair bit CAM (PCAM) cells. This PCAM cell is composed of four conventional RAM bit cells and some hit logic. A PCAM cell can store one out of ten different bit patterns, representing, for example, the four different combinations of two stored bits $(0/0, 0/1, 1/0, 1/1)$, in addition to "don't care" and "cleared" states.

Unorthodox Approaches. Tavangarian [6] generalized the concept of flag-oriented CAMs described in the section on ARAM, from search operations to the processing of data. The operands of these generalized operations are flags. Initially, a number of w-bit data is compressed into one 2^w bit wide flag vector. By extension of the mentioned ARAM structure, several of these flag vectors can be memorized. Moreover, they can be processed efficiently (often in parallel) by appropriate Boolean functions. A complete flag algebra of processing operations has been described. It consists of operations like forming the union or intersection of flag vectors, checking for equivalence or antivalence between the vectors.

Massively Parallel Processing Logic with Associative Features

LUCAS Approach. Fernstrom, Kruzela, and Svensson [25] at the University of Lund developed a bit-sequential, word-parallel associative processor system called LUCAS (Lund University Content Addressable System). Here, the CAM words are very long (4096 bits word length), and to each word a 1-bit ALU is associated (see Fig. 5.10). In hardware, the memory word was very simply realized by ordinary 4-k RAM chips. The entire search process was implemented by transferring the memory content—bit slice by bit slice—to the ALU slice. Here, the bits of a bit slice are compared in parallel with one bit of the given search pattern.

The advantage of this architecture was its easy implementation by already existing hardware building blocks. The trade-off was the (often awkward) bit slice—

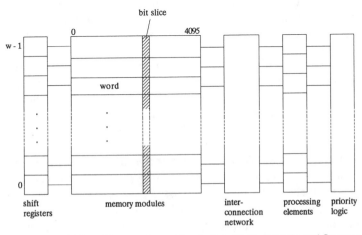

Figure 5.10. *LUCAS architecture (according to Fernstrom, Kruzela and Svensson [25]).*

sequential organization of data processing and even of simple retrieval operations. In their book, the authors also developed a set of benchmark examples for evaluating the time complexity of basic application tasks for CAMs.

ASP. One of the most promising approaches of recent years for general purpose associative systems is the ASP developed by Lea [26] at Brunel University. The ASP system is a dynamically reconfigurable structure of communicating ASP processor substrings. Each of these substrings can communicate with the other substrings via a data buffer ADB and a corresponding communication network (see Fig. 5.11). Each substring comprises a set of identical associative processing elements (APEs, see also Fig. 5.11). Each APE consists of

An *n*-bit data register
An *a*-bit activity register
An *n* + *a*-bit parallel comparator
A single bit full adder and four status flags

As a basic building block, a 256-APE VLSI chip was realized.

CAPRA. Another recent approach by Grosspietsch [27, 28] tries to combine the ideas especially of Lea [26], of Tavangarian [5, 6], and of Waldschmidt [29]. It extends these solutions especially with regard to the following objectives:

• Increase the flexibility of the logic elements
• Combine processor cell arrays with ordinary CAM and RAM parts

This is achieved by inclusion of the new features in an existing RAM structure. RAM, CAM and a content addressable processor/register array (CAPRA) together form a kind of storage hierarchy where the main part can consist of an ordinary RAM (see Fig. 5.12). The additional ''smarter'' components are included as additional memory segments within one uniform physical memory space; their individual capacities can arbitrarily be tailored to the specific needs of the application.

Compatibility between these steps of a hierarchy is achieved in the sense that smarter parts also provide the full functionality of the simpler ones. So, the CAM parts are requested also to be operable as RAMs; the CAPRA is implemented by some functional extension of the CAM architecture.

In Section 5.3, this approach will be discussed in more detail.

Fault Tolerance in Associative Processor Systems. Relatively early, fault tolerance properties of associative processor arrays were investigated. An initial paper of Parhami and Avizienis [30] discussed general strategies and presented, as a case study, the evaluation of a fault tolerant associative processor system by means of modularization and providing spare modules. Subsequent approaches for associative processor arrays usually also comprised some strategy for either gracea)

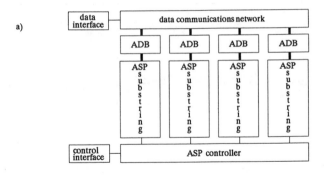

b)

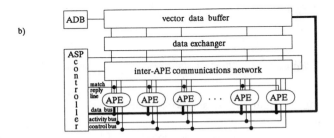

c)

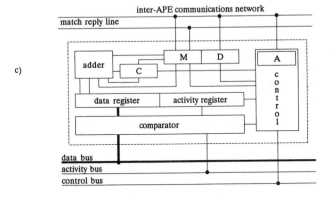

ASP architecture (according to Lea)

a) general structure
b) structure of an ASP substring
c) structure of an APE

ADB   associative data buffer
APE   associative processing element
ASP   associative substring of processing elements
A,C,D,M carry and status flipflops

Figure 5.11. *ASP architecture (according to Lea [26]).*

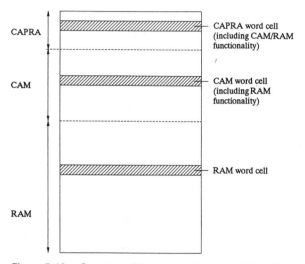

Figure 5.12. *Structure of the proposed memory hierarchy.*

fully degrading faulty arrays by shrinking their size, or by providing spare columns/spare rows.

Relatively little work, however, has been devoted to the area of detailed architecture oriented diagnostic tests for associative processor systems. A recent study was performed by Grosspietsch [9].

5.3 THE PROPOSED APPROACH

5.3.1 Basic Principles and Requirements

For the CAPRA approach, the following architectural properties were felt promising to support more flexible use of content addressable memory/processor systems:

Extension of the usual very simple hit mechanisms of present CAM implementations (equivalence between data, potentially modified by some kind of masking) to more flexible, sophisticated hit evaluation (e.g., by thresholds for the number of equivalent bits, similarity metrics between search pattern and data in storage).

With relatively low hardware effort, extension of the usual comparison logic of a CAM cell to provide an entire set of one bit Boolean operations.

Extension of arithmetics elements from sequential one bit adder elements per word cell to at least 4-bit adder elements.

Features for fully parallel input of data to all bit cells.

Multiaccess features with regard to memory cells and with respect to activation of ALUs.

As a very general example of the cooperative use of CAM and CAPRA parts, consider the case of a parallel programming task where updating and change of sets or arrays of data is to be carried out, and where the control flow is mainly governed by the outcome of checking sets of variables for common properties. This general problem can be elegantly handled by a segment of "intelligent" CAPRA words and a (potentially larger) CAM segment.

The architectural features described nevertheless fit into the usual programming paradigms of the von Neumann machine, the control flow. Therefore, integration of the discussed structure into a conventional system can easily be performed; the architecture introduced is planned to work as a coprocessor of a conventional processor; the instructions of this coprocessor can modularly be added to that of a main processor.

5.3.2 The Resulting Architecture

Our approach specified in general in Section 5.2.1. has the following detail features:

The CAM also has an additional RAM access mode so that it can, for example, be loaded or read like ordinary RAM cells.

In the CAPRA (see Fig. 5.13), as the base cells we again have RAM bit cells. Moreover, to every bit cell a simple logic block is associated, which enables Boolean one-bit operations between two 1-bit operands; this implements bit-parallel and word-parallel execution of a Boolean operation on all words of the CAPRA.

To every word cell in the CAPRA, a simple four-bit arithmetic unit is assigned; so, an arithmetic operation can be performed on all the, for example, 32-bit words of the CAPRA segment in parallel in about eight cycles. The unit size of four bits was chosen mainly because

1. such a restricted ALU size keeps the additional hardware effort, with regard to the extended bit cell, in acceptable limits (the ALU part of a CAPRA word of 32 bits increases the word cell area by about 30 percent)

2. on the other hand, four bits is a natural unit in many pixel oriented applications (coding 16 different grey levels)

Adjacent ALUs are connected by a 4-bit data path so that they can exchange their contents with their upper or lower neighbor ALU.

An additional flag bit is associated with each bit cell of the CAPRA; this enables us to define flexibly arbitrary "activity patterns" for the cells of the array; so it is possible to process data not only on all processor elements, but also on a previously defined arbitrary subpattern of processing elements. In the same way, every 4-bit ALU comprises an activity flag bit ALUF.

An optical transistor together with a simple sense amplifier and an elementary analog/digital converter is integrated into the CAPRA bit cell. Therefore,

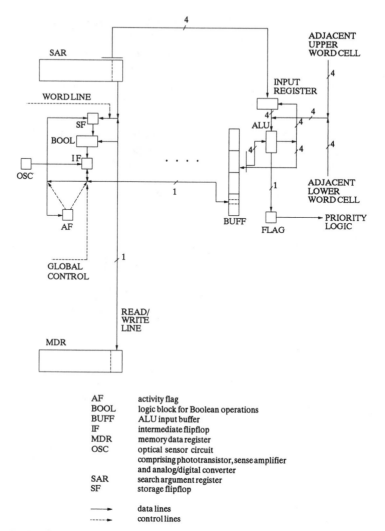

AF	activity flag
BOOL	logic block for Boolean operations
BUFF	ALU input buffer
IF	intermediate flipflop
MDR	memory data register
OSC	optical sensor circuit
	comprising phototransistor, sense amplifier
	and analog/digital converter
SAR	search argument register
SF	storage flipflop
——▶	data lines
------▶	control lines

Figure 5.13.   *Scheme of a one-bit storage cell and a one-bit ALU within a CAPRA word cell.*

analog optical input can be digitized and written into the bit cells of CAPRA in parallel. Thus for certain applications, with regard to the input of data from peripheral devices, the normal narrow bottleneck of von Neumann machines (input only word by word) is removed.

For the RAM access, a simple extension of the memory decoder is provided by means of an additional mask register. This extended (masked) decoder, which was proposed by Tavangarian for a special associative memory of 1-bit word length (see also the section on the ARAM memory), is here applied to more general memory/processor structures: By setting bits of this mask register to 1, an arbitrary part of the address bits can be declared to be "don't care" bits; thus, it is possible to implement concurrent access to word cells which in their addresses have common address bit subpatterns (see again Fig. 5.6). In the word cells, this access mode can be utilized for multiwrite operations, that is, to input the same data value into a set of word cells simultaneously instead of only one. Moreover, the same mechanism can be used to write the same value into the activity flag ALUF of all the ALUs of the accessed word set.

Apart from the write operation mentioned, RAM and CAM parts have the classical functionality of these components, so they will not be described here in more detail. Therefore, in the following section, we shall confine the discussion to the most innovative part of our architecture, the CAPRA.

5.3.3 Operation of the CAPRA

The operation of the CAPRA structure is as follows (see Fig. 5.14): Data can be written into a word cell—controlled by the corresponding word line emanating from the memory decoder—via the MDR and read/write lines. For every bit of a word cell, its content stored in the storage flip-flop *SF* can be combined with the content of the read/write line by a Boolean operation in the functional block BOOL;

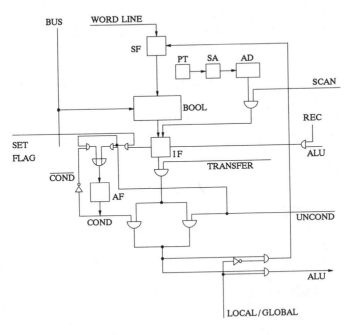

AD analog/digital converter,
PT phototransistor,
SA sense amplifier

Figure 5.14. *Logic structure of a CAPRA bit cell.*

the result of this operation is latched in the intermediate flipflop IF. From there it can be propagated further (control line TRANSFER in Fig. 5.14) either to the adjacent ALU (line GLOBAL/LOCAL = 1) or to be memorized in the storage flip-flop *SF* (GLOBAL/LOCAL = 0). These transfers are performed either unconditionally (control line UNCOND = 1) or dependent on the status of the cell that is memorized in the activity flag *AF* (control line COND = 1, if *AF* stores a 1). As a third sink for the bit transfer from the intermediate flip-flop *IF*, setting of the activity flag is possible (control line SET FLAG). This is performed either unconditionally (control line UNCOND = 1) or dependent on the present status of *AF* (control line $\overline{\text{COND}}$ = 1); in the latter case, setting of *AF* is possible only if *AF* has not yet been set, that is, if *AF* is storing a 0 (control line $\overline{\text{COND}}$ then equals 1).

The intermediate flip-flop may not only receive a data bit from the functional block BOOL, but, alternatively, also from the adjacent ALU (control line REC = 1) or from the optical sensor circuit (control line SCAN = 1).

At transistor level, the extended bit cell can be realized by about 80 transistor functions, that is, about 10 times the number of transistor functions of a conventional static RAM bit cell. This number seems to be still within manageable limits.

5.4 ELEMENTARY OPERATIONS AND PROGRAMMING

5.4.1 Elementary Operations

For the memory structure described we defined the following set of operations:

a. RAM operations

WRITE, ADR; /Normal RAM write raccess (executable in all system parts)

READ, ADR; / Normal RAM read access

MWRITE, ADR, MASK;/Masked RAM write access: multiple access to a set of word cells in memory that have some address subpattern in common

b. CAM operations

LOAD, SAR, SPATTERN; /Load an arbitrary search pattern SPATTERN into the search argument register SAR of the CAM part

ASSOCOMP; /Word-parallel and bit-parallel comparison of the contents of word cells with a predefined search pattern (executable in the CAM and in the CAPRA part)

c. CAPRA operations

c1. bit cell operations

BOOLOP$_i$; /Boolean operation combining the bits of the memory word
- with the bits of an external operand on the read/write lines. The index i ($i = 1, \cdots, 16$) represents the ith operation of the 16 classical Boolean functions of two 1-bit operands

SCAN; /Transfers digitized input from the optical sensors of all bit cells to the intermediate flip-flops *IF*

STORE, $\begin{Bmatrix} \text{COND} \\ \text{UNCOND} \end{Bmatrix}$; /Stores in the storage flip-flops *SF* the content of

the corresponding intermediate flip-flop *IF* either unconditionally (i.e., for all bit cells in the CAPRA) or conditionally (i.e., depending on the local activity flags *AF* of each bit cell)

SET_AF, $\begin{Bmatrix} \text{COND} \\ \text{UNCOND} \end{Bmatrix}$; /Transfers the contents of the intermediate flip-

flop *IF* into the activity flag either unconditionally or conditionally (i.e., only for those bit cells where AF = FALSE)

c2. ALU operations

The ALU operations in the CAPRA can be grouped into two classes:

unconditional ALU operations

conditional ALU operations

Operations of the second class exactly correspond to those of the first class except that they are executed in a local ALU if and only if the activity flag ALUF of this ALU is set to TRUE. The unconditional operations all have the structure

$$
\text{ALU\_OP, BUFFER(j),} \begin{Bmatrix} \text{SAR} \\ \text{REGA} \\ \text{REGB} \\ \text{BUFFER} \end{Bmatrix}, \begin{Bmatrix} \text{BUFFER(j)} \\ \text{REGA} \end{Bmatrix}.
$$

The first operand BUFFER(j) is always a 4-bit sector within the intermediate flip-flops *IF* of all memory words; the position of this segment is given by the index *j*. As the second operand, we may use either the register REGA, REGB, REGC, or SAR. REGA is a 4-bit register corresponding to each ALU in the words of the CAPRA. REGB and REGC simply represent the REGA register of the upper (lower) neighbor ALU. Alternatively, the least significant four bits of the SAR can be used to provide one global 4-bit operand to all the ALUs of the CAPRA.

So, by selection of the second operand, it is possible to combine an operand held in a memory word either with local data residing in the corresponding ALU, or in one of its neighbors (thus enabling communication between neighbors), or with a global operand provided from outside.

The ALU operations are executed either unconditionally in all word cells of the CAPRA or conditionally, controlled by the local ALU flags ALUF. The setting of these flags is performed dependent either on the outcome of certain ALU operations (as usual also in conventional ALUs) or is explicitly carried out from outside. For the latter purpose we have the additional operation

SET_ALU_FLAG, ADR, MASK.

This operation provides (similarly to the masked write operation MWRITE) access to the activity flags ALUF in one or several ALUs, in one cycle.

5.4.2 Elementary Macros and Programming

Based on the introduced machine instruction set, a number of elementary macros have been defined. They are to implement operations that comprise several machine instructions, but represent standard operations for various applications. In addition, to illustrate the programming features especially of the CAPRA, we shall address here two simple examples:

1. The marking of arbitrary bit slices in a set of words the addresses of which have some bits in common is seen in Figure 5.15. The basic idea of this macro is

MARK BIT CELLS / For a set of words given by a common address subpattern,
      mark a selected bit position in the word by setting the activity flags
      AF to 1. BUFFER(i) represents the i'th 4 bit sector of intermediate
      flipflops in the CAPRA words.
SET_ALU_FLAG, 00..00, 11.10; / Activate the ALUs of all even words by
      setting the activity flag of the ALU.
FOR i: = 1 TO 8 DO
   BEGIN
   LOAD, SAR, FOURBITS; / Load 4 mark bits.
   ALUF_TRANS_R_OP,   , SAR, BUFFER (i); / Transfer mark bits to the
      intermediate flipflops IF via the ALUs. The ALU operation routes the
      second ('right') operand without change through the ALU and neglects
      the first operand. The operation is carried out only for ALUs with
      activity flag ALUF = 1.
   END;
SET_AF, COND / Final storage in activity flags of bit cells:
      (UNCOND); / 'Incremental' or 'instantaneous' marking.

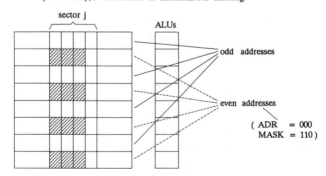

Macro MARK BIT CELLS; as an example, marking of some bit positions
positions in all words with even address is shown.

Example: j'th four bit group from SAR is 1110: The shaded areas represent
the resulting activated bit cells (activity flag AF=1)

Figure 5.15. *Macro* MARK BIT CELLS.

the following: First, the desired word set is activated by one masked addressing of the ALU activity flags ALUF in the word cells of this set. Therefore, the mask parameter exactly has to contain those bits as "1s" ("don't care" bits), which characterize the position of words inside the set. As an example, let us consider the addressing of all even address word cells. To do so, all decoder mask bits except the least significant bit are set to 1; the address ADR is set to 0. By setting the activity flags of the ALUs in the addressed words, the corresponding ALUs are activated. Via these ALUs, a pattern of n bits is routed to all intermediate flip-flops of the word set. This pattern of 1s or 0s marks which of the n bit positions within the addressed words are to be activated. Routing of the pattern has to be performed in units of four bits; so, for example, for a CAPRA word length $n = 32$ bits, eight iterations are necessary. From the ALUs these activity bits are finally stored in the activity flags of the bit cells.

With regard to that, we can distinguish two possible kinds of memorizing: By an unconditional SET__AF operation, the entire old activity status of the addressed word set is destroyed and newly inscribed. On the contrary, the conditional SET__AF operation stores 1s only in those cells that have not yet been set to 1; so here an old 1 value is not destroyed. Therefore, this marking shall be called an "incremental" marking, in contrast to the "immediate" marking of the first way.

The sketched macro enables routing of flexible activity patterns into the bit cells in a few cycles.

2. Another important standard operation needed for neighborhood related operations, as well as data shuffles, is the exchange of the word contents between all pairs of adjacent word cells in memory. To illustrate that, Figure 5.16 shows a macro EXCHANGE, which implements the exchange between words with an odd address and their lower neighbor (exchange with their upper neighbor can be re-

```
EXCHANGE
/ Exchange of the contents of the words with odd address with their next
lower neighbour; BUFFER (i) represents the i'th 4 bit group of intermediate
flipflops in a CAPRA word


BOOL TRANS SF; / Transfer memory contents to intermediate flipflops by
               the Boolean operation BOOL TRANSF SF (transfers SF
               contents to IFs).
FOR i:1 TO 8 DO
    BEGIN
    ALU_TRANS_L_OP, BUFFER (i),    , REGA; / Transfer of first (' left ')
               operand (i.e. BUFFER (i) ) to REGA via ALU.
    SET_ALU_FLAG, 0...0, 11..110; / Sets the activity flag in all
               ALUs with even word address.
    ALUF_TRANS_R_OP,    , REGB, BUFFER (i); / Upper word's 4 bit
               sector into buffer of next lower neighbour.
    SET_ALU_FLAG, 0...001, 11..110; / Activate every ALU which has
               odd address.
    ALUF_TRANS_R_OP,    , REGC, BUFFER (i); / Lower neighbour's
               4 bit sector into buffer flipflops of higher neighbour.
    END;
STORE, UNCOND; / Contents of intermediate flipflops to word cells.
```

Figure 5.16. Macro EXCHANGE.

alized by a similar macro). This exchange is performed sequentially in groups of four bits, as this is the data width of the ALU interconnections. In all words of the CAPRA, 4-bit sectors are routed to the ALU input register REGA (see Fig. 5.16). Then, first the ALUs with even addresses are activated by a masked addressing of their activity flags; these ALUs route a 4-bit sector from their upper neighbor to their own intermediate flip-flop. Subsequently, the odd address ALUs are activated and take a 4-bit sector from their lower neighbor ALU. So, the bits of one sector have been exchanged between the two adjacent words. For exchanging words of a typical CAPRA word length of 32 bits, evidently these steps must be performed eight times in a loop. Finally, all 4-bit groups reside in the intermediate flip-flops of their neighbor word cell. From there, they are then memorized in the storage flip-flops by an unconditional store operation STORE, UNCOND.

5.5 APPLICATION FIELDS

To illustrate the various application fields of the CAPRA, in the following we shall discuss four different application examples:

- Data base support
- Image pixel processing
- Emulation of Petri nets
- Emulation of neural nets

5.5.1 Data Base Support

Associative processing is well known to be especially useful for applications where data are either set structured or array structured. Such set like data organization is found, for example, in database applications, so this field has always been one of the principal applications of associative processing. In the following, we shall illustrate the benefits of our CAPRA approach by considering the classical operations in relational data bases: selection, intersection, difference, union, semijoin and join. As a comparison, we thereby refer to the investigation of Fernstrom, Kruzela, and Svensson [25].

As the basic elements of the database, we consider records of data, that is, ordered tuples of data items. Sets of such records (often also called relations) are represented by tables of records. The mentioned relational operations work on either one or two of such tables as input set operands, producing a third table as the result. Let us call the source relations A and B. Moreover, without loss of generality it is assumed that A contains more data records than B; that is, for the cardinalities NA and NB of A and B we have the condition $NA \geq NB$. Correspondingly, LA and LB denote the bit lengths of the records of relations A and B.

In our CAPRA approach, a record is stored either in one n-bit word or (as the usual case, if the record contains more than n bits) in a number of consecutive words in memory. So, associative checking of the records of relation A or B can be performed in $\lceil LA/n \rceil$ or $\lceil LB/n \rceil$ ($\lceil x \rceil$ denoting the smallest integer $\geq x$)

cycles. It is not necessary to store a table, that is, a set of records, in a segment of consecutive data words. Instead, in an associative system, it is possible to characterize the members of the set by some common properties, namely, values of some items or a common mark bit. The simplest relational data base operation is the selection: This operation selects a subset of the given set A of tuples; the resulting subset comprises those records which for one (or several) tuple items obey certain search criteria. So, in CAPRA this operation can be carried out by a simple associative check that compares the values of these tuple fields with a search pattern in the SAR; hits are memorized by setting a new mark bit in the data record. Thus, the entire select operation can be carried out by $\lceil LA/n \rceil$ ASSOCOMP operations; then in one cycle, a mark bit is written into all records found.

The intersection operation processes two input relations A and B; its result is a subset of one of these relations. This subset consists of those records that belong to both relations. In the CAPRA, this operation is performed by reading out the records of the smaller second relation B, one by one. The records of the first table are associatively compared with such a record of relation B, and hits are noted in the first table. So the entire selection takes a number of cycles of the order $\lceil LA/n \rceil * NB$.

Correspondingly, the difference operation generates a subset of the first relation consisting of all tuples that do not belong to the second relation. Here all records in the first relation are marked where the associative comparison has produced no hit. This can simply be performed by transferring the hit signal of the ASSOCOMP operation into the corresponding ALU and inverting it there. Obviously, the difference operation takes the same time complexity $O(\lceil LA/n \rceil * NB)$ as the intersection operation.

The union operation adds to the first relation all records of the second relation that are not contained in the first one. Here, first in one cycle, the members of the first relation are all marked to also belong to the result relation; subsequently, the members of the second relation B one by one are associatively compared with all of the first relation A. Apparently, again the same time complexity as for the intersection and the difference operation results.

The product operation generates the Cartesian product of two relations. On a sequential von Neumann architecture as well as in the bit-sequential, word-parallel LUCAS approach of Fernstrom, Kruzela, and Svensson [25], this operation has a time complexity of $O(NA * NB)$, where NA and NB again represent the cardinalities of both input relations. In the CAPRA approach, this time complexity can be considerably reduced at the expense of increasing the set cardinalities to the smallest powers of 2 which are $\geq NA$ ($\geq NB$); let us call them NA' and NB'. Then producing the concatenated pairs of data records can be performed in a very efficient way in time complexity $O(\lceil LB/n \rceil * NA' + \lceil LA/n \rceil * NB')$: As shown in Figure 5.17, in one cycle NB', copies of a data word of the first relation are produced by a masked write access. These masked write operations are performed for all members of the first relation. Then, correspondingly, with a changed mask, NA' copies of all the members of the second relation are produced in $NA' * \lceil LB/n \rceil$ masked write operations. Thus, compared to the other mentioned com-

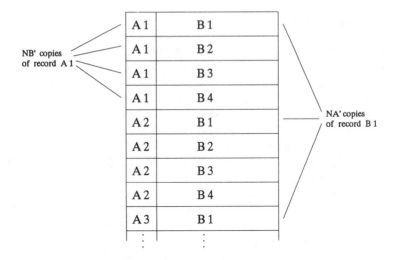

Generation of cartesian products of records by means of masked write operations:

A1, A2, ... records of relation A
B1, B2, ... records of relation B

Figure 5.17. *Generation of Cartesian products of records by means of masked write operations.*

puter architectures, time complexity is reduced by a factor of about *NB* at the expense of a memory space capacity of the order $O(NA' * NB')$; this, however, seems justified as the cost of memory is falling drastically.

As a characteristic example of the semijoin operation, in the study of Fernstrom, Kruzela, and Svensson [25] two relations are considered, one with attributes *g* and *h*, the second one with attribute *h*. The resulting relation is a subset of the first relation, consisting of tuples where the value of the attribute *h* is the same as *some* value of attribute *h* in the second relation. This can be solved by sequentially taking the members of relation *B* and associatively checking it with relation *A*. Apparently, this takes a time complexity of $O(\lceil LA/n \rceil * NB)$.

The join operation is similar to the semijoin, but matching tuples are concatenated, thereby removing the joining attribute. For the CAPRA, we propose to solve this operation in the following way:

1. Scan sequentially through the *NB* tuples of relation *B*, marking in relation *B* to which tuple of relation *A* a match is occurring
2. Form the Cartesian product of the tuples of relations *A* and *B* by $\lceil LB/n \rceil * NA' + \lceil LA/n \rceil * NB'$ masked write operations as described previously
3. Remove tuples not marked as having matched in phase 1 by setting an "invalid" bit
4. From the remaining tuples, remove the attribute to be erased by simply setting another invalid bit in the subfield containing that attribute.

Operation	vNA	LUCAS	CAPRA
Selection	$O(NB)$	$O(10*LB)$	$O(\lceil LA/n \rceil)$
Intersection	$O(NA*NB)$	$O(30*LB*NB)$	$O(\lceil LA/n \rceil *NB)$
Difference	$O(NA*NB)$	$O(30*LB*NB)$	$O(\lceil LA/n \rceil *NB)$
Union	$O(NB)$	$O(30*LB*NB)$	$O(\lceil LA/n \rceil *NB)$
Production	$O(NA*NB)$	$O(22*LB*NA*NB)$	$O(\lceil LB/n \rceil *NA' + \lceil LA/n \rceil *NB')$
Semi-join	$O(NA*NB)$	$O(30\ LB*NB)$	$O(\lceil LA/n \rceil *NB)$
Join	$O(NA*NB)$	$O(48*b'*Z)$	$O(\lceil LB/n \rceil *NA' + \lceil LA/n \rceil *NB')$

Orders O of execution times of typical relational data base operations at the CAPRA, compared with the sequential von Neuman architecture (vNA) and the bit-sequential, word-parallel LUCAS approach (as analyzed by Fernstrom, Kruzela and Svensson). The CAPRA word length is assumed to be 11 bits.

For reasons of simpler representation in the table, the time complexity of the vNA is estimated only roughly. Considering the usual case of records of more than one data word, NA has to be replaced by $NA * \lceil LA/n \rceil$, and NB has to be replaced by $NB * \lceil LB/n \rceil$.

b'	bit length of join attribute
LA, LB	bit length of relation A and B
NA, NB	cardinality (i.e. number of tuples) of relation A and B
NA', NB'	smallest power of 2 which is $\geq NA$, ($\geq NB$)
Z	number of different values in the join attribute of first relation

Figure 5.18. *Orders of execution times of typical data base operations at the CAPRA, compared with the sequential von Neuman architecture (vNA) and the bit-sequential, word-parallel LUCAS approach.*

Figure 5.18 again shows the resulting time complexities of data base operations for the CAPRA architecture in comparison with the von Neumann architecture and the LUCAS approach. It can be seen that the use of CAPRA implies considerable performance gains.

5.5.2 Support for Pixel Processing

One of the standard basic operations for pixel processing is the comparison of the a pixel point with its four or eight nearest neighbors. In the CAPRA, this can be solved as follows (see Fig. 5.19): In a first phase, to compare a bit j in word cell i with its left and right neighbor $j - 1$ and $j + 1$, the ALU of word cell i has to bring three bits from its own word cell. This operation and the subsequent comparison of the bits in the ALU can be performed concurrently for all words in the CAPRA. In a second phase, each ALU i (i being either even or odd) must fetch three bits from the bit positions $j - 1$, j, and $j + 1$ of its upper neighbor word cell via ALU $i - 1$, and compare them with bit j of word i still held in ALU i. This operation can be done concurrently for half of the number of words in the CAPRA.

In a third phase, a corresponding procedure is carried out to bring bits from the lower neighbor word cell and to process them in the same way. The pattern of the basic pixels j that are to be compared with their neighborhoods, is sequentially moved over the 32 bit positions of the CAPRA word length.

Additional communication steps are only necessary when edge points in the memory (bits 0 and $n - 1$) are to be compared with their left or right neighbors,

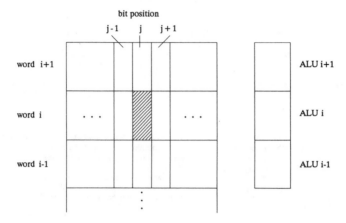

Figure 5.19. *Scheme of a neighborhood comparison for pixel processing.*

respectively. If a pixel array row cannot be placed inside one CAPRA word (this is usually the case), it has to be distributed over several words, as indicated in Figure 5.20. To bring left and right left bit neighbors from the next word, residing in a CAPRA word z words distant, a communication phase by means of z shifts between the ALUs is necessary. This shift operation, however, can be done again concurrently for all z rows of the pixel array.

So, neighborhood comparison in the CAPRA does not depend on the entire number of pixel points in the array, but takes a time complexity of $O(z)$ where z is the number of rows in the pixel array.

5.5.3 Emulation of Petri Nets by the CAPRA Architecture

Petri nets are well known and appreciated modeling and analysis tools for any kind of concurrent systems. They may also be seen as a mathematical low-level formalization of data flow architectures. However, simulation and analysis of Petri nets on conventional sequential computers tends to be slow; speeding up by in-

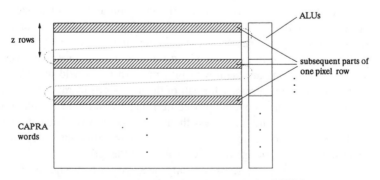

Figure 5.20. *Distribution of pixel points in the CAPRA array.*

herently parallel architectures would here be an ideal solution. We will show in the following that emulation of Petri nets by the CAPRA architecture constitutes interesting progress. Of course, some limitations with regard to data propagation, due to the restricted data exchange mechanism between the CAPRA word cells, still remain. Nevertheless it will turn out that CAPRA provides a considerable speeding up of Petri net execution.

A Petri net is a bipartite graph consisting of two classes of elements, places and transitions. Places are representatives of parts of distributed state conditions. These conditions are encoded by markings of the places with indistinguishable tokens. Transitions represent elementary events (i.e., they are equivalent to state changes). They are enabled (they can "fire") if on all their input places a sufficient number of tokens resides; this number is specified by the weight k of the edge linking the transition to that input place. If a transition fires, it removes from every input place a number of tokens specified by the weight k of the corresponding edge. Similarly, the transition creates new tokens for all its output places; the number of these tokens is given by a weight at the edge leading to that place (see Fig. 5.21).

The basic idea of using the CAPRA architecture for the emulation of Petri nets is to reduce the task to a data base organized approach. Consider a net with k transitions and l places. This net can be emulated by storing in the CAPRA a table that comprises k entries, each representing one transition. Each entry i ($i = 1, \cdots, k$) comprises $2 * l$ subentries and three additional status bits (see Fig. 5.22). For each place j ($j = 1, \cdots l$) of the net there is a subentry $j1$ consisting of the fields I, ANT, and NNT. I (input place) is a mark bit denoting whether place j is an input place of transition i. ANT represents the actual number of tokens that reside on place j; NNT is the necessary number of tokens on place j needed to enable transition i.

In the same way additionally in the entry i for each place there is a subentry characterizing whether this place is an output place of transition i. The subentry consists of a mark bit 0 denoting whether the corresponding place is an output place of transition i, and a field NT (number of token) representing the number of output tokens generated at that output place by the firing of transition i.

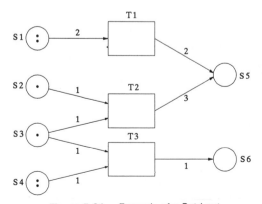

Figure 5.21. *Example of a Petri net.*

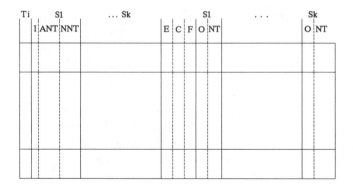

ANT	actual number of tokens
C	status bit 'in potential conflict with other transitions'
E	status bit 'enabled'
F	status bit 'fired'
I	mark bit 'input place'
NNT	necessary number of tokens
NT	number of output tokens
O	mark bit 'output place'
S i	subentry for place i
T i	transition i

Figure 5.22. *Table representation of a Petri net.*

Moreover, in an entry i there are three status bits E, C, and F of transition i. Bit E denotes whether transition i is enabled. C (conflict) represents the case that a transition might be in conflict with at least one other transition (i.e., although both transitions are enabled, they cannot fire concurrently because there are not enough tokens at their input places for firing both together). F is a "fired" bit, set after a firing has been carried out.

Concurrent execution of the Petri net in the CAPRA is performed as follows: The entire table is simultaneously scanned to see whether there are enabled transitions. This is performed by associatively checking all entries as to whether they have $E = 1$ and $C = 0$, that is, whether they are enabled and not in potential conflict with other transitions. This can be carried out in one cycle. All selected entries can fire concurrently; this is emulated as follows: In the corresponding subentries for all input places, the number NNT is subtracted from ANT; E is set to 0, and F set to 1.

If there are enabled transitions with $C = 1$, (let us call their set T'), subsequently each of them is fired sequentially. After each firing of such a transition, for the remaining elements of T', the marking of the input places is updated, and it is checked whether the transitions are still enabled or, instead, must be disabled.

Finally, for all transitions that have fired, the token markings at the output places have to be updated. This is done by reading out the subfields NT of the corresponding entry. To compute the effect of the transitions on a place j ($j = 1$, $\cdots$, l), the values of $NT(j)$ of all entries read out are added together by the main processor outside CAPRA. These cumulated values are then broadcast to all entries i ($i = 1, \cdot \cdot \cdot , k$). Locally, in the entries the values are then added to $ANT(j)$ to update the markings at the input places.

So, the scanning of transitions in the CAPRA takes one cycle, whereas in a sequential computer it has an order of $0(k * f)$, f being the mean number of input places per transition. The recomputing of token markings in the CAPRA needs a time complexity of $0(e)$, where e is the average number of transitions that are concurrently firing. In the sequential computer, for this task we need a time complexity of $0(e * (f + g))$, g being the average number of output places per transition.

5.5.4 Emulation of Neural Nets

In the following, we sketch that the CAPRA architecture also has interesting features as an emulator of neural networks. The basic operations of neural networks (independent of the specific learning model of the net) that could be supported by hardware are

- The multiplication of weights with incoming signals
- The local update of the state function of the nodes and of the weights additionally stored in the nodes
- Routing of data from the output of a node to a (usually large) number of connected nodes

Apart from the development of analog components, in recent years several digital approaches were proposed to either support specific operations of the neural net only or to work as general purpose hardware support for them (see, e.g., the proceedings edited by Delgado-Frias and Moore [31]).

The basic idea of our scheme is to represent the net structure by a data base organized approach. For each node i ($i = 1, \cdot \cdot \cdot , N$) of the neural net, an entry consisting of a segment of adjacent CAPRA words is assigned. In this entry, apart from the internal status of the node, for every node there is a subfield reserved to store potential weights. If the output of node i ($i = 1, \cdot \cdot \cdot , N$) is not connected to node j ($j = 1, \cdot \cdot \cdot , N$), this is simply represented by a 0 in weight subfield j of entry i. By their Boolean and arithmetic units, the words of this CAPRA database have inherently concurrent processing abilities. Thus, local updating of node states and weights can be processed fully in parallel. Moreover, in spite of the restricted interconnection between the ALUs of the CAPRA, this structure exhibits interesting features also with regard to routing: If the output of a node has to be identically distributed to all or to a large fraction of other nodes (e.g., to all input nodes of a next layer in feedforward nets), again the multiwrite access of CAPRA's masked write operation can be applied: The output of a node is read out and, via a masked write, broadcast to all other nodes. These either all store this data unconditionally or, if not logically connected to the input, neglect the data sent to them. So routing of a new output from the N nodes of the net to all nodes takes only N read operations, each followed by one masked write operation. This is much faster than the N^2 communication steps sequentially performed at the von Neumann machine; and on the other side it avoids the vast amount of N^2 physical hardware connections between the N nodes. So, in some way our approach is equivalent to approaches where nodes are linearly connected by means of shift registers. However, in the CAPRA approach, data can be routed bit-parallel in units of entire n-bit words ($n \geq 32$), whereas, in most of the shift register approaches mentioned, routing is confined to the shifting of only few bits in parallel or even only to full bit sequential shifting.

5.6 STATE OF THE IMPLEMENTATION

A simulator of the entire system at register transfer level has been implemented in VHDL. For the machine language introduced in Section 5.4, an assembler was realized. So, actually, programs written in this language can be interpreted by the simulator.

With regard to hardware implementation, electrical simulation and layout of basic cells is currently been carried out. The entire system is planned to work as a coprocessor of conventional widespread main processors. A special coprocessor interface for the Motorola 68000 processor family has already been realized in semicustom technique.

5.7 CONCLUSION

In this paper, we have discussed the architectural properties of a new approach for associative systems. This approach comprises several innovative features as, for example, the combination of memory and processing functions within word cells, multiaccess in one cycle to data words in memory or to activity flags (thus enabling flexible creation of activity patterns), a fully parallel input of data into bit cells via optical sensor elements, and so forth. A resulting machine language (usable in addition to that of a main processor) has been sketched and exemplified by some basic programming examples. Moreover the flexible use of the architecture introduced for various application fields was discussed. This discussion showed a promising potential of performance improvement, compared with conventional computer architectures.

REFERENCES

[1] H. Kadota, J. Miyake, Y. Nishimichi, H. Kudoh, and K. Kagawa, An 8-kbit content-addressable and reentrant memory, *IEEE J. Solid-State Circuits*, 20(5), 951–956 (1985).

[2] T. Ogura, S. Yamada, and T. Nikaido, A 4-kbit associative memory LSI, *IEEE J. Solid-State Circuits*, 20(6), 1277–1282 (1985).

[3] A. Kokubu, M. Kuroda, and T. Furuya, Orthogonal memory—A step toward realization of large capacity associative memory, *Proc. Int. Conf. VLSI '85*, 159–168 (1985).

[4] K. E. Batcher, STARAN parallel processor hardware, *AFIPS Conf. Proc.* 43, 405–410 (1974).

[5] D. Tavangarian, Ortsadressierbarer Assoziativspeicher, *Elektronische Rechenanlagen*, 5(85), 264–278.

[6] D. Tavangarian, Flag-algebra: A new concept for the realisation of fully parallel associative architectures, *IEE Proc.* 136(5), Part E, 357–365 (1989).

[7] K. E. Grosspietsch, H. Huber, and A. Müller, The concept of a full-tolerant and easily-testable associative memory, *Proc. Internat Conf. on Fault-Tolerant Computing, FTCS-16*, 34–39 (1986).

[8] P. Mazumder and J. H. Patel, Methodologies for testing embedded content addressable memories, *Proc. FTCS-17*, 270–275 (1987).

[9] K. E. Grosspietsch, Architectures for testability and fault tolerance in content-addressable memories, *IEE Proc.* 136(5), Part E, 366–373 (1989).

[10] D. B. Sarrazin and M. Malek, Fault-tolerant memories, *Computer*, 17(8), 49–56.

[11] K. E. Grosspietsch, L. Muhlack, K. L. Paap, and G. Wagner, A memory interface chip designed for fault tolerance, *VLSI System Design*, 8(7), 112–118 (1987).

[12] U. Glaeser and U. Steinhausen, Fehlererkennung und Fehlertoleranz beim assoziativen RAM (ARAM)-Speicher, *Proc. 4th Internat. Conf. on Fault-Tolerant Computing Systems*, Baden-Baden 320–333 (1989).

[13] T. Kohonen, *Content-Addressable Memories*, Springer-Verlag, Berlin, Heidelberg, and New York, 1980.

[14] C. C. Foster, *Content-Addressable Parallel Processors*, Van Nostrand, New York, 1976.

[15] K. J. Thurber and L. Wald, Associative and parallel processors, *Computing Surveys*, 7(4), 215–255 (1975).

[16] S. S. Yau and H. S. Fung, Associative processor architecture—A survey, *ACM Computing Surveys*, 9(1), 3–27 (1977).

[17] P. Kogge, J. Oldfield, M. Brule, and C. Stormon, "VLSI and Rule-Based Systems," in J. G. Delgado-Frias and W. R. Moore, Eds., *VLSI for Artificial Intelligence*, Kluwer Academic Pub., Boston, 1989, pp. 95–108.

[18] J. P. Wade and C. G. Sodini, Dynamic cross-coupled bit-line content addressable memory cell for high-density arrays, *IEEE J. Solid-State Circuits*, 22(1), 119–121 (1987).

[19] Y. Ng, R. Glover, and C.-L. Chung, "Unify with Active Memory," in J. G. Delgado-Frias and W. R. Moore, Eds., *VLSI for Artificial Intelligence*, Kluwer Academic Pub., Boston, 1989, pp. 109–118.

[20] I. Robinson, "The Pattern Addressable Memory: Hardware for Associative Processing," in J. G. Delgado-Frias and W. G. Moore, Eds., *VLSI for Artificial Intelligence*, Kluwer Academic Pub., Boston, 1989, pp. 119–130.

[21] A. W. G. Duller et al., Design of an associative processor array, *IEE Proc.*, 136(5), Part E, 374–382 (1989).

[22] Ch. Zeidler, Content-addressable mass memories, *IEE Proc.*, 136(5), Part E, 351–356 (1989).

[23] D. L. Lee and F. L. Lochovsky, HYTREM- a hybrid text-retrieval machine for large data bases, *IEEE Trans. Computers*, 39(1), 111–123 (1990).

[24] H. Yamada, M. Hirata, H. Nagai, and K. Takahashi, A high speed string-search engine, *IEEE J. Solid-State Circuits*, 22(5), 829–834 (1987).

[25] C. F. Fernstrom, I. Kruzela, and B. Svensson, *LUCAS Associative Array Processor*, Springer Verlag, Berlin and New York, 1986.

[26] M. Lea, ASP: A cost-effective parallel microcomputer, *IEEE Micro*, 8(5), 10–29 (1988).

[27] K. E. Grosspietsch, "An Architecture for an Intelligent Multi-Mode WSI Memory," in M. Sami and F. Distante, Eds., *Wafer Scale Integration III*, North Holland, New York, 1990, pp. 211–220.

[28] K. E. Grosspietsch, "An intelligent sensor integrated VLSI preprocessor/emulator facility for neural nets," in M. Sami, J. Calzadilla-Daguerre, Eds., *Silicon Architectures for Neural Nets*, North Holland, New York, 1991, pp. 187–199.

[29] K. Waldschmidt, Associative processors and memories—Overview and current status, *Proc. COMPEURO '87*, 19–26 (1987).

[30] B. Parhami and A. Avizienis, Design of fault-tolerant associative processors, *Proc. Internat Symp. on Computer Architecture*, 141–145 (1973).

[31] J. G. Delgado-Frias and W. L. Moore, Eds., *VLSI for Artificial Intelligence*, Kluwer Academic Pub., 1989.

[32] S.-I. Chae, J. T. Walker, C.-C. Fu, and R. F. Pease, Content addressable memory for VLSI pattern inspection, *IEEE J. Solid-State Circuits*, 23(1), 74–78 (1988).

CHAPTER 6 ———————————————————

Cellular Processing

E. KATONA

6.1 INTRODUCTION

How can we use a homogeneous array of elementary processors (cells) to solve different computational problems? An early answer to this question was the cellular automata concept of J. von Neumann [1]. Later on cellular arrays appeared in (V)LSI circuit design [2], in Programmable Gate Arrays [3], different cellular automata realizations have been proposed [4, 5], and the notion of systolic arrays was created [6]. On the other hand, different massively parallel machines have been constructed (MPP, DAP, GAPP, etc. [7]) based on cellular computing too.

This chapter gives an overview of cellular processing with special respect to cell processors developed by Cellware Ltd. Section 6.2 sketches a general cellular array model forming a common theoretical frame for very different cellular array machines. Sections 6.3 and 6.4 describe basic hardware implementation techniques of cellular arrays illustrated on cellprocessors M1, X1, and SP1 of Cellware Ltd. Sections 6.5 and 6.6 discuss how to realize pipeline processing in cellular arrays. Problems of modeling, partitioning, and I/O management are examined. The different cellular array machines are compared on the basis of the general model of Section 6.2, connections are discovered between inhomogeneity, efficiency, and programming methodology.

6.2 CELLULAR ARRAY MODELS

In this section, a general cellular array model is introduced with special respect to the spatial, temporal, and topological inhomogeneity of the arrays.

Fuzzy, Holographic, and Parallel Intelligence, By Branko Souček and the IRIS Group.
ISBN 0-471-54772-7 © 1992 John Wiley & Sons, Inc.

Consider a rectangular array $C = [c(i, j)]$ of elementary processors, called *cells*. Each cell is connected to a number of other cells, called *neighbors*. The most frequently used interconnection structure is the *von Neumann neighborhood*, where cell $c(i, j)$ is connected to its four orthogonal neighbors and to itself (Fig. 6.1). In general, cell $c(i, j)$ is connected to cells $c(i + p_1, j + q_1)$, $c(i + p_2, j + q_2)$, $\cdots$, $c(i + p_n, j + q_n)$, where the vector $((p_1, q_1), (p_2, q_2), \cdots, (p_n, q_n))$ is called the *neighborhood pattern*, and it is common for each cell in the array. The von Neumann neighborhood pattern is $((0, 0), (-1, 0), (1, 0), (0, -1), (0, 1))$.

Any cell $c(i, j)$ has a *state register* $s(i, j)$ storing a binary information called *cell state*. The so-called *transition function*, denoted by f, determines the next state of a cell, depending on the states of neighbors. Denote $s(i, j, t)$ the state of cell $c(i, j)$ at time step t, then

$$s(i, j, t + 1) = f(s(i + p_1, j + q_1, t), s(i + p_2, j + q_2, t),$$
$$\cdots, s(i + p_n, j + q_n, t))$$

The above described structure corresponds to the *conventional cellular automata definition* and forms the basis of our cellular array model. To ensure more flexibility in processing, inhomogeneity will be introduced in space, time, and topology as follows.

Spatial inhomogeneity means that different cells work with different transition functions:

$$s(i, j, t + 1) = f_{i,j}(s(i + p_1, j + q_1, t), s(i + p_2, j + q_2, t),$$
$$\cdots, s(i + p_n, j + q_n, t))$$

Temporal inhomogeneity means that different transition functions are used in different time steps:

$$s(i, j, t + 1) = f_t(s(i + p_1, j + q_1, t), s(i + p_2, j + q_2, t),$$
$$\cdots, s(i + p_n, j + q_n, t))$$

If spatial and temporal inhomogeneity are used together, then we get

$$s(i, j, t + 1) = f_{i,j,t}(s(i + p_1, j + q_1, t), s(i + p_2, j + q_2, t),$$
$$\cdots, s(i + p_n, j + q_n, t))$$

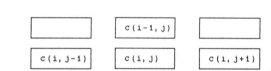

Figure 6.1 *The von Neumann neigh-borhood.*

Topological inhomogeneity means that different cells may have different neighborhood index:

$$s(i, j, t + 1) = f(s(i + p_{i,j,1}, j + q_{i,j,1}, t), s(i + p_{i,j,2}, j + q_{i,j,2}, t),$$

$$\cdots, s(i + p_{i,j,n}, j + q_{i,j,n}, t)).$$

Until now we have concentrated only on the inside of cellular array, but how can we work the border cells, which may have less number of neighbors than the inner ones?

A possible solution is to suppose input buffers on the four edges of the array, and the border cells feel these buffers as "outer neighbors." On the other hand, state registers of border cells are available for the outside world. In this way, border cells perform input–output management for the array.

Another possibility is to connect left border cells to the right ones and upper border cells to the lower ones, but in this case I/O management of the cellular array should be solved in another way.

6.3 CELLULAR ARRAY ARCHITECTURES

There are different ways to realize a cellular array in hardware. In this section three different possibilities are shown demonstrated on the cellprocessors M1, X1, and SP1. These machines have been developed by Cellware Ltd. Under leadership of Thomas Legendi, they have been fabricated and supplied with base software and cellprogram development system. Here only the basic architectural characteristics will be presented; for details see [8–11].

6.3.1 Memory Based Cells—M1 and X1 Cellular Arrays

A *memory based cell* consists of a state register and a transition function memory (Fig. 6.2). The latter is a RAM storing the transition table (look-up table) of the transition function. For example, Figure 6.3 shows the transition table of the cell

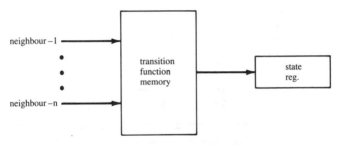

Figure 6.2 *Sketch of a memory based cell.*

s(i, j, t)	s(i-1, j, t)	s(i, j-1, t)	s(i, j, t+1)
0	0	0	0
0	0	1	1
0	1	0	0
0	1	1	1
1	0	0	0
1	0	1	1
1	1	0	1
1	1	1	1

Figure 6.3 *Example of transition table.*

transition function

$$s(i, j, t + 1) = (s(i, j, t) \text{ AND } s(i - 1, j, t)) \text{ OR } s(i, j - 1, t)$$

where two-state cells (1-bit state registers) are supposed. Only the rightmost column of transition table is stored in transition function memory. In each time step neighbors address the memory, and the new state is written into the state register.

Contents of transition function memories may differ from cell to cell, in this way a total *spatial inhomogeneity* is ensured for the cellular array. However, (re)loading of transition function memories is a relatively slow procedure, so the architecture seems to be static in a temporal sense. To offer *temporal inhomogeneity*, several transition functions are stored in a cell, and quick change is ensured from one transition function to the other. The number of transition functions is limited by the storage capacity of the cell transition function memory.

M1 Cellular Array.   The array consists of 16 * 16 cells and is built mainly from standard memory chips [10]. Sixteen state cells are used (i.e., a four-bit state register for each cell) and five neighbors for each cell (including itself). However, a total five-neighbor transition table would consist of 1,048,576 elements; that is why only eight bits of the five neighbors are selected according to the sophisticated neighborhood pattern of Fig. 6.4. In this way only a 256 * 4 bit memory is needed for a transition function. The neighborhood pattern is fixed and common for each

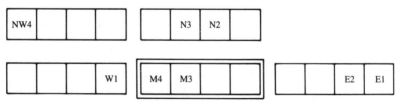

Figure 6.4 *Neighborhood of M1 cells. New state of the double framed cell may depend on the assigned eight state bits of neighboring cells.*

cell, but the ordering of bits supports different kinds of bit pipeline processing very well.

To offer temporal inhomogeneity, 16 transition functions are stored in each cell. A control unit broadcasts a 4-bit control signal to each cell in each clock cycle, this signal selects one of the 16 transition functions. So to say, there are 16 transition function layers and from step to step different transition function layers can be selected.

Summarizing, the M1 cellular array offers unlimited spatial and limited temporal inhomogeneity beside a homogeneous topology.

X1 Cellular Array. Another way to realize memory based cells is to get a Programmable Gate Array (PGA) chip, for instance, XC2064 (product of XILINX Inc. [3]), which contains 8 * 8 configurable logic blocks (cells) and a switching network for cell to cell interconnections.

Each cell contains a single bit state register S and a 16-bit transition function memory. Cells can be configured in three different ways (see Figs. 6.5, 6.6, and

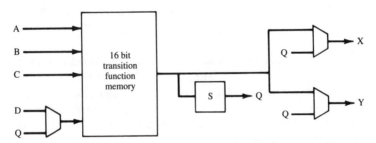

Figure 6.5 *First cell configuration: one function of four variables.*

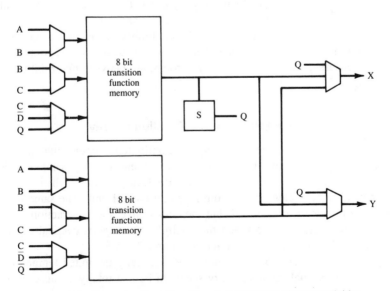

Figure 6.6 *Second cell configuration: two functions of three variables.*

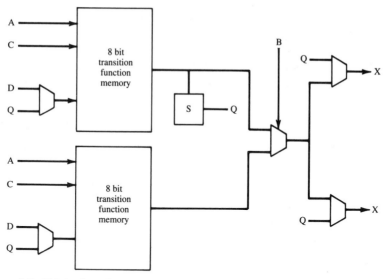

Figure 6.7 *Third cell configuration: dynamic selection of two functions of three variables.*

6.7), in case of second and third cell configurations the 16-bit transition function memory is divided into two 8-bit parts. Each cell has four input points A, B, C, D and two output points *X*, *Y*. Output points of cells can be connected to input points of other cells using a programmable switching network offered by the PGA chip. This ability offers a nearly arbitrary topology for the cellular array, but the number of neighbors is limited.

Cellular array of X1 cellprocessor [11] has been built from 4 * 4 XC2064 PGA chips; in this way a 32 * 32 cellular array is gained. The whole machine is realized on a single plug-in card interfaced to IBM PC/AT and compatibles.

Summarizing, the X1 cellular array offers unlimited spatial inhomogeneity and nearly unlimited topological inhomogeneity, but practically no temporal inhomogeneity is ensured: The only possibility is to choose between two 8-bit transition tables (Fig. 6.7).

6.3.2 Microprogrammed Cells—SPP Cellular Array

If we want to construct a cellular array with unlimited temporal inhomogeneity, then the concept of memory based cells should be rejected. A possible solution is microprogramming: each cell is a universal Boolean processor, which gets a microcommand in each clock cycle from a central control unit. The same microinstruction is broadcast to each cell, but the consecutive microinstructions are read from a microprogram memory and the control unit supports cyclical repetition, subroutine call, and so on, in the microprogram (Fig. 6.8).

It is clear that microprogramming offers practically unlimited temporal inhomogeneity, but spatial inhomogeneity seems to be lost totally because of broad-

address	microprogram memory contents	Sequence of microinstructions broadcast to the cells
0	REPEAT 3	M1
1	M1	M2
2	M2	M1
3	ENDREP	M2
4	M3	M1
5	GOSUB 8	M2
6	M4	M3
7	STOP	M5
8	M5	M6
9	M6	M4
10	RETURN	

Figure 6.8 *Example of microprogramming on the hardware level.*

casting. To get spatial inhomogeneity, some bits of the cell state register are separated and named as internal state, while other bits are named external state. Internal state bits are not "felt" by the neighbors and serve to distinguish cells from each other: Cells, which have different internal states, may behave in different ways while executing the same microprogram. However, microprogram length grows if it involves different subprograms for different cells; consequently, efficiency may be lost when spatial inhomogeneity increases.

The concept of microprogrammed cells is used in massively parallel machines such as MPP and DAP [7]. A further attempt in this direction is the SPP chip and SP1 cellprocessor developed in the United Kingdom by Cellware Ltd. and Densitron Ltd.

The SPP chip [8, 12] contains an 8 * 8 array of microprogrammed cells and a switching network to support programmable interconnection of chips (Fig. 6.9). Each cell has six internal and two external state bits. Getting several chips, arbitrarily large cellular arrays can be built with partial topological inhomogeneity: the 8 * 8 cells in a chip are connected according to von Neumann neighborhood, but border cells of a chip can communicate with border cells of an arbitrarily chosen other chip—using the on-chip switching network (Fig. 6.9).

As a first attempt, a 64 * 64 cellular array has been built from 8 * 8 SPP chips, supplemented with a control unit and a simple I/O processor. This machine, called SP1, works now with a software system including assembly and microassembly languages, simulator, and runtime system.

Further on, Densicell Demo Board [9] has been created and manufactured, including four SPP chips and supplied with a simple development software for demonstration and education of massively parallel processing.

6.4 CELLPROCESSOR ARCHITECTURES

A cellular array is efficient only on problems suitable for massively parallel execution, therefore it is not advisable to apply it as a universal purpose computing unit. It is more advantageous to use a traditional computer as host machine and to attach the cellular array as a peripheral unit to the host.

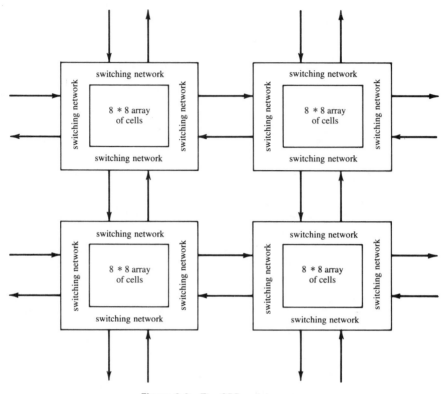

Figure 6.9   *The SPP cellular array.*

A cellular array should be supplemented with some functional units to get a suitable interface to the host. This complex—the cellular array with the required functional units—is called *cellprocessor*.

Figure 6.10 shows the basic structure of cellprocessors M1 and X1. The cellular array is a rectangular matrix of cells surrounded with I/O buffers on the four edges. These I/O buffers communicate with a fast parallel memory, which is connected also to the bus of the host computer. Operation of the cellular array and parallel memory is organized by a (microprogrammed) control unit (Fig. 6.10).

6.5   CELLULAR PROGRAMMING

There are two basic concepts in programming of cellular arrays:

- Array processing: Data are stored in the cellular array while they are processed

system bus
(to the host)

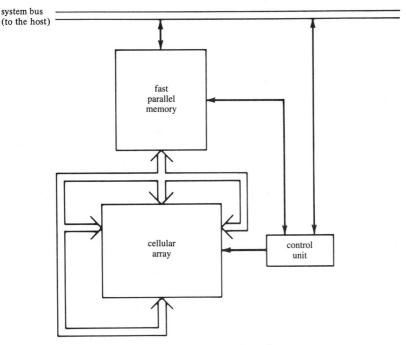

Figure 6.10 *General scheme of a cellprocessor.*

- Pipeline processing: Data are driven through the cellular array while they are processed

Array processing strongly requires temporal inhomogeneity (microprogramming), while spatial and topological inhomogeneity have less importance. In most cases cells are supplied with local memories (MPP, DAP), and the basic problem is to find a low-cost solution for the loading of input data before processing and the unloading of result data after processing.

In case of pipeline processing no loading–unloading is needed because data are in continuous movement and they are processed in a systolic way. Temporal inhomogeneity is not important in this case, but spatial and topological inhomogeneity can be utilized very well. Cells need only a few-bit local memory. Cellular arrays of M1 and X1 support pipeline processing rather than array processing, but SPP assumes both processing modes. (When array processing is applied, internal state bits of SPP cells can be used as local memories.)

In case of *pipeline processing* the cellular array is used as a complex, *dynamically reconfigurable pipeline processor*. Data vectors are read out from parallel memory (Fig. 6.10), driven through the cellular array, and rewritten into parallel memory. This process should be repeated as many times as it is needed to get final result (see Fig. 6.11 and the example of Section 6.6). Although the system is

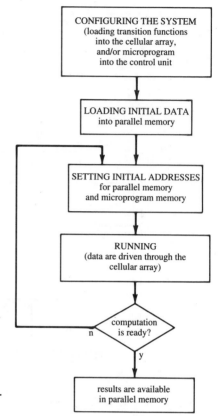

Figure 6.11 *Pipeline processing mode of cell-processors.*

configured only once at the beginning, between computation cycles the cellular array can be reconfigured by using temporal inhomogeneity abilities (to change transition function layers (M1), or to broadcast different microprograms (SPP)).

Pipeline structures, to be embedded into the cellular array, can be modeled by a graph [13] where the nodes are processing elements and the edges represent data transmissions between them. Let us consider a simple example. A polynomial

$$y = a_3 x^3 + a_2 x^2 + a_1 x + a_0$$

should be evaluated for the elements of vector $\mathbf{X} = (x_1, \cdots, x_n)$ to get the resulting vector $\mathbf{Y} = (y_1, \cdots, y_n)$. To solve the problem, the cellular array is configured according to the pipeline structure of Figure 6.12, where squares denote processing elements, $a_3, \cdots, a_0$ are constants stored in the array, x is input, and y is output. Processing elements are realized by groups of cells, the number of cells utilized in a PE depends on the word length. Vector $\mathbf{X}$ is stored in parallel

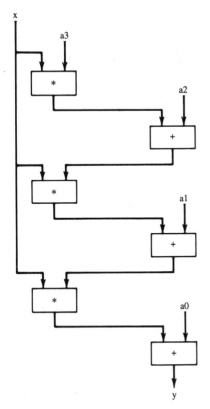

x

Figure 6.12 *Graph model of a pipeline cellular structure for polynomial evaluation.*

memory and after driving through the cellular array, resulting vector **Y** is gained also in parallel memory.

6.6 PARTITIONING

How to solve arbitrarily sized problems with a given sized array of cells? We show that *pipeline processing supports partitioning of problems*. It is clear that a long pipeline can be simulated by a short one if data are driven through several times and the pipeline is reconfigured between driving cycles. This partitioning principle has been generalized in [14] and will be illustrated in this section on a transitive closure algorithm.

Consider a graph of n vertices, and represent it with an $n * n$ matrix **A** where $a(i, j) = 1$ if there is an edge from the ith vertex to the jth one, and $a(i, j) = 0$ otherwise. The task is to compute a matrix **B** representing the transitive closure of the original graph. The problem can be solved with a rhombus form cellular array [15], which gets matrix **A** in delayed form and outputs matrix **B** in the same form, while special signals go downward controlling the computation (Fig. 6.13). Three

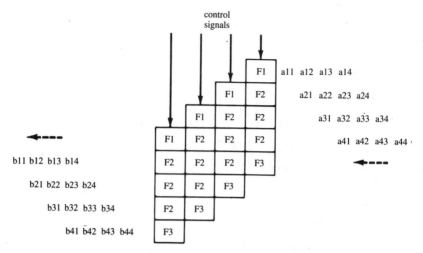

Figure 6.13 Cellular array for transitive closure calculation.

different cell transition functions ($F1$, $F2$, and $F3$) are applied in the array (Fig. 6.14).

This algorithm needs a $2n * n$ cellular array to process $n * n$ matrices. To demonstrate the partitioning method, consider a $16 * 16$ cellular array and matrix size $n = 48$. First, a (virtual) cellular array of size $96 * 48$ is considered, which

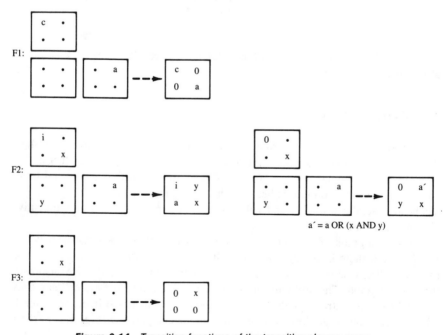

Figure 6.14 Transition functions of the transitive closure array.

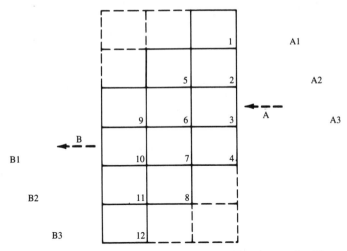

Figure 6.15 Partitioning principle of the transitive closure algorithm.

can solve the problem directly (without partitioning). This array can be divided into 18 partitions each of 16 * 16 size (Fig. 6.15).

Considering the rhombus form of the transitive closure array, six partitions can be omitted and the remaining 12 partitions can be processed one after the other in the sequence of numbers of Figure 6.15 as follows:

In the starting situation matrix **A** is stored in parallel memory.

Cellular array is configured to compute partition 1. Submatrix $A1$ (consisting of the first 16 rows of **A**) is driven through the 16 * 16 array from right to left, while a partial result submatrix $X1$ is generated leaving the array downward (Fig. 6.16). This submatrix is stored into the parallel memory.

Cellular array is configured to compute partition 2. Submatrices $A2$ and $X1$ are driven through the 16 * 16 array, and partial result submatrices $A2'$ and $X1'$ leave the array (Fig. 6.16). They are restored into parallel memory replacing $A2$ and $X1$, respectively.

The process is continued for partitions 3, 4, · · · , 12 according to Figure 6.16 until the resulting submatrices $B1$, $B2$, $B3$ are available in parallel memory.

The presented solution can be considered as typical example for partitioning of two-dimensional pipeline structures. It turns out that partitioning can convert spatial and topological inhomogeneity of the nonpartitioned algorithm into temporal inhomogeneity, because quick change of array configurations should be ensured between simulating different partitions. This kind of temporal inhomogeneity can be solved easily by the 16 transition function layers of M1 cellprocessor. The

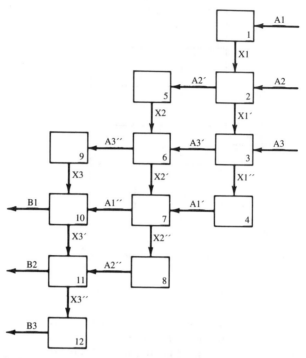

Figure 6.16   *Data management in the partitioned transitive closure algorithm.*

presented partitioned transitive closure algorithm is programmed for M1 and produces a speedup factor 460 compared to an IBM PC-AT on a 640 ∗ 640 matrix.

6.7 CONCLUSIONS

There are two characteristic ways of programming cellular arrays: array processing and pipeline processing. Cellprocessors M1, X1 and SP1 support bit-level pipeline processing, and—although they contain relatively small cellular arrays—they can solve arbitrarily large problems applying the partitioning principle of Section 6.5. These machines produce high efficiency with low hardware cost because simple cells are used and only a few bit memory is needed per cell. For instance, the single card X1 processor involves 1024 Boolean processing elements and can perform 10 GOPS on Boolean operations if it is maximally utilized.

Based on the presented cellprocessor concept large cellular systems can be built [16] involving thousands or millions of cells. Programming of such a system can be modeled by pipeline graphs (Fig. 6.12) and a high level programming language can be used [13]. Application fields of such systems include image processing, associative processing, finite element and related methods (e.g., surface interpolation), neurocomputing, and other fields of artificial intelligence.

REFERENCES

[1] J. von Neumann, *Theory of Self-Reproducing Automata*, A. W. Burks, Ed., University of Illinois Press, Urbana, 1966.

[2] K. Hwang, *Computer Arithmetic*, Wiley, New York, 1979.

[3] *The Programmable Gate Array Design Handbook*, XILINX Inc., 1986.

[4] T. Legendi, Cellprocessors in computer architecture, *Computational Ling. Computer Languages*, II, 147–167 (1977).

[5] T. Toffoli and M. Margolus, *Cellular Automata Machines*, MIT Press, Cambridge, Mass., 1987.

[6] H. T. Kung, "The Structure of Parallel Algorithms," in M.C. Yovits, Ed., *Advances in Computers*, vol. 19, Academic Press, New York, 1980, pp. 65–112.

[7] T. Fountain, *Processor Arrays—Architectures and Applications*, Academic Press, London, 1987.

[8] "The SPP Chip—Product Specification, Description for Assembly and Microassembly Programming," Cellware Ltd., Budapest, 1990.

[9] "Densicell Demo Board—Documentation, Application Notes," Cellware Ltd., Budapest, 1990.

[10] "M1 Processor—User's Manual, Development System, Program Libraries," Cellware Ltd., Budapest, 1991

[11] "X1 Processor—User's Manual, Development System," Cellware Ltd., Budapest, 1991.

[12] J. Tóth, A 64K cell LSI based cellprocessor prototype, *Proc. PARCELLA '84*, 154–161 (1985).

[13] E. Katona, A programming language for cellular processors, *Parallel Computing 85*, 371–376 (1986).

[14] E. Katona, A general partitioning method for cellular algorithms, *Informatik-Skripten 21*, T.U. Braunschweig, 1988, pp. 85–94.

[15] E. Katona, A transitive closure algorithm for a 16-state cellprocessor, *Proc. PARCELLA '88, Mathematical Research 48*, 285–290 (1988).

[16] T. Legendi, E. Katona, J. Tóth, and A. Zsótér, Megacell machine, *Parallel Computing*, 8, 195–199 (1988).

PART II

Parallel Algorithms

An Optimal Partitioning Method for Parallel Algorithms: LSGP

KARL-HEINZ ZIMMERMANN

7.1 INTRODUCTION

It is well known that the optimal scheduling problem is NP-hard [1]. The optimal scheduling problem is the problem to find a schedule such the computation of a given number of tasks on a multiprocessor system becomes minimal. On the other hand, signal and image processing problems usually require real time processing and must therefore be efficiently implemented on a multiprocessor system. For this we require efficient methods to decompose algorithms into subalgorithms and to perform these partitioned algorithms efficiently on multiprocessor systems.

In this chapter we investigate the decomposition of algorithms according to the direct LSGP scheme. For this we study a class $\mathcal{C}$ of algorithms which can be formally described by so-called local, homogeneous, and complete data dependence graphs. In this class we can find a lot of algorithms from linear algebra, signal, and image processing. We first focus on the study of linear schedules for the LSGP scheme. Linear schedules are very important from the practical point of view, since they exhibit several regularity properties and are easy to implement. Then we develop several criteria under which direct LSGP decompositions of algorithms from $\mathcal{C}$ yield minimal overall computation time. In particular, we show that linear schedules can be used to schedule the operations of every subalgorithm. We first discuss two categories of partitioning strategies in general terms [2–5].

1. Direct Versus Indirect Decomposition

- Direct decomposition:
  In the direct partitioning approach, an algorithm represented by a data

Fuzzy, Holographic, and Parallel Intelligence, By Branko Souček and the IRIS Group.
ISBN 0-471-54772-7 © 1992 John Wiley & Sons, Inc.

dependence graph (DG) is directly decomposed into several subalgorithms (or blocks). The blocks are then mapped onto a target array processor.

- Indirect decomposition:

  In the indirect partitioning approach, an algorithm represented by a DG is at first transformed into a virtual array processor structure (also known as signal flow graph [4]). This transformation consists of a node assignment and scheduling part. The resulting virtual array processor structure is then decomposed and mapped onto a target array processor.

2. LSGP versus LPGS scheme

- LSGP scheme:

  In the LSGP scheme an algorithm is partitioned into a number of subalgorithms equal to the number of processing elements (PEs) available in the target array processor. While all subalgorithms are performed in parallel in different PEs, the operations of every subalgorithm are sequentially executed by the associated PE. This kind of partitioning technique is referred to as locally sequential globally parallel (LSGP). The LSGP scheme exhibits simplicity and low communication bandwidth. However the size of the local PE memory directly depends on the size of the problem. Hence every PE requires a sufficiently large data storage.

- LPGS scheme:

  In the LPGS scheme an algorithm is decomposed into subalgorithms such that each subalgorithm is mapped onto an entire array processor. While the operations of each subalgorithm are executed in parallel by different PEs, different subalgorithms are sequentially performed by the array processor. This type of partitioning technique is termed locally parallel globally sequential (LPGS). The LPGS scheme suffers from a high communication bandwidth. Furthermore it is necessary to feed back data via a FIFO storage into the array processor for processing the next subalgorithm. However the local memory size in the PE is generally independent of the problem size and can thus be kept rather small.

The LSGP and LPGS scheme can be used to control the dimensions of the local memory of a PE and the ratio of the I/O speed and the throughput of the array processor. Clearly the direct or indirect partitioning approach can be combined with the LSGP or LPGS scheme.

In the following we investigate the direct partitioning approach combined with the LSGP scheme [5]. This combination, called direct LSGP scheme, is quite appealing if all PEs have a sufficiently large local memory. In opposition this, several researchers have investigated the indirect LGPS scheme [2, 3, 6]. The starting point for indirect partitioning is a virtual array processor structure derived from an algorithm by node assignment and scheduling. In this case, the designer has to take into account the pipelining period of the virtual array processor structure.

7.2 DIRECT LSGP DECOMPOSITIONS OF DEPENDENCE GRAPHS

In this section we introduce the concept of dependence graph (DG) as a formal tool to analyze algorithms [4]. For this we fully restrict our investigations to the class of so-called local, homogeneous and complete DGs. We first study linear schedules for DGs. In particular, we prove that for each n-D DG there are exactly $n!$ different sequential linear schedules with pipelining period 1. We furthermore illustrate how the inverse function of a sequential linear schedule with pipelining period 1 can be efficiently calculated. We then define an equivalence relation on DGs and introduce a standard form of neighborhood stencil. We finally show that every equivalence class of DGs contains a DG with a standard neighborhood stencil.

7.2.1 A Formal Notation for Dependence Graphs

Clearly every algorithm can be transformed into an equivalent single assignment algorithm [4]. A dependence graph (DG) is simply a graphical representation of a single assignment algorithm.

As an example, we consider the algorithm for matrix–vector multiplication $c = Ab$ where $A = (a_{ij})$ is an $n \times n$-matrix, and $b = (b_i)$ and $c = (c_i)$ are vectors of length n (see Kung [4] for details):

$$c_i = \sum_{k=1}^{n} a_{ik}b_k \quad \text{for } i = 1, \cdots, n$$

An equivalent single assignment algorithm is given by

for i, k from 1 to n

$$c(i, k) := c(i, k - 1) + a(i, k) * b(k)$$

with initial conditions $c(i, 0) = 0$, $a(i, k) = a_{ik}$, $b(k) = b_k$ and final result $c(i, n) = c_i$.

The set $\{(i, k) | 1 \le i, k \le n\}$ of pairs of natural numbers is called the *index space* associated with the algorithm, and corresponds to the operations to be performed. The DG of the above single assignment algorithm is shown in Figure 7.1a. The nodes of the DG correspond to the index space of the algorithm. We say that the indexed variable $c(i, k)$ is computed at index point (i, k). The edges represent the data dependencies among the operations represented by the nodes. The index points incidenting with (i, k) correspond to the data required to compute $c(i, k)$. The DG in Figure 7.1a exhibits edges whose length depends upon the problem size n. The data associated with such edges are called *broadcast data*. In our example $b(1), \cdots, b(n)$ are broadcast data. Clearly we can construct from the DG shown in Figure 7.1a a DG without broadcast data by shifting the broad-

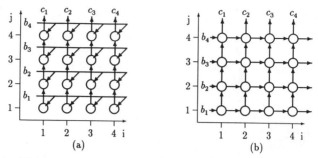

Figure 7.1 *DG for matrix–vector multiplication ($n = 4$): (a) global, (b) localized version.*

cast data $b(1), \cdots, b(n)$ *through* the nodes which depend on them. For this we consider the following equivalent single assignment algorithm:

> for i, k from 1 to n
>
> $b(i, k) := b(i - 1, k)$
>
> $c(i, k) := c(i, k - 1) + a(i, k) * b(i, k)$

with the additional initial condition $b(0, k) = b_k$. The resulting DG of the modified single assignment algorithm exhibits only edges whose length is independent of the problem size and is therefore called a *local* DG (see Fig. 7.1*b*). It should be noted that the problem of deriving a local DG from a single assignment algorithm is yet not completely solved. Indeed, most existing approaches are rather heuristic [4, 7].

Another typical feature of the DG in Figure 7.1*b* is *homogeneity* (or *shift invariance*): All nodes up to the boundary nodes of the DG share a common neighborhood stencil [4]. The *neighborhood stencil* of a node **v** in a local DG consists of all vectors incidenting with **v**. For instance, each nonboundary node of the DG in Figure 7.1*b* has neighborhood stencil $\{(1, 0), (0, 1)\}$. In the following we shall write all vectors as row vectors. Moreover we say that a DG is *complete* if its index space forms an *n*-D cube for some positive integer n.

In the following we apply the direct LSGP scheme to local, homogeneous, and complete DGs. The class of local, homogeneous and complete DGs corresponds to algorithms from linear algebra, signal and image processing like matrix–matrix multiplication, convolution, and mathematical morphology operations. We first provide a formal description for local, homogeneous, and complete DGs.

Definition 7.1 Let $n \in \mathbb{N}$ and $k_1, \cdots, k_n \in \mathbb{N}$. The set $S(k_1, \cdots, k_n)$ of all *n*-tuples $(a_1, \cdots, a_n)$ of nonnegative integers with the property $0 \le a_i < k_i (i = 1, \cdots, n)$ is called an *index space*. We put $\mathbf{0} := (0, \cdots, 0) \in \mathbb{N}_0^n$.

The set $S(k_1, \cdots, k_n)$ can be graphically thought of a mesh consisting of a lattice of finite points. Every nonempty subset N of $\{-1, 0, 1\}^n \setminus \{\mathbf{0}\}$ is a potential neighborhood stencil. If we associate with an index space $S(k_1, \cdots, k_n)$ a neighborhood stencil N, then we have to bear in mind that the arcs of N describe the data dependencies among the index points (and thus among the operations of the underlying algorithm). A pair consisting of an index space $S(k_1, \cdots, k_n)$ and a neighborhood stencil N defines a directed graph (V, E) with vertex set $V := S(k_1, \cdots, k_n)$ and edge set E such that

$$(\mathbf{u}, \mathbf{v}) \in E :\Leftrightarrow \exists \mathbf{s} \in N : \mathbf{v} = \mathbf{u} + \mathbf{s} \quad \text{for all } \mathbf{u}, \mathbf{v} \in V$$

For every edge $(\mathbf{u}, \mathbf{v}) \in E$, $\mathbf{u}$ is said to be a *neighbor of* $\mathbf{v}$, and the set $N(\mathbf{v})$ of all neighbors of $\mathbf{v}$ is called the *neighborhood of* $\mathbf{v}$.

The directed graph defined by an index space as well as a neighborhood stencil may contain cycles. However, the DG of a single assignment algorithm is always acyclic, since each algorithm is by definition computable. This observation suggests the following

Definition 7.2 Let $S(k_1, \cdots, k_n)$ be an index space and $N \subseteq \{-1, 0, 1\}^n \backslash \{\mathbf{0}\}$. The pair $D = (S(k_1, \cdots, k_n), N)$ is called a dependence graph (DG) if the directed graph (V, E) associated with D is acyclic. N is called the neighborhood stencil and n is denoted as the dimension of D.

Clearly every DG described by Definition 7.2 is local, homogeneous, and complete. Figure 7.2 illustrates an example.

7.2.2 Linear Schedules for Dependence Graphs

In this section we investigate schedules for DGs. In general, a *schedule* associates with each node in a DG a nonnegative integer representing the execution time of the node in a target array processor [4]. We shall see that scheduling the operations of a DG is simplified by a linear schedule. A *linear schedule* is mathematically a nonzero linear mapping ϕ from the n-dimensional real vector space $\mathbb{R}^n$, into which the index space of the n-dimensional DG in question is embedded, to a one-dimensional vector space, the set $\mathbb{R}$ of real numbers, so that the image of the restriction of ϕ to the nodes of the DG is a subset of nonnegative integers. Then for each node $\mathbf{v}$ of the DG, $\phi(\mathbf{v})$ is interpreted as the execution time of $\mathbf{v}$ in the associated PE.

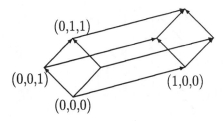

Figure 7.2 *Local, homogeneous, and complete 3-D DG S(2, 2, 2) with neighborhood stencil {(1, 0, 0), (0, 1, 0), (0, 0, 1)}.*

It follows from linear algebra that there exists a vector $\mathbf{c} \in \mathbb{R}^n$ such that

$$\phi(\mathbf{v}) = \langle \mathbf{c}, \mathbf{v} \rangle \quad \text{for all } \mathbf{v} \in \mathbb{R}^n$$

where $\langle , \rangle$ denotes the ordinary inner product. The kernel of ϕ is then the subspace $U := \{\mathbf{u} \in \mathbb{R}^n | \langle \mathbf{c}, \mathbf{u} \rangle = 0\}$ of $\mathbb{R}^n$. Thus we can characterize the linear schedule ϕ by a vector $\mathbf{c}$ orthogonal to U and call $\mathbf{c}$ the *schedule vector* associated with ϕ. By linear algebra, the dimension of U is $n - 1$. Hence every affine subspace $\mathbf{v} + U = \{\mathbf{v} + \mathbf{u} | \mathbf{u} \in U\}$ of $\mathbb{R}^n$ ($\mathbf{v} \in \mathbb{R}^n$) is a hyperplane and has the property

$$\phi(\mathbf{v} + \mathbf{u}) = \langle \mathbf{c}, \mathbf{v} + \mathbf{u} \rangle = \langle \mathbf{c}, \mathbf{v} \rangle + \langle \mathbf{c}, \mathbf{u} \rangle$$
$$= \langle \mathbf{c}, \mathbf{v} \rangle \quad \text{for all } \mathbf{u} \in U$$

Thus all nodes of a hyperplane $\mathbf{v} + U$ are scheduled at the same time step $\langle \mathbf{c}, \mathbf{v} \rangle$. Figure 7.3 illustrates a set of hyperplanes and a schedule vector. In the following we are interested in schedules preserving all data dependencies.

Definition 7.3 We call a schedule ϕ for a nondecomposed DG D *permissible* if it fulfills the *causality constraint*, that is, if node $\mathbf{v}$ depends on node $\mathbf{u}$, then the time step $\phi(\mathbf{v})$ assigned for $\mathbf{v}$ is greater than the time step $\phi(\mathbf{u})$ assigned for $\mathbf{u}$.

If the schedule is linear, then permissibility means that for each node $\mathbf{v}$, all nodes $\mathbf{v} + \mathbf{s}$ ($\mathbf{s} \in N$) directly depending on $\mathbf{v}$ lie on the same side of the hyperplane $\mathbf{v} + U$ (see Section 7.2.4). In the following we choose the positive half space of a hyperplane. Since all DGs are homogenous, it is sufficient to consider the case $\mathbf{v} = \mathbf{0}$. Then the causality constraint becomes

$$\langle \mathbf{c}, \mathbf{s} \rangle > 0 \quad \text{for all } \mathbf{s} \in N$$

The LSGP scheme necessitates that the operations of every subproblem (or block) are sequentially executed by the corresponding PE. Sequential means that at most one node of a block is executed at a time. We therefore investigate sequential linear schedules in more detail. We recall that the *pipelining period* of a processor is the time interval, say α, between two successive computations. In other words, the processor is busy for one out of every α time intervals [4]. In the

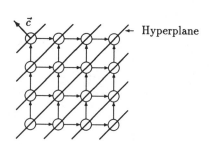

Figure 7.3 *Illustration of a DG S(4, 4) with schedule vector c and some hyperplanes.*

following, we apply the notion of pipelining period also to schedules in the same way.

Lemma 7.1 Let $D = (S(k_1, \cdots, k_n), N)$ be a DG. Then the linear schedule given by schedule vector

$$\mathbf{c} = \left(1, k_1, \cdots, \prod_{i=1}^{n-1} k_i\right) \tag{7.1}$$

is a sequential schedule for D with overall computation time $\prod_{i=1}^{n} k_i$ and pipelining period 1.

Proof: Let $\langle , \rangle$ denote the ordinary scalar product on the vector space $\mathbb{R}^n$. It is sufficient to prove that the mapping

$$\langle \mathbf{c}, \cdot \rangle : S(k_1, \cdots, k_n) \ni \mathbf{x} \mapsto \langle \mathbf{c}, \mathbf{x} \rangle \in \left\{0, 1, \cdots, \left(\prod_{i=1}^{n} k_i\right) - 1\right\}$$

is a bijection. Then vector $\mathbf{c}$ defines a sequential linear schedule. To see this let

$$y \in \left\{0, 1, \cdots, \left(\prod_{i=1}^{n} k_i\right) - 1\right\}$$

We now consider the following sequence of successive divisions with rest:

$$y = q_1 k_1 + x_1 \quad \text{where } 0 \le x_1 < k_1$$
$$q_1 = q_2 k_2 + x_2 \quad \text{where } 0 \le x_2 \le k_2$$
$$\cdots$$
$$q_{n-2} = q_{n-1} k_{n-1} + x_{n-1} \quad \text{where } 0 \le x_{n-1} < k_{n-1} \tag{7.2}$$

Hence we have $y = x_1 + k_1(x_2 + k_2(x_3 + \cdots (x_{n-1} + k_{n-1}q_{n-1}) \cdots))$ and thus by definition of y, $0 \le q_{n-1} < k_n$. If we put $x_n := q_{n-1}$, then we obtain

$$\langle \mathbf{c}, (x_1, \cdots, x_n) \rangle = y$$

Consequently the mapping $\langle \mathbf{c}, \cdot \rangle$ is surjective and therefore bijective since $S(k_1, \cdots, k_n)$ has $\prod_{i=1}^{n} k_i$ elements. $\square$

We now prove the converse of Lemma 7.1, namely, that all vectors, which yield sequential linear schedules *with* pipelining period 1, have the form similar to Eq. (7.1). In order to keep our notation as concise as possible, we use the notion of symmetric group: For each natural number n, the symmetric group Γ_n consists of all bijective mappings on the set $\{1, \cdots, n\}$ together with function composition. The elements of Γ_n are usually called permutations.

Lemma 7.2 Let $D = (S(k_1, \cdots, k_n), N)$ be a DG. Suppose $\psi: \mathbb{R}^n \to \mathbb{R}$ is a nonzero linear mapping, whose restriction to $S(k_1, \cdots, k_n)$ gives a bijection

$$\psi: S(k_1, \cdots, k_n) \to \left\{0, \cdots, \left(\prod_{i=1}^{n} k_i\right) - 1\right\}$$

that is, ψ defines a sequential linear schedule for D. Then there exists a permutation $\pi \in \Gamma_n$ such that the schedule vector $\mathbf{c} \in \mathbb{R}^n$ associated with ψ is given by

$$c_{\pi(1)} = 1 \quad \text{and} \quad c_{\pi(i)} = \prod_{j=1}^{i-1} k_{\pi(j)} \quad \text{for } i = 2, \cdots, n. \tag{7.3}$$

Proof: Let $\mathbf{e}_1, \cdots, \mathbf{e}_n$ denote the unit vectors of $\mathbb{R}^n$, i.e., $\mathbf{e}_1 = (1, 0, \cdots, 0)$ and so on. Then $\{\mathbf{e}_1, \cdots, \mathbf{e}_n\}$ is a basis of $\mathbb{R}^n$. By definition of ψ, there exists a vector $\mathbf{c} = (c_1, \cdots, c_n) \in \mathbb{R}^n$ such that

$$\psi(\mathbf{v}) = \langle \mathbf{c}, \mathbf{v} \rangle \quad \text{for all } \mathbf{v} \in \mathbb{R}^n$$

Then the function

$$\langle \mathbf{c}, \cdot \rangle: S(k_1, \cdots, k_n) \ni \mathbf{x} \mapsto \langle \mathbf{c}, \mathbf{x} \rangle \in \left\{0, 1, \cdots, \left(\prod_{i=1}^{n} k_i\right) - 1\right\}$$

is by hypothesis a bijection. Suppose that $k_i > 1$ for all $i = 1, \cdots, n$. Otherwise, we can replace D by a lower dimensional DG, e.g., $S(5, 1)$ and $S(5)$ specify the same index set. We may assume that the neighborhood stencil of D is standard (see Section 7.2.4 for details). Then the unit vectors $\mathbf{e}_1, \cdots, \mathbf{e}_n \in \mathbb{R}^n$ lie on the same side of the hyperplane determined by $\mathbf{c}$. Thus we have

$$c_i := \langle \mathbf{c}, \mathbf{e}_i \rangle > 0 \quad \text{for } i = 1, \cdots, n$$

By hypothesis, there exists a node $\mathbf{v}_0$ in D with $\langle \mathbf{c}, \mathbf{v}_0 \rangle = 1$. Since $\mathbf{v}_0 = \sum_{i=1}^{n} r_i \mathbf{e}_i$ for some nonnegative integers r_i, we obtain

$$\langle \mathbf{c}, \mathbf{v}_0 \rangle = \sum_{i=1}^{n} r_i c_i = 1$$

Hence there exists $i_0 \in \{1, \cdots, n\}$ so that $\mathbf{v}_0 = \mathbf{e}_{i_0}$ and consequently $c_{i_0} = 1$. Now we proceed by induction. We may renumber the components of $S(k_1, \cdots,$

k_n) such that for some $m < n$:

$$c_1 = 1 \quad \text{and} \quad c_i = \prod_{j=1}^{i-1} k_j \quad \text{for all } i = 2, \cdots, m$$

Let U be the subspace of $\mathbb{R}^n$ spanned by the vectors $\mathbf{e}_1, \cdots, \mathbf{e}_m$ and $U' = U \cap S(k_1, \cdots, k_n)$. (Here we adopt the convention that $\prod_{j=1}^{0} = 1$). Then we have for all $\mathbf{u} = \sum_{i=1}^{m} r_i \mathbf{e}_i \in U'$:

$$\langle \mathbf{c}, \mathbf{u} \rangle = \sum_{i=1}^{m} r_i \langle \mathbf{c}, \mathbf{e}_i \rangle$$

$$= \sum_{i=1}^{m} r_i \prod_{j=1}^{i-1} k_j$$

$$\leq \sum_{i=1}^{m} (k_i - 1) \prod_{j=1}^{i-1} k_j$$

$$= \left(\sum_{j=1}^{m} k_j \right) - 1$$

The last equation follows easily by induction on m. Thus we have shown that the restriction of ψ to U' gives a bijection onto the set $M := \{0, \cdots, (\prod_{j=1}^{m} k_j) - 1\}$. Hence there exists a vector $\mathbf{w}_0 \in S(k_1, \cdots, k_n) \setminus U'$ with the property

$$\langle \mathbf{c}, \mathbf{w}_0 \rangle = \prod_{j=1}^{m} k_j$$

Assume that $\mathbf{w}_0 = \mathbf{x} + \mathbf{y}$ where $\mathbf{x} = \sum_{j=1}^{m} r_j \mathbf{e}_j$ and $\mathbf{y} = \sum_{j=m+1}^{n} r_j \mathbf{e}_j$. Suppose that $\mathbf{x}$ is not the zero vector. Since $\mathbf{x} \in U'$, we obtain

$$\langle \mathbf{c}, \mathbf{y} \rangle = \langle \mathbf{c}, \mathbf{w}_0 - \mathbf{x} \rangle = \langle \mathbf{c}, \mathbf{w}_0 \rangle - \langle \mathbf{c}, \mathbf{x} \rangle \leq \left(\prod_{j=1}^{m} k_j \right) - 1$$

Hence there exists an element $\mathbf{u} \in U'$ such that $\langle \mathbf{c}, \mathbf{u} \rangle = \langle \mathbf{c}, \mathbf{y} \rangle$. But we must have $\mathbf{y} \neq \mathbf{u}$, since $\mathbf{x} \in U$ and $\mathbf{w}_0 \notin U$. Now have derived a contradiction, since $\langle \mathbf{c}, \cdot \rangle$ is sequential. Consequently $\mathbf{w}_0 = \mathbf{y} = \sum_{j=m+1}^{n} r_j \mathbf{e}_j$. Since ψ maps U' onto M, each unit vector $\mathbf{e}_j \notin U'$ is mapped to

$$\psi(\mathbf{e}_j) \geq \prod_{j=1}^{m} k_j$$

The assumption $\psi(\mathbf{e}_j) > \prod_{j=1}^{m} k_j$ for all $j = m + 1, \cdots, n$, leads to a contradiction. Thus there exists $j_0 \in \{m + 1, \cdots, n\}$ such that $\mathbf{e}_{j_0} = \mathbf{w}_0$. Hence the schedule vector $\mathbf{c}$ has the required property, and the proof of the lemma is complete. $\square$

Lemmas 7.1 and 7.2 provide a complete description of all sequential linear schedules for $S(k_1, \cdots, k_n)$ with pipelining period 1.

Corollary 7.1   Let $n \in \mathbb{N}$ and $k_1, \cdots, k_n \in \mathbb{N}$ such that $k_1 > 1, \cdots, k_n > 1$. Then the number of different sequential linear schedules for an n-D DG $D = (S(k_1, \cdots, k_n), N)$ with pipelining period 1 is $n!$.

Proof: Lemma 7.2 shows that every sequential linear schedule for D with pipelining period 1 is given by a schedule vector which is uniquely determined by a permutation of Γ_n. Thereby different permutations π and π' of Γ_n yield different sequential linear schedules for D. Hence the number of different sequential linear schedules for D with pipelining period 1 equals the order of the symmetric group: $|\Gamma_n| = n!$. This proves the corollary. $\square$

For instance, the sequential linear schedules with pipelining period 1 for a 3-D DG with index space $S(k_1, k_2, k_3)$ are summarized in Table 7.1.

Every sequential schedule ψ for an n-D DG $D = (S(k_1 \cdots, k_n), N)$ with pipelining period 1 yields a bijection

$$\psi : S(k_1, \cdots, k_n) \to \left\{ 0, \cdots, \left(\prod_{i=1}^{n} k_i \right) - 1 \right\}$$

The inverse function of a schedule ψ is useful for its implementation (see Section 7.6 for details). While the inverse function of a sequential nonlinear schedule is in general hard to calculate (see Fig. 7.6), the inverse function of a sequential schedule can be easily calculated using the algorithm specified by Eq. (7.2).

TABLE 7.1   Sequential Linear Schedules for 3-D DGs with Pipelining Period 1

Permutation of Γ_3	Schedule vector
(1)	$(1, k_1, k_1 k_2)$
(123)	$(k_2 k_3, 1, k_2)$
(132)	$(k_3, k_1 k_3, 1)$
(12)	$(k_2, 1, k_1 k_2 1)$
(13)	$(k_2 k_3, k_3, 1)$
(23)	$(1, k_1 k_3, k_2)$

Example 7.1 We consider a DG D with index space $S(4, 8, 16)$ and schedule vector $c = (1, 4, 32)$. The coordinates of node v to be executed at time step $t = 401$ according to c can be computed as follows (see Eq. (7.2)):

$$401 = 100 \cdot 4 + 1$$
$$100 = 12 \cdot 8 + 4$$

Therefore we obtain $v = (1, 4, 12)$.

Thus the class of permissible linear schedules offers in opposition to nonlinear schedules the following advantages:

- The evaluation of the values of a sequential linear schedule has time complexity $O(n)$.
- The evaluation of the values of the inverse function of a sequential linear schedule with pipelining period 1 has time complexity $O(n)$, by Eq. (7.2).
- The storage requirement for linear schedules is $O(n)$ since only the components of the schedule vector have to be stored.

(An example of a sequential nonlinear schedule is given in Figure 7.9.)

7.2.3 Permissible Schedules for the Direct LSGP Scheme

The application of the direct LSGP scheme to a DG $D = (S(k_1, \cdots, k_n), N)$ yields a decomposition of D into a number of blocks. In the following we assume for simplicity reasons that D is decomposed into $m_1 \times \cdots \times m_n$ equally sized blocks of the form of $S(l_1, \cdots, l_n)$, where $k_i = l_i \cdot m_i$ for all $i = 1, \cdots, n$. The reader may notice that the theory provided in the next sections is straightforwardly extendable to the general case (see Remark 7.2). Since the blocks are mapped one-to-one onto the PEs of the target array processor, the overall schedule for the decomposed DG has to fulfill certain constraints.

Definition 7.4 A schedule ψ for a direct LSGP decomposition of a DG $D = (S(k_1, \cdots, k_n), N)$ is called *permissible* if

1. ψ defines a permissible sequential schedule for each block of the decomposition (see Definition 7.3), and
2. ψ fulfills the causality constraint for every pair of nodes lying in adjacent blocks.

We say that a permissible schedule ψ for the direct LSGP decomposition of D is linear if ψ is *linear* inside each block of the decomposition.

Clearly ψ consists of two parts, a local scheduling part which specifies the node assignment inside every block, and a global scheduling part that defines the interrelation between adjacent blocks. (Examples of permissible schedules for direct LSGP decompositions of 2-D DGs are given in Figures 7.5–7.8.)

7.2.4 Standardization of Neighborhood Stencils for n-D DGs

We first introduce an equivalence relation on the class of n-D DGs using (geometrical) reflections. Recall that reflections are length and angle preserving linear mappings.

Definition 7.5 Two n-dimensional DGs $D_i = (S_i, N_i)$, $i = 1, 2$, are called *equivalent* if D_1 can be obtained from D_2 by a finite sequence of reflections.

Clearly the notion of equivalent DGs induces an equivalence relation on the set of DGs. As an example, we determine the equivalence classes of all local 2-D DGs.

Example 7.2 Since every DG is by definition acyclic, it is sufficient to restrict the neighborhood stencil N of a local 2-D DG to a subset of

$$N_2 := \{(1, 0), (0, 1), (1, 1), (1, -1)\}$$

This is a consequence of the fact that there exists a hyperplane (line) H through the origin such that among the set

$$\{(1, 0), (0, 1), (1, 1), (1, -1), (-1, 0), (0, -1), (-1, -1), (-1, 1)\}$$

of all dependency arcs, the arcs of N_2 lie on the same side of hyperplane H, and N_2 is a maximal subset with this property. The neighborhood stencils of a complete set of representatives of the equivalence classes of local 2-D DGs are illustrated in Figure 7.4. It should be noted that the equivalence class of 2-D DGs determined by stencil (*c*) also contains those DGs with stencils $[(1, 0), (1, -1)]$ and $\{(1, 0), (1, 1)\}$.

Example 7.2 shows that the neighborhood stencil of a local 2-D DG can be chosen as a subset of N_2. The following definition provides a generalization of this idea.

Definition 7.6 Let $N_2 := \{(1, 0), (0, 1), (1, 1), (1, -1)\}$. For any integer $k > 2$, let

$$N_k := \{(a_1, \cdots, a_{k-1}, 0) | (a_1, \cdots, a_{k-1}) \in N_{k-1}\} \cup$$

$$\{(b_1, \cdots, b_{k-1}, 1) | b_1, \cdots, b_{k-1} \in \{-1, 0, 1\}\}$$

We call any nonempty subset of N_k a *standard* neighborhood stencil.

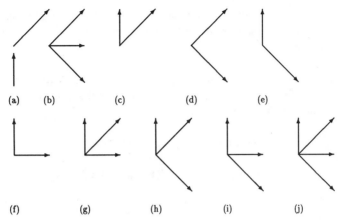

Figure 7.4 *Neighborhood stencils of a complete set of representatives of the equivalence classes of local 2-D DGs.*

We note that N_k is the maximal subset of vectors in $\{1, 0, -1\}^k$ lying on the same side of some hyperplane going through the origin. In fact, an induction argument shows that for all integers $k \geq 2$:

$$|N_k| = \frac{3^k - 1}{2}.$$

Lemma 7.3 For every local k-D DG D with stencil N there exists an equivalent DG D' with standard neighborhood stencil.

Proof: Since D is acyclic, there exists a vector $\mathbf{c} \in \mathbb{R}^n$ such that $\langle \mathbf{c}, \mathbf{s} \rangle > 0$ for all $\mathbf{s} \in N$. Hence all arcs of N lie on the same side of the hyperplane defined by $\mathbf{c}$. By linear algebra, N can be reflected into a standard neighborhood stencil since N_k is a maximal set of dependency arcs lying on the same side of a hyperplane. $\square$

Thus we can restrict our studies to local DGs equipped with a standard neighborhood stencil. We next prove that for any local, complete and homogeneous DG with standard neighborhood stencil a permissible sequential linear schedule with pipelining period 1 exists.

Theorem 7.1 Let $n \geq 2$ and let $l_1, \cdots, l_n$ be positive integers. Suppose $D = (S(l_1, \cdots, l_n), N)$ is an n-D DG such that $N \subseteq N_n$. Then the vector

$$\mathbf{c}_n = (l_2, 1, l_1 l_2, \cdots, l_1 l_2 l_3 \times \cdots \times l_{n-1})$$

defines a permissible sequential linear schedule for D with pipelining period 1. If $N = N_n$, then $\mathbf{c}_n$ is the unique permissible sequential linear schedule for D with pipelining period 1.

Proof: It is sufficient to prove the lemma for $N = N_n$. The proposition is certainly true for $n = 2$. So we assume that the theorem is proved for $n - 1$ ($n > 2$). We consider two cases:

1. Let $\mathbf{a}_n := (a_1, \cdots, a_{n-1}, 0) \in N_n$. Then $\mathbf{a}_{n-1} := (a_1, \cdots, a_{n-1}) \in N_{n-1}$ by definition. Since $\mathbf{c}_{n-1}$ defines a permissible schedule for N_{n-1} by induction hypothesis, we obtain

$$\langle \mathbf{c}_n, \mathbf{a}_n \rangle = \langle \mathbf{c}_{n-1}, \mathbf{a}_{n-1} \rangle > 0.$$

2. Let $\mathbf{b} := (b_1, \cdots, b_{n-1}, 1) \in N_n$. Then an induction argument shows that

$$l_1 \times \cdots \times l_{n-1} > 1 + l_2 + l_2 l_1 + \cdots + l_2 l_1 l_3 \times \cdots \times l_{n-2}.$$

Thus we obtain $\langle \mathbf{c}_n, \mathbf{b} \rangle > 0$.

Hence by Lemma 7.2, $\mathbf{c}_n$ defines a permissible sequential linear schedule for D with pipelining period 1. In view of Lemma 7.2 it is easy to see that in case of $N = N_n$, $\mathbf{c}_n$ is the only permissible sequential linear schedule for D with pipelining period 1. $\square$

7.3 OPTIMAL DIRECT LSGP-DECOMPOSITIONS OF 2-*D* DGs

The designer of a partitioning scheme has to take into account several optimality criteria, like minimum overall computation time, minimum pipelining period, minimum average processing element bandwidth, and minimum control overhead. In this section we apply the direct LSGP scheme to decompose complete, local, and homogenous 2-*D* DGs. Therefore we stipulate that all DGs under consideration are complete, local and homogeneous. The main objective is to design permissible linear schedules for direct LSGP decompositions with minimal overall computation time and minimal pipelining period. Then we discuss the layout of array processors resulting from direct LSGP decompositions. Thus our methodology is strictly top-down, from the algorithm via direct LSGP decomposition to the layout of array processors. In this way, the inherent parallelism of algorithms is best utilized. We finally address further optimality criteria and discuss some examples.

7.3.1 An Optimality Theorem for the Direct LSGP-Decomposition of 2-*D* DGs

In this section we design optimal permissible linear schedules for direct LSGP decompositions of complete, local, and homogeneous 2-*D* DGs w.r.t. overall computation time and pipelining period. In view of Lemma 7.3 we can restrict our investigations to DGs equipped with a standard neighborhood stencil. Recall that the application of the direct LSGP scheme to a 2-*D* DG $D = (S(k_1, k_2), N)$ yields a decomposition of D into $m_1 \times m_2$ blocks

$$B_{i,j} := \{(x + il_1, y + jl_2)|0 \le x < l_1 \wedge 0 \le y < l_2\},$$

for $i = 0, \cdot \cdot \cdot, m_1 - 1$, and $j = 0, \cdot \cdot \cdot, m_2 - 1$, of size $l_1 \times l_2$ (see Section 7.2.3). The blocks are mapped one to one onto the PEs of the target array processor.

Proposition 7.1 A necessary condition for a permissible linear schedule of a 2-D DG D to be optimal w.r.t. overall computation time is that for each node $\mathbf{v}$ of block $B_{0,0} = S(l_1, l_2)$ there exists a directed path from $\mathbf{0}$ to $\mathbf{v}$ and from $\mathbf{v}$ to $(l_1 - 1, l_2 - 1)$. If the condition holds for $B_{0,0}$ then it holds for all blocks since D is homogeneous. This condition is satisfied if and only if the stencil is of the form $(e), \cdot \cdot \cdot, (i)$ or (j) in Figure 7.4.

Indeed, if the stencil is of the form (b), (c), or (d) in Figure 7.4, then there exist permissible nonlinear schedules that have less overall computation time than any permissible linear schedule (see Figs. 7.5, 7.6, and 7.7). However the calculation of their inverse function (for each block) is rather complicated. On the other hand, there seem to be no practical algorithms associated with complete DGs which have stencil (b), (c), or (d). We show that for all 2-D DGs with neighborhood stencil $(e), \cdot \cdot \cdot, (i)$, or (j) there exist direct LSGP decompositions that admit optimal permissible linear schedules.

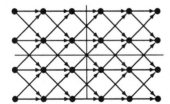

0	2	5	6	9	10
1	3	4	7	8	11
0	2	4	7	8	11
1	3	5	6	9	10

Figure 7.5 DG with stencil (b) partitioned into 2 × 2 blocks and an optimal permissible nonlinear schedule.

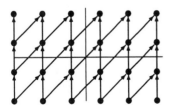

6	8	10	10	8	7
5	7	9	4	5	6
4	5	3	3	4	5
0	1	2	0	1	2

Figure 7.6 DG with stencil (c) partitioned into 2 × 2 blocks and an optimal permissible nonlinear schedule.

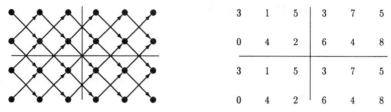

3	1	5	3	7	5
0	4	2	6	4	8
3	1	5	3	7	5
0	4	2	6	4	8

Figure 7.7 DG with stencil (d) partitioned into 2 × 2 blocks and an optimal permissible non-linear schedule.

For this we introduce an algorithm *block_schedule* (i, j) (in symbolic notation) which is associated with block $B_{i,j}$. Since we rely on the neighborhood stencils of Figure 7.4, the execution of *block_schedule* (i, j) requires that *block_schedule* (x, y) was already performed for all blocks $B_{x,y}$ where

$$(x, y) \le (i - l, j + l) \quad \text{or} \quad (x, y) \le (i + k, (j - 1) - k)$$

for $l = 1, \cdots, i, k = 0, \cdots, j - 1$. In this way, a schedule for the whole DG is obtained.

Algorithm 1 procedure *block_schedule* (i, j)

input: 2-D DG $D = (S(k_1, k_2), N)$, partitioned into $m_1 \times m_2$ blocks of size $l_1 \times l_2$, where $k_i = l_i \cdot m_i$ for all $i = 1, \cdots, n$, and a schedule vector $c = (l_2, 1)$. N is one of the stencils $(e), \cdots, (j)$ shown in Figure 7.4 such that $m_1 \le m_2$. (If N has shape (f) or (g), the condition $m_1 \le m_2$ can be omitted.)

output: function $\psi : S(k_1, k_2) \to \mathbb{R}$ determines the execution time of all nodes in D.

1. let $\mathbf{v} := (il_1, jl_2)$;
2. if $N(\mathbf{v}) \ne \emptyset$ then
3. $\quad \psi(\mathbf{v}) := \max \{\psi(\mathbf{u}) | \mathbf{u} \in S(k_1, k_2) \wedge \exists \mathbf{s} \in N : \mathbf{v} = \mathbf{u} + \mathbf{s}\} + 1$;
4. else
5. $\quad \psi(\mathbf{v}) := 0$;
6. fi
7. for $x \leftarrow 0$ step 1 until l_1 do
8. $\quad$ for $y \leftarrow 0$ step 1 until l_2 do
9. $\quad\quad \psi(x + il_1, y + jl_2) := \langle \mathbf{c}, (\mathbf{x}, \mathbf{y}) \rangle > + \psi(\mathbf{v})$;

An example illustrating the application of the algorithm is shown in Figure 7.8.

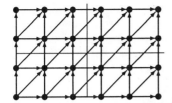

3	5	7	8	10	12
2	4	6	7	9	11
1	3	5	6	8	10
0	2	4	5	7	9

Figure 7.8 *DG decomposed into 2 × 2 blocks and an optimal permissible linear schedule* ψ

Remark 7.1 We have to pinpoint to the case not covered by Algorithm 1. If $m_1 > m_2$ and N is one of the stencils (e), (h), (i), or (j) shown in Figure 7.4, then there exists an optimal permissible nonlinear schedule w.r.t. overall computation time, if the lines 7–9 of Algorithm 1 are replaced by the schedule illustrated in Figure 7.9. The convolution example will show that the condition $m_1 \leq m_2$ is in practice not as restrictive as it seems (see subsection on convolution).

We shall now prove that Algorithm 1 defines an optimal schedule ψ. In fact, schedule ψ is sequential and linear within each block (see lines 7–9) and data-driven between adjacent blocks (see lines 2–6). Clearly node $\mathbf{v} = (il_1, jl_2)$ specifies the first scheduled operation of block $B_{i,j}$. In practice, the value $\psi(\mathbf{v})$ is determined by the arrival of all data necessary to perform the operation specified by $\mathbf{v}$ (see lines 2, 5). The algorithm assumes that the transfer of data between adjacent blocks only takes one time step. It would have been more realistic to assume a constant time delay for data transfer between adjacent blocks. The reader may notice that the following theorem remains valid in this general setting. We now prove the main result of this section.

Theorem 7.2 Under the assumptions made in the input part of Algorithm 1, ψ defines an optimal permissible linear schedule for the direct LSGP decomposition of D w.r.t. overall computation time as well as pipelining period.

Proof: Clearly the function ψ is well-defined. We first show that ψ is permissible for the direct LSGP decomposition of D. Indeed, if $l_2 > 1$, then

$$\langle \mathbf{c}, \mathbf{s} \rangle > 0 \quad \text{for all } \mathbf{s} \in N$$

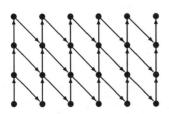

6	10	14	18	21	23
3	7	11	15	19	22
1	4	8	12	16	20
0	2	5	9	13	17

Figure 7.9 *Sequential nonlinear schedule for block S(6, 4).*

and thus ψ defines a permissible schedule for every block of D. If $l_2 = 1$, then ψ is trivially permissible for every block of D. Moreover ψ is in view of Lemma 7.1 sequential inside each block. It remains to prove that ψ fulfills the causality constraint for every pair of nodes lying in adjacent blocks. For this we require the following lemma.

Lemma 7.4   Let $\mathbf{v}$ be a node in $B_{i+1,j+1}$ with nonempty neighborhood, that is, $N(\mathbf{v}) \neq \varnothing$, which is located at the borderline to $B_{i,j+1}$ or $B_{i+1,j}$, that is, $\mathbf{v}$ has some neighbor $\mathbf{u} \in N(\mathbf{v})$ in $B_{i,j+1}$ or $B_{i+1,j}$, respectively.

If D is scheduled by ψ, then the execution time of $\mathbf{v}$ is greater than the execution time of all neighbors $\mathbf{w}$ of $\mathbf{v}$ located in $B_{i,j+1}$ or $B_{i+1,j}$, respectively.

Proof: We first consider the adjacent blocks $B_{i+1,j+1}$ and $B_{i+1,j}$. By lines 2–6 of Algorithm 1, the lemma is certainly true for node

$$\mathbf{v}_0 = ((i + 1)l_1, (j + 1)l_2)$$

Now we proceed by induction and assume that node $\mathbf{v} = ((i + 1)l_1 + k, (j + 1)l_2)$, $k < l_1 - 1$, has some neighbor $\mathbf{u} := \mathbf{v} - \mathbf{s}$ ($\mathbf{s} \in N$) in $B_{i+1,j}$ such that $\psi(\mathbf{v}) > \psi(\mathbf{u})$. For this we put $\mathbf{u} = (x, y)$, and first show that $\mathbf{v}_1 = ((i + 1)l_1 + (k + 1), (j + 1)l_2)$ has neighbor $\mathbf{u}_1 := (x + 1, y) \in B_{i+1,j}$. Indeed

$$\mathbf{v}_1 = \mathbf{v} + (1, 0) = \mathbf{u} + \mathbf{s} + (1, 0) = \mathbf{u}_1 + \mathbf{s}$$

It remains to prove that $\psi(\mathbf{v}_1) > \psi(\mathbf{u}_1)$. In fact, we have

$$\begin{aligned}
\psi(\mathbf{v}_1) &= \psi(\mathbf{v} + (1, 0)) \\
&= \psi(\mathbf{v}) + \langle \mathbf{c}, (1, 0) \rangle \\
&> \psi(\mathbf{u}) + \langle \mathbf{c}, (1, 0) \rangle \quad \text{by induction hypothesis} \\
&= \psi(\mathbf{u} + (1, 0)) \\
&= \psi(\mathbf{u}_1).
\end{aligned}$$

A similar proof establishes the assertion of the lemma for the adjacent blocks $B_{i,j+1}$ and $B_{i+1,j+1}$. $\square$

Thus we have shown that ψ defines a permissible linear schedule for the direct LSGP decomposition of D.

Moreover it follows from Lemma 1 and lines 7–9 of Algorithm 1 that the pipelining period of schedule ψ is 1. It remains to prove that ψ is optimal w.r.t. overall computation time. For this we denote by d_{ij} and e_{ij} the minimal and maximal execution time of the nodes in block $B_{i,j}$ if D is scheduled by ψ, respectively.

Suppose ψ_0 is an arbitrary optimal permissible schedule for the direct LSGP decomposition of D w.r.t. overall computation time. If D is scheduled by ψ_0, let s_{ij} and t_{ij} denote the minimal and maximal execution time of the nodes in block $B_{i,j}$, respectively. Thus we have

$$t_{ij} = s_{ij} + l_1 l_2 - 1 \text{ and } e_{ij} = d_{ij} + l_1 l_2 - 1 \tag{7.4}$$

for all $i = 0, \cdots, m_1 - 1, j = 0, \cdots, m_2 - 1$. Clearly t_{m_1-1,m_2-1} and e_{m_1-1,m_2-1} specify the overall computation time of D if D is scheduled by ψ_0 and ψ, respectively. Since ψ_0 is optimal, we must have

$$t_{m_1-1,m_2-1} \leq e_{m_1-1,m_2-1}. \tag{7.5}$$

For $m_1 \leq m_2$, we consider block B_{0,m_2-m_1}. It follows from Algorithm 1 that

$$d_{0,m_2-m_1} = (m_2 - m_1)l_2$$

since $(0, 1) \in N$ by hypothesis. Because of the dependency arc $(0, 1) \in N$, all nodes in block B_{0,m_2-m_1} have execution time not less than $(m_2 - m_1)l_2$. Thus we have shown that

$$s_{0,m_2-m_1} \geq d_{0,m_2-m_1}$$

and consequently by Eq. (7.4)

$$t_{0,m_2-m_1} \geq e_{0,m_2-m_1}.$$

We next require the following

Lemma 7.5 Let $\mathbf{v}$ be a node in $B_{i+1,j+1}$ with nonempty neighborhood, that is, $N(\mathbf{v}) \neq \varnothing$, which is located at the borderline to $B_{i,j+1}$ or $B_{i+1,j}$, that is, $\mathbf{v}$ has some neighbor $\mathbf{u} \in N(\mathbf{v})$ in $B_{i,j+1}$ or $B_{i+1,j}$, respectively.

If D is scheduled by ψ, then there exists a neighbor $\mathbf{w}$ of $\mathbf{v}$ in $B_{i,j+1}$ or $B_{i+1,j}$, respectively, such that the execution time of $\mathbf{w}$ is one less than the execution time of $\mathbf{v}$, that is, $\psi(\mathbf{w}) = \psi(\mathbf{v}) - 1$.

Proof: We consider the adjacent blocks $B_{i+1,j}$ and $B_{i+1,j+1}$. By lines 2–6 of Algorithm 1, the statement is certainly true for node $\mathbf{v}_0 = ((i + 1)l_1, (j + 1)l_2)$. We now proceed by induction and assume that node $\mathbf{v} = ((i + 1)l_1 + k, (j + 1)l_2)$, $k < l_1 - 1$, has some neighbor $\mathbf{u} := \mathbf{v} - \mathbf{s}$ ($\mathbf{s} \in N$) in $B_{i+1,j}$ such that $\psi(\mathbf{v}) = \psi(\mathbf{u}) + 1$. For this we put $\mathbf{u} = (x, y)$. Then by the proof of Lemma 4, $\mathbf{v}_1 = ((i + 1)l_1 + (k + 1), (j + 1)l_2)$ has neighbor $\mathbf{u}_1 := (x + 1, y) \in B_{i+1,j}$, i.e., $\mathbf{v}_1$

$= \mathbf{u}_1 + \mathbf{s}$. It remains to prove that $\psi(\mathbf{v}_1) = \psi(\mathbf{u}_1) + 1$. In fact, we have

$$
\begin{aligned}
\psi(\mathbf{v}_1) &= \psi(\mathbf{v} + (1, 0)) \\
&= \psi(\mathbf{v}) + \langle \mathbf{c}, (1, 0) \rangle \\
&= \psi(\mathbf{u}) + \langle \mathbf{c}, (1, 0) \rangle + 1 \quad \text{by induction hypothesis} \\
&= \psi(\mathbf{u} + (1, 0)) + 1 \\
&= \psi(\mathbf{u}_1) + 1
\end{aligned}
$$

An analogous proof establishes the assertion for the adjacent blocks $B_{i,j+1}$ and $B_{i+1,j+1}$. $\square$

We have already proved that $t_{0,m_2-m_1} \geq e_{0,m_2-m_1}$. Now we proceed by induction. For this suppose that

$$
t_{i,m_2-m_1+i} \geq e_{i,m_2-m_1+i} \tag{7.6}
$$

holds for some $i < m_1 - 1$. By Proposition 7.1, the upper right node

$$
\mathbf{v} = (il_1 + l_1 - 1, (m_2 - m_1 + i)l_2 + l_2 - 1)
$$

of block B_{i,m_2-m_1+i} must have execution time e_{i,m_2-m_1+i} or t_{i,m_2-m_1+i} if D is scheduled by ψ or ψ_0, respectively. We now consider the "lower left" node

$$
\mathbf{v}_0 = ((i + 1)l_1, (m_2 - m_1 + i + 1)l_2)
$$

of block B_{i+1,m_2-m_1+i+1}. It follows again from Proposition 7.1 that $\mathbf{v}_0$ has execution time d_{i+1,m_2-m_1+i+1} or s_{i+1,m_2-m_1+i+1} when D is scheduled by ψ or ψ_0, respectively. We now require the following

Lemma 7.6 Let τ denote the length (i.e., number of edges) of the longest directed path from $\mathbf{v}$ to $\mathbf{v}_0$. Then we have

$$
d_{i+1,m_2-m_1+i+1} = e_{i,m_2-m_1+i} + \tau
$$

The proof follows directly from Lemma 7.5 (see also Fig. 7.8). Notice that Lemma 7.6 holds independently of the specific blocks under consideration, since D is homogeneous and the neighborhood stencil of D is of the form $(e), \cdots ,$ (i) or (j) (see Fig. 7.4). Lemma 7.6 and Eq. (7.6) imply that

$$
d_{i+1,m_2-m_1+i+1} = e_{i,m_2-m_1+i} + \tau \leq t_{i,m_2-m_1+i} + \tau
$$

Since ψ_0 is permissible, we must have

$$
t_{i,m_2-m_1+i} + \tau \leq s_{i+1,m_2-m_1+i+1}
$$

Thus we obtain

$$e_{i+1, m_2-m_1+i+1} \leq t_{i+1, m_2-m_1+i+1},$$

since ψ and ψ_0 define sequential linear schedules for every block. Our induction argument shows that in particular, $e_{m_1-1, m_2-1} \leq t_{m_1-1, m_2-1}$. This in view of Eq. (7.5):

$$t_{m_1-1, m_2-1} = e_{m_1-1, m_2-1}$$

Hence we have shown that ψ is optimal w.r.t. overall computation time, and the proof of the theorem is complete □

In all cases not covered by Theorem 7.2 it is useful to have at least so-called suboptimal linear schedules.

Definition 7.7 A *suboptimal* linear schedule for a direct LSGP decomposition of a DG D is a permissible linear schedule for D which is optimal among all permissible linear schedules for D w.r.t. overall computation time.

Since the class of sequential linear schedules with pipelining period 1 is fully known, we can find suboptimal linear schedules by enumeration (see Section 7.5). We finally provide a formula for the overall computation time of the global schedule specified by Algorithm 1.

Corollary 7.2 Under the assumptions of the inputs part of Algorithm 1, the overall computation time is given by

$$T = \begin{cases} (m_2 - 1)l_2 + (m_1 - 1)((l_1 - 1)(l_2 - 1) + l_1 + 1) + l_1 l_2 \text{ if } (1, -1) \in N \\ (m_2 - 1)l_2 + (m_1 - 1)((l_1 - 1)(l_2 - 1) + l_1) + l_1 l_2 \quad \text{otherwise} \end{cases}$$

$$(7.7)$$

Proof: The proof of Theorem 7.2 enables us to compute the least execution time for the blocks $B_{i+1, j}$ and $B_{i, j+1}$ in terms of the (i, j)th block. In fact, we know that the nodes

$$\mathbf{v}_{i, j+1} := (il_1, (j + 1)l_2) \quad \text{and} \quad \mathbf{v}_{i+1, j} := ((i + 1)l_1, jl_2)$$

have least execution time, say $d_{i+1, j}$ and $d_{i, j+1}$, among the nodes in $B_{i+1, j}$ and $B_{i, j+1}$, respectively. If $d_{i, j}$ denotes the execution time of $\mathbf{v}_{i, j} := (il_1, jl_2)$ and $(1, -1) \notin N$, then we obtain, by definition of ψ,

$$d_{i+1, j} = d_{i, j} + (l_1 - 1)(l_2 - 1) + l_1 \quad \text{and} \quad d_{i, j+1} = d_{i, j} + l_2$$

Moreover, in case of $(1, -1) \in N$, we obtain

$$d_{i+1,j} = d_{i,j} + (l_1 - 1)(l_2 - 1) + l_1 + 1 \qquad \text{and} \qquad d_{i,j+1} = d_{i,j} + l_2$$

By taking into account that the computation time of a sequentially scheduled block of size $l_1 \times l_2$ is $l_1 l_2$, a simple induction argument yields the desired formula. $\square$

Remark 7.2   Theorem 7.2 is also applicable if a DG cannot be partitioned into equally sized blocks. For instance, let D be a DG of size 18×18 which is to be decomposed into 33 blocks. The D can be decomposed into 16 blocks of size 4×4 and 17 blocks of size 2×2. In this case we first consider the subgraph D' of D partitioned into 16 blocks of size 4×4. By applying Theorem 7.2 we obtain a (sub-)optimal linear schedule ψ' for D'. Next we consider the embedding of D' into D and define a linear schedule ψ for D as an extension of ψ', that is, $\psi(\mathbf{v}) = \psi'(\mathbf{v})$ for all nodes $\mathbf{v}$ in D'. Then we apply Algorithm 1 to the (not yet scheduled) blocks: $B_{4,0}, B_{0,4}, B_{4,1}, B_{1,4}, B_{4,2}, B_{2,4}, B_{4,3}, B_{3,4}$ and $B_{4,4}$ and obtain a well defined linear schedule for ψ. It is easy to see that ψ is also a permissible (sub-)optimal linear schedule for D w.r.t. overall computation time.

7.3.2   Block Dependence Relations and Block Graphs

We now discuss the layout of array processors resulting from direct LSGP decompositions of 2-D DGs. For this we introduce the notion of block graph. Recall that the application of the direct LSGP scheme to a 2-D DG $D = (S(k_1, k_2), N)$ yields a decomposition of D into $m_1 \times m_2$ blocks $B_{0,0}, \cdot \cdot \cdot, B_{m_1-1, m_2-1}$.

A binary relation $\rightarrow$ on the set of blocks is defined as follows:

$$B_{ij} \rightarrow B_{kl} : \Leftrightarrow \exists \mathbf{u} \in B_{ij} : \exists \mathbf{v} \in B_{kl} : (\mathbf{u}, \mathbf{v}) \in E,$$

where (V, E) denotes the directed graph associated with D (see Definition 7.2). The relation $\rightarrow$ is called a *block dependence relation* for D and the elements of $\rightarrow$ are called *block links*. The pair $(\{B_{ij} \mid 0 \le i < m_1, 0 \le j < m_2\}, \rightarrow)$ is called a *block graph* for D.

A block graph reveals the data dependencies among adjacent blocks. We now discuss several interesting cases. For this let N denote a 2-D standard neighborhood stencil:

1. If $(1, -1) \notin N$, then the block dependence relation $\rightarrow$ defines a partial order:

   (a) If $m_1 = 1$ or $m_2 = 1$, then the block dependence relation is a linear order. For instance, in case of $m_1 = 1$ the block graph defines a linear array:

   $$B_{0,0} \rightarrow B_{0,1} \rightarrow \cdot \cdot \cdot \rightarrow B_{0, m_2-1}$$

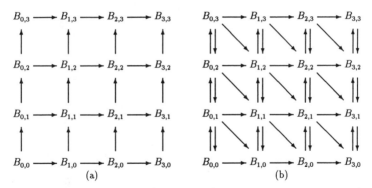

Figure 7.10   *Block graph (a) for N = {(1, 0), (0, 1)}, and block graph (b) for N = {(1, 0), (0, 1), (1, −1)}, where $m_1 = m_2 = 4$.*

(b) In case of $m_1 > 1$ and $m_2 > 1$, the block graph for $N = \{(1, 0), (0, 1)\}$ has an acyclic structure and is illustrated in Figure 7.10a.

2. If $(1, -1) \in N$, then the block dependence relation may not define a partial order:

   (a) In case of $m_1 = 1$ or $m_2 = 1$, the block dependence relation specifies a linear order (see 1a).

   (b) If $m_1 > 1$ and $m_2 > 1$, then, for instance, the block graph for $N = \{(1, 0), (0, 1), (1, -1)\}$ exhibits vertically bidirectional, horizontally and diagonally unidirectional arcs (see Fig. 7.10b).

It should be noted that the definition of block dependence relation and block graph can be easily extended to n-D DGs.

7.3.3   Matching of Block Graphs to Array Processors

In the direct LSGP scheme, the blocks of a DG are mapped one to one onto the PEs of an array processor. This mapping only establishes the correspondence between blocks and PEs, but not between block links $B_{ij} \rightarrow B_{kl}$ and physical communication links of the array processor.

We call a mapping from the block dependence relation to the communication links of an array processor a *matching scheme* [4].

Matching schemes may not be one to one. That means that several block links are mapped onto the same communication link. In this case, the communication channels have to be *time shared* in order to accommodate all block links. A main problem is therefore to specify a proper time division scheme for the communication channels [3, 4].

Example 7.3   The blocks of the block graph shown in Figure 7.10b can be mapped ($B_{i,j} \mapsto z_{i,j}$) one to one onto the 2-D array processor illustrated in Figure 7.11. However, the matching scheme is not one to one. For instance, if the com-

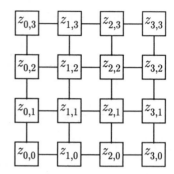

Figure 7.11 Layout of a 2-D array processor.

munication links between $z_{i,j+1}$ and $z_{i,j}$, as well as between $z_{i,j}$ and $z_{i+1,j}$, are time multiplexed, then the array processor can implement all block links (in particular, the diagonal block links $B_{i,j+1} \rightarrow B_{i+1,j}$).

7.3.4 Further Optimality Criteria

Overall computation time and pipelining period are crucial optimality criteria for the implementation of algorithms on constrained array processors. In case of the direct LSGP scheme the storage requirement plays also a very important role. If the matching scheme is not one to one, the communication bandwidth becomes a decisive criterion too.

Storage Requirements. The execution of an operation in a PE requires reading operands from input ports or from local storage, performing the corresponding operation and delivering results to output ports or local storage. Operations corresponding to nodes located at the boundaries of a block access ports, while operations corresponding to interior nodes only access local storage. The storage requirement for a block is given by the number of storage locations required to store input/output data and intermediate results, when the block is executed. We now estimate the storage requirement for a block if the nodes (operations) of a 2-D DG are scheduled by the optimal schedule ψ specified by Algorithm 1. For this we only consider an interior block $B_{i,j}$ of size $l_1 \times l_2$. Then the storage requirement for $B_{i,j}$ is given by

$$SR_2^{\text{int}} := |N|(2l_1 + 4l_2 - 2)$$

In this expression, $l_1 + l_2 - 1$ nodes located at the boundary of $B_{i,j}$ receive input data from adjacent blocks. Therefore we require $|N|(l_1 + l_2 - 1)$ storage locations for the input data. Moreover in view of the definition of ψ, we require at most $2|N|l_2$ locations to store intermediate results. Finally, $l_1 + l_2 - 1$ nodes located at the boundary of $B_{i,j}$ provide data for adjacent blocks. Hence $|N|(l_1 + l_2 - 1)$ storage locations are necessary for storing the output data.

If a DG $D = (S(k_1, k_2), N)$ is decomposed into n blocks according to the LSGP scheme, the minimization of the storage requirement for a block of the decomposition of D requires the minimization of the real valued function $SR_2^{int}(m_1, m_2)$ under the constraints:

$$m_1 \cdot m_2 = n \quad \text{and} \quad m_i \cdot l_i = k_i \text{ for } i = 1, 2$$

Communication Bandwidth. If the overall computation time is affected by the matching scheme, we say that the bandwidth of the target array processor is *limited*. This may be the case if several block links have to share the same physical communication link. Then the minimization of the average communication bandwidth becomes a very important optimality criterion. A coarse measure for the communication bandwidth is the communication requirement:

$$CR = C \frac{|N|(l_1 + l_2 - 1)}{l_1 l_2}$$

which relates the number $l_1 + l_2 - 1$ of nodes at the boundary of a block receiving $|N|$ input data from outside of the block to the total number $l_1 l_2$ of nodes of a block. Improved measures will be necessary in the future.

7.3.5 Examples

We illustrate the theory developed in the previous sections by three examples: matrix–vector multiplication, basic mathematical morphology operations, and convolution.

Matrix–Vector Multiplication. We assume that multiplication of 360×480-matrices by vectors of length 480 is to be performed on an array processor with 24 PEs. In view of Section 7.2.1, the DG D_M for this particular matrix–vector multiplication problem consists of index space $S(360, 480)$ and neighborhood stencil $N = \{(1, 0), (0, 1)\}$. Table 7.2 summarizes all decompositions of D_M into m_1

TABLE 7.2 Decompositions of D_M into 24
Blocks and the Minimal Overall
Computation Time

$m_1 \times m_2$	$l_1 \times l_2$	Computation time
1×24	360×20	7659
2×12	180×40	14800
3×8	120×60	21901
4×6	90×80	28962
6×4	60×120	28922
8×3	45×160	21826
12×2	30×240	14700
24×1	15×480	7544

$\times\ m_2$ blocks of size $l_1 \times l_2$ with the property

$$m_1 \cdot m_2 = 24,\ m_1 \cdot l_1 = 360 \qquad \text{and} \qquad m_2 \cdot l_2 = 480$$

and the associated overall computation time of schedule ψ specified by Algorithm 1. Notice that the given computation times are optimal. While the decomposition into blocks of the form $S(360, 20)$ and $S(15, 480)$ yields linear block graphs, all other decompositions yield 2-D gridlike arrays as illustrated in Fig 7.10a. The decomposition into blocks of size 15×480 yields the highest efficiency: 0.95. The reader may notice that there is a trade-off between storage requirement and computation time.

Mathematical Morphology Operations: Dilation and Erosion.   A systolic array design for the mathematical morphology operations dilation and erosion consisting of 24 PEs has been proposed to process images having the size of 360×480 pixels [8]. By applying some transformations, the DG D has the same structure as for the matrix–vector multiplication problem. We have proposed a systolic array design with implements the most efficient decomposition of D into blocks of size 15×480 (see Table 7.2).

Convolution.   The problem of convolution can be defined in the following way: Given two sequences $(u_0, \cdots, u_{n-1})$ and $(w_0, \cdots, w_{n-1})$ of complex numbers of length n. The convolution of the two sequences yields a sequence $(y_0, \cdots, y_{2n-2})$ such that

$$y_j = \sum_{k=0}^{j} u_k w_{j-k} \quad \text{for } j = 0, \cdots, 2n - 2$$

(see Kung [4] for details). A corresponding single assignment algorithm is given by

$$u_j^k = u_{j-1}^k \qquad w_j^k = w_{j-1}^{k-1}$$
$$y_j^k = y_j^{k-1} + u_j^k \cdot w_j^k$$

with the initial conditions

$$u_0^k = u_k,\ w_{j-k}^0 = w_{j-k} \qquad \text{and} \qquad y_j^0 = 0$$

From this we derive the corresponding DG D' (see Fig. 7.12a). In order to apply our theory we transform D' into a DG D by adopting the following coordinate transformation:

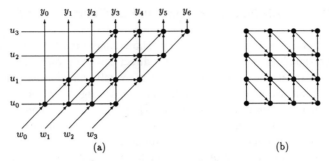

Figure 7.12 Local DGs for convolution ($n = 4$).

$$\begin{pmatrix} j' \\ k' \end{pmatrix} = \begin{pmatrix} 0 & 1 \\ 1 & -1 \end{pmatrix} \begin{pmatrix} j \\ k \end{pmatrix}.$$

D is schematically illustrated in Figure 7.12b. Suppose that convolution of sequences of length $n = 512$ is to be implemented by an array processor of 16 PEs. We then obtain a DG $D = (S(512, 512), N)$, where N is specified as in Figure 7.4i. Table 7.3 summarizes all decompositions of D into $m_1 \times m_2$ blocks of size $l_1 \times l_2$ satisfying the constraints

$$m_1 \cdot m_2 = 16, \quad m_1 \cdot l_1 = 512 \quad \text{and} \quad m_2 \cdot l_2 = 512$$

Notice that the only permissible sequential linear schedule with pipeline period 1 for a block with stencil N is given by $\mathbf{c} = (512, 1)$. Table 7.3 also shows the corresponding overall computation time if D is scheduled by Algorithm 1 together with schedule vector $\mathbf{c}$. The reader may notice that only the overall computation time corresponding to decompositions into blocks of size 512×32, 256×64, and 128×128 are optimal. The most efficient decomposition ($m_1 = 1$ and $m_2 = 16$) yields an implementation of the convolution algorithm with efficiency 0.97, and the resulting block graph is linear. This example demonstrates that the condition $m_1 \le m_2$ occurring in the input part of Algorithm 1 is not a serious restriction. $\square$

TABLE 7.3 Decompositions of D into 16 Blocks

$m_1 \times m_2$	$l_1 \times l_2$	Computation time
16×1	32×512	254493
8×2	64×256	129549
4×4	128×128	65541
2×8	256×64	33153
1×16	512×32	16863

7.4 OPTIMAL DIRECT LSGP DECOMPOSITIONS OF *n-D* DGs

The discussion in the previous section has shown that a fairly large class of algorithms corresponding to 2-*D* DGs admit a direct LSGP decomposition for which an optimal permissible linear schedule w.r.t. overall computation time exists. A similar assertion also holds for algorithms corresponding to 3-*D* DGs [5]. We now show that under certain restrictions every *n-D* DG admits a decomposition according to the direct LSGP scheme for which a permissible optimal linear schedule w.r.t. overall computation time and pipelining period exists. We again stipulate that all DGs under consideration are complete, homogeneous, and local.

7.4.1 An Optimality Theorem for the Direct LSGP Partitioning of *n-D* DGs

We recall that the application of the direct LSGP scheme to an *n-D* DG $D = (S(k_1, \cdots, k_n), N)$ yields a decomposition of D into a number of blocks. In the following we assume for simplicity reasons that D decomposes into $m_1 \times \cdots \times m_n$ equally sized blocks of the form $S(l_1, \cdots, l_n)$, where $k_i = l_i \cdot m_i$ for all $i = 1, \cdots, n$ (see Remark 2). The $(y_1, \cdots, y_n)$th block of the decomposition is then comprised by the set

$$B_{y_1, \ldots, y_n} := \{(x_1 + y_1 l_1, \cdots, x_n + y_n l_n) | 0 \le x_i < l_i \text{ for } i = 1, \cdots, n\}$$

where $y_i = 0, \cdots, m_i - 1$ for $i = 1, \cdots, n$. We now study direct LSGP decompositions of *n-D* DGs, which admit optimal permissible linear schedules. For this we first consider a special case (Theorem 7.3) and then provide several extensions. Therefore we first apply the following procedure *block_schedule*($y_1, \cdots, y_n$), which is obviously a generalization of procedure *block_schedule*(y_1, y_2) given in Section 7.3.1, to *n-D* DGs whose neighborhood stencil consists of the n unit vectors.

Algorithm 2 procedure *block_schedule*($y_1, \cdots y_n$)

input: *n-D* DG $D = (S(k_1, \cdots, k_n), N)$ with standard neighborhood stencil, partitioned into $m_1 \times \cdots \times m_n$ of size $l_1 \times \cdots \times l_n$, where $k_i = l_i \cdot m_i$ for $i = 1, \cdots, n$. Let

$$m_{\pi(1)} \ge \cdots \ge m_{\pi(n)} \quad \text{for some } \pi \in \Gamma_n$$

Then define a schedule vector

$$\mathbf{c} = (c_1, \cdots, c_n) \in \mathbb{R}^n$$

where

$$c_{\pi(1)} = 1 \quad \text{and} \quad c_{\pi(i)} = \prod_{j=1}^{i-1} (l_{\pi(j)} + 1) \quad \text{for } i = 2, \cdots, n$$

output: function $\psi : S(k_1, \cdots, k_n) \to \mathbb{R}$ determines the execution time of all nodes in the DG D.

1.   let $\mathbf{v} := (y_1 l_1, \cdots, y_n l_n)$;
2.   if $N(\mathbf{v}) \neq \varnothing$ then
3. $\psi(\mathbf{v}) := \max \{\psi(\mathbf{u}) \,|\, \mathbf{u} \in S(k_1, \cdots, k_n) \land \exists \mathbf{s} \in N : \mathbf{v} = \mathbf{u} + \mathbf{s}\} + 1$;
4.   else
5. $\psi(\mathbf{v}) := 0$;
6.   fi
7.1. for $x_1 \leftarrow 0$ step 1 until l_1 do $\cdots$
7.n. for $x_n \leftarrow 0$ step 1 until l_n do
8. $\psi(x_1 + y_1 l_1, \cdots, x_n + y_n l_n) := < \mathbf{c}, (x_1, \cdots, x_n) > + \psi(\mathbf{v})$;

Theorem 7.3 Let $D = (S(k_1, \cdots, k_n), N)$ be an n-D DG whose stencil consists of the n unit vectors, that is,

$$N = \{(1, 0, \cdots, 0), \cdots, (0, \cdots, 0, 1)\}$$

Suppose that D is decomposed into $m_1 \times \cdots \times m_n$ blocks of size $l_1 \times \cdots \times l_n$. If Algorithm 2 is applied to this decomposition of D, then ψ is an optimal permissible linear schedule for the direct LSGP decomposition of D w.r.t. overall computation time as well as pipelining period.

Proof: Notice first that Lemmas 7.4, 7.5, and 7.6 can be easily generalized to the n-D case. In fact, their proofs only require the change of a few words. Thus it follows from the generalization of Lemma 7.4 that ψ is permissible according to Definition 7.4. We now apply induction to prove that the proposed schedule ψ is optimal w.r.t. overall computation time. For simplicity we may assume that

$$m_1 \geq \cdots \geq m_n$$

Then the schedule vector defined by Algorithm 2 becomes

$$\mathbf{c} = \left(1, l_1, \cdots, \prod_{i=1}^{n-1} l_i\right)$$

Clearly Theorem 7.2 proves the statement in case of $n = 2$. Suppose that the assertion is proved for $(n\text{-}1)$-dimensional DGs. We first consider the node

$$\mathbf{v} = ((m_1 - m_n)l_1, \cdots, (m_{n-1} - m_n)l_{n-1}, 0)$$

belonging to block $B_{(m_1-m_n, \cdots, m_{n-1}-m_n, 0)}$ and define the $(n\text{-}1)$-D DG

$$D_{n-1} = (S((m_1 - m_n + 1)l_1, \cdots, (m_{n-1} - m_n + 1)l_{n-1}), N')$$

where $N' = N \setminus \{(0, \cdots, 0, 1)\}$. By hypothesis

$$\mathbf{s} = \left(1, l_1, \cdots, \prod_{i=1}^{n-2} l_i\right)$$

defines an optimal permissible linear schedule for D_{n-1}. Notice that $B_{(m_1-m_n, \cdots, m_{n-1}-m_n, 0)}$ belongs to D_{n-1}, and furthermore

$$\mathbf{u} = ((m_1 - m_n)l_1 + l_1 - 1, \cdots, (m_{n-1} - m_n)l_{n-1} + l_{n-1} - 1, 0)$$

is the last node scheduled if Algorithm 2 together with $\mathbf{s}$ is applied to D_{n-1}. Hence if we compare ψ with some optimal permissible schedule ψ_0, then $\mathbf{v}$ is scheduled at $d_{(m_1-m_n, \cdots, m_{n-1}-m_n, 0)}$ and we obtain

$$s_{(m_1-m_n, \cdots, m_{n-1}-m_n, 0)} \geq d_{(m_1-m_n, \cdots, m_{n-1}-m_n, 0)}$$

Here we use the notation as in the proof of Theorem 7.2. For both schedules are sequential inside every book,

$$t_{(m_1-m_n, \cdots, m_{n-1}-m_n, 0)} \geq e_{(m_1-m_n, \cdots, m_{n-1}-m_n, 0)}$$

where $e_{(m_1-m_n, \cdots, m_{n-1}-m_n, 0)}$ is the execution time of $\mathbf{u}$. Now we may proceed by induction using Lemmas 7.5 and 7.6 as in the proof of Theorem 7.2 to see that ψ is optimal w.r.t. overall computation time. Clearly the pipelining period α resulting from schedule ψ is $\alpha = 1$ (see Zimmermann [5] for further details). □

Example 7.4 Let $D = (S(6, 9, 4), N_3)$ be decomposed into 12 blocks of size $3 \times 3 \times 2$. Hence $m_1 = 2$, $m_2 = 3$, and $m_3 = 2$. Figure 7.13 exhibits the block structure of D. The optimal permissible linear schedule ψ for D obtained from Algorithm 2 together with schedule vector $\mathbf{c} = (3, 1, 9)$ is shown in Figure 7.14. In order to illustrate the proof of Theorem 7.3, notice that $\mathbf{v} = (0, 3, 0)$ is an element of block $B_{(0,1,0)}$ belonging to the 2-D DG $D_2 = (S(3, 6), N')$.

Corollary 7.3 Let $D' = (S(k_1, \cdots, k_n)N')$ be an n-D DG such that

$$(1, 0, \cdots, 0), \cdots, (0, \cdots, 0, 1) \in N'$$

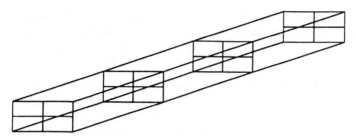

Figure 7.13 Block structure of D.

Suppose that D' is decomposed into $m_1 \times \cdot \cdot \cdot \times m_n$ blocks of size $l_1 \times \cdot \cdot \cdot \times l_n$. If all vectors $\mathbf{v} \in N'$ satisfy the causality constraint

$$\langle \mathbf{c}, \mathbf{v} \rangle > 0$$

then the application of Algorithm 2 to this decomposition of D' yields an optimal permissible linear schedule ψ w.r.t. overall computation time as well as pipelining period.

Corollary 7.4 Let $D = (S(k_1, \cdot \cdot \cdot , k_n), N_n)$ be an n-D DG with neighborhood stencil N_n (see *Definition* 7.6). Then there exists a decomposition of D into $m_1 \times$

	17	20	23		25	28	31
16	19	22		24	27	30	
15	18	21		23	26	29	
	8	11	14		16	19	22
7	10	13		15	18	21	
6	9	12		14	17	20	

	14	17	20		22	25	28
13	16	19		21	24	27	
12	15	18		20	23	26	
	5	8	11		13	16	19
4	7	10		12	15	18	
3	6	9		11	14	17	

	11	14	17		19	22	25
10	13	16		18	21	24	
9	12	15		17	20	23	
	2	5	8		10	13	16
1	4	7		9	12	15	
0	3	6		8	11	14	

$$x_3 \qquad x_2 \qquad x_1$$

Figure 7.14 *Optimal linear schedule for D: The first column shows the blocks $B_{(0,0,0)}$, $B_{(0,1,0)}$, $B_{(0,2,0)}$, the second, $B_{(1,0,0)}$, $B_{(1,1,0)}$, $B_{(1,2,0)}$.*

$\cdots \times m_n$ blocks of size $l_1 \times \cdots \times l_n$ such that the application of Algorithm 2 to this given decomposition of D yields an optimal permissible linear schedule w.r.t. overall computation time and pipelining period.

Proof: We may choose the decomposition such that $m_2 \geq m_1 \geq m_3 \geq \cdots \geq m_n$. Then in view of Theorem 7.1, c_n defines a permissible sequential linear schedule for every block of the decomposition. Hence by Corollary 7.3, Algorithm 2 together with $c := c_n$ applied to this predefined decomposition of D yields an optimal permissible linear schedule ψ w.r.t. overall computation time and pipelining period. $\square$

We now prove the main result.

Theorem 7.4   Let $D = (S(k_1, \cdots, k_n), N)$ be an n-D DG such that the unit vectors are contained in N. Then there exists a decomposition of D into $m_1 \times \cdots \times m_n$ blocks of size $l_1 \times \cdots \times l_n$ for which an optimal permissible linear schedule w.r.t. overall computation time and pipelining period exists.

Proof: We may choose the decomposition such that $m_2 \geq m_1 \geq m_3 \geq \cdots \geq m_n$. Now the proof is literally the same as for Corollary 7.4. $\square$

Theorem 7.4 remains valid if the condition that N contains the set of unit vectors is replaced by to the following more general condition: For every node $\mathbf{v}$ of block $B_{(0, \cdots, 0)}$ there exists a directed (data dependency) path from $\mathbf{0}$ to $\mathbf{v}$ and from $\mathbf{v}$ to node $(l_1 - 1, \cdots, l_n - 1)$ (see Proposition 7.1). Since D is homogeneous, the condition holds for all blocks. Thus optimal permissible linear schedules exist for a large class of problems or algorithms which admit a homogeneous, local and complete DG.

The discussions in the previous section about block graphs, matching of block graphs to array processors, and optimalitiy criteria, like storage requirements and communication bandwidth, can be easily extended to the n-D case.

We illustrate the results of this section by an important example.

7.4.2   Example: Matrix–Matrix Multiplication

We consider the multiplication of matrices $\mathbf{A}$ and $\mathbf{B}$ of size 512×512. The 3-D DG D for this problem consists of index space $S(512, 512, 512)$ together with neighborhood stencil $N = \{(1, 0, 0), (0, 1, 0), (0, 0, 1)\}$. For a detailed discussion of the matrix–matrix multiplication problem the reader is referred to Kung [4]. Suppose that the multiplication is to be performed on an array processor consisting of 16 PEs. By applying the direct LSGP scheme, D is partitioned into $m_1 \times m_2 \times m_3$ blocks of size $l_1 \times l_2 \times l_3$ such that

$$m_1 \cdot m_2 \cdot m_3 = 16 \quad \text{and} \quad m_i \cdot l_i = 512 \quad \text{for } i = 1, 2, 3$$

**TABLE 7.4   The Essentially Different Decompositions
of D into 16 Blocks**

$m_1 \times m_2 \times m_3$	$l_1 \times l_2 \times l_3$	*Computation time*
$16 \times 1 \times 1$	$32 \times 512 \times 512$	8389087
$8 \times 2 \times 1$	$64 \times 512 \times 512$	8405376
$4 \times 4 \times 1$	$128 \times 128 \times 512$	8437762
$2 \times 2 \times 4$	$256 \times 256 \times 128$	16777473

In view of the symmetry of D, there exist four essentially different decompositions of D (see Table 7.4). Theorem 7.3 assures that the computation times of all decompositions shown in Table 7.4 are minimal. The "best" decomposition is in fact $m_1 = 16$, and $m_2 = m_3 = 1$ and yields efficiency 0.9999. $\square$

7.5   Automatic Search for Suboptimal Linear Schedules

The search for suboptimal linear schedules for a given direct LSGP decomposition of an n-D DG can be automatically performed by a computer program [5]. In fact, the program merely implements Algorithm 2 using Lemma 7.2, the generalization of Lemma 7.5 to the n-D case, and the induction principle visualized in the proof of Corollary 7.2. In this manner the framework assists the designer to implement direct LSGP decompositions suitable for his requirements.

7.6   ON THE IMPLEMENTATION OF THE DIRECT LSGP SCHEME

The notions of block graph and matching scheme can be easily extended to the n-D case. In this way we obtain a methodology to design for any direct LSGP decomposition of an n-D DG the layout of an array processor based on the concept of block graph and matching scheme. We now discuss an efficient scheme for the execution of the operations associated to a block. Notice first that we have proposed an algorithm in Section 7.2.2 to compute the inverse function of a sequential linear block schedule. This computation requires $O(n)$ time steps. We can use this inverse function to efficiently implement the direct LSGP scheme. To see this suppose that there exists a host computer which provides the PEs of an array processor with the operations (nodes) of the DG under consideration (by a global bus). Moreover assume that the host transfers the operations of a block to the associated PE in the increasing order of their scheduled time steps. More concretely, let ψ be the sequential linear schedule for a particular block of size $l_1 \times \cdots \times l_n$. Then the host transfers the operations associated to this block in the order

$$\psi^{-1}(0), \psi^{-1}(1), \cdots, \psi^{-1}(k)$$

where $k = (\Pi_{i-1}^{n} l_i) - 1$. The incoming operations may then be stored consecutively in increasing memory locations of the PE associated with the block. Thus the operations of a block are stored in the same way as a sequential program, and hence the overhead required for the block schedules is entirely shifted to the host.

7.7 CONCLUDING REMARKS

We have discussed a mathematical framework for the direct LSGP decomposition of local, complete, and homogeneous n-D DGs. In particular, we have demonstrated that a large subclass of local, homogeneous, and complete n-D DGs admits direct LSGP decompositions for which optimal permissible linear schedules exist. Linear schedules share some outstanding features, they are simple and can be implemented efficiently with minimal control overhead. Nevertheless the quest for a general procedure providing for each decomposition of an n-D DG an optimal schedule goes on. However, in view of the implementation of the direct LSGP scheme, the realization of simple and efficient schedules (for scheduling the operations associated with every block) remains a very important design criterion.

ACKNOWLEDGMENT

Many thanks to S. Y. Kung and all the collaborators of his CE-group, in particular, Kostas Diamantaras, Mike Lee, Weidong Mao, and Andrew Takacz for many valuable discussions.

REFERENCES

[1] N. F. Chen and C. L. Liu, "On a Class of Scheduling Algorithms for Multiprocessor Computing Systems," in T. Feng, Ed., *Parallel Processing*, Lecture Notes in Computer Science, Springer, New York, 1975, pp. 1–16.

[2] K. Jainandunsing, "Optimal Partitioning Schemes for Wavefront/Systolic Array Processors," Tech. Rep., Delft University of Technology, Delft, The Netherlands (1986).

[3] S.-N. Jean, "Mapping/Matching Algorithms to Mesh Processor Arrays," Ph.D. thesis, University of Southern California, Los Angeles (1988).

[4] S. Y. Kung, *VLSI Processor Arrays*, Prentice Hall, Englewood Cliffs, N.J., 1987.

[5] K.-H. Zimmermann, "On Optimal Direct LSGP-partitioning Strategies," Tech. Rep. CE-K90-001, University of Princeton, Princeton, (1990).

[6] D. I. Moldovan and J. A. B. Fortes, Partitioning and mapping of algorithms into fixed size systolic arrays, *IEEE Trans. on Computers*, 1–12 (January 1986).

[7] P. Quinton, Automatic synthesis of systolic arrays from uniform recurrent equations, *Proc. 11th Annual Symposium on Computer Architecture*, pp. 208–214 (1984).

[8] K. Diamantaras, K.-H. Zimmermann, and S. Y. Kung, Integrated fast implementation of mathematical morphology operations in image processing, *Proc. ISCAS 90*, New Orleans (1990).

CHAPTER 8 ⎯⎯⎯⎯⎯⎯⎯⎯⎯⎯⎯⎯⎯

Parallel Matrix Algorithms

D. J. EVANS

8.1 INTRODUCTION

One of the major problems in the mathematical modeling of scientific and engineering problems is that of solving the large sets of linear equations that occur in the discretization of differential equations by both finite difference and finite element methods. With the emergence of parallel computers in recent years much work and attention has been concentrated on designing efficient methods suitable to solve linear systems on these new computer architectures.

In this chapter we present a thorough description and analysis of some new parallel methods for the solution of general linear systems. The new parallel strategies known as Quadrant Interlocking Factorization (Q.I.F.) for solving linear systems directly and Quadrant Interlocking Iterative (Q.I.I.) methods for solving linear systems iteratively consider the interlocking matrix quadrants instead of the standard L and U triangular components of A.

In Sections 8.2–8.8 we present the alternative (Q.I.F.) methods developed by Evans and Hatzopoulos [1]; Evans and Hadjidimos [2]; Evans, Hadjidimos, and Noutsos [3]; and Shanehchi and Evans [4] together with their relative error and computational cost analysis.

Finally in Section 8.9 we present a practical example comparing the Triangular Decomposition and Quadrant Interlocking Factorization methods.

Fuzzy, Holographic, and Parallel Intelligence, By Branko Souček and the IRIS Group.
ISBN 0-471-54772-7 © 1992 John Wiley & Sons, Inc.

8.2 DIRECT METHODS

In the following sections we study alternative direct methods developed to date for the solution of linear systems. The methods correspond to the standard sequential algorithms such as *LU* decomposition, *LDU* factorization, the Gauss–Jordan elimination method for general square matrices, and the Choleski method for a symmetric positive definite coefficient matrix. For the application of these methods and their suitability for different types of parallel computers, see, for example, references [4–10].

8.3 THE FACTORIZATION PROCESS OF THE Q.I.F. METHOD

Consider the following set of linear equations

$$A\mathbf{x} = \mathbf{b} \tag{8.1}$$

where A is a nonsingular $(n \times n)$ matrix, $\mathbf{x}$ is an unknown $(n \times 1)$ column matrix, and $\mathbf{b}$ is a given $(n \times 1)$ column matrix. In this method, the matrix A is factorized into two matrices W and Z [1], such that,

$$A = W * Z \tag{8.2}$$

where the matrices W and Z are of the forms:

$$W = [W_1 W_2 \cdots W_n]$$

and

$$Z^T = [Z_1 Z_2 \cdots Z_n] \tag{8.3}$$

where W_i and $Z_i | i = 1(1) \, n$ are the column vectors of the matrices W and Z^T, which are of the following general forms:

1. For n odd,

$$
W_i \equiv
\begin{cases}
[\underbrace{0 \;\; 0 \cdots \; 0 \;\; 1}_{i} \;\; w_{i+1,i} \cdots \; w_{n-i,i} \;\; 0 \cdots \; 0]^T, & i = 1(1)\dfrac{n-1}{2} \\[3mm]
[\underbrace{0 \;\; 0 \cdots \; 0 \;\; 1}_{i} \;\; 0 \cdots \cdots \cdots \; 0]^T, & i = \dfrac{n+1}{2} \\[3mm]
[\underbrace{0 \;\; 0 \cdots \; 0}_{n-i+1} \;\; w_{n-i+2,i} \cdots \; w_{i-1,i} \;\; 1 \;\; 0 \cdots \; 0]^T, & i = \dfrac{n+3}{2}(1)\,n
\end{cases}
$$

$$\tag{8.4a}$$

and

$$
Z_i \equiv
\begin{cases}
[\underbrace{0 \;\; 0 \;\; \cdots \;\; 0}_{i-1} \;\; z_{i,i} \;\; \cdots \cdots \cdots \;\; z_{i,n-i+1} \;\; 0 \;\; \cdots \;\; 0]^T, & i = 1(1)\,\dfrac{n+1}{2} \\[3em]
[\underbrace{0 \;\; 0 \;\; \cdots \;\; 0}_{n-i} \;\; z_{i,n-i+1} \;\; \cdots \;\; z_{i,i} \;\; 0 \;\; \cdots \;\; 0]^T, & i = \dfrac{n+3}{2}\,(1)\,n
\end{cases}
$$

$$(8.4b)$$

2. For n even,

$$
W_i \equiv
\begin{cases}
[\underbrace{0 \;\; 0 \;\; \cdots \;\; 0}_{i} \;\; 1 \;\; w_{i+1,i} \;\; \cdots \;\; w_{n-i,i} \;\; 0 \;\; \cdots \;\; 0]^T, & i = 1(1)\,\dfrac{n}{2} - 1 \\[3em]
[\underbrace{0 \;\; 0 \;\; \cdots \;\; 0}_{i} \;\; 1 \;\; 0 \;\; \cdots \;\; 0]^T, & i = \dfrac{n}{2},\dfrac{n}{2} + 1 \\[3em]
[\underbrace{0 \;\; 0 \;\; \cdots \;\; 0}_{n-i+1} \;\; w_{n-i+2,i} \;\; \cdots \;\; w_{i-1,i} \;\; 1 \;\; 0 \;\; \cdots \;\; 0]^T, & i = \dfrac{n}{2} + 2(1)\,n
\end{cases}
$$

$$(8.5a)$$

and

$$
Z_i \equiv
\begin{cases}
[\underbrace{0 \;\; 0 \;\; \cdots \;\; 0}_{i-1} \;\; z_{i,i} \;\; \cdots \;\; z_{i,n-i+1} \;\; 0 \;\; \cdots \;\; 0]^T, & i = 1(1)\,\dfrac{n}{2} \\[3em]
[\underbrace{0 \;\; 0 \;\; \cdots \;\; 0}_{n-i} \;\; z_{i,n-i+1} \;\; \cdots \;\; z_{i,i} \;\; 0 \;\; \cdots \;\; 0]^T, & i = \dfrac{n}{2} + 1(1)\,n
\end{cases}
$$

$$(8.5b)$$

For example, when $n = 5$ the matrices W and Z have the following forms:

$$
W \equiv
\begin{bmatrix}
1 & 0 & 0 & 0 & 0 \\
w_{2,1} & 1 & 0 & 0 & w_{2,5} \\
w_{3,1} & w_{3,2} & 1 & w_{3,4} & w_{3,5} \\
w_{4,1} & 0 & 0 & 1 & w_{4,5} \\
0 & 0 & 0 & 0 & 1
\end{bmatrix},
$$

$$Z \equiv \begin{bmatrix} z_{1,1} & z_{1,2} & z_{1,3} & z_{1,4} & z_{1,5} \\ 0 & z_{2,2} & z_{2,3} & z_{2,4} & 0 \\ 0 & 0 & z_{3,3} & 0 & 0 \\ 0 & z_{4,2} & z_{4,3} & z_{4,4} & 0 \\ z_{5,1} & z_{5,2} & z_{5,3} & z_{5,4} & z_{5,5} \end{bmatrix}$$

while for $n = 6$, we have

$$W \equiv \begin{bmatrix} 1 & 0 & 0 & 0 & 0 & 0 \\ v_{2,1} & 1 & 0 & 0 & 0 & w_{2,6} \\ v_{3,1} & w_{3,2} & 1 & 0 & w_{3,5} & w_{3,6} \\ w_{4,1} & w_{4,2} & 0 & 1 & w_{4,5} & w_{4,6} \\ w_{5,1} & 0 & 0 & 0 & 1 & w_{5,6} \\ 0 & 0 & 0 & 0 & 0 & 1 \end{bmatrix}$$

$$Z \equiv \begin{bmatrix} z_{1,1} & z_{1,2} & z_{1,3} & z_{1,4} & z_{1,5} & z_{1,6} \\ 0 & z_{2,2} & z_{2,3} & z_{2,4} & z_{2,5} & 0 \\ 0 & 0 & z_{3,3} & z_{3,4} & 0 & 0 \\ 0 & 0 & z_{4,3} & z_{4,4} & 0 & 0 \\ 0 & z_{5,2} & z_{5,3} & z_{5,4} & z_{5,5} & 0 \\ z_{6,1} & z_{6,2} & z_{6,3} & z_{6,4} & z_{6,5} & z_{6,6} \end{bmatrix}$$

From the given forms of the matrices W and Z in Eq. (8.4) or Eq. (8.5) and the equality (8.2) we can obtain the elements of these matrices in $\left[\dfrac{n-1}{2}\right]$ steps, where $\left[\dfrac{n-1}{2}\right]$ represents the largest integer number, which is $\leq \dfrac{n-1}{2}$. It can easily be seen that the values of the elements of the first and last rows of the matrix Z are as follows:

$$\begin{cases} z_{1,i} = a_{1,i} \\ z_{n,i} = a_{n,i} \end{cases} \quad \text{for } i = 1(1)n \tag{8.6}$$

The elements of the first and last columns of the matrix W are then evaluated by solving $(n - 2)$ sets of (2×2) linear systems given by

$$\text{and} \quad \begin{cases} z_{1,1} w_{i,1} + z_{n,1} w_{i,n} = a_{i,1} \\ z_{1,n} w_{i,1} + z_{n,n} w_{i,n} = a_{i,n} \end{cases} \quad \text{for } i = 2(1)n - 1 \qquad (8.7)$$

Finally, to complete this step of the factorization process the elements of the matrix **A** are modified by the following formula:

$$a_{i,j} = a_{i,j} - w_{i,1} z_{1,j} - w_{i,n} z_{n,j}, \quad i, j = 2(1)n - 1 \qquad (8.8)$$

In general, at ith step of the factorization process we have the relationships

$$\left. \begin{aligned} z_{i,j} &= a_{i,j} \\ z_{n-i+1,j} &= a_{n-i+1,j} \end{aligned} \right\} \quad \text{for } j = i(1)n - i + 1 \qquad \begin{aligned} &(8.9) \\ \\ &(8.10) \end{aligned}$$

and the solution of the $(2 * 2)$ linear systems

$$\begin{cases} z_{i,i} w_{j,i} + w_{n-i+1,i} w_{j,n-i+1} = a_{j,i} \\ z_{i,n-i+1} w_{j,i} + z_{n-i+1,n-i+1} w_{j,n-i+1} = a_{j,n-i+1} \end{cases} \quad j = i + 1(1)n - i \quad (8.11)$$

to give the unknown quantities $w_{j,i}$ and $w_{j,n-i+1}$ for $j = i + 1(1)n - i$, and the modified $a_{i,j}$'s are evaluated from the formula:

$$a_{k,l} = a_{k,l} - w_{k,i} z_{i,l} - w_{k,n-i+1} z_{n-i+1,l}, \quad k, l = i + 1(1)n - i. \qquad (8.12)$$

In order to solve a set of linear equations by the Q.I.F. method it can be seen from Eq. (8.1) and Eq. (8.2) that the system

$$(W * Z)x = b \qquad (8.13)$$

can be solved instead of Eq. (8.1), where we need to solve two related and simpler linear systems of the form

$$Wy = b \qquad (8.14)$$

and

$$Zx = y \qquad (8.15)$$

The system (8.14) is first solved for the intermediate vector **y** and then the final solution of the system (8.1) can be obtained by solving the linear system (8.15) for **x**.

The solution of linear system (8.14) can be obtained in $\left\lceil\dfrac{n-1}{2}\right\rceil$ steps where from the structure of the matrix W it can be seen that y_1 and y_n are evaluated first, then y_2, y_{n-1}, and so on working in pairs from the top and rear of the vector $\mathbf{y}$. The following procedure typifies the step i $\left(i = 1, 2, \cdots, \left\lceil\dfrac{n-1}{2}\right\rceil\right)$ of the solution process:

$$\begin{cases} y_i & = & b_i \\ y_{n-i+1} & = & b_{n-i+1} \end{cases} \tag{8.16a}$$

and

$$b_j = b_j - w_{j,i}y_i - w_{j,n-i+1}y_{n-i+1}, \quad j = i + 1(1)n - i \tag{8.16b}$$

and then we proceed to the next step.

For the solution of the linear system (8.15), we proceed as follows:

If n is odd, we can find that

$$x_l = y_l/z_{l,l}, \quad l = \frac{n+1}{2} \tag{8.17}$$

and in preparation for the next step we have

$$y_j = y_j - x_l * z_{j,l}, \quad j = 1(1)n \qquad \text{and}$$

$$j \neq \frac{n+1}{2} \tag{8.18}$$

It can be seen that the elements of the vector $\mathbf{x}$ can be obtained in pairs by solving $\dfrac{n-1}{2}$ sets of $(2 * 2)$ linear systems in $\dfrac{n-1}{2}$ distinct steps. In general, for the ith step we solve the following $(2 * 2)$ linear system:

$$\begin{cases} z_{i,i}x_i + z_{i,n-i+1}x_{n-i+1} = y_i \\ z_{n-i+1,i}x_i + z_{n-i+1,n-i+1}x_{n-i+1} = y_{n-i+1}, \end{cases} \quad i = l - 1(-1)1 \tag{8.19}$$

Furthermore, to compute x_i and x_{n-i+1}, we then set

$$y_j = y_j - x_iz_{j,i} - x_{n-i+1}z_{j,n-i+1} \quad \left|\begin{array}{l} i = l - 1(-1)1 \\ j = 1(1)i - 1 \quad \text{and } n - i(1)n \end{array}\right. \tag{8.20}$$

and proceed to the next step.

However, if n is even, then all the components of the vector x are found in pairs. To find all the pairs, the linear system (8.19) and the formula (8.20) are executed respectively in turn for $i = \left[\frac{n}{2}\right](-1)1$.

8.4   COMPUTATIONAL COST ANALYSIS OF THE Q.I.F. METHOD

In order to analyze the computational cost of the Q.I.F. method we adopt a similar procedure to that described in Shanehchi and Evans [4]. For this, we consider two different strategies which may be used to solve the set of $(2 * 2)$ linear equations encountered during the factorization and the solution process.

1. **Cramer's rule:** Each of the $(2 * 2)$ linear systems in (8.11) is solved by the following procedure.

    1.a   Define the quantities T_1, T_2, and T_3 (say) as

    $$T_1 = z_{i,i} * z_{n-i+1,n-i+1} - z_{n-i+1,i} * z_{i,n-i+1}$$

    $$T_2 = a_{j,i} * z_{n-i+1,n-i+1} - a_{j,n-i+1} * z_{n-i+1,i}$$

    $$T_3 = a_{j,i} * z_{i,n-i+1} - a_{j,n-i+1} * z_{i,i}$$

    1.b   Compute $w_{j,i} = T_2/T_1$ and $w_{j,n-i+1} = T_3/T_1$.
    It is clear from the definition of T_1 that if any of the quantities

    $$T_1 \equiv \det \begin{bmatrix} z_{i,i} & z_{i,n-i+1} \\ z_{n-i+1,i} & z_{n-i+1,n-i+1} \end{bmatrix} = 0 \qquad (8.21)$$

    then the method will break down. In order to avoid such an event we can adopt two well established pivotal strategies used in the well known standard elimination methods. These are as follows:

    Partial pivoting: This corresponds to the partial pivoting strategy used in the Gaussian elimination process. In this strategy row interchanges are made wherever necessary to result in the highest determinantal value defined in Eq. (8.21). This method solves the linear system PAx and Pb instead of Eq. (8.1) where P is a permutation matrix. In order to locate the pivot at the ith, $i = 1, 2, \cdots, n$, stage of the factorization process a search is carried out amongst the elements $a_{j,i}$, $a_{j,n-i+1}$ $i \le j \le n - i + 1$ to find the value of α defined as

    $$\alpha = \max \left\{ \text{abs} \begin{vmatrix} a_{p,i} & a_{p,n-i+1} \\ a_{q,i} & a_{q,n-i+1} \end{vmatrix} \right\}, \quad i \le p, q \le n - i + 1 \qquad (8.22)$$

then rows p and q of the matrix A and the right hand side vector $\mathbf{b}$ are interchanged (if necessary) with rows i and $n - i + 1$ (or alternatively with rows $n + i + 1$ and i) respectively, and the factorization process is continued. It can be easily seen that at each stage i, $i = 1, 2, \cdots,$ $\left[\dfrac{n + 1}{2}\right]$, of the scheme a number of $(n - 2i + 1)(n - 2i + 2)/2$ determinant evaluations are necessary to locate the required pivot.

Full pivoting: In this method, the linear system (8.1) is changed to an equivalent system $PAQ\mathbf{y} = P\mathbf{b}$ where $\mathbf{y} = Q^{-1}\mathbf{x}$ and P and Q are two permutation matrices which hold the record of row and column interchanges. The pivot at stage i of the factorization process is determined as follows: A search is carried out among the elements of the submatrix A_i which is formed from A by deleting all rows and columns which are less than i or greater than $(n - i + 1)$. Then we evaluate α as

$$\alpha = \max\left\{\text{abs}\begin{vmatrix} a_{p,j} & a_{p,k} \\ a_{q,j} & a_{q,k} \end{vmatrix}\right\}, \quad i \leq p, q, j, k \leq n - i + 1 \quad (8.23)$$

and the necessary row and column interchanges are made before continuing the procedure. As can be seen this form of pivoting corresponds to the full pivotal strategy used in the standard Gauss elimination process. It can be shown that $(n - 2i + 1)^2(n - 2i + 2)$ determinant evaluations are required at stage i, $i = 1, 2, \cdots,$ $\left[\dfrac{n + 1}{2}\right]$ to locate the pivot.

2. Gauss elimination method: Alternatively in order to solve each of $(2 * 2)$ linear system in Eq. (8.11), the Gauss elimination method can be used. In this case the procedure is based on the following algorithms.

2.a Compute $\rho = z_{i,i} - z_{i,n-i+1}$.
   If $\rho \geq 0$ then the values of $w_{j,i}$ and $w_{j,n-i+1}$ are obtained by the following procedure:

$$2.\text{b}.1 \quad m = z_{i,n-i+1}/z_{i,i}$$

$$2.\text{c}.1 \quad w_{j,n-i+1} = (a_{j,n-i+1} - m * a_{i,j})/ \qquad (8.24)$$
$$(z_{n-i+1,n-i+1} - m * z_{n-i+1,i})$$

$$2.\text{d}.1 \quad w_{j,i} = (a_{j,i} - z_{n-i+1,i} * w_{j,n-i+1})/z_{i,i}$$

whereas if $\rho < 0$ then we have

2.b.2 $m = z_{i,i}/z_{i,n-i+1}$

2.c.2 $w_{j,n-i+1} = (a_{j,i} - m * a_{j,n-i+1})/$

$(z_{n-i+1,i} - m * z_{n-i+1,n-i+1})$

2.d.2 $w_{j,i} = (a_{j,n-i+1} - z_{n-i+1,n-i+1} * w_{j,n-i+1})/z_{i,n-i+1}$

$$(8.25)$$

If we adopt the basic assumptions made in Shanehchi [5] and a parallel replacement statement requires negligible time, while any other parallel arithmetic operation needs the same time that is referred to as a unit time step, we can easily determine that for the complete factorization process, if Cramer's rule is used for the solution of the (2×2) linear systems in Eq. (8.11), then we shall require either a total number of $6 \left\lceil \dfrac{n-1}{2} \right\rceil$ time steps and a maximum number of P processors where

$$P \equiv \max \{6(n-2), 2(n-2)^2\} \qquad (8.26)$$

or a total number of $7 \left\lceil \dfrac{n-1}{2} \right\rceil$ time steps and a maximum number of P processors where

$$P \equiv \max \{6(n-2), (n-2)^2\} \qquad (8.27)$$

and if the Gauss elimination method is employed, then we shall need either a total of $11 \left\lceil \dfrac{n-1}{2} \right\rceil$ time steps and a maximum of $2(n-2)^2$ number of processors or a total number of $12 \left\lceil \dfrac{n-1}{2} \right\rceil$ time steps and a maximum number of P processors where

$$P \equiv \max \{2(n-2), (n-2)^2\} \qquad (8.28)$$

Moreover, it can be seen that the complete evaluation of the components of the auxiliary vector y in Eq. (8.16) requires a total number of $3 \left\lceil \dfrac{n-1}{2} \right\rceil$ time steps and a maximum number of $2(n-2)$ processors. However, it can easily be seen that for the solution of the linear system (8.15), if Cramer's rule is used for solving the (2×2) linear systems in Eq. (8.19), then a total number of $6 \left\lceil \dfrac{n-1}{2} \right\rceil + \frac{3}{2}(3 + (-1)^n)$ time steps and a maximum number of $6(n-2)$ processors are required, while if the Gauss elimination method is employed, then a total number of $11 \left\lceil \dfrac{n-1}{2} \right\rceil + 7 + 4(-1)^n$ time steps and a maximum number of $2(n-2)$ processors are needed.

TABLE 8.1 Computational Costs of the QIF Method.

Solution method of the (2 × 2) linear system	Total number of time steps	Maximum number of processors working in parallel
Cramer's rule	$15\left[\dfrac{n-1}{2}\right] + \dfrac{3}{2}[3 +(-1)^n]$	$\max\{6(n-2), 2(n-2)^2\}$
	$16\left[\dfrac{n-1}{2}\right] + \dfrac{3}{2}[3 +(-1)^n]$	$\max\{6(n-2), (n-2)^2\}$
Gauss elimination method	$25\left[\dfrac{n-1}{2}\right] + 7 + 4(-1)^n$	$2(n-2)^2$
	$26\left[\dfrac{n-1}{2}\right] + 7 + 4(-1)^n$	$\max\{2(n-2), (n-2)^2\}$

Table 8.1 illustrates the alternative computational costs for the complete quadrant interlocking factorization of the coefficient matrix A and the solution of the linear system (8.1).

8.5 ROUNDING ERROR ANALYSIS OF Q.I.F. METHOD

Because of the rounding errors that occur during the Q.I.F. of a coefficient matrix A, it can be said that the computed quadrant factors of A, that is, W and Z, correspond to the exact factorization of $A + E$, where E is a perturbation matrix.

It can be shown that the Q.I.F. of a coefficient matrix A is true for computed values of the matrix W and Z such that

$$W * Z = A + E \tag{8.29}$$

where E is given by

$$\begin{cases} |E| < \rho * N_1, & \text{for } n \text{ odd} \\ |E| < \rho * N_2, & \text{for } n \text{ even} \end{cases} \tag{8.30}$$

where

$$\rho = \max\left\{2^{-t}\left(3.09 + \frac{4.12 * g^2}{\alpha}\right),\ g * 2^{-t} * 5.01\right\} \tag{8.31}$$

and N_1, N_2 are the matrices of the form:

$$N_1 \equiv \begin{bmatrix} 0 & 0 & 0 & \cdot & \cdot & \cdot & \cdot & 0 & 0 & 0 \\ 1 & 1 & 1 & \cdot & \cdot & \cdot & \cdot & 1 & 1 & 1 \\ 1 & 2 & 2 & \cdot & \cdot & \cdot & \cdot & 2 & 2 & 1 \\ 1 & 2 & 3 & \cdot & \cdot & \cdot & \cdot & 3 & 2 & 1 \\ \cdot & \cdot & \cdot & \cdot & \frac{n+1}{2} & \cdot & \cdot & \cdot & \cdot & \cdot \\ \cdot & \cdot & \cdot & \cdot & \cdot & \cdot & \cdot & \cdot & \cdot & \cdot \\ \cdot & \cdot & \cdot & \cdot & \cdot & \cdot & \cdot & \cdot & \cdot & \cdot \\ 1 & 2 & 3 & \cdot & \cdot & \cdot & \cdot & 3 & 2 & 1 \\ 1 & 2 & 2 & \cdot & \cdot & \cdot & \cdot & 2 & 2 & 1 \\ 1 & 1 & 1 & \cdot & \cdot & \cdot & \cdot & 1 & 1 & 1 \\ 0 & 0 & 0 & \cdot & \cdot & \cdot & \cdot & 0 & 0 & 0 \end{bmatrix}, \quad \text{for } n \text{ odd} \tag{8.32a}$$

$$N_2 \equiv \begin{bmatrix} 0 & 0 & 0 & \cdot & \cdot & & \cdot & \cdot & 0 & 0 & 0 \\ 1 & 1 & 1 & \cdot & \cdot & & \cdot & \cdot & 1 & 1 & 1 \\ 1 & 2 & 2 & \cdot & \cdot & & \cdot & \cdot & 2 & 2 & 1 \\ 1 & 2 & 3 & \cdot & \cdot & & \cdot & \cdot & 3 & 2 & 1 \\ \cdot & \cdot & \cdot & \cdot & \cdot & & \cdot & \cdot & \cdot & \cdot & \cdot \\ \cdot & \cdot & \cdot & \cdot & \frac{n}{2}-1 & \frac{n}{2}-1 & \cdot & \cdot & \cdot & \cdot & \cdot \\ \cdot & \cdot & \cdot & \cdot & \frac{n}{2}-1 & \frac{n}{2}-1 & \cdot & \cdot & \cdot & \cdot & \cdot \\ \cdot & \cdot & \cdot & \cdot & \cdot & & \cdot & \cdot & \cdot & \cdot & \cdot \\ 1 & 2 & 3 & \cdot & \cdot & & \cdot & \cdot & 3 & 2 & 1 \\ 1 & 2 & 2 & \cdot & \cdot & & \cdot & \cdot & 2 & 2 & 1 \\ 1 & 1 & 1 & \cdot & \cdot & & \cdot & \cdot & 1 & 1 & 1 \\ 0 & 0 & 0 & \cdot & \cdot & & \cdot & \cdot & 0 & 0 & 0 \end{bmatrix}, \quad \text{for } n \text{ even} \tag{8.32b}$$

where

$$\alpha = \text{Min} \left\{ \det \begin{bmatrix} a_{i,i} & a_{i,p} \\ a_{p,i} & a_{p,p} \end{bmatrix}, \quad i = 1, 2, \cdots, \frac{(n-1)}{2} \right\} \tag{8.33}$$

and g is the largest in absolute value of the elements of the matrix Z evaluated during the factorization process.

For a detailed discussion on this error analysis and also the error bounds for the solution of the linear system, see Shanehchi and Evans [4] or Shanehchi [5].

8.6 THE MODIFIED Q.I.F. METHOD

In this section, we now present a modification to the Q.I.F. method, whereby the two matrix factors, W and Z are chosen to be slightly different in structure from the matrix factors involved in the original method; see Evans and Hadjidimos [2].

Consider the system of Eq. (8.1) and assume that there exists two matrices W and Z such that

$$A = W * Z \tag{8.34}$$

where the matrices W and Z are defined as follows:

$$W_i \text{ and } Z_i \quad i = 1(1)n$$

are the column vectors of the matrices W and Z^T, then we have

$$W = [W_1 W_2 \cdots W_n] \tag{8.35}$$

$$Z^T = [Z_1 Z_2 \cdots Z_n] \tag{8.36}$$

where the column vectors W_i and Z_i are of the following general forms:

$$
W_i \equiv
\begin{cases}
[\underbrace{0 \cdots 0}_{i-1} \ 1 \ w_{i+1,i} \cdots w_{n-i,i} \ 0 \cdots 0]^T, & i = 1(1)\left[\dfrac{n}{2}\right] \\[2em]
[\underbrace{0 \cdots 0}_{i-1} \ 1 \ 0 \cdots 0]^T, & i = \left[\dfrac{n}{2}\right] + 1 \\[2em]
[\underbrace{0 \cdots 0}_{n-i+1} \ w_{n-1+2,i} \cdots w_{i-1,i} \ 1 \ 0 \cdots 0]^T, & \\[1em]
\qquad\qquad i = \left[\dfrac{n}{2}\right] + 2(1)n
\end{cases}
$$

and $\tag{8.37}$

$$
Z_i \equiv
\begin{cases}
[\underbrace{0 \cdots 0}_{i-1} \ z_{i,i} \cdots z_{i,n-i+1} \ 0 \cdots 0]^T & i = 1(1)\left[\dfrac{n+1}{2}\right] \\[2em]
[\underbrace{0 \cdots 0}_{n-i} \ z_{i,n-i+2} \cdots z_{i,i} \ 0 \cdots 0]^T, & i = \left[\dfrac{n+1}{2}\right] + 1(1)\, n
\end{cases}
$$

$$\tag{8.38}$$

Also it can be easily seen from Eqs. (8.34), (8.35), and (8.36) that the following relationship holds;

$$A = \sum_{i=1}^{n} W_i Z_i^T \tag{8.39}$$

For example, when $n = 5$ we have

$$W \equiv \begin{bmatrix} 1 & 0 & 0 & 0 & 0 \\ w_{2,1} & 1 & 0 & 0 & w_{2,5} \\ w_{3,1} & w_{3,2} & 1 & w_{3,4} & w_{3,5} \\ w_{4,1} & w_{4,2} & 0 & 1 & w_{4,5} \\ w_{5,1} & 0 & 0 & 0 & 1 \end{bmatrix},$$

$$Z \equiv \begin{bmatrix} z_{1,1} & z_{1,2} & z_{1,3} & z_{1,4} & z_{1,5} \\ 0 & z_{2,2} & z_{2,3} & z_{2,4} & 0 \\ 0 & 0 & z_{3,3} & 0 & 0 \\ 0 & 0 & z_{4,3} & z_{4,4} & 0 \\ 0 & z_{5,2} & z_{5,3} & z_{5,4} & z_{5,5} \end{bmatrix}$$

while for $n = 6$, the matrices W and Z have the following forms:

$$W \equiv \begin{bmatrix} 1 & 0 & 0 & 0 & 0 & 0 \\ w_{2,1} & 1 & 0 & 0 & 0 & w_{2,6} \\ w_{3,1} & w_{3,2} & 1 & 0 & w_{3,5} & w_{3,6} \\ w_{4,1} & w_{4,2} & w_{4,3} & 1 & w_{4,5} & w_{4,6} \\ w_{5,1} & w_{5,2} & 0 & 0 & 1 & w_{5,6} \\ w_{6,1} & 0 & 0 & 0 & 0 & 1 \end{bmatrix}$$

and

$$Z \equiv \begin{bmatrix} z_{1,1} & z_{1,2} & z_{1,3} & z_{1,4} & z_{1,5} & z_{1,6} \\ 0 & z_{2,2} & z_{2,3} & z_{2,4} & z_{2,5} & 0 \\ 0 & 0 & z_{3,3} & z_{3,4} & 0 & 0 \\ 0 & 0 & 0 & z_{4,4} & 0 & 0 \\ 0 & 0 & z_{5,3} & z_{5,4} & z_{5,5} & 0 \\ 0 & z_{6,2} & z_{6,3} & z_{6,4} & z_{6,5} & z_{6,6} \end{bmatrix}$$

It can readily be seen that the elements of the matrices W and Z are evaluated in $\left[\dfrac{n+1}{2}\right]$ stages where at the commencement of the kth stage, we define the matrix A_k, $k = 1(1)\left[\dfrac{n-1}{2}\right]$ as follows:

$$A_1 = A,$$

$$A_k = A - \sum_{i=1}^{k-1} W_i Z_i^T - \sum_{i=n-k+2}^{n} W_i Z_i^T, \quad k = 2(1)\left[\frac{n-1}{2}\right] \qquad (8.40)$$

It is easily seen that the first and the last $(k-1)$ rows and columns of any matrix A_k defined by Eq. (8.40) are zero. Thus, to evaluate the elements that are different from 0 and 1 in the kth and $(n-k+1)$th rows and columns of W and Z we have the following algorithm:

$$z_{k,j} = a_{k,j}^{(k)}, \quad j = k(1)n - k + 1 \qquad (8.41a)$$

$$w_{j,k} = a_{j,k}^{(k)}/z_{k,k}, \quad j = k + 1(1)n - k + 1 \qquad (8.41b)$$

$$z_{n-k+1,j} = a_{n-k+1,j}^{(k)} - w_{n-k+1,k} * z_{k,j}, \quad j = k + 1(1)n - k + 1 \qquad (8.41c)$$

$$w_{j,n-k+1} = (a_{j,n-k+1}^{(k)} - w_{j,k} * z_{k,n-k+1})/z_{n-k+1,n-k+1},$$
$$j = k + 1(1)n - k \qquad (8.41d)$$

$$A_{k+1} = A_k - W_k Z_k^T - W_{n-k+1} * Z_{n-k+1}^T,$$
$$\text{for all } k = 1(1)\left[\frac{n-1}{2}\right] \qquad (8.41e)$$

To complete the computation of all the elements of the matrices W and Z, a further step (8.41a) has to be carried out for n odd, to evaluate the center element

$$z_{(n+1)/2,(n+1)/2}$$

while if n is even, the further steps of Eqs. (8.41a) and (8.41c) have to be carried out in order to find the central elements $z_{k,k}$, $z_{k,k+1}$, $w_{k+1,k}$, and $z_{k+1,k+1}$, where $k = \dfrac{n}{2}$.

For the solution of linear system (8.1) we again need to solve two linear systems of the form:

$$W\mathbf{y} = \mathbf{b} \qquad (8.42)$$

and

$$Z\mathbf{x} = \mathbf{y} \qquad (8.43)$$

where the linear system (8.42) is first solved for the auxiliary vector **y** then the solution of the linear system (8.43) for the vector **x**, which is a final solution.

For the solution of the system (8.42) we let

$$Wy = b = b^{(1)} \tag{8.44}$$

therefore,

$$\sum_{i=1}^{n} y_i w_i = b^{(1)} \tag{8.45}$$

Hence,

$$y_k = b_k^{(k)} \tag{8.46a}$$

$$y_{n-k+1} = b_{n-k+1}^{(k)} - y_k * w_{n-k+1,k} \tag{8.46b}$$

$$b^{(k+1)} = b^{(k)} - y_k * w_k - y_{n-k+1} * w_{n-k+1} \tag{8.46c}$$

for $k = 1(1)\left[\dfrac{n-1}{2}\right]$. If n is odd, step (8.46a) has to be executed for $k = \left[\dfrac{n+1}{2}\right]$ to find the center element y_k, while for n even, steps Eqs. (8.46a) and (8.46b) have to be executed for $k = \left[\dfrac{n+1}{2}\right]$ to find the two elements in the middle that are y_k and y_{k+1}.

We now carry out the following algorithm for the solution of the linear system (8.43); first we let

$$Zx = y = y^{(1)} \tag{8.47}$$

so that

$$\sum_{i=1}^{n} x_i Z_i^* = y^{(1)} \tag{8.48}$$

where $Z_i^* | i = 1(1)n$ are the column vectors of the matrix Z, that is,

$$Z = [Z_1^* Z_2^* \cdots Z_n^*] \tag{8.49}$$

Hence, if we set $l = \dfrac{n+1}{2}$, then for n odd we can find that

$$x_l = y_l^{(1)} / Z_{l,l} \tag{8.50}$$

and

$$y^{(2)} = y^{(1)} - x_l Z_l^*, \tag{8.51}$$

while for n even, we have

$$x_{l+1} = y_{l+1}^{(1)}/z_{l+1,l+1}$$
$$x_l = (y^{(1)} - x_{l+1}z_{l,l+1})z_{l,l} \tag{8.52}$$

and

$$y^{(2)} = y^{(1)} - x_l Z_l^* - x_{l+1}Z_{l+1}^* \tag{8.53}$$

Then we proceed by using the following relationships:

$$x_{n-k+1} = y_{n-k+1}^{(l-k+1)}/z_{n-k+1,n-k+1} \tag{8.54a}$$

$$x_k = (y_k^{(l-k+1)} - x_{n-k+1} * z_{k,n-k+1})/z_{k,k} \tag{8.54b}$$

$$y^{(l-k+2)} = y^{(l-k+1)} - x_k * Z_k^* - x_{n-k+1} * Z_{n-k+1}^* \tag{8.54c}$$

for all $k = \left[\dfrac{n-1}{2}\right](-1)1$ where stage (8.54c) is not executed for $k = 1$.

Under the same assumption as in Section 8.2, it can be seen that the complete factorization of the coefficient matrix A and the solution of the linear system (8.1) need either a total number of $21\left[\dfrac{n-1}{2}\right] + \frac{9}{2}(1 + (-1)^n)$ time steps and a maximum number of $2(n-1)^2$ processors, or a total number of $22\left[\dfrac{n-1}{2}\right] + \frac{9}{2}(1 + (-1)^n)$ time steps and a maximum number of $(n-1)^2$ processors.

8.7 THE WDZ FACTORIZATION

In this section we study the factorization of the matrix A into three matrices W, D, and Z [5], such that,

$$A = W * D * Z \tag{8.55}$$

where the matrices W and Z have the following form:

1. If W_i and $Z_i | i = 1(1)n$ are the column vectors of the matrices W and Z^T, then we have

$$W = [W_1 W_2 \cdots W_n] \tag{8.56}$$

and

$$Z^T = [Z_1 Z_2 \cdots Z_n] \tag{8.57}$$

where the column vectors W_i's are the following general form:

(a) for n odd,

$$
W_i \equiv \begin{cases}
[\underbrace{0 \;\cdots\; 0 \;\; 1}_{i} \;\; w_{i+1,i} \;\cdots\; w_{n-i,i} \;\; 0 \;\cdots\; 0]^T, & i = 1(1)\dfrac{n-1}{2} \\[3ex]
[\underbrace{0 \;\cdots\; 0 \;\; 1}_{i} \;\;\;\; 0 \;\cdots\; 0]^T, & i = \dfrac{n+1}{2} \\[3ex]
[\underbrace{0 \;\cdots\; 0}_{n-i+1} \;\; w_{n-i+2,i} \;\cdots\; w_{i-1,i} \;\; 1 \;\; 0 \;\cdots\; 0]^T, & i = \dfrac{n+3}{2}(1)n
\end{cases}
$$

$$(8.58)$$

(b) for n even,

$$
W_i \equiv \begin{cases}
[\underbrace{0 \;\cdots\; 0 \;\; 1}_{i} \;\; w_{i+1,i} \;\cdots\; w_{n-i,i} \;\; 0 \;\cdots\; 0]^T, & i = 1(1)\dfrac{n}{2}-1 \\[3ex]
[\underbrace{0 \;\cdots\; 0 \;\; 1}_{i} \;\;\;\; 0 \;\cdots\; 0]^T, & i = \dfrac{n}{2}, \dfrac{n}{2}+1 \\[3ex]
[\underbrace{0 \;\cdots\; 0}_{n-i+1} \;\; w_{n-i+2,i} \;\cdots\; w_{i-1,i} \;\; 1 \;\; 0 \;\cdots\; 0]^T, & i = \dfrac{n}{2}+2(1)n
\end{cases}
$$

$$(8.59)$$

2. The column vectors Z_i's are of the following form:

$$
Z_i \equiv \begin{cases}
[0 \;\cdots\; 0 \;\; 1 \;\; z_{i+1,i} \;\cdots\; z_{i,n-i+1} \;\; 0 \;\cdots\; 0]^T, & i = 1(1)\dfrac{n+1}{2} \\[3ex]
[0 \;\cdots\; 0 \;\; z_{i,n-i+1} \;\cdots\; z_{i,i-1} \;\; 1 \;\; 0 \;\cdots\; 0]^T, & i = \dfrac{n+3}{2}(1)n
\end{cases}
$$

$$(8.60)$$

For example, when $n = 5$, the matrices W and Z have the following forms:

$$W \equiv \begin{bmatrix} 1 & 0 & 0 & 0 & 0 \\ w_{2,1} & 1 & 0 & 0 & w_{2,5} \\ w_{3,1} & w_{3,2} & 1 & w_{3,4} & w_{3,5} \\ w_{4,1} & 0 & 0 & 1 & w_{4,5} \\ 0 & 0 & 0 & 0 & 1 \end{bmatrix},$$

$$Z \equiv \begin{bmatrix} 1 & z_{1,2} & z_{1,3} & z_{1,4} & z_{1,5} \\ 0 & 1 & z_{2,3} & z_{2,4} & 0 \\ 0 & 0 & 1 & 0 & 0 \\ 0 & z_{4,2} & z_{4,3} & 1 & 0 \\ z_{5,1} & z_{5,2} & z_{5,3} & z_{5,4} & 1 \end{bmatrix}$$

while for $n = 6$, we have

$$W \equiv \begin{bmatrix} 1 & 0 & 0 & 0 & 0 & 0 \\ w_{2,1} & 1 & 0 & 0 & 0 & w_{2,6} \\ w_{3,1} & w_{3,2} & 1 & 0 & w_{3,5} & w_{3,6} \\ w_{4,1} & w_{4,2} & 0 & 1 & w_{4,5} & w_{4,6} \\ w_{5,1} & 0 & 0 & 0 & 1 & w_{5,6} \\ 0 & 0 & 0 & 0 & 0 & 1 \end{bmatrix}$$

$$Z \equiv \begin{bmatrix} 1 & z_{1,2} & z_{1,3} & z_{1,4} & z_{1,5} & z_{1,6} \\ 0 & 1 & z_{2,3} & z_{2,4} & z_{2,5} & 0 \\ 0 & 0 & 1 & z_{3,4} & 0 & 0 \\ 0 & 0 & z_{4,3} & 1 & 0 & 0 \\ 0 & z_{5,2} & z_{5,3} & z_{5,4} & 1 & 0 \\ z_{6,1} & z_{6,2} & z_{6,3} & z_{6,4} & z_{6,5} & 1 \end{bmatrix}$$

It can be seen that the matrices W and Z by the above definitions have the same structure as the W and Z matrices in the original Q.I.F. method, except that the diagonal elements of Z are now all unity. The matrix D is a diagonal matrix with its elements denoted by $d_{i,i}$.

For a computation of the elements of the matrices W, D, and Z we have a similar procedure as mentioned before for the Q.I.F. method in Section 8.3, Eq. (8.2), that is, the process is executed in $\left[\dfrac{n-1}{2}\right]$ steps where, in general, at the ith step we have the solution of (2×2) linear system:

$$
\begin{cases}
a_{i,i}w_{j,i} + a_{n-i+1,i}w_{j,n-i+1} = a_{j,i} \\
a_{i,n-i+1}w_{j,i} + a_{n-i+1,n-i+1}w_{j,n-i+1} = a_{j,n-i+1}
\end{cases}
, \quad j = i + 1(1)n - i
$$

$$(8.61)$$

and the relationships,

$$
\begin{cases}
z_{i,j} = a_{i,j}/a_{i,i} \\
z_{n-i+1,j} = a_{n-i+1,j}/a_{n-i+1,n-i+1}
\end{cases}
, \quad \text{for } j = i(1)n - i + 1 \quad (8.62)
$$

and

$$
\begin{cases}
d_{i,i} = a_{i,i} \\
d_{n-i+1,n-i+1} = a_{n-i+1,n-i+1}
\end{cases}
\tag{8.63}
$$

Finally, in preparation for the next stage we calculate the quantities

$$
a_{k,l} = a_{k,l} - w_{k,i}a_{i,l} - w_{k,n-i+1}a_{n-i+1,l}, \quad k, l = i + 1(1)n - i \quad (8.64)
$$

For the solution of the linear system (8.1) we need to solve the following three simpler systems:

$$
W\mathbf{y} = \mathbf{b} \tag{8.65}
$$

$$
D\mathbf{u} = \mathbf{y} \tag{8.66}
$$

and

$$
Z\mathbf{x} = \mathbf{u} \tag{8.67}
$$

The solution process of the systems (8.65), (8.66), and (8.67) for the auxiliary vectors $\mathbf{y}$, $\mathbf{u}$, and the final solution vector $\mathbf{x}$, we have the following procedure:

1. The intermediate vector **y** can be obtained from the following algorithm: At step i for $i = 1, 2, \cdots, \left[\frac{n-1}{2}\right]$, we compute

(a) $\begin{cases} y_i = b_i \\ y_{n-i+1} = b_{n-i+1} \end{cases}$ (8.68)

(b) $b_j = b_j - w_{j,i}y_i - w_{j,n-i+1}y_{n-i+1}, \quad j = i + 1(1)n - i.$ (8.69)

We then proceed to the next step.
2. The auxiliary vector **u** can be found by formula

$$u_i = y_i/d_{i,i}, \quad i = 1(1)n$$ (8.70)

3. The final solution vector **x** can be obtained as follows: If n is odd, we have

$$x_l = u_l, \quad l = \frac{n+1}{2}$$ (8.71)

$$u_j = u_j - x_l * z_{i,l}, \quad j = 1(1)n \quad \text{and} \quad j \neq \frac{n+1}{2}$$ (8.72)

The rest of the elements of the vector **x** are found in pairs, by solving $\left[\frac{n-1}{2}\right]$ systems of (2×2) linear system in $\left[\frac{n-1}{2}\right]$ distinct steps. In general, at the ith step we solve the (2×2) linear system

$$\begin{cases} x_i + z_{i,n-i+1}x_{n-i+1} = u_i \\ z_{n-i+1,i}x_i + x_{n-i+1} = u_{n-i+1}, \end{cases} \quad i = l - 1(-1)n$$ (8.73)

Then we set

$$u_j = u_j - x_i z_{j,i} - x_{n-i+1}z_{j,n-i+1} \begin{vmatrix} i = l - 1(-1)1 \\ j = 1(1)i - 1 \end{vmatrix} \quad \text{and} \quad n - i + 2(1)n$$ (8.74)

If n is even, then all the components of the vector **x** are found in pairs, by the solution of the linear system (8.73) and the formula (8.74), respectively, for $i = \frac{n}{2}(-1)1.$

The Table 8.2 illustrates the alternative computational costs for the complete factorization of a coefficient matrix A in the form $A = W * D * Z$ together with the computational cost for the solution of the linear system $A\mathbf{x} = \mathbf{b}$.

TABLE 8.2 Computational Costs of the WDZ Method.

Solution method of the (2 × 2) linear system	Total number of time steps	Maximum number of processors working in parallel
Cramer's rule	$17\left[\dfrac{n-1}{2}\right] + 2(2 + (-1)^n)$	$\max\{6(n-2), 2(n-2)^2\}$
	$18\left[\dfrac{n-1}{2}\right] + 2(2 + (-1)^n)$	$\max\{6(n-2), (n-2)^2\}$
Gauss elimination method	$27\left[\dfrac{n-1}{2}\right] + 7 + 4(-1)^n$	$2(n-2)^2$
	$28\left[\dfrac{n-1}{2}\right] + 7 + 4(-1)^n$	$\max\{2(n-2), (n-2)^2\}$

8.8 THE CHOLESKI Q.I.F. METHOD

We now study the Q.I.F. method in which the coefficient matrix A of (8.1) is a symmetric positive definite matrix. It will be shown that the symmetric positive definite matrix A can be factorized as follows [5]:

$$A = W * W^T \tag{8.75}$$

where the matrix W has the following form: If W_i, $i = 1, 2, \cdots, n$, is a column vector of W, then we have

$$W = [W_1 W_2 \cdots W_n] \tag{8.76}$$

and where the general form of W_i, $i = 1, 2, \cdots, n$, is as follows:

1. For n odd,

$$W_i \equiv \begin{cases} \underbrace{[0 \cdots 0}_{i-1} \; w_{i,i} \cdots w_{n-i+1,i} \; 0 \cdots 0]^T, & i = 1(1)\dfrac{n-1}{2} \\[2em] \underbrace{[0 \cdots 0}_{(n-1)/2} \; w_{i,i} \; 0 \cdots 0]^T, & i = \dfrac{n+1}{2} \\[2em] \underbrace{[0 \cdots 0}_{n-i+1} \; w_{n-i+2,i} \cdots w_{i,i} \; 0 \cdots 0]^T, & i = \dfrac{n+3}{2}(1)n \end{cases}$$

$$\tag{8.77}$$

2. For n even,

$$
W_i \equiv \begin{cases}
[0 \cdots 0 \underbrace{}_{i-1} w_{i,i} \cdots w_{n-i+1,i} \ 0 \cdots 0]^T, & i = 1(1)\dfrac{n}{2} \\[4mm]
[0 \cdots 0 \underbrace{}_{i-1} w_{i,i} \ 0 \cdots 0]^T, & i = \dfrac{n}{2} + 1 \\[4mm]
[0 \cdots 0 \underbrace{}_{n-i+1} w_{n-i+2,i} \cdots w_{i,i} \ 0 \cdots 0]^T, & i = \dfrac{n}{2} + 2(1)n
\end{cases}
$$

$$(8.78)$$

Thus, when $n = 5$ we have

$$
W \equiv \begin{bmatrix}
w_{1,1} & 0 & 0 & 0 & 0 \\
w_{2,1} & w_{2,2} & 0 & 0 & w_{2,5} \\
w_{3,1} & w_{3,2} & w_{3,3} & w_{3,4} & w_{3,5} \\
w_{4,1} & w_{4,2} & 0 & w_{4,4} & w_{4,5} \\
w_{5,1} & 0 & 0 & 0 & w_{5,5}
\end{bmatrix}
$$

while for $n = 6$, we have

$$
W \equiv \begin{bmatrix}
w_{1,1} & 0 & 0 & 0 & 0 & 0 \\
w_{2,1} & w_{2,2} & 0 & 0 & 0 & w_{2,6} \\
w_{3,1} & w_{3,2} & w_{3,3} & 0 & w_{3,5} & w_{3,6} \\
w_{4,1} & w_{4,2} & w_{4,3} & w_{4,4} & w_{4,5} & w_{4,6} \\
w_{5,1} & w_{5,2} & 0 & 0 & w_{5,5} & w_{5,6} \\
w_{6,1} & 0 & 0 & 0 & 0 & w_{6,6}
\end{bmatrix}
$$

The elements of the matrix W can be computed in $k = \left\lceil \dfrac{n+1}{2} \right\rceil$ distinct stages and we define at the start of the kth stage, the matrix A_k, $k = 1(1)\dfrac{n-1}{2}$, with elements $a_{i,j}^{(k)}$, $i, j = 1(1)n$ as follows:

$$A_1 = A$$

$$A_k = A - \sum_{i=1}^{k-1} W_i * W_i^T - \sum_{i=n-k+2}^{n} W_i * W_i^T, \quad k = 2(1)\left\lceil \dfrac{n-1}{2} \right\rceil \quad (8.79)$$

It can be seen, from the definition (8.79) that the first and last $(k - 1)$ rows and columns of any A_k matrix are zero. Thus, by starting with $A_1 = A$ we evaluate at the kth step, $k = 2(1) \left[\dfrac{n - 1}{2}\right]$, the elements that are nonzero in the kth and $(n - k + 1)$th columns of W by the following algorithm:

$$w_{k,k} = \sqrt{a_{k,k}^{(k)}} \tag{8.80a}$$

$$w_{i,k} = a_{i,k}^{(k)}/w_{k,k}, \quad i = k + 1(1)n - k + 1 \tag{8.80b}$$

$$w_{n-k+1,n-k+1} = (a_{n-k+1,n-k+1}^{(k)} - w_{n-k+1,k}^2)^{1/2} \tag{8.80c}$$

$$w_{i,n-k+1} = (a_{i,n-k+1}^{(k)} - w_{i,k}w_{n-k+1,k})/w_{n-k+1,n-k+1},$$
$$i = k + 1(1)n - k \tag{8.80d}$$

$$A_{k+1} = A_k - W_k * W_k^T - W_{n-k+1} * W_{n-k+1}^T \tag{8.80e}$$

To complete the computation of all the elements of W we need one more step in which, for n odd, the $\left[\dfrac{n + 1}{2}\right]$th step is carried out to evaluate the center element $w_{i,i}$ for $i = \dfrac{n + 1}{2}$ from the formula (8.80a), and for n even, the $\left(\dfrac{n}{2}\right)$th step is carried out to evaluate the elements $w_{k,k}$, $w_{k+1,k}$ and $w_{k+1,k+1}$ from the formulas (8.80a), (8.80b), and (8.80c).

In order to solve the linear system of Eq. (8.1), where the matrix A is factorized as Eq. (8.75), we need first to solve the linear system

$$W\mathbf{y} = \mathbf{b} \tag{8.81}$$

for the auxiliary vector $\mathbf{y}$ with its components denoted by $y_i | i = 1(1)n$, and then the final solution $\mathbf{x}$ is obtained by solving the linear system

$$W^T\mathbf{x} = \mathbf{y} \tag{8.82}$$

We can solve the linear system (8.81) for $k = 1(1)\left[\dfrac{n - 1}{2}\right]$ by the following algorithm:

$$y_k = b_k^{(k)}/w_{k,k} \tag{8.83a}$$

$$y_{n-k+1} = (b_{n-k+1}^{(k)} - y_k * w_{n-k+1,k})/w_{n-k+1,n-k+1} \tag{8.83b}$$

$$b^{(k+1)} = b^{(k)} - y_k W_k - y_{n-k+1} * w_{n-k+1} \tag{8.83c}$$

If n is odd, step (8.83a) has to be carried out for $k = \dfrac{n + 1}{2}$ to find the element in the center of the auxiliary vector, y_k, while if n is even, then steps (8.83a) and (8.83b) have to be executed for $k = \dfrac{n}{2}$ to find the two center elements $y_{n/2}$ and $y_{n/2+1}$ of the vector $\mathbf{y}$.

For the solution of the linear system (8.82) we shall use the algorithm presented by Evans and Hadjidimos [2] (see Section 8.6) for the solution of the linear system $Z\mathbf{x} = \mathbf{y}$, since the structure of the matrices Z and W^T is the same.

We first let

$$W^T\mathbf{x} = \mathbf{y} = \mathbf{y}^{(1)}$$

so that

$$\sum_{i=1}^{n} x_i W_i^* = y^{(1)} \tag{8.84}$$

where W_i^*, $i = 1, 2, \cdots, n$, are the column vectors of the matrix W^T, that is,

$$W^T = [W_1^* W_2^* \cdots W_n^*]. \tag{8.85}$$

Hence, if we set $l = \left[\dfrac{n+1}{2}\right]$ then for n odd, the center element of the vector $\mathbf{x}$, that is, x_l can be evaluated as

$$x_l = y_l^{(1)}/wt_{l,l} \tag{8.86}$$

and

$$y^{(2)} = y^{(1)} - x_l W_l^*$$

while for n even we find that

$$\begin{cases} x_{l+1} = y_{l+1}^{(1)}/wt_{l+1,l+1} \\ x_l = (y^{(1)} - x_{l+1} wt_{l,l+1})wt_{l,l} \end{cases} \tag{8.87}$$

and

$$y^{(2)} = y^{(1)} - x_l W_l^* - x_{l+1} W_{l+1}^*$$

where $wt_{i,j}$, $i, j = 1, 2, \cdots, n$ denotes the elements of the matrix W^T. Then we proceed using the following algorithm:

$$x_{n-k+1} = y_{n-k+1}^{(l-k+1)}/wt_{n-k+1,n-k+1} \tag{8.88a}$$

$$x_k = (y_k^{(l-k+1)} - x_{n-k+1} wt_{k,n-k+1})/wt_{k,k} \tag{8.88b}$$

$$y^{(l-k+2)} = y^{(l-k+1)} - x_k W_k^* - x_{n-k+1} W_{n-k+1}^* \tag{8.88c}$$

for all $k = \left[\dfrac{n-1}{2}\right](-1)1$ where step (8.88c) is not executed for $k = 1$.

Under the same assumptions as before (Section 8.2), it can be seen that the complete factorization of the matrix A and the solution of the linear system (8.1) requires either a total number of $15n + 23 \left[\dfrac{n-1}{2}\right] + 6 + 5(-1)^n$ time steps and a maximum of $2(n-1)^2$ processors, or a total number of $15n + 24 \left[\dfrac{n-1}{2}\right] + 6 + 5(-1)^n$ time steps and a maximum number of $(n-1)^2$ processors.

It can be shown that there exists a relationship between the Choleski Q.I.F. method and the Choleski factorization method.

Let A be a symmetric positive definite matrix, then by the Choleski factorization method we would obtain a lower triangular matrix L (say) with its elements $l_{i,j}$, $i = 1(1)n$ and $j = 1(1)i$ defined by

$$l_{i,i} = \left(a_{i,i} - \sum_{k=1}^{i-1} l_{i,j}^2 \right)^{1/2}$$

and (8.89)

$$l_{i,j} = \left(a_{i,i} - \sum_{k=1}^{j-1} l_{i,k} l_{j,k} \right) \Big/ l_{j,j}, \quad j < i$$

such that

$$A = L * L^T \tag{8.90}$$

Consider the following permutation matrix P with its element denoted by $p_{i,j}$, $j, i = 1, 2, \cdots, n$ where the nonzero elements of P are defined as

1. For n odd,

$$p_{i,2i-1} = 1, \quad i = 1(1)\frac{n+1}{2}$$

$$p_{n+1/2+i,n-2i+1} = 1, \quad i = 1(1)\frac{n-1}{2} \tag{8.91a}$$

2. For n even,

$$p_{i,2i-1} = 1, \quad i = 1(1)\frac{n}{2}$$

$$p_{n/2+i,n-2i+2} = 1, \quad i = 1(1)\frac{n}{2} \tag{8.91b}$$

Theorem 8.1 In the Choleski form of the quadrant interlocking factorization method of the matrix PAP^T, where A is a symmetric positive definite matrix and

P a permutation matrix defined by (8.19a) and (8.19b), the resulting matrix W which is of the form shown in (8.77) or (8.78) is a permutated form of the matrix L where L is the lower triangular matrix defined by (8.89) for which the relation (8.90) holds, that is,

$$W = PLP^T \tag{8.92}$$

Proof For proof see Shanehchi and Evans [2]. □

8.9 COMPARISON OF SEQUENTIAL AND PARALLEL MATRIX METHODS

In this final section we compare the triangular decomposition and quadrant interlocking matrix methods.

Given a matrix A, that is,

$$\begin{bmatrix} a_{11} & a_{12} & a_{13} & a_{14} \\ a_{21} & a_{22} & a_{23} & a_{24} \\ a_{31} & a_{32} & a_{33} & \mathring{a}_{34} \\ a_{41} & a_{42} & a_{43} & a_{44} \end{bmatrix} \quad \det A^{-1} \neq 0 \text{ nonsingular} \tag{8.93}$$

we now attempt to find matrix factors L and U of the following form:

$$L = \begin{bmatrix} 1 & & & \\ l_{21} & 1 & 0 & \\ l_{31} & l_{32} & 1 & 1 \\ l_{41} & l_{42} & l_{43} & \end{bmatrix}$$

and   (8.94)

$$U = \begin{bmatrix} u_{11} & u_{12} & u_{13} & u_{14} \\ & u_{22} & u_{23} & u_{24} \\ & 0 & u_{33} & u_{34} \\ & & & u_{44} \end{bmatrix}$$

such that

$$A \equiv LU$$

By equating coefficients we can derive the following relations to determine the coefficients of L and U:

$$u_{11} = a_{11}, \quad u_{12} = a_{12}, \quad u_{13} = a_{13}, \quad u_{14} = a_{14}$$

$$l_{21}u_{11} = a_{21}, \, l_{21}u_{12} + u_{22} = a_{22}, \, l_{21}u_{13} + u_{23} = a_{23}, \, l_{21}u_{14} + u_{24} = a_{24}$$

$$l_{31}u_{11} = a_{31}, \, l_{31}u_{12} + l_{32}u_{22} = a_{32}, \, l_{31}u_{13} + l_{32}u_{23} + u_{33} = a_{33}, \text{ etc.}$$

$$(8.95)$$

and similarly for the last row. All these are essentially sequential relations, since each of the unknowns $l_{i,j}$ and $u_{i,j}$ are brought into the above relations one at a time and so can be determined.

The reason why such a factorization is sought in $L. U.$ form is that to obtain the solution of the linear system,

$$Ax = b \tag{8.96}$$

thus, by making use of the substitution $A = LU$, then the problem reduces to the solution of the coupled system,

$$Ly = b \tag{8.97}$$

and

$$Ux = \mathbf{y} \tag{8.98}$$

where $\mathbf{y}$ is an intermediate vector.

The systems (8.97) and (8.98) are easily solvable systems and can be solved by forward or backward substitution processes, that is, the following manner,

$$Ly = b$$

$$\begin{bmatrix} 1 & & & \\ l_{21} & 1 & & 0 \\ l_{31} & l_{32} & 1 & \\ l_{41} & l_{42} & l_{43} & 1 \end{bmatrix} \begin{bmatrix} y_1 \\ y_2 \\ y_3 \\ y_4 \end{bmatrix} = \begin{bmatrix} b_1 \\ b_2 \\ b_3 \\ b_4 \end{bmatrix} \tag{8.99}$$

can be solved as follows:

$$\begin{aligned} y_1 &= b_1 & &\rightarrow y_1 = b_1 \\ l_{21}y_1 + y_2 &= b_2 & &\rightarrow y_2 = b_2 - l_{21}y_1 \\ l_{31}y_1 + l_{32}y_2 + y_3 &= b_3 & &\rightarrow y_3 = b_3 - l_{31}y_1 - l_{32}y_2 \\ l_{41}y_1 + l_{42}y_2 + l_{43}y_3 + y_4 &= b_4 & &\rightarrow y_4 = b_4 - l_{41}y_1 - l_{42}y_2 - l_{43}y_3 \end{aligned} \tag{8.100}$$

Similarly a backsubstitution process can be derived for $Ux = \mathbf{y}$.

Again these are all sequential processes since they have to be solved in the manner indicated by the arrow. Finally it is well known that the LU triangular decomposition method requires $O(n^3)$ operations.

The interesting question now is this: Can we find a factorization that is more suitable for a parallel computer?

Consider a factorization of A of the form,

$$A = WZ \tag{8.101}$$

where

$$W = \begin{bmatrix} 1 & 0 & 0 & \\ w_{21} & 1 & 0 & w_{24} \\ w_{31} & 0 & 1 & w_{34} \\ 0 & 0 & 1 \end{bmatrix} \quad \text{and} \quad Z = \begin{bmatrix} z_{11} & z_{12} & z_{13} & z_{14} \\ & z_{22} & z_{23} & \\ 0 & & & 0 \\ & z_{32} & z_{34} & \\ z_{41} & z_{42} & z_{43} & z_{44} \end{bmatrix} \tag{8.102}$$

Thus, in general W and Z will have the form,

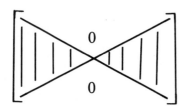   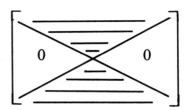

and are termed quadrant interlocking factors (Q.I.F.), which have a Butterfly design.

To determine the coefficients of W and Z, again we proceed to equate coefficients.

Thus,

I. $z_{11} = a_{11},\ z_{12} = a_{12},\ z_{13} = z_{13},\ z_{14} = a_{14}$ \hfill (8.103a)

IV. $z_{41} = a_{41},\ z_{42} = a_{42},\ z_{43} = a_{43},\ z_{44} = a_{44}$ \hfill (8.103d)

II. $\overset{①}{w_{21}z_{11}} + w_{24}z_{41} = a_{21}; \qquad \overset{②}{w_{21}z_{12} + z_{22} + w_{24}z_{42}} = a_{22}$ \hfill (8.103b)

$\overset{③}{w_{21}z_{13} + z_{23} + w_{24}z_{43}} = a_{23}; \qquad \overset{④}{w_{21}z_{14} + w_{24}z_{44}} = a_{24}$

By eliminating ① and ④ we can obtain w_{21} and w_{24}. Then we substitute in ② and ③ to obtain z_{22} and z_{23}.

III. $\overset{\textcircled{1}}{w_{31}z_{11}} + w_{34}z_{41} = a_{31};$ $\overset{\textcircled{2}}{w_{31}z_{12}} + z_{32} + w_{34}z_{42} = a_{32}$ (8.103c)

$\overset{\textcircled{3}}{w_{31}z_{13}} + z_{33} + w_{34}z_{43} = a_{33};$ $\overset{\textcircled{4}}{w_{31}z_{14}} + w_{34}z_{44} = a_{34}$

Similarly, again we can eliminate ① and ④ to obtain w_{31} and w_{34} and substitute in ② and ③ to obtain z_{32} and z_{33}. Thus, we can see from these operations that the first and last rows of Z are given immediately. Then, (2×2) sets of linear equations are required to be solved to obtain the $w_{i,1}$ and $w_{i,4}$ for $i = 2, 3$.

Thus, the calculation proceeds as follows:

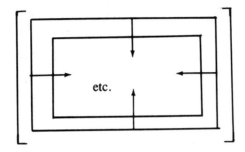

the outermost elements of the matrices W and Z are obtained. Then, the calculation proceeds on the innermost next layer of elements. Thus, only $\left(\dfrac{n-1}{2}\right)$ stages are required to compute all the elements of W and Z.

Further it must be noticed that for $n =$ odd, special consideration has to be provided to cope with the center element separately. In comparison, the LU decomposition procedure to determine the matrix coefficients of L and U are given by

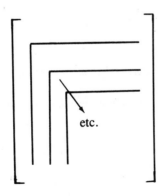

Again by using the relationship

$$A = WZ$$

the linear system

$$Ax = b$$

can be reformulated as the solution of two related linear systems,

$$Wy = b \quad \text{and} \quad Zx = y \tag{8.104}$$

To solve $Wy = b$ we proceed as follows

$$
\begin{bmatrix}
1 & 0 & 0 & 0 \\
w_{21} & 1 & 0 & w_{24} \\
w_{31} & 0 & 1 & w_{34} \\
0 & 0 & 0 & 1
\end{bmatrix}
\begin{bmatrix}
y_1 \\
y_2 \\
y_3 \\
y_4
\end{bmatrix}
=
\begin{bmatrix}
b_1 \\
b_2 \\
b_3 \\
b_4
\end{bmatrix}
\tag{8.105}
$$

from which we see immediately that

$$y_1 = b_1 \quad \text{and} \quad y_4 = b_4 \tag{8.106}$$

and

$$w_{21} y_1 + y_2 w_{24} y_4 = b_2 \quad \text{and} \quad w_{31} y_1 + y_2 + w_{34} y_4 = b_3 \tag{8.107a}$$

or

$$y_2 = \tilde{b}_2 = (b_2 - w_{21} y_1 - w_{24} y_4)$$

and

$$y_3 = \tilde{b}_3 = (b_3 - w_{31} y_1 - w_{34} y_4) \tag{8.107b}$$

Thus the solutions for **y** are obtained in pairs working from the top and bottom of the intermediate vector **y**.

Once the vector **y** has been determined then to solve $Zx = y$ we proceed as follows:

$$
\begin{bmatrix}
z_{11} & z_{12} & z_{13} & z_{14} \\
 & z_{22} & z_{23} & \\
 & z_{32} & z_{33} & \\
z_{41} & z_{42} & z_{43} & z_{44}
\end{bmatrix}
\begin{bmatrix}
x_1 \\
x_2 \\
x_3 \\
x_4
\end{bmatrix}
=
\begin{bmatrix}
y_1 \\
y_2 \\
y_3 \\
y_4
\end{bmatrix}
\tag{8.108}
$$

Starting at the center we solve the (2×2) linear system,

$$z_{22}x_2 + z_{23}x_3 = y_2$$

$$z_{32}x_2 + z_{33}x_3 = y_3 \qquad (8.109)$$

for x_2 and x_3

Then, we proceed outward and solve the (2×2) linear system,

$$z_{11}x_1 + z_{14}x_4 = y_1 = (y_1 - z_{12}x_2 - z_{13}x_3)$$

$$z_{41}x_1 + z_{44}x_4 = y_4 = (y_4 - z_{42}x_2 - z_{43}x_3) \qquad (8.110)$$

for x_1 and x_3

Thus, the solution $\mathbf{x}$ can be obtained in $O(n)$ stages on a parallel SIMD computer with n^2 processors.

REFERENCES

[1] D. J. Evans and M. Hatzopoulos, The parallel solution of linear systems, *Internat. J. Computer Maths.*, 7, 227–238 (1980).

[2] D. J. Evans and A. Hadjidimos, A modification to the quadrant interlocking factorisation parallel method, *Internat. J. Computer Maths.*, 8, 149–166 (1980).

[3] D. J. Evans, A. Hadjidimos, and D. Noutsos, The parallel solution of banded linear equations by the new quadrant interlocking factorisation (Q.I.F.) method, *Internat. J. Computer Maths.*, 9, 151–162 (1981).

[4] J. Shanehchi and D. J. Evans, New variants of interlocking factorisation (Q.I.F.) method, in *Computer Science III Proc. of Conpar 81 Conf.*, lecture notes 1981, W. Handler, Ed., Springer Verlag, Berlin, 493–507 (1981).

[5] J. Shanehchi, "The Determination of Sparse Eigensystems and Parallel Linear System Solvers," Ph.D. thesis, Loughborough University of Technology U.K., (1980).

[6] H. S. Stone, "Problems of Parallel Computation," in, J. F. Traub, Ed., *Complexity of Sequential and Parallel Numerical Algorithms*, Academic Press, San Diego, Calif., 1–16 (1973).

[7] J. F. Traub, *Complexity of Sequential and Parallel Numerical Algorithms*, Academic Press, San Diego, Calif., 1973.

[8] M. J. Flynn, Very High Speed Computing Systems, *Proc. IEEE*, 54, 1901–1909 (1966).

[9] D. J. Kuck, "Multioperation Machine Computation," in J. F. Traub, Ed., *Complexity of Sequential and Parallel Numerical Algorithms*, Academic Press, San Diego, Calif., 17–47 (1973).

[10] R. C. Dunbar, "Analysis and Design of Parallel Algorithms," Ph.D. thesis, Loughborough University of Technology U.K., (1978).

CHAPTER 9 ⎯⎯⎯⎯⎯⎯⎯⎯⎯⎯⎯⎯⎯

Parallel Matrix Iterative Algorithms

D. J. EVANS

9.1 INTRODUCTION

As is well known, all the known iterative methods such as Jacobi, Gauss–Seidel, and the S.O.R. method for solving the linear system of equations $A\mathbf{x} = \mathbf{b}$ are built around a partition (or splitting) of A into the form

$$A = D - L - U$$

where D is the main diagonal elements of A and $-L$ and $-U$ are strictly lower and strictly upper triangular elements of A, respectively.

Now a new splitting of A is introduced and corresponding iterative methods developed for solving a linear system of equations. These iterative schemes are called Quadrant Interlocking Iterative (Q.I.I.) methods. In Section 9.2 we introduce the Quadrant Interlocking Splitting, in Section 9.3 we present the basic iterative methods based on quadrant interlocking splitting, in Section 9.4 we prove the essential theorems for convergence of the basic parallel iterative schemes, and in Section 9.5 we give the practical implementation of these parallel schemes.

9.2 THE QUADRANT INTERLOCKING (Q.I.) SPLITTING METHOD

Consider the linear system of equations

$$A\mathbf{x} = \mathbf{b} \tag{9.1}$$

Fuzzy, Holographic, and Parallel Intelligence, By Branko Souček and the IRIS Group.
ISBN 0-471-54772-7 © 1992 John Wiley & Sons, Inc.

where A is a nonsingular matrix of order n, with elements $a_{i,j}$, $i, j = 1(1)n$ and $\mathbf{x}$ and $\mathbf{b}$ are two n-dimensional vectors with $\mathbf{x}$ (unknown) and $\mathbf{b}$ (known) given by

$$\mathbf{x} = [x_1, x_2, \cdots, x_n]^T$$

$$\mathbf{b} = [b_1, b_2, \cdots, b_n]^T \tag{9.2}$$

We can partition the matrix A into the form

$$A = X - W - Z \tag{9.3}$$

where the structure of the matrices X, $-W$, and $-Z$ is defined as follows:

If X_i, W_i, and Z_i, $i = 1, 2, \cdots, n$, are the column vectors of the matrix X, $-W$, and $-Z^T$, we have

$$X = [X_2, \cdots, X_n] \tag{9.4}$$

$$-W = [W_1, W_2, \cdots, W_n] \tag{9.5}$$

and

$$-Z^T = [Z_1, Z_2, \cdots, Z_n] \tag{9.6}$$

The column vectors X_i have the following general form:

$$X_i \equiv \begin{cases} [\underbrace{0 \cdots 0}_{i-1} \; a_{i,i} \, 0 \cdots 0 \, a_{n-i+1,i} \, 0 \cdots 0]^T, & i = 1(1) \left[\dfrac{n+1}{2}\right] \\[2em] [\underbrace{0 \cdots 0}_{n-i} \; a_{n-i+1,i} \, 0 \cdots 0 \, a_{i,i} \, 0 \cdots 0]^T, & i = \left[\dfrac{n+3}{2}\right] (1)n \end{cases} \tag{9.7}$$

where the symbol $[n]$ denotes the largest integer $\le n$. The column vectors W_i and Z_i have the following general forms:

1. For n odd,

$$W_i \equiv \begin{cases} [\underbrace{0 \cdots 0}_{i} \; a_{i+1,i} \cdots a_{n-i,i} \, 0 \cdots 0]^T, & i = 1(1)\dfrac{n-1}{2} \\[2em] [0 \cdots 0]^T, & i = \dfrac{n+1}{2} \\[2em] [\underbrace{0 \cdots 0}_{n-i+1} \; a_{n-i+2,i} \cdots a_{i-1,i} \, 0 \cdots 0]^T, & i = \dfrac{n+3}{2}(1)n \end{cases} \tag{9.8a}$$

and

$$
Z_i \equiv \begin{cases}
[\underbrace{0 \;\cdots\; 0}_{i} \quad a_{i,i+1} \;\cdots\; a_{i,n-i}\, 0 \;\cdots\; 0]^T, & i = 1(1)\dfrac{n-1}{2} \\[2em]
[0 \;\cdots\; 0]^T, & i = \dfrac{n+1}{2} \\[2em]
[\underbrace{0 \;\cdots\; 0}_{n-i+1} \quad a_{i,i+2} \;\cdots\; a_{i,i-1}\, 0 \;\cdots\; 0]^T, & i = \dfrac{n+3}{2}(1)n
\end{cases}
$$

$$(9.8b)$$

2. For n even,

$$
W_i \equiv \begin{cases}
[\underbrace{0 \;\cdots\; 0}_{i} \quad a_{i+1,i} \;\cdots\; a_{n-i,i}\, 0 \;\cdots\; 0]^T, & i = 1(1)\dfrac{n}{2} - 1 \\[2em]
[0 \;\cdots\; 0]^T, & i = \dfrac{n}{2}, \dfrac{n}{2} + 1 \\[2em]
[\underbrace{0 \;\cdots\; 0}_{n-i+1} \quad a_{n-i+2,i} \;\cdots\; a_{i-1,i}\, 0 \;\cdots\; 0]^T, & i = \dfrac{n}{2} + 2(1)n
\end{cases}
$$

$$(9.9a)$$

and

$$
Z_i \equiv \begin{cases}
[\underbrace{0 \;\cdots\; 0}_{i} \quad a_{i,i+1} \;\cdots\; a_{i,n-i}\, 0 \;\cdots\; 0]^T, & i = 1(1)\dfrac{n}{2} - 1 \\[2em]
[0 \;\cdots\; 0]^T, & i = \dfrac{n}{2}, \dfrac{n}{2} + 1 \\[2em]
[\underbrace{0 \;\cdots\; 0}_{n-i+1} \quad a_{i,n-i+2} \;\cdots\; a_{i,i-1}\, 0 \;\cdots\; 0]^T, & i = \dfrac{n}{2} + 2(1)n
\end{cases}
$$

$$(9.9b)$$

For example when $n = 5$, we have

$$
X \equiv \begin{bmatrix}
a_{1,1} & 0 & 0 & 0 & a_{1,5} \\
0 & a_{2,2} & 0 & a_{2,4} & 0 \\
0 & 0 & a_{3,3} & 0 & 0 \\
0 & a_{4,2} & 0 & a_{4,4} & 0 \\
a_{5,1} & 0 & 0 & 0 & a_{5,1}
\end{bmatrix},
$$

$$-W \equiv \begin{bmatrix} 0 & 0 & 0 & 0 & 0 \\ a_{2,1} & 0 & 0 & 0 & a_{2,5} \\ a_{3,1} & a_{3,2} & 0 & a_{3,4} & a_{3,5} \\ a_{4,1} & 0 & 0 & 0 & a_{4,5} \\ 0 & 0 & 0 & 0 & 0 \end{bmatrix},$$

$$-Z \equiv \begin{bmatrix} 0 & a_{1,2} & a_{1,3} & a_{1,4} & 0 \\ 0 & 0 & a_{2,3} & 0 & 0 \\ 0 & 0 & 0 & 0 & 0 \\ 0 & 0 & a_{4,3} & 0 & 0 \\ 0 & a_{5,2} & a_{5,3} & a_{5,4} & 0 \end{bmatrix}$$

while for $n = 6$ we have

$$X \equiv \begin{bmatrix} a_{1,1} & 0 & 0 & 0 & 0 & a_{1,6} \\ 0 & a_{2,2} & 0 & 0 & a_{2,5} & 0 \\ 0 & 0 & a_{3,3} & a_{3,4} & 0 & 0 \\ 0 & 0 & a_{4,4} & a_{4,4} & 0 & 0 \\ 0 & a_{5,2} & 0 & 0 & a_{5,5} & 0 \\ a_{6,1} & 0 & 0 & 0 & 0 & a_{6,6} \end{bmatrix}$$

$$-W \equiv \begin{bmatrix} 0 & 0 & 0 & 0 & 0 & 0 \\ a_{2,1} & 0 & 0 & 0 & 0 & a_{2,6} \\ a_{3,1} & a_{3,2} & 0 & 0 & a_{3,5} & a_{3,6} \\ a_{4,1} & a_{4,2} & 0 & 0 & a_{4,5} & a_{4,6} \\ a_{5,1} & 0 & 0 & 0 & 0 & a_{5,6} \\ 0 & 0 & 0 & 0 & 0 & 0 \end{bmatrix}$$

$$-Z \equiv \begin{bmatrix} 0 & a_{1,2} & a_{1,3} & a_{1,4} & a_{1,5} & 0 \\ 0 & 0 & a_{2,3} & a_{2,4} & 0 & 0 \\ 0 & 0 & 0 & 0 & 0 & 0 \\ 0 & 0 & 0 & 0 & 0 & 0 \\ 0 & 0 & a_{5,3} & a_{5,4} & 0 & 0 \\ 0 & a_{6,2} & a_{6,3} & a_{6,4} & a_{6,5} & 0 \end{bmatrix}$$

9.3 BASIC QUADRANT INTERLOCKING ITERATIVE (Q.I.I.) METHOD

We now define four basic (Q.I.I.) methods. We illustrate the methods for the systems:

$$
\begin{bmatrix}
a_{1,1} & a_{1,2}, & \cdots , & a_{1,n} \\
a_{2,1} & a_{2,2}, & \cdots , & a_{2,n} \\
\vdots & & \vdots & \\
a_{n,1}, & a_{n,2}, & \cdots , & a_{n,n}
\end{bmatrix}
\begin{bmatrix}
x_1 \\
x_2 \\
\vdots \\
x_n
\end{bmatrix}
=
\begin{bmatrix}
b_1 \\
b_2 \\
\vdots \\
b_n
\end{bmatrix}
\tag{9.10}
$$

We can obtain the elements of the vector $\mathbf{x}$ in $\left[\frac{n+1}{2}\right]$ distinct steps, where in each step we solve (2×2) linear systems. In general, at the ith step we solve the following linear system:

$$
\begin{cases}
a_{i,i}x_i + a_{i,n-i+1}x_{n-i+1} = c_i \\
a_{n-i+1,i}x_i + a_{n-i+1,n-i+1}x_{n-i+1} = c_{n-i+1}
\end{cases}
, \quad i = 1(1)\left[\frac{n+1}{2}\right] \tag{9.11}
$$

where

$$
\left.
\begin{aligned}
c_i &= -\sum_{j=1}^{n} a_{i,j}x_j + b_i \\
c_{n-i+1} &= -\sum_{j=1}^{n} a_{n-i+1}x_j + b_{n-i+1}
\end{aligned}
\right\}, \quad j \neq i \, \& \, n - i + 1 \tag{9.12}
$$

therefore, if

$$
\Delta_i \equiv \det \begin{bmatrix}
a_{i,i} & a_{i,n-i+1} \\
a_{n-i+1,i} & a_{n-i+1,n-i+1}
\end{bmatrix} \neq 0 \tag{9.13}
$$

we obtain the unknown x_i and x_{n-i+1}, $i = 1, 2, \cdots , \left[\frac{n+1}{2}\right]$ from the formulas

$$
x_i = (c_i * a_{n-i+1,n-i+1} - c_{n-i+1} * a_{i,n-i+1})/\Delta_i \tag{9.14}
$$

and

$$
x_{n-i+1} = (c_{n-i+1} * a_{i,i} - c_i * a_{n-i+1,i})/\Delta_i \tag{9.15}
$$

Note that if n is odd Eq. (9.10) is a single equation at the step $i = \frac{1}{2}(n+1)$.

We have thus replaced the system (9.1) by the equivalent system

$$\mathbf{x} = B\mathbf{x} + \mathbf{c} \tag{9.16}$$

where

$$B = X^{-1}(W + Z) \tag{9.17}$$

and

$$\mathbf{c} = X^{-1}\mathbf{b} \tag{9.18}$$

Clearly, if the $\Delta_i \neq 0$, $i = 1, 2, \cdots, \left\lceil \frac{n+1}{2} \right\rceil$ then X^{-1} exists.

1. With the Simultaneous Quadrant Interlocking Iterative method (S.Q.I.I.) we choose arbitrary starting values $x_i^{(0)}$, $i = 1, 2, \cdots, n$, and compute $x_i^{(1)}$ from Eqs. (9.14) and (9.15) in pairs, using $x_i^{(0)}$ in the right hand side vector of Eqs. (9.12) then determine $x_i^{(2)}$ from the values $x_i^{(1)}$, and so forth. Thus, in general, given $x_i^{(k)}$ we can determine $x_i^{(k+1)}$ by

$$\begin{cases} a_{i,i}x_i^{(k+1)} + a_{i,n-i+1}x_{n-i+1}^{(k+1)} = c_i^{(k)} \\ a_{n-i+1,i}x_i^{(k+1)} + a_{n-i+1,n-i+1}x_{n-i+1}^{(k+1)} = c_{n-i+1}^{(k)} \end{cases}, \quad i = 1(1)\left\lceil \frac{n+1}{2} \right\rceil$$

$$\tag{9.19}$$

where

$$\left. \begin{aligned} c_i^{(k)} &= -\sum_{j=1}^{n} a_{i,j}x_j^{(k)} + b_i \\ c_{n-i+1}^{(k)} &= -\sum_{j=1}^{n} a_{n-i+1,j}x_j^{(k)} + b_{n-i+1} \end{aligned} \right\}, \quad j \neq i \ \& \ n-i+1 \tag{9.20}$$

(note that for n odd, the linear system (9.19) reduces to a single equation), when $i = \frac{1}{2}(n+1)$ or equivalently,

$$\mathbf{x}^{(k+1)} = B\mathbf{x}^{(k)} + \mathbf{c} \tag{9.21}$$

2. Related to the S.Q.I.I. method we have the Simultaneous Overrelaxation Quadrant Interlocking Iterative method (S.O.Q.I.I.). In this method we choose a real parameter ω and replace Eqs. (9.19) by

$$\begin{cases} a_{i,i}x_i^{(k+1)} + a_{i,n-i+1}x_{n-i+1}^{(k+1)} = \omega c_i^{(k)} \\ \qquad\qquad + (1 - \omega)(a_{i,i}x_i^{(k)} + a_{i,n-i+1}x_{n-i+1}^{(k)}) \\ a_{n-i+1,i}x_i^{(k+1)} + a_{n-i+1,n-i+1}x_{n-i+1}^{(k+1)} = \omega c_{n-i+1}^{(k)} \\ \qquad\qquad + (1 - \omega)(a_{n-i+1,i}x_i^{(k)} + a_{n-i+1,n-i+1}x_{n-i+1}^{(k)}) \end{cases} \tag{9.22}$$

where $c_i^{(k)}$ and $c_{n-i+1}^{(k)}$ are defined as in Eqs. (9.20); then equivalently the (S.O.Q.I.I.) is defined as

$$\mathbf{x}^{(k+1)} = B_\omega \mathbf{x}^{(k)} + \omega \mathbf{c} \tag{9.23}$$

where

$$B_\omega = \omega B + (1 - \omega)I \tag{9.24}$$

With $\omega = 1$, we have the (S.Q.I.I.) method.

3. The Successive Quadrant Interlocking Iterative method (S.U.Q.I.I.) is the same as the S.Q.I.I. method except that at each step we use the values of $x_i^{(k)}$ when available. Thus, instead of Eqs. (9.20) we have

$$
\left.
\begin{aligned}
c_i^{(k)} &= -\sum_{j=1}^{i-1} a_{i,j} x_j^{(k+1)} - \sum_{j=n-i+2}^{n} \\
&\quad \cdot a_{i,j} x_j^{(k+1)} - \sum_{j=i+1}^{n-i} a_{i,j} x_j^{(k)} + b_i \\
c_{n-i+1}^{(k)} &= -\sum_{j=1}^{i-1} a_{n-i1,j} x_j^{(k+1)} - \cdot \sum_{j=n-i+2}^{n} \\
&\quad \cdot a_{n-i+1,j} x_j^{(k+1)} - \sum_{j=i+1}^{n-i} x_j^{(k)} + b_{n-i+1}
\end{aligned}
\right\} , \; j \neq i, j \neq n-i+1
$$

$$\tag{9.25}$$

so the S.U.Q.I.I. method can be defined as

$$\mathbf{x}^{(k+1)} = (X - W)^{-1} Z \mathbf{x}^{(k)} + (X - W)^{-1} \mathbf{b} \tag{9.26}$$

or

$$\mathbf{x}^{(k+1)} = \mathcal{L} \mathbf{x}^{(k)} + \mathbf{c} \tag{9.27}$$

where

$$\mathcal{L} = (X - W)^{-1} Z \tag{9.28}$$

and

$$\mathbf{c} = (X - W)^{-1} \mathbf{b} \tag{9.29}$$

4. We now define the Successive Overrelaxation Quadrant Interlocking Iterative method (S.U.O.Q.I.I.), which is related to the S.U.Q.I.I. method. We choose

a real parameter ω and replace Eqs. (9.25) by

$$\left.\begin{array}{l} c_i^{(k)} = \omega c_i^{(k)} + (1 - \omega)(a_{i,i}x_i^{(k)} + a_{i,n-i+1}x_{n-i+1}^{(k)}) \\ c_{n-i+1}^{(k)} = \omega c_{n-i+1}^{(k)} + (1 - \omega)(a_{n-i+1,i}x_i^{(k)} + a_{n-i+1,n-i+1}x_{n-i+1}^{(k)}) \end{array}\right\} \quad (9.30)$$

or equivalently we have

$$\mathbf{x}^{(k+1)} = \mathcal{L}_\omega \mathbf{x}^{(k)} + \omega\mathbf{c} \quad (9.31)$$

where

$$\mathcal{L}_\omega = (X - \omega W)^{-1}(\omega Z + (1 - \omega)X) \quad (9.32)$$

If $\omega = 1$, then the S.U.O.Q.I.I. method reduces to the S.U.Q.I.I. method.

Finally, for the explicit block iterative methods given by Eqs. (9.21), (9.23), (9.27) and (9.31) the iteration matrices B, B_ω, $\mathcal{L}$, and $\mathcal{L}_\omega$ can be evaluated explicitly by the simple inversion and product of (2×2) submatrices.

9.4 CONVERGENCE OF THE BASIC QUADRANT INTERLOCKING METHOD

In this section, the convergence of the basic (Q.I.I.) methods which were considered in Section 9.3 is studied. We will first give theorems on the convergence of the S.O.Q.I.I. and S.U.O.Q.I.I. methods, which are applicable for any matrix, and we will then study the cases where the coefficient matrix A is diagonally dominant or positive definite, or where A is an L-matrix. We assume that the crossed diagonals matrix X of the matrix A is nonsingular.

Theorem 9.1   For any coefficient matrix A, if the S.Q.I.I. method converges, then the S.O.Q.I.I. method will also converge for

$$0 < \omega \leq 1$$

Proof   By relation (9.24), that is,

$$B_\omega = \omega B + (1 - \omega)I,$$

we have the following relationship between the eigenvalues ρ_i of the S.O.Q.I.I. and the eigenvalues μ_i of the S.Q.I.I. methods:

$$\rho_i = \omega\mu_i + (1 - \omega) \quad (9.33)$$

Consider $\mu_i = re^{i\theta}$ where $r \leq 1$ as a result of the convergence of the S.Q.I.I. method. Thus we have

$$|\rho_i|^2 = \omega^2 r^2 + 2\omega(1 - \omega)r \cos\theta + (1 - \omega)^2 \tag{9.34}$$

If $0 < \omega \leq 1$, then we obtain

$$|\rho_i|^2 < 1 \tag{9.35}$$

which implies the convergence of the S.O.U.Q.I.I. method.

Following Kahan [1] we have the following general convergence theorem for the S.U.O.Q.I.I. method.

Theorem 9.2   For the S.U.O.Q.I. I. matrix $\mathcal{L}_\omega$ and for all real ω we have

$$\rho(\mathcal{L}_\omega) \geq |\omega - 1| \tag{9.36}$$

Moreover, if the S.U.O.Q.I.I. method converges, then we have the result

$$0 < \omega < 2 \tag{9.37}$$

Proof   Let $\tilde{W} = X^{-1}W$ and $\tilde{Z} = X^{-1}Z$, then from Eq. (9.32) we have

$$\mathcal{L}_\omega = (I - \omega\tilde{W})^{-1}(\omega\tilde{Z} + (1 - \omega)I) \tag{9.38}$$

We know that

$$\det \mathcal{L}_\omega = \prod_{i=1}^{n} \lambda_i,$$

where $\lambda_i | i = 1(1)n$ are the eigenvalues of $\mathcal{L}_\omega$. Since $\tilde{W}$ and $\tilde{Z}$ have the same structure as the matrices W and Z, respectively, and since

$$\det (I - \omega\tilde{W}) = 1$$

then we have

$$\det \mathcal{L}_\omega = \det (\omega\tilde{Z} + (1 - \omega)I)$$
$$= (1 - \omega)^n$$

Hence

$$\rho(\mathcal{L}_\omega) \geq (|1 - \omega|^n)^{1/n} = |\omega - 1|$$

Now, if the S.U.O.I.I. method converges then we have

$$\rho(\mathcal{L}_\omega) \leq 1$$

Hence

$$|\omega - 1| < 1$$

or

$$0 < \omega < 2$$

We now seek to establish convergence theorems where the coefficient matrix A is diagonally dominant.

Theorem 9.3   Let A be an $(n \times n)$ diagonally dominant matrix. Then the S.Q.I.I. method converges.

Proof   By Eq. (9.17) (i.e., $B = X^{-1}(W + Z)$) we have

$$\left. \begin{matrix} b_{i,i} = 0 \\ b_{n-i+1,i} = 0 \end{matrix} \right\}, \quad i = 1(1)n \qquad (9.39)$$

Then

$$b_{i,j} = (a_{n-i+1,n-i+1} * a_{i,j} - a_{i,n-i+1} * a_{n-i1,j}) / \left| \begin{matrix} i = 1(1)n, j \neq i, \\ j \neq n - i + 1 \end{matrix} \right. \qquad (9.40)$$
$$(a_{i,i} * a_{n-i+1,n-i+1} - a_{i,n-i+1} * a_{n-i+1,i}),$$

For proof of the theorem, it is sufficient to show that

$$\Sigma |b_{i,j}| < 1 \quad \text{for all} \quad i \qquad (9.41)$$

From Eq. (9.40) we have

$$\Sigma |b_{i,j}| = (1/(a_{i,i} * a_{n-i+1,n-i+1} - a_{i,n-i+1} * a_{n-i+1,i})) \qquad (9.42)$$
$$\underset{\substack{j \neq i \\ j \neq n-i+1}}{\Sigma} |a_{n-i+1,n-i+1} * a_{i,j} - a_{i,n-i+1} * a_{n-i+1,j}|$$

Since A has diagonal dominance, it can be seen that

$$\sum_{\substack{j \neq 1 \\ j \neq n-i+1}} |a_{n-i+1,n-i+1} * a_{i,j} - a_{i,n-i+1} * a_{n-i+1,j}| \leq |a_{n-i+1,n-i+1}|$$

$$\sum_{\substack{j \neq 1 \\ j \neq n-i+1}} |a_{i,j}| + |a_{i,n-i+1}| \sum_{\substack{j \neq i \\ j \neq n-i+1}} |a_{n-i+1,j}|$$

$$< |a_{n-i+1,n-i+i1}| \, (|a_{i,i}| - |a_{i,n-i+1}|) + |a_{i,n-i+1}|$$

$$\cdot \, (|a_{n-i+1,n-i+1}| - |a_{n-i+1,i}|)$$

$$= |a_{n-i+1,n-i+1}| * |a_{i,i}| - |a_{i,n-i+1}| * |a_{n-i+1,i}|$$

$$\leq |a_{n-i+1,n-i+1} * a_{i,i} - a_{i,n-i+1} * a_{n-i+1,i}|$$

Thus, by Eq. (9.42) it is clear that

$$\sum_{\substack{j \neq i \\ j \neq n-i+1}} |b_{i,j}| < 1 \quad \text{for all } i \quad \square$$

Theorem 9.4 Let A be an irreducible and diagonally dominant matrix, then the (S.U.Q.I.I.) method converges, and the (S.U.O.Q.I.I.) method converges for $0 < \omega \leq 1$.

Proof Suppose that $\rho(\mathfrak{L}_\omega) \geq 1$, then for some eigenvalue λ of $\mathfrak{L}_\omega$ we have

$$|\lambda| \geq 1 \quad (\text{i.e., } |\lambda^{-1}| \leq 1)$$

and

$$\det(\mathfrak{L}_\omega - \lambda I) = \lambda^n * \det(I - \lambda^{-1}\mathfrak{L}_\omega) = 0 \tag{9.43}$$

Let $\tilde{W} = X^{-1}W$ and $\tilde{Z} = X^{-1}Z$, as before; then from Eq. (9.32) we have

$$I - \lambda^{-1}\mathfrak{L}_\omega = I - \lambda^{-1}[(I - \omega\tilde{W})^{-1}(\omega\tilde{Z} + (1 - \omega)I)] \tag{9.44}$$

or

$$\lambda(I - \omega\tilde{W})(I - \lambda^{-1}\mathfrak{L}_\omega) = (\lambda + \omega - 1)I - \lambda\omega\tilde{W} - \omega\tilde{Z} \tag{9.45}$$

If $0 < \omega \leq 1$, then $\lambda + \omega - 1 \neq 0$ and we have

$$\frac{\lambda}{\lambda + \omega - 1}(I - \omega\tilde{W})(I - \lambda^{-1}\mathfrak{L}_\omega) = I - \frac{\lambda\omega}{\lambda + \omega - 1}\tilde{W} - \frac{\omega}{\lambda + \omega - 1}\tilde{Z}$$

$$\tag{9.46}$$

Since Eq. (9.43) we have

$$\det\left[I - \frac{\lambda\omega}{\lambda + \omega - 1}\tilde{W} - \frac{\omega}{\lambda + \omega - 1}\tilde{Z}\right] = 0 \qquad (9.47)$$

Let $\lambda^{-1} = \delta e^{i\theta}$, where δ and θ are real and $\delta \le 1$. Thus,

$$\left|\frac{\lambda\omega}{\lambda + \omega - 1}\right| = \frac{\omega}{[1 - 2\delta(1 - \omega)\cos\theta + \delta^2(1 - \omega)^2]^{1/2}}$$

$$\le \frac{\omega}{1 - \delta(1 - \omega)} \qquad (9.48)$$

It can easily be seen that

$$1 - \frac{\omega}{1 - \delta(1 - \omega)} = \frac{(1 - \delta)(1 - \omega)}{1 - \delta(1 - \omega)} \ge 0 \qquad (9.49)$$

Hence, we have

$$\left|\frac{\omega}{\lambda + \omega - 1}\right| \le \left|\frac{\omega\lambda}{\lambda + \omega - 1}\right| \le 1 \qquad (9.50)$$

Since A is a diagonally dominant matrix, it can readily be seen that the matrix $X^{-1}A$ expressed as

$$X^{-1}A = I - \tilde{W} - \tilde{Z}$$

$$= I - B$$

is also a diagonally dominant matrix, so by Eq. (9.50), it follows that the matrix

$$I - \frac{\lambda\omega}{\lambda + \omega - 1}\tilde{W} - \frac{\omega}{\lambda + \omega - 1}\tilde{Z}$$

is diagonally dominant and it is also irreducible; then we have

$$\det\left[I - \frac{\lambda\omega}{\lambda + \omega - 1}\tilde{W} - \frac{\omega}{\lambda + \omega - 1}\tilde{Z}\right] \ne 0 \qquad (9.51)$$

which is a contradiction. Therefore, $\rho(\mathcal{L}_\omega) < 1$ and the S.U.O.Q.I.I. method converges. $\square$

We now develop some theorems in the case where the matrix A is positive definite. To begin, we first mention the following lemma, due to Wachspress [2].

Lemma 9.1 If A is a positive definite matrix, the iterative method with iteration matrix G is convergent if the matrix

$$M = Q + Q^T - A \tag{9.52}$$

is positive definite, where

$$Q = A(I - G)^{-1} \tag{9.53}$$

Moreover, we have

$$\|A^{1/2} G A^{-1/2}\| < 1 \tag{9.54}$$

Conversely, if Eq. (9.54) holds, then M is positive definite.

Theorem 9.5 Let A be a real, symmetric, nonsingular matrix, and let the crossed diagonals matrix of A (i.e., X) be positive definite. Then the S.O.Q.U.I.I. method converges if and only if A and $2\omega^{-1}X - A$ are positive definite. The condition that $2\omega^{-1}X - A$ is positive definite may be replaced by the condition

$$0 < \omega < 2/(1 - \mu_{\min}) \le 2 \tag{9.55}$$

where $\mu_{\min} \le 0$ is the smallest eigenvalues of the S.Q.I.I matrix B.

Proof Since X is positive definite, then $X^{1/2}$ exists and we define

$$\tilde{B} = X^{1/2} B X^{-1/2} = X^{-1/2}(W + Z)X^{-1/2} \tag{9.56}$$

which is symmetric because $W + Z = X - A$ is. Hence $\tilde{B}$ and therefore B have real eigenvalues. Since $B_\omega = \omega B + (1 - \omega)I$, it follows that the eigenvalues ρ_i of B_ω are given in terms of the eigenvalues μ_i of B of

$$\rho_i = \omega\mu_i + 1 - \omega \tag{9.57}$$

Thus, the S.O.Q.I.I. method will converge if and only if

$$-1 < \omega\mu_i + 1 - \omega < 1 \tag{9.58}$$

for all eigenvalues μ_i of B. Since trace $(B) = 0$ and since the eigenvalues of B are real, it follows that $\mu_{\min} \le 0$; then the condition (9.58) can be written as follows:

$$\begin{cases} 1 - \mu_i > 0, \\ \mu_i > 1 - 2\omega^{-1} \end{cases} \quad \omega > 0 \tag{9.59}$$

Since from Eq. (9.56) we have

$$\hat{A} = X^{-1/2} A X^{-1/2} = X^{-1/2}(X - W - Z)X^{-1/2}$$

$$= I - \tilde{B} \tag{9.60}$$

by the first of the conditions (9.59) it can be seen that all the eigenvalues of $\hat{A}$ are positive. Hence $\hat{A}$ and A must be positive definite. From Eq. (9.60) it can be seen that the eigenvalues $\hat{\nu}_i$ of $\hat{A}$ satisfy

$$\hat{\nu}_i = 1 - \mu_i \tag{9.61}$$

Therefore, by the second of the conditions of Eqs. (9.59) we have

$$\hat{\nu}_i < 2\omega^{-1} \tag{9.62}$$

thus, the matrix $2\omega^{-1}I - \hat{A}$ is positive definite. Moreover, since

$$X^{1/2}(2\omega^{-1}I - \hat{A})X^{1/2} = 2\omega^{-1}X - A \tag{9.63}$$

it follows that $2\omega^{-1}X - A$ is positive definite. $\square$

The sufficiency of the conditions of the theorem follows from Lemma 9.1. If A is positive definite, then we have

$$Q = A * (I - B_\omega)^{-1}$$

$$= A * [I - \omega B - (1 - \omega)I]^{-1}$$

$$= A * [\omega(I - B)]^{-1}$$

$$= \omega^{-1}A(X^{-1}A)^{-1} = \omega^{-1}X$$

Since X is symmetric then $X^T = X$, we obtain

$$M = 2\omega^{-1}X - A$$

which is a positive definite matrix.

Now, by Eq. (9.60) we have

$$2\omega^{-1}I - \hat{A} = (2\omega^{-1} - 1)I + \tilde{B} \tag{9.64}$$

the matrix $(2\omega^{-1} - 1)I + \tilde{B}$ is positive definite since $2\omega^{-1}I - \hat{A}$ is also. Then we have

$$2\omega^{-1} - 1 + \mu_i > 0 \tag{9.65}$$

where the μ_i are the eigenvalues of B. Thus, we have

$$0 < \omega < 2/(1 - \mu_{min}) \le 2$$

Therefore Eq. (9.55) can be replaced by the condition that $2\omega^{-1}X - A$ is positive definite and the proof of the theorem is complete.

Corollary 9.1   Under the hypotheses of Theorem 9.5, the S.Q.I.I. method converges if and only if A and $2X - A$ are positive definite.

Theorem 9.6   If A is a real symmetric matrix with positive definite crossed diagonals matrix X, then the S.S.O.Q.I.I. method converges if and only if A is positive definite and $0 < \omega < 2$.

Proof   Consider that λ is an eigenvalue of $\mathcal{L}_\omega$, then for some $\mathbf{v} \ne 0$ we have $\mathcal{L}_\omega \mathbf{v} = \lambda \mathbf{v}$ and hence

$$(\omega Z + (1 - \omega)X)\mathbf{v} = \lambda(X - \omega W)\mathbf{v} \tag{9.66}$$

Multiplying both sides on the left by $\mathbf{v}^H$ and solving for λ we obtain

$$\lambda = [\omega(\mathbf{v}, Z\mathbf{v}) + (1 - \omega)(\mathbf{v}, X\mathbf{v})]/[(\mathbf{v}, X\mathbf{v}) - \omega(\mathbf{v}, W\mathbf{v})] \tag{9.67}$$

where $(.,.)$ is an inner product. Since A is symmetric then by definition of the matrices W and Z it is evident that $Z^T = W$; thus we have

$$(\mathbf{v}, Z\mathbf{v}) = (Z^T\mathbf{v}, \mathbf{v}) = (W\mathbf{v}, \mathbf{v}) = (\overline{\mathbf{v}, W\mathbf{v}}) \tag{9.68}$$

If we let

$$y = (\mathbf{v}, W\mathbf{v})/(\mathbf{v}, X\mathbf{v}) \tag{9.69}$$

we have

$$\lambda = [\omega\bar{y} + 1 - \omega]/[1 - \omega y] \tag{9.70}$$

Suppose that $y = re^{i\theta}$, where r and θ are real, then we obtain

$$|\lambda|^2 = 1 - [\omega(2 - \omega)(1 - 2r\cos\theta)]/[(1 - \omega r\cos\theta)^2 + \omega^2 r^2 \sin^2\theta] \tag{9.71}$$

Therefore, we will have $|\lambda| < 1$ for $0 < \omega < 2$, if and only if

$$1 - 2r\cos\theta > 0 \tag{9.72}$$

But, by Eqs. (9.68) and (9.69) we have

$$2r \cos\theta = 2Re(y) = y + \bar{y}$$
$$= (\mathbf{v}, W\mathbf{v})/(\mathbf{v}, X\mathbf{v}) + (\mathbf{v}, Z\mathbf{v})/(\mathbf{v}, X\mathbf{v})$$

or

$$2r \cos\theta = (\mathbf{v}, R\mathbf{v})/(\mathbf{v}, X\mathbf{v}) \tag{9.73}$$

where

$$R = W + Z = X - A \tag{9.74}$$

Therefore, we have

$$2r \cos\theta = 1 - (\mathbf{v}, A\mathbf{v})/(\mathbf{v}, X\mathbf{v}) < 1 \tag{9.75}$$

if A is positive definite, since $(\mathbf{v}, X\mathbf{v}) > 0$. Thus $|\lambda| < 1$ and the convergence follows.

The sufficiency of the conditions of the theorem follows from Lemma 9.1, if the corresponding matrix M is positive definite. We have

$$Q = \omega^{-1}X - W$$

Since the matrix A is symmetric then we have

$$X^T = X, \ W^T = Z$$

Thus, we obtain

$$M = Q + Q^T - A = (2\omega^{-1} - 1)X$$

which is positive definite for $0 < \omega < 2$ since X is also. This completes the proof of the theorem. $\square$

Corollary 9.2   Under the hypotheses of Theorem 9.6, the S.U.Q.I.I. method converges if and only if A is positive definite.

We now consider the case where the coefficient matrix A is an L-matrix and study the convergence properties of the basic Q.I.I. methods in order to compare the spectral radii of the methods. This comparison is based on the work of Stein and Rosenberg [3].

Before going into any further details of the process, we state the following Lemmas.

Lemma 9.2 (Oldenberger [4]) Let A and B be two $n \times n$ matrices if $A \geq |B|$, then

$$\rho(A) \geq \rho(B)$$

Lemma 9.3 (Frobenius [5]) If matrix A is a nonnegative matrix, that is, $A \geq 0$, then $\rho(A)$ is an eigenvalue of A and there exists a nonnegative eigenvector of A and there exists a nonnegative eigenvector of A associated with $\rho(A)$.

Lemma 9.4 Let A be an L-matrix, and its crossed diagonals matrix X be positive definite. Then A is an M-matrix if and only if $\rho(B) < 1$, where

$$B = X^{-1}(W + Z)$$

and

$$A = X - W - Z$$

Proof If $\rho(B) < 1$, then $I - B$ is nonsingular and it can be shown that the series $I + B + B^2 + \cdots$ Converges to $(I - B)^{-1}$. Since X is a positive definite L-matrix, then X is, in fact, a Stieltjes matrix, and it can be seen, Young [6] that a Stieltjes matrix is an M-matrix, thus we have $X^{-1} > 0$. Since $W + Z \geq 0$, we have $B \geq 0$ and therefore $(I - B)^{-1} \geq 0$, the matrix $A = X(I - B)$ is a nonsingular since X and $I - B$ are nonsingular. Then we have

$$A^{-1} = [X(I - B)]^{-1} = (I - B)^{-1}X^{-1} \geq 0$$

it follows that A is an M-matrix.

Now, we will show if A is an M-matrix then we have $\rho(B) < 1$. We define the matrix $\hat{A}$ as follows

$$\hat{A} = X^{-1/2} AX^{-1/2} = X^{-1/2}(X - W - Z)X^{-1/2}$$
$$= I - X^{-1/2}(W + Z)X^{-1/2}$$

It can readily be seen that $\hat{A}$ is also an M-matrix. Consider the matrix $\tilde{B}$, which is similar to B by the following definition

$$\tilde{B} = X^{1/2}BX^{-1/2}$$

By direct calculation we see that

$$(I - \tilde{B}) * (I + \tilde{B} + \tilde{B}^2 + \cdots + \tilde{B}^m) = I - \tilde{B}^{m+1}$$

From the definition of $\hat{A}$ and $\tilde{B}$ it is clear that

$$\hat{A} = I - X^{-1/2}(XB)X^{-1/2} = I - \tilde{B}$$

hence we have

$$(\hat{A})^{-1} = (I - \tilde{B})^{-1} = (I + \tilde{B} + \tilde{B}^2 + \cdots + \tilde{B}^m) + (I - \tilde{B})^{-1}\tilde{B}^{m+1}$$

Since $(I - \tilde{B})^{-1} \geq 0$ and $\tilde{B} \geq 0$, it follows that the elements of the matrix $I + \tilde{B} + \tilde{B}^2 + \cdots + \tilde{B}^m$ must be nondecreasing functions of m and each element is bounded by the corresponding element of $(I - \tilde{B})^{-1}$. Thus, we know that the series $I + \tilde{B} + \tilde{B}^2 + \cdots + \tilde{B}^m$ is convergent and, therefore, $\rho(\tilde{B}) = \rho(B) < 0$. $\square$

Let the crossed diagonals matrix X of A be nonsingular, that is, $X^{-1/2}$ exists; then we can express the matrix B of Eq. (9.17) as

$$B = \tilde{W} + \tilde{Z} \tag{9.76}$$

and the matrix $\mathcal{L}_\omega$ of Eq. (9.32) as

$$\mathcal{L}_\omega = (I - \omega\tilde{W})^{-1}(\omega\tilde{Z} + (1 - \omega)I) \tag{9.77}$$

where

$$\tilde{W} = X^{-1}W, \qquad \tilde{Z} = X^{-1}Z \tag{9.78}$$

and it is evident that the matrices $\tilde{W}$ and $\tilde{Z}$ have the same structure as the definition (9.8) or (9.9). We can now prove the following theorem.

Theorem 9.7. Let A be an L-matrix with positive definite crossed diagonals matrix X, and $0 < \omega \leq 1$, then

(a) $\rho(B) < 1$, if and only if $\rho(\mathcal{L}_\omega) < 1$
(b) $\rho(B) < 1$ (and $\rho(\mathcal{L}_\omega) < 1$), if and only if A is an M-matrix if $\rho(B) < 1$, then

$$\rho(\mathcal{L}_\omega) \leq 1 - \omega + \omega\rho(B)$$

(c) If $\rho(B) \geq 1$ and $\rho(\mathcal{L}_\omega) \geq 1$, then

$$\rho(\mathcal{L}_\omega) \geq 1 - \omega + \omega\rho(B) \geq 1$$

Proof   By the structure of the matrix $\tilde{W}$ it can easily be seen that $\tilde{W}^{[n+1/2]} = 0$, and since A is an L-matrix and $0 < \omega \leq 1$, we have

$$(1 - \omega\tilde{W})^{-1} = I + \omega\tilde{W} + \omega^2\tilde{W}^2 + \cdots + \omega^{[n+1/2]-1}\tilde{W}^{[n+1/2]-1} \geq 0$$

$$(9.79)$$

and

$$\mathcal{L}_\omega = (I - \omega \tilde{W})^{-1}(\omega \tilde{Z} + (1 - \omega)I) \geq 0 \tag{9.80}$$

Let $\bar{\lambda} = \rho(\mathcal{L}_\omega)$ and $\bar{\mu} = \rho(B)$; then by Lemma 9.3, $\bar{\lambda}$ is an eigenvalue of $\mathcal{L}_\omega$ and for some $\mathbf{u} \neq 0$ we have

$$\mathcal{L}_\omega \mathbf{u} = \bar{\lambda} \mathbf{u} \tag{9.81}$$

and

$$(\bar{\lambda} \tilde{W} + \tilde{Z})\mathbf{u} = [(\bar{\lambda} + \omega - 1)/\omega]\mathbf{u} \tag{9.82}$$

Thus, $(\bar{\lambda} + \omega - 1)/\omega$ is an eigenvalue of the matrix $\bar{\lambda} \tilde{W} + \tilde{Z}$.

Then we have

$$\bar{\lambda} + \omega - 1 \leq \omega \rho(\bar{\lambda} \tilde{W} + \tilde{Z}) \tag{9.83}$$

If $\bar{\lambda} \leq 1$, then

$$\bar{\lambda} \tilde{W} + \tilde{Z} \leq \tilde{W} + \tilde{Z} \tag{9.84}$$

From Lemma 9.2 we have

$$\rho(\bar{\lambda} \tilde{W} + \tilde{Z}) \leq \rho(\tilde{W} + \tilde{Z}) = \bar{\mu} \tag{9.85}$$

hence,

$$\bar{\lambda} \leq \omega \bar{\mu} + 1 - \omega$$

On the other hand, if $\bar{\lambda} \geq 1$, then

$$\bar{\lambda} \tilde{W} + \tilde{Z} \leq \bar{\lambda}(\tilde{W} + \tilde{Z}) \tag{9.86}$$

Therefore, we obtain the result

$$(\bar{\lambda} + \omega - 1)/\omega \leq \rho(\bar{\lambda} \tilde{W} + \tilde{Z}) \leq \rho(\bar{\lambda} \tilde{W} + \bar{\lambda} \tilde{Z}) = \bar{\lambda} \bar{\mu} \tag{9.87}$$

and hence

$$\bar{\mu} \geq (\bar{\lambda} + \omega - 1)/(\omega \bar{\lambda}) = 1 + [(1 - \omega)(\bar{\lambda} - 1)/(\omega \bar{\lambda})] \geq 1 \tag{9.88}$$

By the above discussion we have the following results:

(i) if $\bar{\lambda} \leq 1$, then $\bar{\lambda} \leq \omega \bar{\mu} + 1 - \omega$

(ii) if $\overline{\lambda} \geq 1$, then $\overline{\mu} \geq 1$

(iii) if $\overline{\mu} < 1$, then $\overline{\lambda} < 1$

Since X is positive definite and A is an L-matrix, then X is an M-matrix, that is, $X^{-1} > 0$. Therefore, $B \geq 0$ and thus from Lemma 9.3 $\overline{\mu}$ is an eigenvalue of B. Hence, for some $v \neq 0$ we have $Bv = \overline{\mu}v$.

If we let

$$R = (I - \alpha\tilde{W})^{-1}(\omega\tilde{Z} + (1 - \omega)I) \tag{9.89}$$

and

$$\alpha = \omega/(1 - \omega + \omega\overline{\mu}) \tag{9.90}$$

then we have

$$Lv = (1 - \omega + \omega\overline{\mu})v \tag{9.91}$$

Hence

$$1 - \omega + \omega\overline{\mu} \leq \rho(R) \tag{9.92}$$

Since $\alpha \leq \omega$, therefore, it can be seen that if $\overline{\mu} < 1$ we have

$$(I - \alpha\tilde{W})^{-1} = I + \alpha\tilde{W} + \cdots \alpha^{[n+1/2]-1}\tilde{W}^{[n+1/2]-1}$$

$$\leq I + \omega\tilde{W} + \cdots \omega^{[n+1/2]-1}\tilde{W}^{[n+1/2]-1} = (I - \omega\tilde{W})^{-1} \tag{9.93}$$

Therefore, we have $R \leq \mathcal{L}_\omega$ and hence

$$1 - \omega + \omega\overline{\mu} \leq \rho(R) \leq \rho(\mathcal{L}_\omega) = \overline{\lambda} \tag{9.94}$$

Thus, it has been shown that

(iv) if $\overline{\mu} \geq 1$, then $\overline{\lambda} \geq 1 - \omega + \omega\overline{\mu} \geq 1$

(v) if $\overline{\lambda} < 1$, then $\overline{\mu} < 1$

By (iii) and (v) we have (a). Also by (i) and Lemma 9.4 we have (b). Finally, by (iv) we have (c). This completes the proof of the theorem. □

Corollary 9.2 Let A be an L-matrix with positive definite crossed diagonals matrix X, then

(a) $\rho(B) < 1$, if and only if $\rho(\mathcal{L}) < 1$

(b) $\rho(B) < 1$ and $\rho(\mathcal{L}) < 1$, if and only if A is an M-matrix, it can also be shown that in the case where $\rho(B) < 1$,

$$\rho(\mathcal{L}) \leq \rho(B) \tag{9.95}$$

(c) if $\rho(B) \geq 1$ and $\rho(\mathcal{L}) \geq 1$, then

$$\rho(\mathcal{L}) \geq \rho(B) \tag{9.96}$$

Theorem 9.8   If A is an M-matrix and if

$$0 < \omega < 2/[1 + \rho(B)] \tag{9.97}$$

then

$$\rho(\mathcal{L}_\omega) < 1$$

Proof If $0 < \omega \leq 1$, the convergence follows from Theorem 9.7. If $\omega \geq 1$, the by Eq. (9.79) we have

$$T_\omega = (I - \omega\tilde{W})^{-1}[\omega\tilde{Z} + (\omega - 1)I] \geq 0 \tag{9.98}$$

and

$$|\mathcal{L}_\omega| \leq T_\omega \tag{9.99}$$

If we let $\bar{\nu} = \rho(T_\omega)$, from Eq. (9.98) and Lemma 9.3 for some $\mathbf{v} \neq 0$ we have $T_\omega \mathbf{v} = \bar{\nu}\mathbf{v}$ and

$$(\omega\tilde{Z} + \omega\bar{\nu}\tilde{W})\mathbf{v} = (\bar{\nu} + 1 - \omega)\mathbf{v} \tag{9.100}$$

Hence,

$$\bar{\nu} + 1 - \omega \leq \rho(\omega\tilde{Z} + \omega\bar{\nu}\tilde{W}) \tag{9.101}$$

and if $\bar{\nu} \geq 1$, then by Lemma 9.2

$$\bar{\nu} + 1 - \omega \leq \omega\bar{\nu}\rho(B) \tag{9.102}$$

or

$$\omega \geq (1 + \bar{\nu})/[1 + \bar{\nu}\rho(B)] \geq 2[1 + \rho(B)] \tag{9.103}$$

therefore, if Eq. (9.97) holds, then we must have $\bar{\nu} < 1$. By Eq. (9.99) and Lemma 9.2 it follows that $\rho(\mathcal{L}\omega) \leq \bar{\nu} < 1$ and the theorem is proved. $\square$

We now develop a relation between the eigenvalues of the matrix $\mathcal{L}_\omega$ associated with the S.U.O.Q.I.I. method and the eigenvalues of the matrix B associated with the S.Q.I.I. method. We first derive this relation in the case where the coefficient matrix A is a tridiagonal matrix.

Theorem 9.9 Let A be a tridiagonal matrix of the form

$$
\begin{bmatrix}
a_{11} & a_{12} & & & & & \\
& & & & & 0 & \\
a_{21} & a_{22} & a_{23} & & & & \\
& \diagdown & \diagdown & \diagdown & & & \\
& & a_{k,k-1} & a_{k,k} & a_{k,k+1} & & \\
0 & & \diagdown & \diagdown & \diagdown & & \\
& & & & a_{n,n-1} & a_{n,n} &
\end{bmatrix}
\qquad (9.104)
$$

where $k = \left\lceil \frac{n+1}{2} \right\rceil$. Consider the Quadrant Interlocking Splitting (Q.I.S.) of the matrix X of the form $A = X - W - Z$, then

$$
\det(X - W - Z) = \det(X - \alpha W - \alpha^{-1} Z) \qquad (9.105)
$$

where α is any nonzero number.

Proof Consider the diagonal matrix R of the form

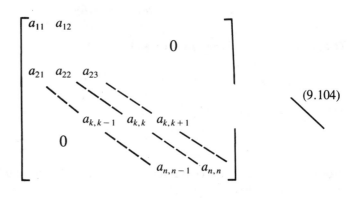

$$
R = \begin{bmatrix}
1 & & & & & & & \\
& \alpha & & & & & 0 & \\
& & \alpha^2 & & & & & \\
& & & \alpha^{n-3/2} & & & & \\
& & & & \alpha^{n-1/2} & & & \\
& & & & & \alpha^{n-1/2} & & \\
& 0 & & & & & \alpha^2 & \\
& & & & & & & \alpha \\
& & & & & & & & 1
\end{bmatrix}, \quad \text{for } n \text{ odd}
$$

$$
(9.106a)
$$

or

$$
\begin{bmatrix}
1 & & & & & & & & \\
& \alpha & & & & & & & \\
& & \alpha^2 & & & & & & \\
& & & \alpha^{n/2-2} & & & & 0 & \\
& & & & \alpha^{n/2-1} & & & & \\
& & & & & \alpha^{n/2-1} & & & \\
& & & & & & \alpha^{n/2-2} & & \\
& 0 & & & & & & \alpha^2 & \\
& & & & & & & & \alpha & 1
\end{bmatrix}, \quad \text{for } n \text{ even}
$$

(9.106b)

it can easily be seen that

$$
X - \alpha W - \alpha^{-1} Z = RAR^{-1}
$$

(9.107)

Therefore,

$$
\begin{aligned}
\det (X - \alpha W - \alpha^{-1} Z) &= \det (RAR^{-1}) \\
&= \det (R) * \det(A) * \det(R^{-1}) \\
&= \det (A) \ \square
\end{aligned}
$$

Theorem 9.10   Let the matrix A be of the form of Eq. (9.104), then the S.Q.I.I. matrix B corresponding to A is

$$
B = X^{-1}(W + Z) = \tilde{W} + \tilde{Z}
$$

(9.108)

where $X^{-1}W = \tilde{W}$ and $X^{-1}Z = \tilde{Z}$ are the form

$$
\tilde{W} =
\begin{bmatrix}
0 & 0 & & & & & & 0 \\
w_{2,1} & 0 & & & & & & \\
& & \ddots & & & & & \\
& & w_{n/2,n/2-1} & 0 & & & & \\
& & & 0 & 0 & w_{n/2+1,n/2+2} & & \\
0 & & & & & & \ddots & \\
& & & & & & & w_{n-1,n} \\
& & & & & 0 & & 0
\end{bmatrix}
$$

(9.109a)

$$\tilde{Z} = \begin{bmatrix} 0 & z_{1,2} & & & & & \\ 0 & 0 & z_{2,3} & & & 0 & \\ & & & z_{n/2-1,n/2} & & & \\ & & & 0 & & & \\ & & & 0 & & & \\ & 0 & & & 0 & & \\ & & & & 0 & & \\ & & z_{n/2+2,n/2+1} & & & 0 & \\ & & & & & z_{n,n-1} & 0 \end{bmatrix}, \quad \text{for } n \text{ even}$$

or

$$\tilde{W} = \begin{bmatrix} 0 & 0 & & & & \\ & 0 & 0 & & 0 & \\ w_{21} & & 0 & & & \\ & & & 0 & & \\ & w_{n+1/2,n-1/2} & 0 & w_{n+1/2,n+3/2} & \\ 0 & & 0 & 0 & \\ & & & & w_{n-1,n} \\ & & & 0 & & 0 \end{bmatrix} \tag{9.109b}$$

$$\tilde{Z} = \begin{bmatrix} 0 & z_{1,2} & & & & \\ & 0 & z_{2,3} & & 0 & \\ & 0 & & & & \\ & & z_{n-1/2,n+1/2} & & & \\ & & 0 & 0 & 0 & \\ 0 & z_{n+3/2,n+1/2} & 0 & & 0 & \\ & & & & & 0 \\ & & & z_{n,n-1} & 0 \end{bmatrix}, \quad \text{for } n \text{ odd}$$

Then we have that

(i)   the nonzero eigenvalues of the matrix B occur in pairs $\pm\mu_i$
(ii) there exists a relationship between the nonzero eigenvalues λ of the

S.U.O.Q.I.I. matrix $\mathcal{L}_\omega$ and the nonzero eigenvalues μ of B, of the form

$$(\lambda + \omega - 1)^2 = \lambda\omega^2\mu^2. \qquad \text{(Young, [6])} \qquad (9.110)$$

Proof

(i) The characteristic polynomial of B is

$$P(\mu) = \det[\mu I - B]$$
$$= \det[\omega I - \tilde{W} - \tilde{Z}]$$

where $\mu I - B$ is a tridiagonal matrix. Therefore, by Theorem 9.9 we have

$$\det[\mu I - \tilde{W} - \tilde{Z}] = \det[\mu I - \alpha\tilde{W} - \alpha^{-1}\tilde{Z}] \qquad (9.111)$$

By choosing $\alpha = -1$ in Eq. (9.115) we have

$$\det[\mu I - \tilde{W} - \tilde{Z}] = \det[\mu I + \tilde{W} + \tilde{Z}]$$
$$= (-1)^n \det[-\mu I - \tilde{W} - \tilde{Z}]$$

that is,

$$P(\mu) = (-1)^n P(-\mu) \qquad (9.112)$$

It follows, therefore, that if n is odd, $P(\mu) = -P(-\mu)$, so $P(\mu)$ is a polynomial in μ of odd degree. Similarly, $P(\mu)$ is an even polynomial of μ when n is even. Hence $P(\mu)$, for some integer $r \geq 0$ will either have the form

$$P(\mu) = \mu^{2r}g(\mu^2)$$

when n is even, or have the form

$$P(\mu) = \mu^{2r+1}f(\mu^2)$$

when n is odd, where $g(x)$ and $f(x)$ denote polynomials in x such that $g(0) \neq 0$ and $f(0) \neq 0$; then the nonzero roots of $P(\mu) = 0$ are given either by $g(\mu^2) = 0$ or by $f(\mu^2) = 0$, thus proving that the nonzero eigenvalues of B occur in pairs $\pm\mu_i$.

(ii) We know that the S.U.O.Q.I.I. matrix is of the form

$$\mathcal{L}_\omega = (I - \omega X^{-1}W)^{-1}\{(1 - \omega)I + \omega X^{-1}Z\} \qquad (9.113)$$

Let $\tilde{W} = X^{-1}W$ and $\tilde{Z} = X^{-1}Z$, then we have

$$\mathfrak{L}_\omega = (I - \omega\tilde{W})^{-1}\{(1 - \omega)I + \omega\tilde{Z}\} \tag{9.114}$$

The eigenvalues λ of $\mathfrak{L}_\omega$ are the roots of

$$\det(\lambda I - \mathfrak{L}_\omega) = 0$$

By expressing λI as

$$\lambda I = \lambda(I - \omega\tilde{W})^{-1}(I - \omega\tilde{W}) \tag{9.115}$$

we can define $\lambda I - \mathfrak{L}_\omega$ as

$$\lambda I - \mathfrak{L}_\omega = (I - \omega\tilde{W})^{-1}\{\lambda(I - \omega\tilde{W}) - (1 - \omega)I - \omega\tilde{Z}\}$$
$$= (I - \omega\tilde{W})^{-1}\{(\lambda + \omega - 1)I - \lambda\omega\tilde{W} - \omega\tilde{Z}\}$$

Hence

$$\det(\lambda I - \mathfrak{L}_\omega) = \det(I - \omega\tilde{W})^{-1} * \det\{(\lambda + \omega - 1)I - \lambda\omega\tilde{W} - \omega\tilde{Z}\} \tag{9.116}$$

Now, we have

$I - \omega\tilde{W}$

$$= \begin{bmatrix} 1 & & & & & & \\ -\omega w_{2,1} & 1 & & & 0 & & \\ & -\omega w_{k,k-1} & 1 & 0 & & & \\ & & 0 & 1 & -\omega w_{k+1,k+2} & & \\ & 0 & & & & -\omega w_{n-1,n} & \\ & & & & & & 1 \end{bmatrix}, \quad \text{for } n \text{ even} \tag{9.117a}$$

$I - \omega\tilde{W}$

$$= \begin{bmatrix} 1 & & & & & \\ -\omega w_{2,1} & 1 & & 0 & & \\ & -\omega w_{k,k-1} & 1 & -\omega w_{k,k+1} & & \\ & 0 & & & -\omega w_{n-1,n} & \\ & & & & & 1 \end{bmatrix}, \quad \text{for } n \text{ odd} \tag{9.117b}$$

Then, it is not difficult to see that

$$\det(I - \omega \tilde{W}) = 1 \tag{9.118}$$

therefore, we have

$$\det(I - \omega \tilde{W})^{-1} = 1 \tag{9.119}$$

so

$$\det(\lambda I - \mathcal{L}_\omega) = \det\{(\lambda + \omega - 1)I - \lambda\omega\tilde{W} - \omega\tilde{Z}\} \tag{9.120}$$

Since A is a tridiagonal matrix then $\lambda\omega\tilde{W}$ and $\omega\tilde{Z}$ are of the form of Eqs. (9.109) and thus $(\lambda + \omega - 1)I - \lambda\omega\tilde{W} - \omega\tilde{Z}$ is also a tridiagonal matrix from Theorem 9.9 by choosing $\alpha = 1/\sqrt{\lambda}$ we obtain

$$\det\left\{(\lambda + \omega - 1)I - \frac{\lambda\omega}{\sqrt{\lambda}} \tilde{W} - \sqrt{\lambda}\,\omega\tilde{Z}\right\} = 0 \tag{9.121}$$

If the order of the coefficient matrix A is n, then Eq. (9.121) can be rewritten as

$$\omega^n\lambda^{n/2} * \det\left\{\left(\frac{\lambda + \omega - 1}{\sqrt{\lambda}\omega}\right)I - (\tilde{W} + \tilde{Z})\right\} = 0 \tag{9.122}$$

which implies that $\frac{\lambda + \omega - 1}{\sqrt{\lambda}\omega}$ is an eigenvalue of matrix $B = \tilde{W} + \tilde{Z}$; therefore, if we denote the eigenvalue of matrix B by μ, then we have

$$\frac{\lambda + \omega - 1}{\sqrt{\lambda}\omega} = \mu \tag{9.123}$$

or

$$(\lambda + \omega - 1)^2 = \lambda\omega^2\mu^2 \tag{9.124}$$

and the proof of Theorem 9.10 is complete. $\square$

We now calculate the value of ω which minimizes the spectral radius of the S.U.O.Q.I.I. matrix.

Consider $\mu_i^2 < 1$, that is, a convergent S.Q.I.I. with real eigenvalues. Let

$$y_1(\lambda) = \frac{(\lambda + \omega - 1)}{\omega} = \frac{1}{\omega}\lambda + 1 - \frac{1}{\omega}, \quad \omega \neq 0 \tag{9.125}$$

and

$$y_2(\lambda) = \lambda^{1/2}\mu \tag{9.126}$$

Equation (9.125) is the equation of a line through the point (1, 1) whose slope $1/\omega$ decreases as ω increases. Equation (9.124) can be rewritten in the form

$$\frac{\lambda + \omega - 1}{\omega} = \pm \lambda^{1/2}\mu \tag{9.127}$$

which gives the points of intersection of the line, Eq. (9.125), and the parabola, Eq. (9.126). It can be seen that the largest coordinate λ_i of the points of intersection for a fixed $\mu = \mu_i$ decreases as ω increases until the line is a tangent to the parabola. This occurs in Figure 9.1.

For this value of ω, $\min_{\omega} \lambda_0 = \omega_0 - 1$, when $\omega > \omega_i$, the roots of Eq. (9.124) are complex and it is easily shown that $|\lambda| = \omega - 1$, which increases as ω increases. Therefore, ω_0 is the value of ω that minimizes the largest root (i.e., λ) of Eq., (9.124) for a fixed μ_i, where $\mu_i^2 < 1$. For the maximum rate of convergence of the S.U.O.Q.I.I. method we are concerned with finding the minimum value of the largest $\lambda_i(\omega) = \lambda_1(\omega)$, say. It can be seen from Eq. (9.124) that for $\omega = 1$ we have

$$\lambda_1(1) = \min_i \mu_i^2 = \mu_1^2, \quad \text{say}$$

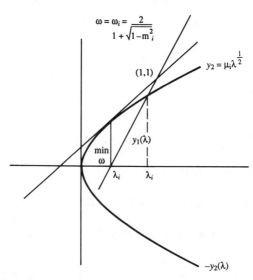

Figure 9.1 *Optimization of over-relaxation parameter ω.*

As ω increases from 1, $\lambda_1(\omega)$ decreases until $\omega = \omega_0$ is reached, where

$$\omega_{opt} = \omega_0 = \frac{2}{1 + \sqrt{1 - \mu_1^2}} \qquad (9.128)$$

For this value of ω, we have

$$\min_{\omega} \lambda_1(\omega) = \min_{\omega} \quad \text{(spectral radius of the S.U.O.Q.I.I. matrix)}$$

$$= \omega_0 - 1 \qquad (9.129)$$

Note that, by Figure 9.1, ω_0 is larger than ω_i, $i = 2, 3, \cdots$, which minimizes $\lambda_i(\omega)$ corresponding to the root pairs $\pm \mu_i$, where

$$|\mu_1| > |\mu_2| > |\mu_3| > \cdots \qquad (9.130)$$

Hence, the roots λ of Eq. (9.124) are complex for $\omega = \omega_b$, $\mu = \mu_i$, and each root has a modulus equal to $(\omega_0 - 1)$; that is, for $\omega = \omega_0$ every eigenvalue of the S.U.O.Q.I.I. matrix $\mathcal{L}_\omega$ has the same modulus $(\omega_0 - 1)$. In other words, each eigenvalue is represented by a point on the circle $|\lambda| = \omega_b - 1$.

It can also be shown that much of the above theoretical results on the tridiagonal matrices can be easily extended to hold for a wider class of matrices, namely the class of group consistently ordered (G.C.O.) matrices. We first develop a relation between the Q.I.I. methods and a special case of group iterative methods.

Definition 9.1   Consider the $(n \times n)$ coefficient matrix A, we define an ordered grouping of the n first integer numbers $1, 2, \cdots, n$ as follows:

$$G_1 = \{1, n\}, \qquad G_2 = \{2, n - 1\}, \cdots, G_{[n - 1/2]}$$

$$= \left\{ \left[\frac{n + 1}{2} \right], n - \left[\frac{n + 1}{2} \right] + 1 \right\} \qquad (9.131)$$

(Note that if n is odd, then $G_{[n + 1/2]}$ has a single element $\left| \frac{n + 1}{2} \right|$.)

We divide the matrix A into submatrices $A_{k,l}$, $k, l = 1, 2, \cdots, \left| \frac{n + 1}{2} \right|$, where each $A_{k,l}$ is formed from A by deleting all the rows except those corresponding to G_k and all the columns except those corresponding to G_l.

For example, when $n = 5$ we have

$$G_1 = \{1, 5\}, \qquad G_2 = \{2, 4\}, \qquad G_3 = \{3\}$$

and submatrices

$$A_{1,1} = \begin{pmatrix} a_{1,1} & a_{1,5} \\ a_{5,1} & a_{5,5} \end{pmatrix}, \quad A_{2,1} = \begin{pmatrix} a_{1,2} & a_{1,4} \\ a_{5,2} & a_{5,4} \end{pmatrix}, \quad A_{1,3} = \begin{pmatrix} a_{1,3} \\ a_{5,3} \end{pmatrix}$$

$$A_{2,1} = \begin{pmatrix} a_{2,1} & a_{2,5} \\ a_{4,1} & a_{4,5} \end{pmatrix}, \quad A_{2,2} = \begin{pmatrix} a_{2,2} & a_{2,4} \\ a_{4,2} & a_{4,4} \end{pmatrix}, \quad A_{2,3} = \begin{pmatrix} a_{2,3} \\ a_{4,3} \end{pmatrix}$$

$$A_{3,1} = (a_{3,1} \quad a_{3,5}), \quad A_{3,2} = (a_{3,2} \quad a_{3,4}), \quad A_{3,3} = (a_{3,3})$$

We now define a permutation matrix P with elements $P_{i,j}$, $1, 2, \cdots, n$, such that its nonzero elements are as follows:

Case (i)   for n odd,

$$\begin{cases} P_{i,2i-1} = 1, & i = 1(1) \dfrac{n+1}{2} \\ \\ P_{n+1/2+i,n-2i+1} = 1, & i = 1(1) \dfrac{n-1}{2} \end{cases} \qquad (9.132)$$

Case (ii)   for n even,

$$\begin{cases} P_{i,2i-1} = 1, \\ P_{n/2+i,n-2i+2} = 1 \end{cases}, \quad i = 1(1) \dfrac{n}{2} \qquad (9.132)$$

It can easily be seen that

$$P^T A P = \tilde{A} = \begin{bmatrix} A_{1,1} & A_{1,2} & \cdots & A_{1,[n+1/2]} \\ A_{2,1} & A_{2,2} & \cdots & A_{2,[n+1/2]} \\ \vdots & & & \vdots \\ A_{[n+1/2],1} & A_{[n+1/2],2} & \cdots & A_{[n+1/2],[n+1/2]} \end{bmatrix} \qquad (9.133)$$

where each $A_{k,l}$ is a (2×2) matrix is defined in Definition 9.1.
We now have the following theorem:

Theorem 9.11   Consider the $(n \times n)$ matrix A and a permutation matrix P defined by Eqs. (9.132). Let the splitting of the matrix $\tilde{A} = P^T A P$ be of the form,

$$\tilde{A} = D - C \qquad (9.134)$$

where

$$D = \begin{bmatrix} A_{11} & & \\ & A_{2,2} & 0 \\ & 0 & \ddots \\ & & A_{[n+1/2],[n+1/2]} \end{bmatrix} \tag{9.135}$$

and

$$C = L + U$$

where L and U are, respectively, strictly lower and strictly upper block triangular matrices. Then, if we split A as $A = X - W - Z$, we have

$$X = PDP^T \tag{9.136}$$

$$W = PLP^T \tag{9.137}$$

$$Z = PUP^T \tag{9.138}$$

where X is defined by Eq. (9.4) and W and Z are defined by Eqs. (9.5) and (9.6).

9.5 PRACTICAL IMPLEMENTATIONS OF PARALLEL MATRIX ALGORITHMS

The basic classifications made by Flynn [7] define a general class of parallel computers of which the most important two are Single Instruction Stream Multiple Data Stream (SIMD) and Multiple Instruction Stream Multiple Data Stream (MIMD) computers. See also Stone [8].

The SIMD type of parallel computer consists of an array of processors. Each of these processors executes the same string of instructions on different sets of data. Unlike a sequential computer, each of the processors in a SIMD computer are unable to generate their own instructions, and the instructions are provided by a central control unit, which is usually a computer by itself. The data streams provide data for each of the processors from private memories, each of which is associated with a processor. Each processor executes the same instructions generated by the control unit on its own data simultaneously.

The MIMD computer or multiprocessor system is basically a minicomputer network. Unlike the SIMD computer, each processor of an MIMD computer generates its own instruction stream, which it executes on its own data stream. In an MIMD computer system, each processor has its own control unit and so is able to generate its own and generally different instruction stream. Therefore, it is possible to execute different instructions simultaneously. The processors need not be identical because they are independent of one another; however, they are compatible with each other. Each processor has its own data stream, which is obtained from two sources: a large primary shared memory and a private memory associated with each processor.

For a full description of SIMD and MIMD and other parallel computers, see Dunbar [9] and Flynn [7].

Generally, a parallel computer with p identical processors is potentially p times as fast as a single computer. However, this limit can only be achieved in idealized situations where the following assumptions made by Kuck [10] hold.

1. Any number of processors and memories may be used at any time.
2. Each processor may perform any of the basic arithmetic operations (i.e., addition, subtraction, multiplication, and division) at any time, but different processors may perform different operations at the same time.
3. No time is required to communicate data between the processors and memories.
4. Instructions are always available for execution as required and are never held up by a control unit.
5. There are no accessing conflicts in the memory.
6. Each operation takes the same amount of time, which will be referred to as a unit step.

Indeed, the above assumptions are used in the computational cost analyses of the methods and are our chosen essential criteria in the computational costs of the methods that we discuss here.

Consider the system of equations $A\mathbf{x} = \mathbf{b}$ and the Q.I.S. of the $(n \times n)$ coefficient matrix A in the form $A = X - W - Z$; we now define the alternative parallel schemes for solution of the systems with the S.Q.I. and S.U.O.Q.I. iteration methods.

In order to illustrate the scheme, we consider the S.Q.I.I. (9.21) in the matrix form shown in Figure 9.2 with n as an even number, where $\alpha = n/2$.

As mentioned before, the unknowns $x_i^{(k+1)}$, $i = 1(1)n$, can be found in pairs, by solving $n/2$ systems of (2×2) linear systems of equations,

$$\begin{cases} a_{i,i}x_i^{(k+1)} + a_{i,n-i+1}x_{n-i+1}^{(k+1)} = c_i^{(k)} \\ a_{n-i+1,i}x_i^{(k+1)} + a_{n-i+1,n-i+1}x_{n-i+1}^{(k+1)} = c_{n-i+1}^{(k)} \end{cases}, \quad i = 1(1)\frac{n}{2} \quad (9.139)$$

In Figure 9.2 the right hand side vector $\mathbf{c}^{(k)}$(say) with components $c_i^{(k)}$, $i = 1, 2, \cdots, n$, can be found by the following formulas,

$$c_i^{(k)} = \sum_{j=1}^{n} a_{l,j}x_j^{(k)} + b_i, \quad l = 1(1)n$$
$$l \neq i \notin n - i + 1 \quad (9.140)$$

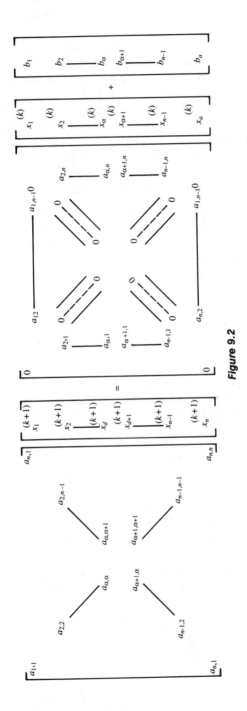

Figure 9.2

331

The implementation of the above method on an SIMD type of computer, where many processors are available, can be formulated as follows:

(i)   The matrix–vector multiplication of the right hand side of Figure 9.2 can on most SIMD computers be performed in "$1 + \log_2(n - 2)$" time steps; this is illustrated in the following manner: The first step consists of the evaluation of each $a_{i,j} * x_j$ for $i, j = 1, 2, \cdots, n, j \neq i \notin n - i + 1$. All such multiplications can be performed simultaneously in one time step (i.e., one multiplication) if $n(n - 2)$ number of processors are available. This would yield a matrix with elements $r_{i,j} = a_{i,j} * x_j$, $i, j = 1, 2, \cdots,$ n, and $j \neq i \notin n - i + 1$; the final step of the product vector is evaluated by summing up of all the elements of each row, which can be done in $\log_2(n - 2)$ time steps and therefore requires $(n - 2)/2$ processors.

(ii)   The summation of the above vector evaluated in (i) to the vector $\mathbf{b}$ is carried out in one step with n processors (i.e., one addition).

(iii) Once the $c_i^{(k)}$, $i = 1, 2, \cdots, n$, are evaluated then the solution in the $(k + 1)$th step of iteration, $k = 0, 1, 2, \cdots$, is determined by solving the (2×2) linear systems in Eqs. (9.139). This can be achieved as follows:

Evaluate

$$\Delta_i = a_{i,i} * a_{p,p} - a_{i,p} * a_{p,i}, \quad i = 1, 2, \cdots, \frac{n}{2} \quad (9.141)$$

where $p = n - i + 1$.

This would require two time steps (one multiplication and one subtraction) and two processors for each Δ_i, which results in requiring n processors to evaluate Δ_i for all $i = 1, 2, \cdots, n/2$.

(b) We then evaluate

$$x_i^{(k+1)} = (c_i^{(k)} * a_{p,p} - c_p^{(k)} * a_{i,p})/\Delta_i, \quad i = 1, 2, \cdots, n \quad (9.142)$$

where $\Delta_i = \Delta_{n-i+1}$, $i = 1, 2, \cdots, n/2$, which again requires three time steps (one multiplication, one subtraction, and one division) and two processors per $x_i^{(k+1)}$ and, hence, $2n$ processors to evaluate all $x_i^{(k+1)}$ values.

Therefore, the complete solution of the method in each iteration requires $7 + \log_2(n - 2)$ time steps and a maximum number of p processors where

$$P = \max\{2n, n(n - 2)\} \quad (9.143)$$

We now consider the S.U.O.Q.I.I. Iteration method for solving the linear system $A\mathbf{x} = \mathbf{b}$. By Eq. (9.31) we have

$$(X - \omega W)\mathbf{x}^{(k+1)} = ((1 - \omega)X + \omega Z)\mathbf{x}^{(k)} + \omega\mathbf{b} \quad (9.144)$$

or in the matrix form shown in Figure 9.3, where n is again an even number and $\alpha = n/2$.

With the value of $\mathbf{x}^{(k)}$ the right hand side of Figure 9.3 easily be computed, that is,

$$c_i^{(k)} = \sum_{j=i+1}^{n-i} -\omega a_{i,j} * x_j^{(k)} + (1 - \omega) * (a_{i,i} x_i^{(k)} + a_{i,p} x_p^{(k)}) + \beta b_i,$$

$$i = 1(1)\frac{n}{2} \tag{9.145}$$

$$c_p^{(k)} = \sum_{j=i+1}^{n-i} -\omega a_{p,j} * x_j^{(k)} + (1 - \omega) * (a_{p,i} x_i^{(k)} + a_{p,p} x_p^{(k)}) + \omega b_p,$$

where $p = n - i + 1$.

Then, the components of unknown vector $\mathbf{x}^{(k+1)}$ can be found in pairs, by solving $n/2$ linear systems of (2×2) equations in $n/2$ distinct steps.

The solution process of the S.U.O.Q.I.I. method for each iteration can be formulated as shown. The first step is to evaluate the right hand side vector $\mathbf{x}^{(k)}$. It can be achieved as follows:

(1) Each $-\omega * a_{i,j}$ must be evaluated for $i = 1(1) \ n/2 - 1$, $j = i + 1(1)n - i$ and $i = n/2 + 2(1)n$, $j = n - i + 2(1)i - 1$. All these multiplications can be performed in one time step (i.e., one multiplication) and require $n(n/2 - 1)$ processors.

(b) $(1 - \omega) * a_{i,i}$ and $(1 - \omega) * a_{i,n-i+1}$ for $i = 1(1)n$. These can be evaluated in one time step (i.e., one multiplication) if $2n$ number of processors are available.

(c) This step consists of the evaluation of each $\mathbf{a}_{i,j}$ is the element of the right hand side matrix after the evaluations in steps (a) and (b). All such multiplications can be performed simultaneously in one time step on $n/2 \ (n + 2)$ number of processors.

(d) Summing up all the elements of each row can again be done in $\log_2 n$ time steps and requires $n/2$ number of processors.

(e) The evaluation of $\omega * \mathbf{b}$ which requires n number of processors and needs just one time step (i.e., one multiplication) to complete.

(f) The summation of the vectors evaluated in steps (d) and (e) can be carried out in one time step (i.e., one addition) with n processors.

With the right hand side vector $\mathbf{x}^{(k)}$, the solution process in the $(k + 1)$th, $k = 0, 1, \cdots$, iteration is carried out as follows:

(i) Evaluate

$$\Delta_i = a_{i,i} * a_{p,p} - a_{i,p} * a_{p,i}, \quad i = 1(1)\frac{n}{2}$$

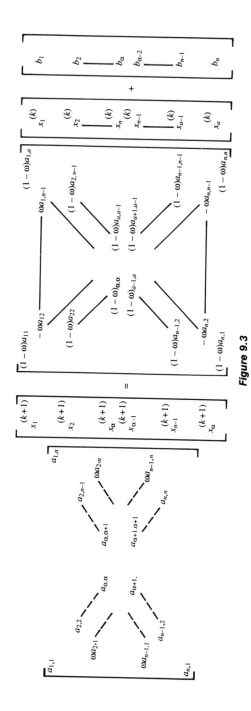

Figure 9.3

where $p = n - i + 1$. As we have seen previously, this can be performed in two time steps and requires n processors.

(ii) Solve the (2×2) linear systems

$$\begin{cases} a_{1,1}x_1^{(k+1)} + a_{1,n}x_n^{(k+1)} = c_1^{(k)} \\ a_{n,1}x_1^{(k+1)} + a_{n,n}x_n^{(k+1)} = c_n^{(k)} \end{cases} \tag{9.146}$$

by using the formulas

$$x_1^{(k+1)} = (c_1^{(k)} * a_{n,n} - c_n^{(k)} * a_{1,n})/\Delta_1 \tag{9.147}$$
$$x_n^{(k+1)} = (c_n^{(k)} * a_{1,1} - c_1^{(k)} * a_{n,1})/\Delta_1$$

(Cramer's rule).

It can be seen that the solution of this system requires just three time steps (one multiplication, one subtraction, and one division) with a total number of four processors. Then before proceeding to evaluate the next pair, we modify the right hand side vector $\mathbf{c}^{(k)}$ as

$$c_j^{(k)} = c_j^{(k)} = \omega * (a_{j,1} x_1^{(k+1)} + a_{j,n} x_n^{(k+1)})$$

$$, \quad j = 2(1)\frac{n}{2} \tag{9.148}$$

$$c_{n-j+1}^{(x)} = c_{n-j+1}^{(k)} - \omega * (a_{n-j+1,1}x_1^{(k+1)} + a_{n-j+1,n}x_n^{(k+1)})$$

This requires four time steps (two multiplication, one addition, and one subtraction) and a total number of $2(n - 2)$ processors to modify all the elements of the vector $\mathbf{c}^{(k)}$. This completes this step of the algorithm.

In general, at the beginning of the lth stage, $l = 1, 2, \cdots, n/2$, we have the solution of (2×2) systems,

$$\begin{cases} a_{l,l}x_l^{(k+1)} + a_{l,p}x_p^{(k+1)} = c_l^{(k)} \\ a_{p,l}x_l^{(k+1)} + a_{p,p}x_p^{(k+1)} = c_p^{(k)} \end{cases} \tag{9.149}$$

where $p = n - l + 1$, to give the unknowns $x_l^{(k+1)}$ and $x_p^{(k+1)}$ and the modification of the right hand side vector according to the following updating formulas,

$$c_j^{(k)} = c_j^{(k)} - \omega * (a_{j,l}x_l^{(k+1)} + a_{j,p}x_p^{(k+1)}) \tag{9.150}$$
$$c_{n-j+1}^{(k)} = c_{n-j+1}^{(k)} - \omega * (a_{n-j+1,l}x_l^{(k+1)} + a_{n-j+1,p}x_p^{(k+1)})$$

N.B., For $l = n/2$ the formula (9.150) is not evaluated.

Therefore, the complete solution of the method in the $(k + 1)$th, $k = 0, 1, 2, \cdots$, step of the iteration requires $14 + \log_2 n$ time steps and a total of $n/2 (n + 2)$ number of processors.

The above algorithm was also implemented on the Sequent Balance system of the Parallel Algorithms Research Centre of Loughborough University, which is an MIMD-type system with 10 National Semiconductor 3200 multiprocessors able to work simultaneously on different tasks.

The way in which the algorithm was designed for use on the Balance system is briefly described below.

The shared memory of the system was arranged to hold the coefficient matrix A, the right hand side vector $\mathbf{b}$, and the solution at each iteration so that each processor can access any part of the above data. The solution process at each iteration was carried out in $\left[\frac{n+1}{2}\right]$ distinct stages where at the stage i the components $x_i^{(k+1)}$ and $x_{n-i+1}^{(k+1)}$, $i = 1, 2, \cdots, \left[\frac{n+1}{2}\right]$ and $k = 0, 1, 2, \cdots$, were evaluated. In this way, the algorithm uses only two processors at any one time, where all the computations related to the determination of $x_i^{(k+1)}$ and $x_{n-i+1}^{(k+1)}$ are carried out on the two processors independently and simultaneously. As soon as a component is evaluated it is tested for convergency and the process will continue to the next iteration if the accuracy test is not satisfied for all the components.

REFERENCES

[1] W. Kahan, "Gauss-Seidel Methods of Solving Large Systems of Linear Equations," Ph.D. thesis, University of Toronto, Canada (1958).

[2] E. L. Wachspress, *Iterative Solution of Elliptic Systems and Applications to the Neutron Diffusion Equations of Reactor Physics*, Prentice-Hall, Englewood Cliffs, N.J., 1966.

[3] P. Stein and R. Rosenberg, On the Solution of linear simultaneous equations by iteration, *J. Lond. Math. Soc.* 23, 111–118 (1948).

[4] R. Oldenburger, Infinite powers of matrices and characteristic roots, *Duke Math. J.*, 6, 357–361 (1940).

[5] G. Frobenius, *Uber matrizen aus positiven elementen*, S. B. Deutsch, Akad. Wiss. Berlin, pp. 471–476, 1908.

[6] D. M. Young, "Iterative Methods for Solving Partial Difference Equations of Elliptic Type," Ph.D. thesis, Harvard University, Cambridge, Mass. (1950).

[7] M. J. Flynn, Very high speed computing systems, *Proc. IEEE.*, 54, 1901–1909 (1966).

[8] H. S. Stone, "Problems of Parallel Computation," in J. F. Traub, Ed., *Complexity of Sequential and Parallel Numerical Algorithms*, Academic Press, San Diego, Calif., 1–16 (1973).

[9] R. C. Dunbar, "Analysis and Design of Parallel Algorithms," Ph.D. thesis, Loughborough University of Technology, U.K., (1978).

[10] D. J. Kuck, "Multioperation Machine Computation," in J. F. Traub, Ed., *Complexity of Sequential and Parallel Numerical Algorithms*, Academic Press, San Diego, Calif., 17–47 (1973).

INDEX